AF328750

BEDFORD
Buses and Coaches

TROSSACHS
McDOUGALL'S MOTOR EXCURSION TOURS OBAN
HET 177
The New
Bedford
26-SEATER
COACH
COACHWORK BY DUPLE

BEDFORD
Buses and Coaches

Nigel R.B. Furness

THE CROWOOD PRESS

First published in 2016 by
The Crowood Press Ltd
Ramsbury, Marlborough
Wiltshire SN8 2HR

www.crowood.com

British Library Cataloguing-in-Publication Data
A catalogue record for this book is available from the British Library.

ISBN 978 1 78500 207 6

Typeset by Jean Cussons Typesetting, Diss, Norfolk

Printed and bound in Malaysia by Times Offset (M) Sdn Bhd

CONTENTS

INTRODUCTION AND ACKNOWLEDGEMENTS

On mentioning to my wife that I intended to write a book about Bedford buses and coaches, amongst her many observations there was one that stood out – 'you used to see them everywhere, didn't you?', although by this time the Bedford name had all but disappeared. Indeed, buses and coaches of Bedford manufacture had not actually been made for nearly thirty years. This shows how strongly the Bedford name had been impressed upon the public consciousness. The irony is that Bedford once used almost the very same words – 'you see them everywhere' – in its advertising. It has also been said that in their most popular days, of all the buses and coaches on the road in the UK, almost half were Bedfords.

Being the progeny of Vauxhall, a volume car manufacture, the characteristics of the Bedford were those of a mass production vehicle: light weight, relatively cheap to buy and easy to service and maintain. As such, Bedford buses and coaches were the ideal rolling stock for the smaller independent operator of private hire and coach tours, who, almost as an addition, might run a single local service to the nearest town on market day. While they naturally became the mainstay of such operators, a use could still be found for them in the fleets of the large territorial company operators. The Bedford OB and OWB in particular were bought by both the Tilling and BET groups during the Second World War and the early 1950s. While Tilling preferred to buy its home-produced Bristol/ECW buses and coaches wherever possible, the role the lightweight bus could play was acknowledged and Tilling/BTC built its own version of the Bedford SB, which they called the Bristol SC, utilizing many Bedford components in its construction. Other Bedfords in due course found their way in small numbers into those fleets, and those of the BET federation too.

Interestingly, the large territorial bus companies that once flourished have now, like Bedford, passed into history, victims all of high finance and changing times, while many small family businesses that built themselves on Bedford and stayed loyal to the marque until the very end are still with us. Coaches may still be hired from Kenzies, Jeffs or Lodge's and one can still 'Go Whittle', though the latter is no longer family owned. On a recent trip north I noticed at least half-a-dozen coaches bearing names that will be familiar to readers who make it to the end of this book.

My own introduction to the Bedford came at the age of eight, when my family first holidayed in Devon. We stayed (in a caravan, naturally, as any working-class family of the time would have done) at Woolacombe. The beach there had this most wonderful of things for the embryonic engineer – a freshwater stream that ran down to the sea that could be dammed and diverted, keeping an eight-year-old boy occupied for hours. I digress, but only slightly; on our first visit to the beach and even before I discovered the pleasures of the stream, my attention was caught by a handsome two-tone blue 1953 Duple Vega-bodied Bedford SB, the property of Blue Coaches of Ilfracombe. This vehicle provided the direct bus service between Woolacombe and Ilfracombe via Mortehoe, as announced by a neatly painted board mounted on the front of the bus, precisely the sort of job the Bedford was made for. I pestered and pestered my parents for a ride on the bus, but my mother was far too proud of our brand-new Vauxhall Viva to consider foregoing its pleasures in favour of its more antiquated and much bluer big brother. So I was denied the opportunity to make a more intimate acquaintance with ODV 38. We returned, year on year, to North Devon well into the 1970s and my blue friend was always there, patiently waiting, until one year it wasn't, and that was that. I missed it, and regretted an opportunity lost.

By that time I had, however, become much more familiar with the products of Dunstable; they were much favoured by the luxury coach operators in Bristol, the largest of which traded as Wessex and operated a fleet of quite modern Bedfords. Thus I got my first ride on an SB, a Duple Bella Vega coach, the luxury version of my old friend ODV

38. The occasion was less joyous, though, as my school used Wessex to provide transport to their playing fields in the Somerset countryside, where I was able to spend several hours being legally abused by my peers in the name of sport. The one thought that kept me going though this iniquity was of course the pleasure of the ride back on the Wessex Bedford. However, Wessex must have tired of the destruction wreaked by unappreciative schoolboys on its smart grey and red luxury coaches and replaced them for this purpose with a somewhat more robust, but oh, so much slower and more uncomfortable, former London Transport RTW double-decker. This dark blue heap of shivering rust and dripping nicotine did nothing to endear me to London buses. Thus my interest in and affection for Bedford began over fifty years ago and continues to this day. I have found, like my father before me, much to commend in the Vauxhall marque and have owned a number, including Bedford light vans, over the years and have always found them enduring and reliable.

In writing *Bedford Buses and Coaches*, it was not my intention to set forth the definitive history of Bedford but rather to provide a comprehensive survey of the buses and coaches produced through the years. The UK once had a flourishing and diverse coachbuilding industry, with coachbuilders large and small building on the Bedford chassis. Small operators in the UK often ordered their chassis in ones and twos through the local Vauxhall/Bedford dealer such as Arlington Motor Co., Vincent Greenhous, SMT and others and had them bodied at the nearest coach works. Others still, such as Shreeve, who traded as Belle Coaches of Lowestoft, built their own bodies on Bedford chassis, so diversity was inherent. Because such large quantities were sold in this way throughout the United Kingdom and the wider world, it has not been possible to trace every instance of a Bedford sale and every operator who used them. To do so would be an enormous task. I have therefore included only those sales that I considered significant or interesting; in doing so, I realize that this might be subjective so I apologize if I have neglected to mention the reader's favourite vehicle or operator. I have also tended to concentrate on the UK market, though Bedford was responsible for significant exports throughout the world. The subject of Bedford overseas remains to be properly addressed and would be an interesting, though challenging, piece of research. I am aware that a number of individuals are pursuing this currently; I look forward to reading the results in due course.

One of the consequences of their ubiquity is that for many years Bedford tended not to be of great interest to the keen public transport enthusiast, whose attentions were often focused on the heavyweight products from manufacturers like AEC, Bristol, Daimler, Guy, Leyland and others. The humble Bedford was ignored because 'you see them everywhere'. Also, for the die-hard bus-spotters of the author's teenage years, who immersed themselves in fleet numbers and esoteric details of allocations, transfers and routes, the Bedford was a slippery so-and-so, sold and resold through a network of dealers and in some cases spending only a few years with each owner before passing on to another — much like Vauxhall's family cars — making them difficult to keep track of, although *Buses Illustrated* magazine and its contributors recorded as many movements as they could. Without the spotter's attention to detail the records would be far less complete, and to them we owe a debt of gratitude. Fully detailed records of the sales, resales and movement of Bedford buses and coaches are therefore hard to find and the PSV Circle has only recently been able to produce some data on Bedford chassis.

In the early years of the preservation movement Bedford similarly tended to be neglected, with the exception of the OB/Duple Vista combination, which must surely equal the Routemaster in being instantly recognizable to the general public and in numbers in preservation. With the passage of time, a new generation of preservationists has grown up and thankfully taken the Bedford under its wing, so now we are seeing many of the later models entering preservation. New age travellers need to be mentioned here for they have been instrumental in saving many old buses and coaches, including Bedfords, and many of whom were and continue to be enthusiasts for the vehicles. It is in no small way due to them that such vehicles have survived to find their way into the hands of restorers and preservationists.

In consideration of the vehicles themselves, I have tried to provide as full technical details as possible for all the principal models — that is those specifically intended for Public Service Vehicle (PSV) use. This was the term used to describe buses and coaches that was in common use during the era of Bedford so I have used it throughout; such vehicles are now referred to as PCVs — Passenger Carrying Vehicles. Such is the adaptability and versatility of the Bedford lightweight chassis, however, that many Bedford-based passenger vehicles have been built on chassis whose primary function was as light trucks or vans; these have not been ignored but have been given a somewhat more generalized treatment due to their diversity and the fact that, once purchased, a Bedford chassis could be used for anything the owner could find to do with it within the law. I have, however, tried to describe a good selection of these in the appropriate chapter. It is perhaps surprising that Bedford did not produce a low-cost double-deck chassis in the same idiom as its single-deck coaches and buses. In fact Bedford did consider building a double-deck bus in collaboration with a major coachbuilder in the 1970s, but nothing came of the idea.

In researching this book, my sources have been the manufacturer in the case of technical information, the range of Bedford instruction books and service manuals containing a wealth of detail – though it must be noted that Bedford's own advertising and technical literature was prone to errors and inconsistencies, so if I have failed to identify (and therefore propagated) any of these errors, I apologize. A particular idiosyncrasy of Bedford was to refer to the capacity of its engines in cubic inches, rather than the more common cubic centimetres or litres. I suspect the reason for this lies in Bedford's overlord, the General Motors Corporation of America. US car manufacturers were long wedded to imperial dimensions, demonstrating a useful consistency not always found in the European motor industry. Where I quote measurements, I have generally given the metric equivalent in parentheses. The exception to this rule is the chapters on the Y-series chassis and YNV; these chassis were built to metric dimensions and legal limits that were defined in metric units and so, rightly, these take precedence and their imperial equivalent is less meaningful. Where Vauxhall and Bedford used dimensions as proper names, as in 'the 214cu in engine', I have not given an equivalent metric dimension in this context as these will be found in the text describing the detailed specifications of the engines.

In pursuance of production and sales figures, it is sad to relate that Vauxhall no longer have any records from that period of their history that covers the Bedford marque and indeed, with the passage of time, no one within the company now or at Vauxhall Heritage knows when, where and how they were disposed of. The PSV Circle records, 'Bus Lists on the Web', contemporary press reports and other secondary sources of data have therefore provided the majority of the statistics for numerical analysis and information on individual vehicles. Photographic and other evidence, including comments from acknowledged experts, has suggested that the published records are quite incomplete and contain many errors, so numbers are for guidance and purposely approximate; in their defence it must be stated that the collators of these data have a different agenda and generally focus on the history of individual vehicles.

I have perhaps laboured this point, but feel obliged to do so in light of recent calls in the enthusiast media for authors of bus and coach books to take more care over the accuracy of facts and figures. While an easy request to make, it is somewhat harder to fulfil in practice with anything like the degree of confidence implied, as any researcher into historical data will confirm. However, such calls are well meant so with that in mind, I would be very pleased to hear from anyone who disagrees with my facts and figures – please contact me via the publisher, but in doing so I would ask that you include your provenance and sources for any data you challenge so I can confirm and report the conclusions of your research with confidence.

ACKNOWLEDGEMENTS

A work of this complexity could not have been achieved without assistance from others, so now is the time to acknowledge and thank them for giving freely of their time. Andrew Duerden at Vauxhall Heritage, Luton, provided a number of historic images and brochures and expressed his views on the subject matter. Images from the Vauxhall Heritage archive are credited 'VH' in the captions. George Atkin, Roger Chambers and William Staniforth provided me with many useful contacts, vehicle details and other information. Bedford bus and coach owners Terry Jones, Cyril Kenzie, Andrew Lodge, Andy Mccarthy, Dave Prosser, Mike Walker and Mark Withers all provided me with information about and images of their vehicles and patiently endured my questions, as did the aforementioned George Atkin and Roger Chambers. I must also mention my Bedford expert proofreader who prefers to remain anonymous (as he put it, 'I don't want to have to buy a tin hat'), but he knows who he is.

Uncredited colour images are drawn from my own collection, to which the photography of Stuart J. Brown, Hugh Jones, Kevin Lane and Cliff Essex has made a significant contribution. Other images have come courtesy of Paul Bateson, Les Simpson, Andy Strong and Terry Walker, who also supplied information about the Cravens Homalloy bus, and others as acknowledged in the captions. Terry Jones needs a further mention for reading the manuscript and correcting a number of errors.

My wife Anne made many phone calls on my behalf to badger various people into providing information and vehicle profiles and proofread the manuscript. I know very well that she would really rather I finished all my outstanding preservation and restoration projects rather than spend my time sat in front of a computer surrounded by technical manuals. My daughter Rebecca also performed secretarial duties for me from time to time and helped organize meetings with vehicle owners.

CHAPTER ONE

THE BEDFORD STORY

ORIGINS

Vauxhall Motors has its origin in the firm of Alex Wilson & Co. Engineers, a business established by Alexander Wilson in 1857 at premises near to Vauxhall Gardens, a large park and pleasure gardens originally laid out in the late seventeenth century. By Alexander Wilson's time the place had acquired something of an unsavoury reputation for being the haunt of vagabonds and 'ladies of easy virtue' and so the gardens closed in 1859.

The company had principally been involved in the manufacture of marine engines and pumps. Wilson left the company in 1897 and it was at this time that the firm's name was changed to the Vauxhall Ironworks Company Ltd. This event has some bearing on the history of Bedford owing to speculation on how the name 'Bedford' came to be adopted. The first motor car appeared from the Ironworks in 1903 and was called a Vauxhall – clearly in the tradition of names related to place of origin – so it is perfectly reasonable to conclude that the Bedford name is the consequence of the product having been manufactured at Dunstable in Bedfordshire. One might argue that a logically correct consequence would have been to name the product 'Dunstable', but Bedford is nearby and trips off the tongue somewhat more easily, an important marketing consideration. It is hard to imagine a purveyor of seaside tours calling out 'come for a ride in my new Dunstable!' – with due respect to the denizens of that town, of course.

The griffin emblem associated with Vauxhall and Bedford was chosen by Alexander Wilson for his company as a result of a legend concerning the name of the area known as Vauxhall; allegedly the name is a corruption of 'Fulke's Hall', after Fulk le Breant, a minor thirteenth-century nobleman of Normandy whose coat of arms included the griffin. By curious coincidence, le Breant held the manor of Luton, whence the car manufacturing side of the Vauxhall Ironworks came in 1905, bringing the griffin back to Luton, as it were.

Vauxhall Arrives in Luton

The expansion of the business soon started to put pressure on the south London site, which was leased rather than owned, so Vauxhall Motors came to Luton in 1905. There they found a seven-acre site in Kimpton Road on which they could set up manufacturing premises. On 29 March 1905 the first Luton-built car left the factory. The cars produced by Vauxhall at Luton in the period up to the early 1920s acquired a reputation for quality and reliability as well as achieving a good deal of success in sporting events. These included the famous 'Prince Henry' models, which have been called the first true British sports car – entirely fitting, then, that one of best performing and best looking of the recent crop of small sports cars is the Vauxhall VX220. The early cars were not particularly cheap and indeed were often to be found in the possession of the wealthier motorist. By 1922, sporting success was becoming rarer for Vauxhall and sales were dropping off, so the emphasis changed to producing a cheaper range of cars for the 'ordinary' motorist in the hope of increasing sales. It was during this period that the name 'Bedford' first appeared, being used for a saloon car body produced on the L-type 14/40 chassis.

GENERAL MOTORS TAKES AN INTEREST

Vauxhall was struggling to compete in the mass car market in the early 1920s – its production methods were outdated and expensive and they had yet to apply the techniques of mass production pioneered by Ford and others in the USA. The company tried to address this by reorganizing the Luton factory to incorporate a production line, but as this was largely applied only to engine manufacture it did not achieve the success that was hoped for. It didn't help that there seemed little will from the most senior management; Leslie Walton, the company chairman, claimed that the Vauxhall workforce was neither trained, nor equipped nor had the desire to produce large quantities of mass produced cars and so would continue the policy of producing a limited number of quality cars at a commensurate price. This 'can't do' attitude, the fall-off in sales and a growing financial crisis within the company put Vauxhall Motors in a position where it was ripe for absorption by a larger manufacturer.

At the same time, US automotive manufacturer General Motors Corporation (GM) was looking for a way to build its market in the UK. GM had established a small plant at Hendon, Middlesex, in 1923 to build cars from its US product range and Chevrolet light commercials for sale in the UK. These were imported in kit form then assembled at Hendon in order to benefit from lower import tariffs compared with bringing in complete cars. This enterprise did not grow as rapidly as hoped, being disadvantaged by competition from cheaper mass-produced models from Austin and Morris; the Buicks, Cadillac, La Salle and Chevrolets attracting higher engine size tax, more expensive insurance and higher servicing costs compared with home-grown models. The Hendon plant was turned over to the production of Chevrolet commercial vehicles utilizing locally built bodies and GM decided that its best option to maintain a slice of the UK automobile market was to acquire a ready-made UK operation. GM's first choice was Austin. While Herbert Austin himself was favourably disposed to the proposed purchase, the majority of Austin's board of directors were not, favouring a modest expansion plan of their own rather than allow the company to fall into US ownership, something that was felt would damage the company's standing in the eyes of the public and attract criticism from the motoring press.

Vauxhall, on the other hand, had no such qualms. Negotiations took around two months and Vauxhall passed into GM ownership on 25 November 1925. GM paid $2,575,291 for Vauxhall, which, taking the gold-standard exchange rate for 1925 at $4.87 to the pound amounted to £528,807. Despite the takeover, Vauxhall's problems were not over; financial losses continued through 1927 to 1929. As Austin's directors had feared, the British motoring press were scathing in their criticism of Vauxhall, *Motor* being the most vociferous in its attacks to the point where Vauxhall withdrew its advertising and loan of cars for testing with the magazine for nearly two years.

BEDFORD
COMMERCIALS BEGIN

A significant event resulting from the takeover was the transfer of manufacture of Chevrolet trucks from Hendon

to Luton in 1929. This included the LQ model, which could be bodied as a small bus with around fourteen to sixteen seats and from 1928 onwards was fitted with the 'Stovebolt Six' Chevrolet straight-six ohv petrol engine. This engine became the foundation from which all Bedford petrol engines would be derived. One of the problems faced by General Motors was that Chevrolet was also an American company, the products of which were not allowed to be exported from the UK. Thus it was necessary to establish a British brand if GM were to break into the export market with commercials made in the UK. It is most likely this factor that prompted the establishment of 'Bedford' as a brand for commercials built at Vauxhall's Luton plant.

This WHB is described by Vauxhall as the first purpose-built Bedford bus. New in August 1931 with a fourteen-seat body by Waveney of Lowestoft, remarkably the bus remained in service until 1956, when it was sold into preservation. It is now owned by Vauxhall at Luton and is looked after by the Vauxhall Heritage Collection. VH

In the early years of production at Luton, the name Bedford was used purely as a model name, and the manufacturer's name that appeared on the instruction book was that of Vauxhall Motors, the address being The Hyde, Hendon, as it had been in the General Motors period before. Indeed, the look and feel of the instruction books for the Bedford models was exactly the same as those of the Chevrolet predecessors, although the latter of course had the General Motors name on the front cover.

The first commercials to carry the Bedford name were the WHG and the WLG light 2-ton (2,032kg) trucks and vans. These were developments of the Chevrolet LQ, the WHG sharing the same 10ft 11in wheelbase as the LQ and powered by a Bedford-modified version of the Stovebolt Six petrol engine. The WHG and the WLG appeared in April 1931, closely followed by the first proper bus chassis, the WHB and WLB, which were intended for fourteen-seat and twenty-seat bus bodies, respectively. Luton could and did build complete trucks, but the passenger chassis were always bodied by independent specialist coachbuilders, although there were small 'station bus' or 'hotel bus'-type conversions seating around seven passengers based on the standard 12cwt (610kg) van. The light weight per passenger of the Bedford passenger chassis soon became a major selling point — a fully laden twenty-seat 'Sun Saloon' body by Duple Bodies and Motors Ltd on a Bedford chassis weighed only 4.25 tons (4,318kg) and was the first laden twenty-seat bus allowed to cross the Menai Strait suspension bridge in north Wales, which at the time had, by coincidence, a weight limit of 4.25 tons!

The last Chevrolets were delivered in early 1932, the overseas success of the new Bedfords being cited as the reason for ending Chevrolet production.

The new Bedford models had a 6-cylinder engine as in their Chevrolet forebears, though this had four main crankshaft bearings as against the three of the Chevrolet, and pressure-feed lubrication instead of the combined pressure-and-splash lubrication of the Chevrolet. Lucas electrical systems appeared for the first time in place of US-made Delco-Remy components.

DUPLE MAKES AN ENTRANCE

It is probably no coincidence that Duple of Hendon emerged as the most prolific body builder on Bedford chassis, being physically located almost next door to the site of Vauxhall's sales office. The introduction of the Certificate of Fitness (COF) by the Ministry of Transport in the Road Traffic Act 1930 encouraged

chassis builders to work more closely with coachbuilders to ensure that requirements of the certificate could be met — this affected things like the size and positions of entrances

Small operators would often have their Bedford chassis bodied locally. Townsend's Tours of Torquay owned this 1935 WTL with Mumford of Plymouth coachwork. It had twenty-six seats, a sunshine roof and a rear entrance. A. CROSS

The 1935 WLB with Duple twenty-seat forward-entrance body was new to T. J. Roberts of Bethesda in northwest Wales. The driver stands proudly by waiting to take the bus to Bangor, his fare collection bag over his shoulder. Roberts traded as Purple Motors. VH

and gangways, seat spacing and so on. As far as Bedford was concerned, this meant building relationships with coach-builders constructing complete vehicles that could be sold through the Vauxhall dealer network. Duple thus became a principal, though not the only, approved body supplier for Bedford chassis.

At the 1931 Commercial Motor Show, twenty-seat buses based on the WLB chassis were on show from: Waveney of Lowestoft (who had bodied the first WHB); Grose, who also built bespoke car bodies on Vauxhall chassis; and Duple. All were similarly priced at £545 for a complete bus from Waveney and Grose and £550 for that from Duple. Interestingly, Waveney had a history of supplying typically fourteen-seat buses on the earlier Chevrolet LM and LQ chassis, Lincolnshire Road Car Co. Ltd and the United Automobile Omnibus Co. Ltd being just two of the larger territorial bus companies that took a number of these in the late 1920s. Waveney was based at Lowestoft and its fourteen- to sixteen-seat bus bodies were marketed as the 'Hendon' – clearly intended to associate them with the Chevrolet make; however, the association did not prosper and while Waveney continued to trade throughout the 1930s, it did not survive the Second World War.

While there was some competition from the likes of Morris Commercial, Dennis, Guy and others, these products tended to be more expensive, so by 1932 Bedford had made the small-bus market its own; 65 per cent of the twenty-seat-and-under buses registered in the UK in that year were made by Bedford.

Spurling Motor Bodies Ltd was another company located close to the Vauxhall sales office in Hendon and also became closely associated with Bedford over the years, particularly in the manufacture of twelve- to fourteen-seat bodies on Bedford goods chassis. However, the first reference to Spurling in connection with Bedford comes in a review in 1934 of a power-assisted brake conversion for current Bedford chassis, which at that time were powered only by the strength of the driver's leg applied to the pedal and thence through mechanical rods and linkages to the brake linings.

Bedfords continued to sell well throughout the early 1930s, and in 1934 the WT 3-ton (3,050kg) range was introduced. A passenger version built by Duple from the WTL lorry chassis was not available until later in the year and the WLB continued in production alongside the WTL. This was only a stop-gap measure as a passenger chassis proper – the WTB – appeared in November 1935 and superseded both the WLB and the WTL. The same straight-six engine was employed as before, although now the power had increased to 64bhp at 2,800rpm.

The rapid success of Bedford stabilized the fortunes of Vauxhall and by the end of 1937 Bedford sales in the one-ton and heavier commercial market were exceeding 26,000 per year. In 1938 the Luton factory gained a new engineering block, known rather appropriately as the 'V Block'. It cost £175,000 and provided accommodation for 335 staff, giving Vauxhall the most up-to-date design and development facility in the UK at the time. Production was now running along modern lines and Vauxhall was in a strong position by 1939, with several new models ready to come to market, notably the new OB bus and coach chassis, introduced in August as successor to the WTB. However, on 1 September 1939 Germany invaded Poland and the deadliest conflict of all time began.

New in March 1936 to Enterprise & Silver Dawn of Scunthorpe, this series I WTB has a rare twenty-six-seat body by Layne & Co. Ltd of Brigg, Lincolnshire. VH

This 1937 WTB bus belonged to the Lancashire Electric Power Co. Ltd, seen here on a works outing in Manchester. The body was the standard Duple twenty-six-seat product. VH

The 1946 OB brochure issued by Bedford. GM

THE RISE OF MOTOR COACH TRAVEL

It was the arrival of the railway as a common carrier in the early nineteenth century that brought the idea of leisure travel to the general public. The roads in Britain had suffered little attention since Roman times and had largely fallen into disrepair until the emergence of the turnpike trusts in the seventeenth century. This brought some improvement, but the canals provided a better way of moving goods so there was little impetus to invest heavily in the roads. Despite this, the need for good roads was recognized and Telford's great highway from London to Holyhead (today the A5) was completed in 1826. Such was the success of the Holyhead road that plans were immediately drawn up to improve the Great North Road (today the A1) on the same model. However, the demonstration of railway locomotive power at the Rainhill trials of 1829 brought a premature end to road development, at least for the next couple of decades, and a rapid rise in the fortunes of the Stephenson family. Long-distance travel before the railways was generally by stagecoach and something one undertook only if absolutely necessary; there are numerous horror stories of the tribulations that befell travellers on the roads at the time. The rapid development of railways meant that for long distance, rail would be the only real choice until the second decade of the twentieth century.

The formation of the county councils under the 1888 Local Government Act brought with it some responsibility for maintaining the highways in the counties but it was the emergence of the internal combustion engine motor vehicle in the first decade of the twentieth century that stimulated improvement in the roads, largely as a result of private individuals acting in cooperation with the county surveyors and engineers. By 1907, things had advanced sufficiently that mechanized road maintenance was taking place. By 1913, Great Britain had a greater mileage of properly built roads than any other country. A Roads Board was set up and funded through new taxes on fuel and a great deal of work was done as a result, then the First World War intervened and the labour force was sent off to war.

Work on the roads resumed after the war and, by the 1930s, the roads in Britain were in a good state. A good network of stage carriage bus services was in place; similarly express services with more luxurious vehicles, some even with toilet facilities, had been in operation since 1925 and were already challenging the supremacy of the railway. Charabancs, long vehicles with car-type bench seats and often a door for each row, provided opportunities for outings that became a way to enjoy precious leisure time in the Edwardian period before the First World War, and their popularity grew throughout the 1920s.

Bedford arrived on the scene just too late to be part of the heady days when the bus and coach industry was a free-for-all and an operator had great freedom over where and when they undertook journeys carrying passengers. In those days, operators would often compete on the same route and drivers of rival companies would sometimes engage in racing, with the consequent effect on health and safety. The 1930 Road Traffic Act brought regulation into the industry; it defined the term 'Public Service Vehicle' as a motor vehicle capable of carrying eight passengers or more for the purpose of hire and reward and brought the term 'PSV' (currently PCV) into common usage. Amongst other far-reaching effects it introduced licensing administered by regional Traffic Commissioners, in particular the Road Service Licence, which an operator needed in order to run buses or coaches on scheduled services, tours and excursions. A Road Service Licence did not apply to private hire work, but because the scope of 'private hire' was not clearly defined this led to anomalies and on occasions absurd cases in the traffic courts when the organizers of annual holiday outings were fined for running a regular scheduled express service without the appropriate licence! Following the Second World War there was something of an upsurge in such cases as small operators sought to reinforce their earnings, which as the 1950s wore on tended to decline in proportion with the rise in private car ownership. By the mid-1970s, the golden age of motor coaching was really over.

One effect of the licensing of operators was to promote a division between those for whom the main business was stage carriage and express services and those whose main business became excursions and tours, a separate licence and costly quasi-legal process being required for each. It has been said that the these proceedings were weighted in favour of the large companies, and indeed the vast majority of stage-carriage services were run by the major bus groups and only the largest of the independents played any significant part in this. Many existing smaller operators sold out to the territorial companies rather than face the cost and difficulties involved in applying for a Road Service Licence for stage carriage services.

For the small operator, an 'E&T' licence required that the operator's vehicle or vehicles complied with a level of fitness for purpose defined by the Ministry of Transport – Bedford was soon advertising that their products complied fully with these new regulations! The lightweight, low-cost Bedford made an ideal E&T and private hire coach, which goes some way to explaining why so many were purchased in just ones and twos by so many businesses throughout the period that Bedford's star was in the ascendancy.

W. S. Hunt's OB/Duple Vista passes the Downlands Cafe and Garage on the A23 near Brighton in the early 1950s. Neither NGP 750 nor the Downlands Cafe and Tea Lounge are still with us, although the pub in the background is still open and Downlands Garage now operates out of the service area on the A23 dual carriageway that now runs a few hundred yards to the left of the road in this picture. VH

JTN 915. The OWB was the wartime version of the OB and the only single-deck bus available for operators to buy new during the war. This is the 1,000th OWB leaving Duple's works. VH

LUTON DURING THE SECOND WORLD WAR AND AFTER

During the First World War, Vauxhall had manufactured 25hp staff cars for the British army. The Second World War brought a much larger role for Vauxhall; car production was suspended except for a few for the military and the factory turned over to the war effort, initially manufacturing large numbers of Bedford trucks for the British services and later the OWB bus chassis for civilian use. The OWB was a slightly modified version of the new OB, fitted with very austere bodywork for wartime production. For a time the OWB was the only bus chassis available until a few other manufacturers were allowed to restart production in a small way. Over the course of the war, 250,000 Bedford trucks were supplied to the services.

The Luton factory's most significant contribution to the war effort was undoubtedly the Churchill tank. Designed and brought to production at Luton in less than twelve months, ten other factories were soon building Churchill tanks from Luton-manufactured components. Over 5,000 tanks had been built by the time the war was over. But that was not all: Luton's contribution included armour-

David MacBrayne was the name for transport in the highlands and islands of Scotland. Here is one of its OB/Duple Vista coaches having just turned off the A9. The destination blind suggests the coach is en route for Carrick Castle, some distance from its pictured location.

The Dunstable factory from the air. The rail connection, abandoned by the time this undated image was taken, can be seen curving in from the bottom right of the picture. GM

piercing shells and components for rocket projectiles, 750,000 steel helmets and panel work for millions of jerricans. The first twelve aircraft jet engines were largely built at Luton, a fact that is rarely mentioned. Given Vauxhall's role in the war effort, the Luton factory attracted attention from the German air force, the worst raid taking place on 30 August 1940, when thirty-nine people lost their lives. Despite this, production of the Churchill tank, which had just started, was not interrupted. The work was divided over the ten 'shadow' factories set up to ensure that production would not be stopped if one received serious bombing damage.

When the war was over, it took until early in 1946 for the factory to return to something like normal and no new car models appeared until 1948.

Production of 'civilian' Bedfords resumed towards the end of 1945 and the OB now became the standard production bus and coach chassis from Bedford. While mechanically similar to the WTB in many ways, the OB came with hydraulic brakes, a longer wheelbase and a new-look V-fronted cab and scuttle shared with the 5-ton (5,080kg) O-series trucks.

The Dunstable Factory Opens

The Dunstable factory was opened in 1942 to provide additional space to assist with Bedford's contribution to the war effort. The new plant was opened at Boscombe Road. Covering 98 acres (40 hectares), the plant was served by a rail connection to the Midland main line at Luton and the West Coast main line at Leighton Buzzard, which enabled efficient distribution of Bedford products. After the war, production of Bedford models continued at both Luton and Dunstable, but by the early 1950s demand for Vauxhall cars was putting pressure on space at Luton so all Bedford bus and truck production was moved to Dunstable, leaving only the light vans to be made at Luton. Between 1955 and 1957 two new two-storey factories were built on the Dunstable site, creating a production line nearly a mile in length. At the time, over 5,000 workers were employed on building Bedfords.

BEDFORD THROUGH THE 1950S

Changes in the maximum dimensions of PSVs became effective on 1 June 1950, making it legal to operate coaches and buses of 30ft overall length, paving the way for new models from a number of manufacturers. Petrol came off ration and there were fears in the bus and coach industry that unless it was made easier for operators to obtain tours licences, the public would take to their cars instead – a touch of crystal-ball gazing that proved remarkably accurate in the long term.

From February 1950 hydraulic shock absorbers became standard equipment on all Bedford PSV chassis, those at the front being mounted directly to the chassis frame; at the rear a bracket was added, allowing the shock absorbers to be mounted horizontally.

For 1950, the bare OB chassis retailed at £533; a similar chassis from Austin, never as popular as the Bedford, was £559. Complete Bedford-Duple vehicles were priced as follows: those with the 'MkIV' thirty-seat service bus

Bedfords were popular in the Antipodes. This Australian Bedford is a 1949 OB with a thirty-one-seat forward-control conversion body by CAC – Commonwealth Air Corporation (later Comair) – of Australia. General Motors held an interest in CAC. H. SCHICK

body cost £1,571; for the Duple Vista luxury coach, the twenty-seven seat version was £1,725 and the twenty-nine seat version was £11 more.

Although the OB had proved tremendously successful, by 1950 it had become outdated and a new passenger chassis, the SB, was introduced as a part of the Bedford 'S' range of 7-ton (7,112kg) payload commercials. A new version of the straight-six petrol engine had been introduced in 1950, producing up to 84bhp; with the commencement of the SB came a new 300cu in (4.9-litre) 110bhp engine. An example with a thirty-two-seat Duple body was exhibited along with the S-series trucks at the 1950 Commercial Motor Show at Earls Court. The SB in time was enormously successful and would prove to be incredibly long-lived for a PSV chassis,

its main appeal being its rugged simplicity – though it did undergo a number of revisions as time went by, keeping pace with Bedford's developments in other spheres. Indeed, the SB would remain available until the end of Bedford production at Dunstable, though in later years the majority of sales were overseas once more sophisticated Bedford chassis became available.

At this time the range of available bus and coach chassis was essentially divided into what were considered 'heavyweight' – the products of, typically, AEC, Bristol, Daimler, Guy, Leyland and, to a lesser extent, Foden, Maudsley and Tilling Stevens – and 'lightweight', made by Bedford, Ford, Commer and Karrier. The manufacturers of heavy chassis also often included double-decks in their range. All had their role to play, though there was a degree of overlap and tradition and politics that influenced sales, but in the main the heavyweights were diesel-powered, designed for long life and day-in day-out stop-start service or regular long-distance express services, where the lightweights were expected to be cheaper to buy, have a shorter life, be serviced more regularly, carry fewer passengers and generally be powered by petrol engines.

As the 1950s wore on, the desire for economy (intensified by the Suez crisis of 1956) meant that operators of lightweight Bedfords were now looking for the kind of the

ABOVE: **Richards Bros' SB8 is a 1962 model with Leyland O.350 engine and Plaxton Embassy body. The Leyland engine had been available as an option on the SB from 1957.**

LEFT: **This 1952 SB with Duple Vega thirty-five coach seat body was photographed in the livery of J. A. Harvey of Evie, Orkney. It later passed to J. D. Peace of Kirkwall, Orkney.**

fuel consumption figures enjoyed by the operators of heavy-weight chassis, which, since the war, had been fitted with diesel engines. Proprietary conversions had been available from several sources since 1950, usually based on the Perkins P6, R6 or Leyland O.350 diesels, and from 1954 the SB was available from Bedford with the Perkins R6 as an option. Despite the economies available with diesel, petrol engines remained available in Bedfords well into the 1970s. Bedford launched its own 300cu in (4.9-litre) diesel in 1957.

KEN 381G. The J2 chassis was a popular choice for small buses. This example with a bus version of the Duple Compact body was owned by Bury Corporation. This photograph was taken on 8 August 1969, when the bus would have been about a year old.

The Small Coaches

With the demise of the OB in 1950, the market for small coaches with seating capacity in the range twenty to twenty-nine had not been specifically catered for. A number of small coaches were built by Duple on the OLAZ 4-ton (4.064kg) long-wheelbase lorry chassis during this period. In 1956 the forward control four-ton C4 and five-ton C5 lorry models were introduced, and these became quite popular as the basis for modifying to suit a small coach body, Duple and Plaxton building bodies that were a scaled-down version of those built for the SB. A further basis for smaller buses and coaches appeared in 1958, with the introduction of the TJ range of trucks. What became known as the J1 and J2 chassis were bodied as PSVs.

In the smaller PSV range, the CA van introduced in 1952, based on running units taken from the contemporary range of Vauxhall cars, was the starting point for a conversion into a twelve-seat mini-bus passenger carrier. Martin Walter, another Hendon business, in particular became associated with light van conversions into small buses and coaches.

in the product line previously occupied by adapted goods chassis. It was announced in August 1961, and both Duple and Plaxton designed twenty-nine seat bodies for it. With its smaller-than-usual 16in wheels it had echoes of Issigonis' Mini about it and seemed entirely in keeping with the new decade.

The Bedford torch was, however, not held by the VAS for long, for at the Commercial Motor Show at Earls Court in 1962 Bedford introduced to the world the VAL – a 36ft-long (11m) maximum-dimension coach with three axles,

THE SWINGING 60S

The 1960s was to be a decade of innovation for Bedford, with a new range of passenger chassis that, while clearly descended from what had gone before, set new standards for lightweight PSV chassis.

The first to appear was the VAS, which at least partially took on the role

FIREFLY

**by
DUPLE**

41 passenger
Luxury Coach
body for Bedford
S.B., Thames P.S.V.
and Albion
Victor chassis

The Duple Firefly body was introduced in 1961. GM

DUPLE GROUP SALES Ltd. EDGWARE RD., THE HYDE, LONDON N.W.9
FOR BODYWORK BY
DUPLE — WILLOWBROOK

TEL:- COLINDALE 6412   BLACKPOOL 62251

IN PRESERVATION

Bedford J2/Plaxton Embassy KNK 373H

Year new: 1969
Engine: Bedford 4-cylinder 220cu in (3.6-litre) diesel
Gearbox: Bedford four-speed
Body: Plaxton Embassy coach, fifteen seats
Current owner: Cyril Kenzie

History

KNK 373H was one of fifteen identical vehicles purchased new by Rickards to run a service between each of the main line stations in London and Heathrow Airport. For this service, several seats were removed at the rear and an additional luggage shelf fitted in the space created. However, the service annoyed the taxi drivers who worked the stations, who saw the coaches as competing for their jobs and so they boycotted the stations. The Ministry of Transport stepped in and Rickards was forced to abandon the service. The J2s were all sold and the luggage racks were replaced with five seats to provide the twenty seats usually found in bodies on the J2 chassis, with the exception of this example, which retains the luggage rack and is therefore unique. After being sold by Rickards, the coach passed through a number of owners, including the brewing firm of Greene King of Bury St Edmunds, Suffolk, who used it to take ex-employee pensioners on outings and the brewery bowls team to matches. The coach ended its working life with Felix Coaches of Long Melford, Suffolk, from whom Cyril bought the coach around fifteen years ago.

Owner's Experience

Cyril Kenzie is perhaps not a typical preservationist. Far from being an amateur enthusiast working out of shed on a farm, Cyril was Chief Engineer of Kenzies Coaches of Shepreth, Hertfordshire for many years. He is also a highly experienced coach driver, and three times winner of Coach Driver of The Year and many other awards at the annual British Coach Rally

KNK 373H. Cyril Kenzie's superb and very original J2/Plaxton Embassy coach, finished in its original Rickards colours.

at Brighton in the 1960s and 1970s; he even starred in a film about coaching made by the BBC in 2010.

Cyril joined his father's coach firm in 1946, having previously worked in a garage from leaving school at the age of fourteen. His employment was interrupted by two years' National Service in the army as a mechanic, where it was, in his own words, 'all fix this! Fix that!' Cyril's father started the business that became Kenzies Coaches with just two taxis, and then expanded it with the acquisition of a twenty-seat Bedford WTB. Kenzies went on to purchase many more Bedfords over the years, as well as AECs and Leylands; these days the fleet is largely Volvo, though most of Cyril's awards were won in Bedfords.

Cyril now maintains a fleet of vintage coaches (which he calls his museum) for Kenzies, exclusively Bedford with two OBs (his personal favourite), the only surviving VAL with a Harrington Legionnaire body and several other Bedfords, including another VAL, a YLQ and the J2.

Cyril recalls that in the early days of his career as an engineer and driver, he would take oil and water out with a coach and service it while waiting for his passengers to return. 'No rules or regulations in those days!', he says.

In Cyril's opinion, his J2 is the best surviving example. Apart from the external paintwork and routine mechanical servicing, no restoration has been performed on the coach and it is completely original, even down to the vinyl antimacassars on the seats. The red moquette trim on the seats is the original and typical Plaxton; it is in fine condition and appears neither worn nor faded given its forty-six years of use. The floor covering is in equally good condition. It is clear, despite the goods origins of the chassis, that this is no simple conversion but a proper small luxury coach. The J2 was painted by Cyril in Kenzies' own body shop, and the finish is superb. Of driving the J2, Cyril says 'Because it is a diesel, it doesn't have much go. Whoever drove it between northern and southern Ireland (one of its regular trips as a touring coach) was a hero. The brakes are good – hydraulic with a servo – and there is no power steering but that's OK as it is so small'.

The Golden Age of Coach Travel, a BBC4 Timeshift documentary featuring Cyril Kenzie and his Bedford OB, was first broadcast in 2011 and is available as a YouTube download.

twin steering wheels and capable of seating fifty-two passengers. The show example was fitted with a Duple Vega Major body. The 1960s was perhaps the last period when elegance in engineering was considered important; one thinks of Concorde and the first River Severn road bridge, both of which combined imagination and engineering excellence. The VAL became a symbol of modernity and a film star, featuring most famously in *The Italian Job* (alongside a fleet of Issigonis' Minis) and in the Beatles' *Magical Mystery Tour*. While the latter was perhaps not the Fab Four's finest hour, it helped to strengthen the image that Bedford was in tune with the times.

Bedford's Market Position in the 1960s

The market for Bedford throughout the 1960s continued to be largely the independent operator who favoured lightweight chassis and body combinations; the only real rivals for Bedford in this market were Commer and Ford with its 'Thames' range. No real attempt seems to have been made at this time by Bedford to break into the market almost totally occupied by the heavyweights – the large bus groups of BET and the government-owned BTC group of bus companies (the former Tilling group) and the municipal fleets. For example, It was reported in November 1962 that UK municipal fleets were operating just twenty-eight Bedfords and, of these, remarkably, twenty-two had petrol engines with just six being diesel powered. Even this small total showed a slight decline on the previous year and serves to illustrate well the role that Bedford was expected to play in the industry. One municipal operator who had some success in the tours market was Edinburgh Corporation Transport, who were operating a fleet of a dozen Bedfords in 1963, consisting of nine SBs with Duple Bella Vega bodies and three VAS with Duple Bella Vista bodies, all painted in a special black and white livery in contrast to the corporation's usual madder red and white livery. These coaches operated a series of two- and three-hour tours to places of interest in Scottish history in and around the city, including a boat trip to Inchcolm Island.

Orders for Bedford/Duple coaches for delivery in late 1964 and early 1965 remained healthy; a snapshot of the order book for 1965 shows the following: for George Ewer and Co. Ltd (Grey-Green and Orange Luxury Tours), ten Duple Bella Vega on SB13 chassis; for Wessex Coaches Ltd of Bristol, seven forty-one-seat Duple Firefly coaches on SB5 chassis; and five forty-one-seat Bella Vega on SB5 for Wilts & Dorset Motor Services, an unusual purchase for a former Tilling group company.

Coachbuilders Consolidate

Some consolidation in the coachbuilding industry took place in the late 1950s and early 1960s. Having acquired Nudd Bros & Lockyer of Kegworth to form Duple Motor Bodies (Midland) Ltd in the 1955, followed by Willowbrook of Loughborough in 1958, Duple acquired H. V. Burlingham of Blackpool in 1960, followed by the coachbuilding activities of W. S. Yeates of Loughborough in 1963. The latter had built a few bodies on OB chassis in 1948 and 1949, but made a larger contribution on the SB chassis. Yeates continued to trade as a dealer in the PSV and general motor trade until the 1980s, when the company ceased these activities and became involved in property development. Another reduction in the number of coachbuilders took place when Martin Walter acquired Kenex and its product range in 1963.

The former Burlingham works in Blackpool subsequently traded as Duple (Northern), while the Yeates' operation became part of Duple (Midland). Willowbrook continued to trade under its own name, while financial control passed to George Hughes, who also owned Duple, in 1971. The Duple (Midland) and Willowbrook factories came to concentrate on bus body production while Willowbrook was part of Duple, whereas the Hendon and Blackpool factories' output became predominantly coach bodies, sometimes producing the same bodies with slight differences. Willowbrook closed in 1984; however, the business restarted in

This 1972 SB has a Willowbrook bus body to a Duple (Midland) design. It was owned by Rochester & Marshall, part of the Moor-Dale Group, and used on Hexham town services, where it is seen in September 1980.

alternative premises in Loughborough in 1985, with two new bodies – the Crusader, intended for the Bedford YNV Venturer chassis, and the Warrior bus body.

The range of bodies available for the larger Bedford chassis in the early years of the 1960s was quite extensive. From Duple, the smallest body in its range was the nineteen-seat metal-framed bus body manufactured at Blackpool for the J2 goods chassis converted to forward control. Next in line was the Bella Vista twenty-nine-seat body for the VAS, with a larger version known as the Bella Vega and capable of seating forty-one passengers. From the Duple (Northern) factory again came the Firefly, also seating forty-one but in a style that harked back a decade rather than looking forward like the Bella Vista and Vega bodies. The largest model for Bedford was the Vega Major, with fifty-two seats for the VAL.

From Plaxton there was the Embassy II, seating forty-one when mounted on

Hulley's of Baslow ran this 1961 SB with striking Yeates Fiesta coachwork until 1975. It is seen here in the picturesque Derbyshire town of Bakewell in the late 1960s.

the SB chassis, twenty-nine in the version for the VAS and eighteen to twenty in that for the J2 chassis. The Embassy had replaced the Consort body in 1960. The Plaxton Panorama body with its trademark panoramic side windows, unique for the time, had first appeared in 1959 and was available for the SB with forty-one to forty-three seats. A restyled version appeared at the 1964 Commercial Motor Show and could be had with forty-nine to fifty-two seats on the Bedford VAL chassis in addition to the smaller-capacity version on the SB.

From Thurgood of Ware there was the Forerunner, available in various seating capacities up to twenty-nine and with versions to suit the J2 and VAS, while Thomas Harrington of Hove was building the Crusader MkIII with thirty-seven or forty-one seats for the SB. A body rarely seen in practice was the Metropolitan-Cammell-Weymann (MCW) Amethyst, whose appearance was somewhat less attractive than its name might suggest; it was described as having a seating capacity of 'as required' but nominally forty-one for the SB.

Another distinctive, though fairly uncommon, body was the Yeates Fiesta Continental, a forty-one-seat model for the SB chassis with quite purposeful and individual looks. Of special note was the FE44 version of this body, which embodied a conversion of the SB chassis to allow the entrance to be positioned in the front overhang ahead of the front wheels. A bus version was also available, called the Pegasus. The conversion caused some discomfort to Bedford and was never supported by them. Another well-known name in other branches of PSV manufacture was Strachans (and Brown) Ltd, originally at North Acton but by this time based in Hamble, Hampshire. Strachans also

Strachans of Hamble was advertising its Pacesaver body on the SB in 1965.

built on Bedford chassis, offering utility bus bodies on the Bedford SB chassis.

Prices for bare PSV chassis from Bedford in 1963 were as follows: VAS with petrol engine £860, with diesel engine £1,045. The SB petrol chassis was £1,035, SB with Bedford diesel £1,165; SB with Leyland diesel £1,465. The VAL was £1,820. In comparison, lightweight chassis from Ford cost £1,040 for a petrol-powered Thames Trader and £1,170 for a diesel version of the same chassis, which competed directly with the SB. Another rival for the SB was the Commer Avenger, priced at £1,580. To compete with the VAL, Ford was offering the new Thames36 chassis. This was quite a bit cheaper than the VAL at £1,500 for a petrol-powered chassis and £1,620 for a version with a diesel engine, but of course was of conventional design with the less exciting configuration of only two axles! All of these were classified as lightweight chassis; if one wanted a heavier chassis from AEC, Daimler, Guy or Leyland then prices started at around £2,500 and ranged to £3,000, so a VAL at just over £1,800 seemed like a good buy in the short term for a fifty-two-seat coach.

A New Chassis

New for 1965 was the VAM. This was an entirely new chassis, not just an updated version of the SB and was designed for true front-entrance bodywork from the start and therefore rendered redundant the disapproved-of conversion of the SB chassis offered by Yeates. The VAM was suitable for bus and coach bodies of around forty-five seats. Despite the almost universal adoption of horizontal, amidships-mounted underfloor diesel engines by the heavier chassis manufacturers, the traditional vertical front engine, including a

Barton Transport of Chilwell fleet no. 1027 was one of the unapproved Yeates Fiesta front-entrance conversions on the SB chassis. Originally owned by Price of Halesowen, it was bought by Barton in 1965.

petrol option, and unit-mounted gearbox were retained. Though clearly intended to replace the SB, such was the popularity of the latter that Bedford continued to produce it, while the VAM carved its own niche in the market. VAM chassis commenced production at the end of June 1965, a year that had seen the 50,000th chassis leave the Dunstable plant, a VAL chassis bound for Australia, thirty-four years after the first Bedford passenger chassis appeared.

The VAM quickly became popular and highly thought of in the industry and soon built up a strong following. Bedfords were already popular in Scotland, and the Scottish Bus Group had taken a small number of twenty-nine-seat VAS coaches and forty-one-seat SBs in 1962. Quite significant purchases by the group followed later on in the 1960s and 1970s, Highland Omnibuses Ltd having six VAMs and six VASs, and Scottish Omnibuses Ltd twenty VAMs in 1968; similarly, in Northern Ireland the newly formed Ulsterbus company ordered seventy Duple (Northern) forty-five-seat coaches on VAM chassis worth around a quarter of a million pounds in 1966. Many more Bedfords crossed the Irish Sea bound for Ulsterbus over the years.

The Transport Holding Company (THC) took some VAMs with ECW bus bodies in 1967/8 for several former Tilling group companies while the Bristol LH was under development. These were part of an order for sixty-four VAM and VAL chassis from the Tilling Association – other

NMU 552E. Good night-time pictures are rare, so the opportunity to include this shot of Grey-Green's VAM14 with Duple Bella Venture body could not be missed. Grey-Green was part of the George Ewer Group of companies and this coach was new to the company in January 1967.

coachbuilders fulfilling this order included Duple, Plaxton and Strachans, the latter supplying some dual-entrance thirty-three seat buses on VAM chassis for Hants & Dorset Motor Services.

Some BET companies also took a few Bedfords. The East Kent Road Car Co. Ltd, for example, ordered ten twenty-nine-seat buses on VAS chassis with bodies by Marshall of

A forty-five-seat Alexander Y-type body is fitted to Highland Scottish's fleet no. CD20, a 1967 VAM5, seen on 6 June 1981.

Cambridge (Engineering) Ltd in 1966 for delivery in 1967; very similar bodies were supplied to a number of operators on Bristol LHS chassis so this did not necessarily reflect a growing market for Bedford. Indeed, the Bristol LH range would in time become a quite severe thorn in Bedford's side. Other significant orders for delivery in early 1967 included thirty-eight units with Duple coachwork for T. J. Whittle & Son, Bridgwater, this order alone being worth £900,000; and sixteen VAMs with Duple coachwork for the George Ewer group.

Welfare and School Buses

Bedfords found a useful niche in the welfare market over time. These were specially adapted passenger carriers, suited to the needs of those with a variety of disabilities who relied on the local authority for transport, and generally operated as a unit separate from local authority-controlled municipal bus fleets. Such vehicles were more expensive and in 1965 a typical budget for a VAS with suitably adapted coachwork for use by the London Borough of Islington Welfare Committee was £4,000. Coventry Corporation bought seven thirty-seat VASs with Marshall bodies for use by the education committee for transporting children to and from school in 1966.

The London borough of Haringey received eight VAS with thirty-two-seat bodies by Strachans (Coachbuilders) Ltd of Hamble in August 1967, intended to be the forerunners of replacements for those currently used for school and welfare duties in the borough's fleet of approximately 200 vehicles. A further two were supplied with wheelchair accommodation and Ratcliffe electro-hydraulic tail-lifts. The chassis for all ten were supplied through Bedford dealer Capitol Motor Co. Ltd of Tottenham.

In the Republic of Ireland, a free school transport scheme was introduced and Coras Iompair Eireann (CIE), the Irish state-owned transport undertaking, was tasked with providing vehicles for the scheme, which became something of a phenomenon in time with drivers being largely part-time but specially trained and drawn from the ranks of agricultural workers, teachers, garage owners, clerks and housewives. Research predicted a need for 760 vehicles for this purpose in the short term. Some were provided by refurbishing older vehicles, but 230 new vehicles were needed to fulfil requirements. These came in two sizes, 130 larger vehicles based on Bedford SB chassis seating sixty-seven children or forty-five adults (no seat belt regulations in those days), while the remainder were smaller vehicles

'Functional' might describe this Lex body on a 1980 VAS5 chassis for the Metropolitan Police.

based on VAS chassis and seating forty-nine children or thirty-three adults. The bodies on the SB chassis were built at CIE's famous works at Spa Road, Inchincore, while the VAS bodies were divided between McArdle, Duffy and Murphy, all Dundalk-based coachbuilders. A distinctive livery of golden brown with a broad white horizontal stripe was chosen for the new fleet. Over the years 1968–1974 the CIE fleet of Bedfords grew to an astonishing total of 800, one of the largest fleets of Bedfords in the world, of which 150 were VAS5, the remainder mostly SB5.

The early 1970s was the time when large centralized comprehensive schools were becoming widespread and Local Education Authorities (LEAs) in rural areas were discovering the problems of getting children to school, especially where the usual forms of public transport were unable to cope or simply unavailable. In 1972, West Suffolk County Council bought a fleet of eleven SBs with Strachans bodies supplied by dealer O. G. Barnard and Sons Ltd of Stowmarket, Suffolk, the fifty-one-seat capacity being achieved by a three-and-two seat arrangement and, with safety in mind, painted in an appealing tangerine livery. The Greater London Council (GLC) bought seventy-seven VAS with Dormobile thirty-one-seat bodies for the Inner London Education Authority (ILEA).

Certain coachbuilders specialized in this kind of vehicle, such as J. H. Sparshatt and Sons Ltd, Burrfields Road, Portsmouth and Lex Vehicle (Engineering) Ltd, of Totton. Hampshire and Reeve Burgess of Chesterfield all built what could be described as basic welfare-type bus bodies. Reeve

Burgess had good sales of its highly adaptable Reebur range of mini-coach bodies based on Bedford CF and Ford Transit chassis. Options included wide rear doors incorporating a tail-lift.

Lex introduced a fairly heavy-duty body in 1979; known as the Maxeta, it typified the specification for this kind of vehicle. The Maxeta was of all-metal construction in steel and aluminium, with pressed-steel floor and cant rails. A heavy-duty roll bar and anti-crush roof were features that addressed concerns raised in the 1970s about roll-over protection in PSVs. The roof was panelled in aluminium alloy sheet while other internal and external panels were of zinc-coated steel sheet secured to the framework by rivets. The floor was generally of resin-bonded plywood with a hard-wearing bonded fibreglass non-slip surface for safety. Wheelchair lifts, quick-release seats and wheelchair anchorage fittings, passenger harnesses and crutch racks were available as options. The body could be fitted to a number of chassis, including the J-series, SB and VAS, with seats ranging from twenty-eight to fifty-four.

A Glimpse of the Future

A portent of the future was a photograph that appeared in *Commercial Motor* for the 24 December 1965, showing a Bedford VAS fitted with an attractive coach body built by Bova N. V. of Valkenswaard, Holland. Bova would become a familiar name in the UK coaching industry in years to come. Another interesting venture of the time was a small all-metal single-deck bus, also on a VAS chassis supplied by dealer Bently Bros and built by Cravens Homalloy Ltd as a private speculative venture. This bus was purchased by Sheffield Corporation, presumably to show its support for local industry, for £2,400.

BORDER COURIERS AND BEDFORD

An interesting example of welfare operations is provided by the Borders Courier service, which over the years has been contracted to a number of operators, including Eastern Scottish, Lowland Scottish and First group. A consistent feature of operations throughout the 1980s and 1990s was the use of Bedford-based small buses of the welfare type. The Borders region of Scotland had at that time just one general hospital, at Peel, Galashiels. What distinguished the 1979 Border Courier from other rural bus services was the pick-up and delivery service provided for the local Health Board. The service started with five Bedford CFs fitted with Reeve Burgess bodies, each with thirteen seats for passengers and luggage space at the rear for medical and other supplies. Access to the storage compartment was by rear doors.

The journeys ran inwards to Peel in the morning and outwards into the region in the afternoon. In the course of its inward journey the Courier stopped at health centres and cottage hospitals to collect supplies and samples for Peel, then during the lunch layover the supplies were sorted and the Courier buses reloaded, often with bulk supplies from the smaller hospitals to be delivered back to the outlying health centres and small hospitals. In addition to the hospital run, a useful rural bus service was provided for people living in remote corners of the region. So successful was the service that it was not long before the CFs were replaced with VAS seventeen-seat buses with luggage compartments. By 1982 it was reported that the service was carrying 419 passengers per week, more than double the expected 200 passengers. Though heavily subsidized, the service was found to be substantially more economical to run than conventional services. The VASs were obviously well thought of, being replaced with brand new VASs in 1987 – some of the last Bedfords made.

Bedfords were found to be highly suitable for the Border Courier service. This VAS5 with Reebur (Reeve Burgess) body replaced an earlier CF with a smaller-capacity Reebur body; it is seen here at Peebles on a wet day in June 1984.

Throughout the 1960s the existing bodies suitable for Bedford chassis from Duple and Plaxton were revised generally almost annually and the results usually shown at the various shows around the UK and at the biennial Commercial Motor Show at Earls Court in September. Now and then new models were introduced to take account of advances in manufacturing and the expectations of customers and the travelling public. The Duple Viceroy was one such new product and was unveiled at Hendon on 4 July 1966, bringing a new and fresh look from Duple. Intended for the VAL and VAM chassis, it cost £3,825 for a forty-five-seat body for a petrol VAM and £40 more for the diesel version. For the VAL, the body was known as the Viceroy 36 and cost £4,280 – the chassis not included! Also announced was a slightly longer body for the VAS, the Vista 25, though still with twenty-nine seats and costing £2,875 for the petrol version and once again £40 more for the diesel.

Bedfords continued to sell well overseas; export orders for 1966 included eighteen units shared between VAM and VAS chassis for municipal services in Mauritius, ten SBs for Barbados and twelve VASs for Finland.

Advances in Bedford's goods range usually found applications in the passenger chassis in due course. From August 1967 the 70-series diesel engine developed for the KM range of heavy goods chassis became available for the VAL and VAM. The smaller J2 forward-control conversion and CA conversions were still selling well in the twelve- to twenty-seat range.

Showing off its Wares

From time to time, small shows would be laid on by the coachbuilders and by Bedford dealers to enable customers to gain an intimate view of new products. For example, Duple held its own show at Hendon every two years, the twelfth such show occurring in October 1967. The kind of thing that might be seen included improved entrance arrangements for the Viceroy body with easier steps. The high frames of the contemporary range of lightweight coaches meant the floor level was generally a lot higher than today, where ease of access has become a priority in body design. However, coachbuilders were beginning to recognize these factors and the revised Viceroy entrance had three 8in (20cm) steps in place of the two 12in (30cm) steps of the original design. Additional improvements to the Viceroy included improved seating, three-way opening Weathershield roof lights and better sound insulation. For the driver there was a more adjustable seat and a compact instrument and switch binnacle.

Duple was keen to show off its versatility, and the exhibits included a twenty- or twenty-one-seat Compact luxury coach built on a J2L chassis that had been designed in conjunction with United Transport International – a company that shared its roots with the Red & White group in the UK – for operation in the game reserves of South Africa, Tanzania, Uganda and Kenya.

Such shows could be quite major events. For example, at another event in October 1967, Vauxhall and Bedford dealer E. J. Baker and Co. (Dorking) Ltd of Chertsey had more than a hundred coaches on show at the premises of Creamline Motor Services (Bordon) Ltd, an operator recently acquired by Baker's parent company, Dorada Investment Group. On show at this event was a Bedford VAL70 with a Plaxton Panorama body fitted with forty-four reclining seats, designed for continental touring. Costing just £10,000, it was fitted with a two-speed rear axle and Telma retarder and was operated by Coliseum Coaches Ltd of Southampton. While prices are in mind, inflation determined a price increase from March 1968, the petrol VAS now costing £959, the diesel VAM £1,675, the VAL £1,971 and the ever-popular SB £1,137.

New Bodies for Bedford

The Duple Group and Plaxton continued to be the main suppliers of the bodies on Bedford chassis into 1968, though there had been attempts by other coachbuilders to break into the market for Bedford. MCW notably produced a stylish and advanced body called the Metropolitan, and a few were built, not only on Bedford but also on Ford chassis. Park Royal Vehicles Ltd had announced a suitable body in 1966 but this did not sell well and was not listed by 1968. Duple and Plaxton continued to build bodies on the J2 chassis, generally much as designed for the VAS. For the VAL and VAM, Duple now only offered the Viceroy. Plaxton's new Panorama Elite became the main body from the Scarborough factory, superseding both the Panorama I and the Panorama II, the latter still being available but now with little demand. Most coaches by now had forced air ventilation combined with non-opening windows; however, both Duple and Plaxton did offer a sliding-window ventilation option, though this was available only on the Panorama II from Plaxton. The SB continued to sell well and for this chassis Duple was still building the Bella Vega, while a version of the Panorama was available from Plaxton.

Bedford continued to sell well overseas; of interest in 1968 and 1969 were orders from Caltex Services Ltd for the Bahrain Petroleum Co. Ltd. These were for fifteen in total VAM chassis, with ten fifty-three-seat bodies built by MCW to a style developed by the Superior Coach

Corporation of Lima, Ohio, USA, the remaining five being built by Strachans, who had taken over the rights to the Superior body in the UK and was marketing it as the Superior 5100 body.

Continuing demand for the SB had meant that Duple was still building the Bella Vega to the 1960 design. Around fifty coaches of this forty-one-seat style were produced in 1968 and demand outstripped supply. With this in mind, Duple sought to replace the Bella Vega with a suitable body for the SB but of modern appearance. One hundred coaches with this new body, known as the Vega 31, were therefore planned for 1970. All had been sold to customers or dealers before production got fully underway, some operators reverting to the SB after having operated the VAM, reinforcing once again how popular was the SB. The Vista 25 body for the VAS was also restyled for 1970 production.

New Codes for Old Chassis

Computers were finding their way into the automotive industry for accounting and stock control during the late 1960s, so Bedford introduced new chassis identification codes in connection with computerization at Vauxhall. The SB3 (petrol) became the NFM and the SB5 (diesel) the NJM; in time the system renamed the VAS1 (petrol) the POK and the VAS5 (diesel) the PJK, though the use of these codes outside of Bedford seemed to be half-hearted at best and the industry generally continued to the refer to all chassis by their more familiar designations of SB, VAS, VAL, VAM and so on right until the end of production.

Continental Drift

If the UK coachbuilding industry had been contracting as suggested in the media at the time, then the range of bodies available to customers was about to increase and the complacency of UK manufacturers challenged even further. In 1968, in quite a small way, a revolution began that would see the UK coaching scene eventually dominated by products from continental Europe. At the Commercial Motor Show that year, dealer Alf Moseley and Sons Ltd of Loughborough, Leicestershire showed a coach of typically continental design based on a Leyland Leopard chassis. The all-metal body, of welded frame construction, had been built by the Portuguese coachbuilder IMVT Salvador Caetano SARL. Two Caetano bodies had been imported by John Willment, Ford dealers, earlier in the year, one fitted to a Ford D500 goods chassis, the other it is thought to a Ford R226, which was the first example of a full-size coach from Caetano. However, following the Motor Show the names Moseley and Caetano would be forever linked and the Loughborough company bought a substantial share of the Portuguese coachbuilder in 1986.

A subsidiary of the Moseley group, Moseley Continental Coachwork Ltd, was formed for the purpose of importing coaches from continental Europe, and its first product for a Bedford chassis came not from Caetano but from Belgian coachbuilder Van Hool. The prototype was a fifty-three-seat body on a VAL chassis; a forty-five-seat version for the VAM would soon follow, the body having been adapted from the company's current product range in conjunction with Moseley. By the end of 1969, Moseley was offering a

This smart **YRQ** with Van Hool Vistadome forty-five-seat body was operated by Basil Williams of Emsworth, Hampshire, who traded as Southern Motorways. It was new in January 1972. A Van Hool body on a Bedford chassis was quite rare at this time.

twenty-nine-seat body branded the Caetano Sintra on the VAS; a fifty-three-seat body for the VAL, named the Estoril; and a forty-five-seat body, called the Cascais, on the VAM.

While the largest proportion of Bedford's market (leaving aside the huge school bus commitment for CIE) had been for luxury and touring coaches, there had been a steady though proportionately smaller trade in bus versions of the VAM. Moseley held its own exhibition at its Shepshed, Leicestershire coach works in October 1969. On show, in addition to the Caetano range, were a Plaxton Derwent forty-seven-seat express bus body and Willowbrook forty-five-seat express bus body, both on Bedford VAM 70 chassis.

A MID-ENGINE BEDFORD AT LAST

By 1970 the industry press was reporting that UK operators were expressing a degree of dissatisfaction with the available range of lightweight coach chassis. Bedford in particular was criticized for high noise levels and poor braking – many operators were finding it necessary to fit retarders – and operators now wanted a chassis with the engine anywhere but at the front. The continuing success of the SB seems at odds with this, though the SB was by this time finding its role in more utilitarian duties so perhaps should not be part of the argument. In fairness, the body-builders equally came in for criticism, though it seems that operators were not totally in agreement regarding the desirable features – forced-air ventilation versus sliding windows, radios and PA systems were all subjects for discussion. Considered a 'must' were power-operated doors and competent heaters. Further, operators were asking for another quality body in competition with Duple and Plaxton at the same price, opening the door for the likes of Van Hool and Caetano to step in, though there were questions over the expected life of these bodies and the potential after-sales service.

Bedford responded for its part by introducing an entirely new chassis, announced in September 1970. Intended to supersede the VAM, the YRQ had its new 466cu in (7.6-litre) diesel engine mounted vertically amidships in the chassis under the floor, allowing bodies to be built with wider entrance areas and easier engine access. Given that the centrally mounted underfloor-engine arrangement had been adopted by the heavy chassis makers since around 1950, it seems remarkable that Bedford took twenty years to produce a chassis of this type. Even when they did, the engine stubbornly remained vertically mounted whereas in all the traditional underfloor-engine chassis, the engines were fitted horizontally to lower the floor line. It could be argued that Bedford was reluctant to use a proprietary engine in the YRQ and that the cost of developing a horizontal version of the 466 range was prohibitive, yet this had not prevented the adoption of a Leyland engine for the VAL. Having said that, the new YRQ instantly found favour with operators and rapidly became popular. The YRQ's more robust construction showed that Bedford was aware of the competition from the traditional heavyweight chassis manufacturers and in particular the Bristol LH, which was gaining considerable popularity with independent operators and other regular Bedford customers. The VAM was now no longer available for the UK market, although it remained in the export catalogue and continued to sell well overseas, as did the SB.

A bare YRQ chassis was on show at the Commercial Motor Show in September 1970, as well as examples with bodies from both Duple and Plaxton. For 1970, further rationalization of Duple's product line meant that only the Viceroy was available with forty-five seats and upwards, a forty-five seat version being mounted on the YRQ, while an updated Duple (Northern) Viscount body was now available for the VAS. The forty-one-seat Duple Vega continued to be available for the SB. The latter body remained of traditional jig-built composite construction incorporating a great deal of wood. Externally the design had been updated, with some of the contemporary Viceroy features, though still resembling the superseded Viscount design in outline. A contemporary observer noted that the improvements to the Vega gave it a better entrance than the Viceroy on the YRQ, so not all progress was in the right direction! Brightwork and fittings on all Duple coaches were in stainless steel, providing an interesting contrast with the Moseley Continental Caetano bodies on show, whose brightwork was formed of anodized aluminium profiles and heavily chromed brass. Indeed, the Caetano bodies were of modern all-metal construction, utilizing arc-welded box-section frames assembled in jigs.

Plaxton's only offering on show was the Panorama Elite II luxury coach, another forty-five-seat luxury coach on a YRQ chassis with restyled interior and a facelifted frontal design with a larger grille for easier access and four headlamps, grouped in pairs.

Economically, the coachbuilding industry seemed on the up slightly in 1970. There was a growing choice, with offerings from Caetano and Van Hool and a surprising challenge from Eastern Coachworks Ltd (ECW) of Lowestoft, with a new luxury coach body on the prototype AEC Sabre chassis. While well built, as all ECW products tended to be, the body clearly exhibited styling cues drawn from the products of both Duple and Plaxton, in particular the Panorama Elite and, as was usually the case with ECW products, a bit behind the times. Whilst the AEC/ECW combination would not materialize in production, the body was revised and formed the basis of a new body for the Bristol RE and Leyland Leopard, though it was really dead in the water from the start in the wider lightweight luxury coach market. The Leyland Leopard chassis, by contrast, was highly thought of and became a serious competitor in Bedford's market in 1970s and 1980s, though generally with Plaxton coachwork of the same style as fitted to the YRQ.

Duple took orders worth £1.48m at the show itself, bringing the total orders for 1970 to £3.5m, 10 per cent up on those for 1968. A review of the orders gives an interesting window on Bedford's customers at the time, with Viceroy, Vega and Vista bodies on YRQ, SB and VAS chassis being ordered by Salopia Saloon Coaches of Whitchurch, Shropshire; J. T. Whittle and Sons of Highley, near

Kidderminster, Worcestershire; Don Everall Travel Ltd of Wolverhampton; Fred Winkle of Willenhall, Staffordshire; Wye Valley Motors of Hereford; Dodds of Troon; Travel House of Luton; Stanley Hughes Hire of Gomersal, West Yorkshire (forerunner of Arriva Bus & Coach Ltd); Hutchinson's Coaches of York; West Coast Motor Services of Campbeltown, Argyll; Park's Thistle Coaches of Hamilton, Lanarkshire; Golden Eagle Coaches of Motherwell, Lanarkshire; Shamrock and Rambler Motor Coaches Ltd of Bournemouth; the Metropolitan Police; Roseland Coaches of Truro; Wessex of Bristol; Thorpe's Coaches of Walthamstow; and Mayfair Coaches of London.

The Era of the Executive Coach

By 1972 the VAL was becoming outdated and Bedford needed to offer a modern chassis in the 11m-long (36ft), fifty-plus-seats market. This duly appeared in early 1972 as the YRT, which followed the pattern established with the YRQ of engine and gearbox mounted amidships. With the YRT, some of the criticisms that had been levelled at Bedford were addressed, particularly that of interior noise. The length of the YRT made it a good basis for the emerging style of executive coaches, with reduced seating capacity, independent generators to provide on-board power, catering facilities, and TV and bathroom facilities. At the 1972 Commercial Motor Show, Caetano, Plaxton, Van Hool and Willowbrook all had coaches of this type on show; all were on YRT chassis except the Van Hool body, which was mounted on a Leyland Leopard. Willowbrook was also showing a service bus based on the YRT.

1972 Bedford brochure announcing the new 11m (36ft) YRT chassis. GM

The YRT was Bedford's first 11m (36ft) chassis. Lothian Transport's YRT with Alexander Y-type coach body with fifty-three bus seats was photographed in Edinburgh on 1 April 1977. It survives in preservation.

This YRT with Plaxton Supreme fifty-three-seat body was new to Braybrooks of Mendlesham, Suffolk, in whose livery it was photographed in December 1975. It later passed to County Travel of Loughborough, where it received a new front end and radiator grille from the later Paramount body.

Also new at the show was a body from Jonckheere, and, while mounted on an AEC Reliance chassis, gave further evidence of the increasing competition from mainland Europe; portentous also was Willowbrook's 007 integral model with running units from the Mercedes-Benz 0.302 coach, though it was at least partially UK-built so perhaps not in itself the vanguard of the European invasion. Integral construction with a monocoque body utilizing mechanical units from a suitable source was not new in the bus field and there were some notably successful examples, the most obvious being the Leyland National bus, which had appeared in 1972, though all parts had been Leyland-sourced. According to Salvador Caetano's own records, the company built seven semi-integral Cascais II coaches with rear-mounted 466cu in (7.6-litre) engines and Bedford YRQ running units during 1974–5. The term 'semi-integral' in this context means that while there is a separate underframe, it is designed specifically to be integrated into a single body design, and when the two are joined together they form a single structure that shares all the loads. The concept proved

ultimately not to be popular and production did not continue, an echo of the late 1940s when J. C. Beadle of Dartford built several buses utilizing Bedford OWB mechanical components. While larger coaches were in the limelight, the VAS continued to be popular, Dormobile (successor to Martin Walter) showing a school bus-type body of around thirty seats.

The appearance of the YRT provided an opportunity for long-standing customers to consider updating their Bedford fleets; George Ewer placed a substantial order for twenty YRQs and four VASs, all with Plaxton bodies to replace a number of older coaches, including four-year-old VALs, which they were advertising for sale at £4,500. A Grey-Green (a member of the Ewer group) order for YRTs

OLJ 404M. Strachans' bodies were sometimes something of an acquired taste, styling-wise. This 1973 twenty-seven-seat VAS5 fleet no. M4 was operated by Yellow Buses, successors to Bournemouth Corporation Transport.

followed in 1973, as did one for twenty-five from Ulsterbus followed by another for 100 YRQs, all with locally built bus bodies, the YRQs having forty-five seats and the YRTs fifty-five. The total order value to Bedford was £400,000 and the largest order to date for Y-series Bedfords for bus use.

By 1974 the influence of the all-metal bodies from the continent was becoming apparent. Both Duple and Plaxton were in the process of converting their construction methods to eliminate composite construction, employing all-steel, tubular-framed construction methods, firstly on their smaller models for the VAS – the growing need for economy reflected by a resurgence of interest from operators in coaches in the twenty-nine- to thirty-five-seat range. Duple had achieved all-metal construction with three models by September 1974, having started with a new body, the Dominant, introduced in 1972, which was largely all-metal with a small amount of wood used where the external panels were attached to the all-metal frame. It was intended eventually to extend the style of construction to the rest of the range, forgoing all wood in the construction of the body. Plaxton had introduced the new metal-framed Panorama Supreme model to replace the aging Panorama Elite, though in appearance the new body was clearly based on the earlier one. The VAS was at this time, according to Vauxhall, selling around 750 units annually, of which 80 per cent were for the UK market.

Willowbrook continued its excursion into the executive coach arena with its super-luxury 008 body on the YRT chassis, while Alf Moseley introduced a new twenty-seat luxury coach, called the Faro, on the evergreen J2 chassis.

The continental invasion continued, with the import of sixty Mercedes O.608D chassis by the manufacturer. Mercedes had yet to make much of an impact in the full-size coach market in the UK, so, taking advantage of the upturn in the small coach market, these were intended for bodying by Duple and Plaxton with adapted versions of the bodies already available on the VAS and J2 chassis. The product was reasonably competitively priced at around £1,000 more than the VAS.

A new body by Duple was launched at the 1974 Commercial Motor Show; this was the Dominant Bus body, intended for the YRQ chassis for the around forty-five-seat light bus market. The Dominant Bus was based on the all-metal Dominant coach body introduced in 1972 and the show model seated forty-seven. The coach version received a facelift at the same time, with an improved level of interior trim, along with an alarm system and a host of other small changes.

The New Bus Grant introduced by the UK Ministry of Transport in 1967 had made it worthwhile for many operators of stage and contract hire services to buy brand-new vehicles to 'Grant specification' at prices as low as they would have previously paid for second-hand vehicles. Thus the price of second-hand coaches had fallen dramatically over the years, meaning that that those operators who traditionally replaced their fleets every two to three years were now finding it economically necessary to keep their vehicles longer on front-line service. The knock-on effect was that operators were now looking for more robust vehicles with potentially longer, lower-maintenance lives to counter this. The new Bedford Y-series was more robustly built, in an attempt to claw back sales that might have been lost to the Bristol LH and Leyland Leopard, further strengthened by the introduction in autumn 1975 of more powerful engines for the YRT and YRQ – which now became the YMT and YLQ. Interest in these new chassis grew quickly and Bedford initially struggled to meet demand; some criticism was received from dealers over delay in deliveries and reluctance on Bedford's part to discuss the situation at the time.

Generally speaking, the mechanical specification of Bedford's PSV chassis had been simple and conservative, with straightforward engines and axles and manual gearboxes. However, there was growing demand in the industry for the driver's conditions to be improved. A batch of YRTs with Allison automatic transmission had already been exported to Australia under a special order and from early 1976 this transmission became an option on the YRT, YMT and YLQ chassis.

State of the Market in the mid-1970s

The policy of pedestrianizing town and city centres to relieve them of congestion from private cars was gaining sway in the mid-1970s. A number of such schemes were in existence; these placed emphasis on providing frequent local bus services using buses small enough to be safely used in restricted areas. Initially, many of these schemes made use of converted light vans of around twelve to sixteen seats; in Bournemouth, however, the services were so popular that larger vehicles had to be used and the corporation transport department, having operated small Bedfords in the past, naturally turned to Bedford again for two twenty-seven-seat buses based on VAS chassis.

By the mid-1970s the only realistic choices in the lightweight bus and coach market lay between the products of Bedford and Ford. This was the view of T. F. Mclachlan, a director and the general manager of Grey-Green Coaches, writing on the state of the market in *Commercial Motor*. The British lightweights were saving as much as 25 per cent in fuel consumption over the popular imported types at the time and the continentals were significantly more expensive to buy new. Bedford parts were also 25–50 per cent cheaper than those from Leyland, though Mclachlan acknowledged that over five years the costs would probably even out, with the more robust Leyland Leopard needing less attention. To place these comments in context, the George Ewer group was one of the largest users of Mercedes-Benz 0.302s at the time.

Mclachlan's view was that the reason the market was not dominated by lightweights was due to the ongoing maintenance costs, which included employment of skilled fitters, parts, time the vehicle was off the road and the availability of workshop space; however, the purchase price of a lightweight was significantly low enough – 30–60 per cent cheaper than a similar-sized heavyweight chassis – for an operator to have a rolling replacement programme in place so the average age of the fleet was kept low, maintenance costs in the first twelve months of a vehicle's life being very low. Costs, he said, rose very steeply after the first two to three years of life, though he felt that both Bedford and Ford offered good value for money.

The growing popularity of the Leyland Leopard was highlighted; Mclachlan's view was that of the heavyweights, now the Bristol RE was no longer available, it was the most robust and for express services had no equal. Mclachlan was also of the view that the main areas of competition were not between Bedford and Ford but between the lightweights as a whole and the heavyweights, in particular the Leopard and the Bristol LH. Bedford had to some extent countered this threat with the introduction of the YLQ and YMT mid-engine chassis, which, while more expensive than their predecessor the VAM, were more robustly built with more powerful engines and power steering that positioned the YLQ and YMT somewhere between the Bristol and the Leyland. Mclachlan felt that while the YMT was now capable of taking on some of the roles previously best suited to the Leopard, the latter was still likely to be the best buy for long-distance express services. In practice this meant being thrashed up and down the motorways, the network having been largely completed during the 1970s, with only the M25 and M40 remaining to complete the plan.

There was some criticism of Bedford for making larger chassis only available in 33ft (10m) or 36ft (11m) lengths; most operators, he felt, would think there was little to be lost and much to be gained by buying only the 36ft (11m) version with a fifty-three-seat body, which could be put to the majority of jobs not serviced by twenty-nine-seat coaches, at little extra cost over the shorter version; the 33ft (10m) coach would find most use in a large fleet with a large variety of work where a forty-one- to forty-five-seat coach would always find a use. As a result, the forty-one- to forty-five-seat coach had gone into decline.

The twenty-nine-seat coach based on the VAS could accommodate parties of fourteen and upwards who would be lost in a fifty-three-seat coach, so most operators found a use for one or two. The VAS therefore continued to be in demand and retained its second-hand value well, though there were still complaints of engine noise and poor quality of ride from its small wheels. The short version of the Bristol LH, the LHS, gave better riding qualities, was quieter and was achieving some success in Bedford's traditional market, though it was more expensive. In evaluating it as a competitor, it was difficult to see how Bedford could only

The JJL was Bedford's innovative midi bus concept introduced in 1976. Alas, the industry was not quite ready for the JJL and the project foundered. L. SIMPSON

provide a 33ft (10m) or 36ft (11m) chassis and miss out on an opportunity in the 30ft (9m) market while Bristol could make the LH in what amounted to four separate lengths. Mclachlan felt that a 9m (30ft) Bedford YRQ would be more acceptable to operators than the Bristol LHS – cheaper to buy, cheaper on parts and for fitters the familiar mechanical units would ease maintenance time and costs.

Operators tended to keep with the same body manufacturer, partly for continuity and consistency of appearance, particularly where coaches were going to stay in the same fleet for more than two or three years, as stocks of spares could be built up. Bodies that were only produced for a short period of time became expensive to repair, leading to a drop in their value on the second-hand market, though some of the new continental styles that had appeared were attractive to customers because they were noticeable, stood out from the uniformity of what had gone before and were fresh and appealing. Executive coaches had not turned out to be a good purchase; their special features often did not age well and needed a lot of attention to keep them working properly. After two or three years the special features were often removed and the coaches re-trimmed as standard coaches at additional expense.

Midi Buses from Bedford

The trend for introducing small buses on frequent headways in restricted town and city centres led Bedford to embark on an ambitious new project, announced in 1976. This was an integral, rear-engine 25ft (7.5m) vehicle developed in conjunction with specialist coachbuilders Marshall of Cambridge, who were well thought of in the industry and part of a group with wide-ranging engineering capability, including aerospace. The prototype appeared on the Bedford stand at the Commercial Motor Show for 1976 (the last to be held at Earls Court) and was labelled the JJL. Also from Marshall at the same show was a school bus-type body on the venerable SB chassis – and if further proof was necessary of the popularity of the SB, Van Hool had a 'multipurpose' body mounted on the same chassis.

Continuing the small bus theme at the show was a twelve-seat Dormobile SL Utilabus, based on the CF van chassis. An all-steel Dominant I body of updated appearance with twenty-nine seats on a VAS chassis was exhibited on the Duple stand. A potential challenger for the VAS appeared in the form of the Moseley-Continental alloy-framed 'Faro III' twenty-five-seat dual-purpose body, mounted on a Ford A0609 chassis. B. Walker and Son Ltd of Watford also showed its updated 'Walkerbus' conversion on the CF.

New from Belgium were two Jonckheere Bermuda bodies on YMT chassis, while on the YLQ Plaxton was showing the latest version of its Supreme forty-five-seat body.

Steady Sales in the Late 1970s

Bedford's position in the UK export market remained strong, figures from Vauxhall for 1978 showing the company in second place only to Leyland by supplying 2,743 bus and coach chassis to world markets. Included in this figure were no fewer than 1,400 SB chassis for Pakistan alone, while large numbers of SBs went to Australia, Malaysia, Bangladesh, New Zealand and Hong Kong. YMTs went to Australia, some with Duple bodies, but most were supplied as chassis for bodying locally. Denmark received thirty-one YMTs, many with UK-built bodies and sixty-eight VAMs were supplied to Guatemala, with others going to Australia, where the chassis remained extremely popular with operators. An interesting development was the Unicar body from the Spanish coachbuilder Barro-Chavin group, which made its first appearance at the 1978 British Coach Rally mounted on a YMT chassis. The Moseley group was the sole concessionaire for Unicar bodies and a number were sold in the UK in 1978–80, many on YMT chassis.

A quick review of the coachbuilding scene in the UK in 1978 reveals that Duple's production was concentrated on the steel-framed Dominant range of bodies, with the Dominant I available on VAS, SB, YLQ and YMT chassis. The Dominant II coach body was Duple's prestige offering, designed for coaches of 33–39ft (10–12m) length, and was in greater demand than the Dominant I. Suitable for the YLQ and YMT chassis, standard features included a heated, top-tinted laminated windscreen, rectangular quartz halogen headlamps and polished stainless steel side-trims.

Things were somewhat less happy at Plaxton in 1978. A prolonged industrial dispute meant that plans to introduce a new, metal-framed body to replace the Derwent bus body (which had been in production since 1962, ceasing in 1977) had to be postponed, although a range of coach bodies based on the Supreme was in full production and available for fitting on VAS, YLQ and YMT chassis. 'New Bus Grant' specification versions were available for all Bedford models except the VAS. All the bodies from both Plaxton and Duple were, of course, available for fitting to other manufacturer's chassis.

At the end of the 1970s the Y series and the VAS were all still selling well – in particular, the Plaxton Supreme made a very pretty little coach on the VAS that was appealing both to passengers and operators. Competition was never far away, however, and the twenty-nine-seat market was

New to the Eastern National Omnibus Co. Ltd in 1981 was this YMQ/S with a thirty-three-seat dual-purpose Wadham Stringer Vanguard body. Such combinations of chassis and body provided a somewhat simpler and more economic solution to the desire for a midi bus compared with the innovative JJL. A Bristol RE of the same company lurks in the background of this charming image. S. RAY

now attracting attention from the likes of Mercedes and Ford, both of whom were offering modified goods chassis suitable for small coach bodies by the end of the decade. Another contender in the small coach market appeared in 1979, the Leyland Cub – the second time Leyland had used the Cub name for a small PSV chassis – intended for bodies in the twenty-five- to twenty-nine-seat range. With its simplicity and lack of sophistication, the Cub was clearly aimed at the same market as the VAS and was shown for the first time at the 1979 Scottish Commercial Motor Show at Kelvin Hall. The Scottish show was a biennial event held alternately with the Earls Court Show on 'odd' years. No Bedford PSVs were shown, but examples of YLQ, YMT and VAS coaches were displayed at the premises of dealers SMT Ltd of Finnieston Street, Glasgow during the period of the show. Two YMTs were shown, both seating fifty-three, one with a Duple Dominant II body and the other with a Plaxton Supreme body. Forty-five-seat versions of the Dominant and Supreme bodies were shown on the YLQs and twenty-nine-seat versions on the VAS.

Small is Beautiful

Conversions of the CF van were very popular, proving economical to operate in a climate of rising costs; Plaxton had a Mini Supreme seventeen-seat coach while Reebur (Reeve Burgess) was showing a similar capacity bus on the same chassis. A twelve-seat Dormobile PSV conversion completed the line-up on the CF.

The most interesting Bedford on show was, however, a special adaptation of the YLQ chassis by Tricentrol. Known as the YLQ/S, the conversion was intended to produce an 8m (26ft) thirty-five-seat coach, thus answering the call from operators for a Bedford to compete with the Bristol LHS in the midi bus and midi coach markets.

Large Group Customers

The large bus groups had generally not purchased Bedfords in any great quantities, though there was a steady influx of small numbers of Bedford coaches and occasionally buses. The Tilling group had sold out to the British Transport Commission (BTC) in 1948, which became the Transport Holding Company (THC) in 1962, which then purchased the British Electric Traction group (BET) in 1968, leading to the formation of the National Bus Company (NBC) on 1 January 1969. NBC had in the main gradually refined its purchasing until the single-deck bus need was satisfied by the Leyland National integral and Bristol LH, while the Bristol VR became the standard double-deck bus. The standard NBC coach was the Leyland Leopard with Plaxton body, but NBC still had some requirements that could be met by Bedford, typically where one of its subsidiary companies had once been a strong Bedford customer. NBC orders for 1980, for example, called for 413 single-decks, of which eighteen were Bedford YLQ buses and three were YMT coaches. The order also called for two Reebur mini-buses on CF chassis.

Customer Service is Everything

Complaints of poor customer service and back-up from Bedford led to Vauxhall introducing the Bedford 'Road-call' service, a 24-hour nationwide recovery service that was provided with all new Bedford coaches from 1979; while this was intended to support brand-new coaches with the occasional teething trouble, operators with older Bedford buses and coaches could also subscribe to the scheme, which was operated by Nationwide Break Down Recovery Services Ltd. Roadside repair and recovery costs up to a maximum of £200 for vehicles less than twelve months old were provided by the service, which also included windscreen replacement. For older vehicles, the operator had to foot the bill but even so it was a useful and innovative scheme for the time.

THE 1980S – BEDFORD'S LAST STAND

New for 1980 was the YNT chassis, essentially a more powerful version of the YMT. Shown at the Birmingham Motor Show, the YNT was intended for 36ft (11m) and 39ft (12m) bodies and had Bedford's 500cu in (8.2-litre) 206bhp turbocharged Blue series diesel engine, making it a powerful coach for its class; however, it was the only PSV chassis on show on Bedford's stand. The VAS continued to be available to fill the gap in the market between these and the twelve-to twenty-seat mini-to-midi range, but Reeve Burgess, a long-standing supplier of bus bodies on Bedford chassis, unveiled its RB26, based on the MAN-VW 8.36 light goods chassis. Scottish dealer SMT's annual show included the YNT chassis and the new Plaxton Bustler service bus body on the YMT chassis.

Military contracts played a large part in Bedford's output for many years and carried the Bedford name to all parts of the world. The Bedford SB in particular provided transport for soldiers, RAF and Navy personnel throughout the 1950s, 1960s and 1970s and continued to be built right until the close of production at Dunstable.

By the early 1980s Bedford's star was on the wane and the company in the form in which it had existed since 1931 was struggling, particularly in the Far East; sales of the SB in Malaysia, one of the territories in which the SB had been very popular, declined rapidly between 1980 and 1982. Problems of poor customer service caused by the switch from Bedford in the UK to GM in Singapore and all-too-common arguments over warranty claims were cited as contributing to the decline. Another factor was competition from other manufacturers, particularly from Volvo,

who were now supplying small buses to challenge the SB; and from the Japanese, who were building modern, more reliable vehicles based on newer technology and with better back-up. Poor trading relations caused by UK government policy at the time outweighed the traditional customer loyalty that Bedford had previously enjoyed. The UK-bodied YNT coach failed to make any impact in the blossoming tourist market, in part due to the availability of the small Isuzu integral-body coach, which, even though there was a connection with GM, was competing with Bedford in the same market.

Back in the UK, the Transport Act of 1980 provided for deregulation of coach services of over 30 miles in length. Traditionally these services had been operated mainly by subsidiaries of the National Bus Company and its forebears, who found the more heavily built chassis from the likes of AEC, Bristol and Leyland more suitable for this kind of work; the Leyland Leopard, in particular, outstripped its counterparts in sales, and when the independent sector moved into deregulated long-distance services this trend continued. The market for lightweight coaches from Bedford and similar products from Ford became substantially reduced as the range of services operated by the independents increased and vehicles were needed that were suited to the full range of work now on offer.

Despite this, Bedford struggled on, and collaboration with Robert Wright and Sons of Ballymena produced an all-aluminium coach body with relatively low floor-line for mounting on the 39ft (12m) Bedford YNT chassis. Known as the Wright Contour and styled at Luton, an example was shown at the SMT Coach Show in Glasgow in November 1982, to be sold in the UK through the established network of coach dealers, including Shaw and Kilburn Ltd in London, the Vincent Greenhous group of Hereford and SMT Ltd in Scotland.

Turbocharged engines were introduced across the entire Bedford range in 1981, resulting in some changes to model computer-code designations. A review of the model list at the start of the 1980s revealed that apart from the CF-based minibuses and coaches, the smallest available chassis was now the VAS. This venerable product had been in continuous production since 1960 and now had the option of a turbocharged 5.4-litre engine, although the 4.9-litre petrol option remained available. The VAS was also referred to by Bedford's computer codes as the PFE, PJK or POK, according to which engine was fitted. SB production continued, though largely for the overseas market for bodies of between thirty-six and forty-one seats. It too acquired a turbocharged diesel but remained listed as the SB, though with additional computer codes of NJM and NOM. The front-line chassis was now the YNT, which had grown up from the YRT, became the YMT when the 500-series engine was introduced and then the YNT when the turbo-charged engine became available. This chassis was designed for 36ft (11m) bodies, though by this time lengths were usually quoted and discussed in metric units. The 33ft (10m) YLQ became the YMQ and then the YMP when the turbocharged engine was introduced, the designation changing because the 'Q' was not an allowable character within international regulations for vehicle identification codes. The YMQ was not listed by 1982. At the end of 1981, it was reported that Bedford was intending to phase out all the naturally aspirated Blue series diesels for the Y-series in favour of smaller turbocharged units.

Despite the more powerful engines and the more robust nature of the Y series, Bedford still had not made major inroads in the long-distance market. For example, County Travel of Leicester found that while it was generally happy with its fleet of Duple- and Plaxton-bodied Bedford YMTs, it had quickly become apparent that they were not suited to the long-distance runs from Leicester to the south of France that the company was running in connection with camping holidays. However, instead of perhaps turning to the ubiquitous Leyland Leopard (which by now was itself fairly long in the tooth) County bought five DAF MB200 DKTLs with Plaxton bodies, which were found much more suited to the high-mileage, intensive summer journeys to France and back – a poor reflection on the state of UK chassis builders at the time.

Clearly this was not good news for Bedford. The Society of Motor Manufacturers and Traders (SMMT) published figures for 1981 that showed that sales generally were down on the same period in 1980; for example, in July 1981 only nineteen new Bedford PSVs were registered, against seventy-three in July 1980. By comparison, in the same month, 220 Leylands PSVs were registered. Over a ten-month period, only 408 Bedfords were registered, compared with 684 in 1980. Interestingly, over this period forty-seven new DAF coaches and 236 Volvos were registered.

The figures did not only affect Bedford, of course; overall registrations of light- and middle-weight coaches had shown a dramatic reduction in 1981 over 1980. Bedford remained, however, the most likely chassis one might find under a new Duple body in 1980, with Ford in second place. The prices of Duple and Plaxton bodies on Bedford chassis were generally very closely matched, making the choice for operators more one of personal preference and experience. The exception to this was the Duple Dominant III, first seen at the 1980 show with the Dominant IV and

which was now available in a 'super deluxe' specification. For an additional £2,000 over the basic cost, this included double-glazed bronze-tinted side windows, power door, and audio systems in addition to full insulation of the body sides and roof.

A hope for a new area of market growth appeared in 1984 with the revival of interest in dial-a-ride services; these had first appeared in 1972 in Oxford and were a cross between a taxi and a bus service that used small-capacity PSVs typical of those produced on CF chassis and the ubiquitous Ford Transit. When they started they were well received and popular with the travelling public. Without doubt they provided a useful social service, but the schemes rarely, if ever, covered their operating costs and by 1979 had largely died out or undergone metamorphosis into more traditional bus services. However, the service started by Ringwood Coaches of Chesterfield, Derbyshire in March 1984 was sponsored by Derbyshire County Council and primarily aimed at disabled customers, though to ensure that the service qualified for fuel tax rebate it was available to all potential riders. It was operated by two Bedford VAS vehicles with Chesterfield-built Reeve Burgess bodies equipped with tail-lifts, and with a capacity for fourteen seated passengers and five wheelchairs.

Bedford Stands Alone

Vauxhall had been experiencing widespread financial problems for a number of years, operating at a loss covered by parent General Motors, which was performing generally well in the world markets. However, by 1982 Bedford was the only part of Vauxhall still in the red. Bedford was in fact GM's only interest in commercial vehicles outside North America, and GM Vice President Donald J. Attwood warned that specific changes would need to be made to Bedford to enable it to be competitive in world markets – this would include new manufacturing facilities to enable Bedford's participation in GM's new 'World Truck' programme. This was a common platform for goods vehicles that would be manufactured in both Europe and the USA, in the same way as the 'J Car' formed the basic platform of GM's worldwide production of front-wheel-drive cars, sold in the UK as the Cavalier and its derivatives. That there was no mention of the future Bedford's PSV range suggested that these were not at the top of GM's agenda.

In order to protect Vauxhall from Bedford's losses, it was announced in December 1982 that as from 1 January 1983, Bedford would be separated from Vauxhall and became an entity known as Bedford Commercial Vehicles Ltd, a division of GM's recently formed Overseas Commercial

Vehicle Corporation, itself a part of GM's worldwide Truck and Bus Group. The commercial vehicle division at Luton and the Dunstable plant were both transferred to the new company, and for the first time in fifty-two years Bedford stood on its own feet as a manufacturing company. Initially, there was an upsurge in demand for vehicles from Bedford; however, this was short lived and sales once again took a downturn into 1984.

Back on the shop floor, as it were, new bodies with higher specifications were in the news for 1983. Improved sound and thermal insulation, a higher standard of interior trim, improved glazing, sound systems, catering and toilets and washrooms were all seen as useful marketing tools to meet the expectations of the travelling public and to compete with rail and air travel. At the Birmingham Motor Show in 1983, Plaxton was showing the new Paramount range with variable specification, the 3200 being the basic model and the 3500 having a more lavish specification. The 3500, though, was suitable only for heavyweight chassis, which put Bedford at a disadvantage, as only the 3200 could be built on the YMP and YNT chassis. Despite the widespread

use of bonded glazing by this time, the Paramount range retained rubber-mounted glazing, the argument being that operators preferred the ease and speed with which glass could be replaced when mounted this way.

Duple was also offering two new bodies, the Laser and Caribbean, a Laser-bodied YNT being displayed at Coach Fair '83 at Syon Park – the first such event at this venue organized jointly by *Commercial Motor* and *Travel News*.

Development of a new chassis to complement the existing range of the Y-series was announced in 1984, with full air suspension for the first time on a Bedford chassis. This materialized as the YNV, to which Bedford gave the name 'Venturer', the first time a model name had been used for a Bedford PSV chassis; though clearly in the Vauxhall tradition of names beginning with the letter V, there was perhaps an element of pathos as Bedford was no longer a part of the Vauxhall nuclear family.

The continentals were by now a familiar part of the coaching scene in the UK, with integral coaches accounting for about 6 per cent of the market, mainly from Bova, Van Hool, Kassbohrer Setra and Neoplan. The Setra range

Bebb of Llantwit-Fardre, Pontypridd, South Wales could be relied upon for its coaches to be modern and well turned out. Here are three brand-new and as yet unregistered YNV Venturers with Duple 320 bodies awaiting delivery from the coachbuilder in 1986.

in particular featured 10m (33ft) and 12m (39ft) coaches with either high- or low-floor format and the Setra Imperial double-deck coach, one of the new breed of coaches seen on the UK roads in the early 1980s. Bedford was still in the game, though, and the first Wright Contour body on a YNT chassis was delivered to Go Whittle in Shropshire in summer 1983.

Another significant event for 1983 was the sale of Bedford's long-established partner Duple to the Hestair group, amongst whose members was Dennis Bros of Guildford. Dennis, like Robert Wright of Ballymena, was on the up and up, part of the new vanguard of bus and coach builders in the UK. The new order included more and more overseas manufacturers and, as if to prove the point, while the 1984 Brighton Coach Rally marked the first appearances of a Dennis Dorchester with Duple Caribbean body, there was also to be seen several Bova Futuras and a DAF MB200 with Berkhof Everest coachwork finished in Green Line livery and entered by London Country Bus Services.

The continuing trend towards heavier chassis caused by the increasing size and weight of highly specified coach bodies was not good news and, although the Plaxton Paramount 3200 body continued to be available on Bedford chassis, the Paramount range was more often to be seen on a heavyweight Leyland Tiger chassis. There were also clear indications in the industry of a move towards integral construction to compete with the invaders from the continent, with collaborations between body-builders and suppliers of mechanical units; while it would not have been impossible for Bedford to embrace the technology, the company showed little interest in this area.

There was one glimmer of hope on the horizon; in February 1984, Transport Minister Lynda Chalker's main message to delegates at the Bus and Coach Council symposium at the Birmingham Metropole Hotel was that the government would like the independent sector to take more of an interest in stage-carriage operation, a sector which she observed had traditionally concentrated on contract carriage and private hire work, perhaps as a result of the difficulties in obtaining stage-carriage licences. The independent sector had been by far Bedford's largest market, so operators who felt obliged to take up the minister's offer might similarly feel obliged to turn to Bedford for their new buses, particularly as the Plaxton Derwent and Duple Dominant had proved themselves eminently equitable service bus bodies for Bedford chassis, and the ubiquitous Alexander Y-type bus body had been mounted on many Bedford chassis for the Scottish Bus Group.

The reality was, though, that the minster's speech was really a part of the run-up to deregulation of the major sec-

tor of the bus industry to which she had referred, and the current operators in that sector were already preparing themselves for battle. A survey of the sector that included all municipal undertakings, passenger transport executives (PTEs), NBC subsidiaries and Scottish Bus Group Subsidiaries revealed that of the approximately 36,000 PSVs licensed for stage-carriage operation by those operators, only 134 were manufactured by Bedford. This was a market Bedford clearly needed to be in if it wished to continue to be a leading supplier of PSVs.

A comparison of prices in 1984 showed that, on price at least, Bedford remained a good buy; the list price of an 11m YNT with Plaxton Paramount 3200 or Duple Laser bodies was around £52,000, while several dealers were able to offer these coaches at only £42,000. This compared well with a DAF SB2300 with a Paramount 3200 body at £55,750. To place these figures in context, this was about one-and-a-half times as much as the average price of a house in many parts of the UK at the time. Heavyweight coaches like the DAF MB200, Volvo B10M and Leyland Tiger could be bought for around £60,000. At this time Bedford was still selling in fifty-five countries around the world, though GM had sales offices in over 200 countries.

Back to Earls Court

Nine years after the last annual Commercial Motor Show at Earls Court, commercial vehicles returned to the venue for the First International Bus and Coach Exhibition in September 1985, but Bedford was not on the list of exhibitors. Perhaps with the end in sight there was no longer any enthusiasm for pushing the company's products; yet the Bedford name was not entirely absent. Robert Wright, who was becoming a major force in the UK bus-building industry, showed a body on a SB chassis, one of the few 'welfare' buses on show – Bedford had always been a favourite with local authorities for this application. The SB by this time was the longest-running PSV chassis from any manufacturer, having been in continuous production for thirty-five years. Also on show was an example of the Wright Contour body on a 12m (39ft) YNV Venturer chassis, as was the Hestair Duple 425 fully integral coach, first seen at the previous motor show in Birmingham. The 425 was indicative of the way the wind was blowing and the fifty-four-year relationship between Bedford and Duple had about run its course. Also introduced in 1985, with an eye on the forthcoming deregulation of stage carriage services, was a new bus body, the Wright TT, an example of which was on display at SMT's own show at Finnieston Street in Glasgow. The show TT was mounted on a YMT chassis fitted with

Allison fully automatic transmission. Of fairly uninspiring, box-like appearance, there was also a version of the TT suitable for mounting on the VAS.

Bedford in Decline

Bus and coach registrations in the UK continued to decline, although in part this was probably due to the impending change in operating regulations; in the first five months of 1985 Bedford reported a fall from 210 to 137 registrations over the same period for 1984, though monthly figures for May 1985 showed a rise, due to deliveries of the new YNV. This must have still been somewhat disappointing as Bedford PSV sales had actually shown a significant upturn in the last quarter of 1984. Sadly, despite optimistic figures here and there, it was simply not enough to save the company. SMMT figures for the whole of 1985 revealed that annual registrations of Bedford PSVs had fallen from 356 to 253.

Attempts were made to save Bedford. GM explored potential arrangements with various European manufacturers, including Enasa, the Spanish state-owned group that built Pegaso trucks and owned Seddon Atkinson, and MAN of West Germany. Talks with Leyland regarding a potential merger came to nought, blocked by the UK government, who had seen the proposed deal as a potential takeover of Leyland by GM and felt that there would be hostility from the public over US ownership of Leyland. There is some irony in this, as the Tory MP for Dunstable, David Madel, pointed out in an interview by the BBC that workers at the Dunstable plant were used to US ownership and management methods and had no fear of these. The industry press were scathing in their criticism of the government's handling of the situation, blaming the failure of the Leyland deal on the ineptitude of Margaret Thatcher's government.

Bedford truck and bus production finished at the end of 1986. At its peak, the Dunstable plant had employed over 10,000 people; by the end, fewer than 4,000 were working at the site.

The Dunstable factory, along with the rights to some goods models, was sold to AWD Ltd, who had been working alongside Bedford in truck manufacture since the 1970s. At first there was some speculation in the industry media that AWD would gradually reintroduce the Bedford PSV range, most likely with proprietary engines instead of the Bedford units, but this was not to be. AWD went bankrupt in 1992 and the Dunstable site was cleared for a new retail park and industrial estate. Light commercials were produced by IBC Vehicles (Isuzu Bedford Company Ltd) at the Luton Vauxhall factory until 1992. The Bedford name continued to be used on light commercials until about 1994, the last use being on the Bedford Rascal micro-van and pick-up manufactured jointly with Suzuki. The Bedford name finally disappeared from wider view when production of the Rascal moved to Japan in 1993. AWD was purchased by another division of Marshall, Marshall SPV Ltd, who was given permission to continue to use the Bedford name.

The end of Bedford was seen as a major disappointment within the UK industry. Sam Newton, chairman of the Leyland Truck Distributor Association, said that the closure of Bedford was 'a tragedy for the industry' and 'another example of how Britain has let its own manufacturers down to the advancement of foreign competition'. He went on to say, 'It would be easy for us to gloat at Bedford's demise, but that is definitely not our reaction. We would have preferred to see Bedford and Leyland working together…'.

The last words on the subject cannot be better expressed than in this quote from *Commercial Motor* on 13 September 1986:

> *The warnings could hardly have been spelled out more clearly. For years various GM executives have been asserting publicly that, like the overcapacity in the European truck manufacturing industry, the losses at Bedford could not continue indefinitely. Judging by the sense of outrage in the transport industry and elsewhere which greeted this week's news that production of all Bedford civilian medium and heavy trucks and buses and coaches will cease by the end of this year, those warnings were not generally taken as seriously as they should have been.*

CHAPTER TWO

THE WLG, WHB, WLB, WTL AND WTB

THE WLG

The WLG was a 3- to 4-ton (3,050–4,064kg) goods chassis of 13ft 1in (3.9m) wheelbase, which preceded the introduction of the WLB PSV chassis by a few months in April 1931. As a result, in order to meet demand, somewhere between 180 and 200 were bodied as passenger vehicles and thus became the first Bedford buses and coaches. The ear-liest WLG chassis number recorded as a PSV had a Duple twenty-seat front-entrance bus body for Felday Coaches, of Forest Green, Dorking, Surrey, so this may have been the first ever Bedford bus. The data are somewhat patchy in their detail, but it seems at least 200 WLGs were bodied as buses or coaches, the largest number being built in 1931, though penny numbers continued to be built with passenger bodies until at least 1938. While there are a large number

BEDFORD WLG

Layout and Chassis: Single-deck bus or coach with 14–20 seats (WLB). Frame: reinforced pressed-steel channel section, 6 cross-members

Engine
Type: 6-cylinder petrol
Capacity: 194cu in (3.2 litres)
Carburettor: Zenith model 30U downdraught with accelerator pump
Max. power (DIN): 57bhp at 2,800rpm
Fuel capacity: 18gal (82ltr)

Transmission
Gearbox: 4-speed selective sliding gear (sliding mesh)
Clutch: Single dry plate with pedal adjustment to compensate for wear. Self-aligning clutch release bearing
Ratios
  1st: 7.22:1
  2nd: 3.5:1
  3rd: 1.7:1
  4th: 1:1
Final drive: Fully enclosed in torque tube, twin propeller shafts with intermediate universal joint
Rear axle: Spiral-bevel, ratio: 5.83:1 and optional 6.2:1

Suspension and Steering
Suspension: Semi-elliptic leaf spring, front and rear

Steering: Semi-irreversible worm and wheel, with adjustable ball joints on the track rods and drag link
Front axle: Forged I-beam with inclined swivel pins; hubs carried on taper-roller bearings
Tyres: 6 × 32in
Wheels: Pierced steel disc wheels with integral rim, singles at the front and twin at the rear
Rim width: 5in × 32in

Brakes
Type: Drums with internally expanding shoes, mechanically operated by rods and cables; handbrake entirely independent of footbrake with its own shoes at the rear
Size: 11.5 × 1.75in (front); 16 × 2.5in (rear)

Dimensions
Track
  Front: 57in (1,448mm)
  Rear: 61in (1,549mm)
Frame: 7 × 2.25 × 0.22in (178mm × 57.14mm × 5.55mm)
Wheelbase: 157in (3,987mm)
Overall length: 220.6in (5,603mm)
Electrical system: 12v with Lucas starter and CAV dynamo with third-brush regulation; half-charge/full-charge change-over switch combined with lighting on the driver's instrument panel to ensure full charge when the lights were on

of chassis for whom the original owner is not recorded, the biggest single fleet of WLGs seems to have been those of Walter Alexander of Falkirk. Curiously, the largest number of bodies built for the WLG was also by Alexander, but this was Alexander Motors of Semple Street, Edinburgh – a completely separate concern from Walter Alexander the operator and also a coachbuilder.

The vast majority of bodies on the WLG seated twenty, though capacities as low as fourteen and as high as twenty-six have been recorded. Most, if not all, had the entrance at the front beside the driver. As the WLB was generally very similar with just a few differences in specifications, a fuller description will be found in the next section.

WHB AND WLB

The first true Bedford PSV chassis, the WHB and the WLB chassis were intended to offer two size options for light buses and coaches of around two tons. The style of construction and all major components were common with the WS van and WHG/WLG range of light truck chassis and the driving position was 'normal control', with the driver sat conventionally behind the engine. Where the WHG and the WLG had been primarily intended for goods use and had only been bodied as buses or coaches out of necessity, the WHB and WLB were designed specifically as passenger carriers. General dimensions were shared with their goods predecessors, as were the engine, gearbox, general method of construction and final drive. The WHB had a wheelbase of 10ft 11in (3.33m), while the WLB's wheelbase was 13ft 1in (3.99m). The WHB was intended for completed vehicles of typically 18ft 4in (5.6m) overall length, while the WLB produced a vehicle of around 21ft 4in (6.5m).

It has been suggested that the WHB was simply the Chevrolet LQ rebadged as a Bedford. While there are definite similarities with the 1929 Chevrolet LQ, particularly in the appearance of the front end, bonnet and radiator assemblies, there were also significant differences. The LQ's wheelbase was the same as that of the WHB; the same pressure-lubricated version of the Stovebolt Six engine was fitted to the WHB and the WLB and both models inherited the universal joint inside a 'torque ball' mounted on the rear of the gearbox to transfer drive to the propeller shaft. The general layout of the chassis frame was also the same as the LQ. However, the WHB and the WLB had twin rear wheels where the LQ only had singles, these being of one-piece pierced-disc type where the LQ wheels had demountable rims, and the brakes were quite different and improved compared with the primitive arrangements at the rear on the LQ. The electrics on the WHB and WLB were 12v, utilizing two 6v batteries in series, whereas the LQ had a 6v system with a single battery.

While the front end was of similar appearance to the LQ, it was not identical. The radiator surround lacked the sharp edges of the Chevrolet and the casing was more rounded; most importantly, though, there now resided at the top centre a griffin instead of a Chevrolet badge, under which the word 'Bedford' and 'Made in England' appeared in an attempt to appease those who felt that Vauxhall should not be US-owned.

The chassis frames were constructed from flanged pressings in 0.22in (5.55mm) steel, the flanges being of 2.25in (57mm) width. The WHB frame pressings were 6.375in (162mm) deep while the WLB frame was 7in (178mm) deep. Pressed-steel cross-members of similar dimensions to the mainframe members were incorporated into a simple ladder frame, six in the case of the WHB and eight in the case of the WLB. The frames were parallel from the back to the forward rear spring mountings then tapered inwards to the front end of the chassis, where a front bumper terminated the ladder. A spare-wheel carrier was provided under the rear of the chassis frame between the rear spring mountings.

To accommodate the extra length of the WLB, the propeller shaft was divided into two sections

This WLB with Duple twenty-seat bus body was new to F. Cross of Bury St Edmunds, Suffolk, who traded as Safety Coaches. When this picture was taken the bus was in service with Mulley's Motorways of Ixworth, Suffolk, who had acquired it from Cross. VH

with an additional universal joint. Torque tubes enclosed the propeller shafts, which were supported within the tubes by phosphor-bronze bushings. No universal joint was provided at the rear axle, a simple sliding spline joint being employed. The rear axle itself was fully floating and consisted of a banjo casing with a spiral-bevel differential and half-shaft drive to the rear hubs. A differential with a final drive ratio of 5.83:1 was fitted to the WHB, that for the WLB having a ratio of 6.2:1, reflecting the expected heavier gross vehicle weight of the longer chassis.

The gearbox fitted to these chassis was of the simple sliding-mesh type, where the gears on the gearbox main shaft are slid onto the countershaft (layshaft) gears by a yoke, in contrast to the constant mesh gearbox, where the mainshaft gears are constantly in mesh with the countershaft gears and drive is transmitted by locking the selected gear to the mainshaft. An interesting feature of the WHB/WLB gearbox was the mechanical tyre pump fitted to the nearside of the vehicle and driven from the third-speed layshaft gear. A spiral-bevel gear at the rear of the gearbox drove the speedometer. Transmission of power from the gearbox to the final drive was by a propeller shaft with a single Hardy Spicer universal joint mounted at the gearbox end. The WLB had an additional universal joint supported by one of the chassis cross-members. On both chassis the propeller shafts were fully enclosed by a torque tube with drive reaction forces being taken by the road springs. The universal joint at the gearbox was enclosed in a spherical housing, which served to support the front end of the torque tube; on the WLB the intermediate universal joint was enclosed in a similar housing supported by an additional cross-member in the chassis frame.

Brakes were mechanically operated drum brakes with self-servo-action expanding shoes, this being achieved by the use of different-sized shoes offset across a diameter drawn through the axle. At the rear, the handbrake was provided by an additional small pair of shoes mounted between the long and short shoes looking towards the front of the vehicle. Operation of the handbrake was completely independent of the foot brake. The front brakes were operated by cable to allow for steering movement, the rears by rods and a cross shaft mounted on the differential casing. The braking system for the WHB and WLB was entirely new and shared with the WHG and WLG trucks; the LQ, in contrast, while having expanding shoe brakes on the front, had more primitive external contracting brake bands on the rear.

The front axle was a forged I-beam with steering swivels of 'Reverse Elliott' type, where the hub carrier is forked and the axle beam is drilled and inserted into the fork. The

Many operators in the 1930s favoured local coachbuilders. The body on J. W. Newton & Son's 1931 WLB was built by Mumford of Plymouth and seated twenty. Newton traded as Star Motor Service based in Down Thomas, Devon and his WLB is pictured here on a one-person-operated service from Down Thomas to Elburton. Mr Newton lived at nearby Staddicombe and died in 1949. VH

swivel, or king, pin is then inserted though the hub carrier and the swivel pin hole in the I-beam axle. It must be remembered that even in the 1930s, development and refinement of mechanical systems for motor vehicles was still going on. The 'Reverse Elliott' system became almost universal in the UK bus and coach manufacturing industry. On the WHB and WLB chassis, the swivel pin is parallel, unlike the tapered, adjustable kngpins of later commercial vehicles.

The fuel system was petrol and the well-appointed dash panel included a fuel gauge. The tank itself was situated beneath the driver's seat, perhaps not an ideal place given the effect petrol fumes might have on the driver's concentration, not to mention the possibility of fire giving him a warm backside!

In common with most of its contemporaries, the WHB/WLB needed frequent and regular maintenance. The steering pivots and joints and the propeller shaft joints had to be lubricated with heavy gear oil every 500 miles, gearbox oil level had to be checked every 1,000 miles, engine oil had to be changed every 2,000 miles, wheel bearings greased every 5,000 miles. No sealed-for-life bearings in those days! The more frequent tasks were often undertaken by the driver, though it was not uncommon for the owner, driver and mechanic to be all the same person anyway in the 1930s.

BEDFORD WHB AND WLB

Layout and Chassis: Single-deck bus with 14 seats (WHB) or 16–20 seats (WLB). Frame: reinforced pressed-steel channel section, 6 (WHB) or 8 (WLB) cross-members

Engine
Type: 6-cylinder petrol
Capacity: 194cu in (3.2 litres)
Carburettor: Zenith model 30U downdraught with accelerator pump
Max. power (DIN): 57bhp at 2,700rpm
Fuel capacity: 18gal (82ltr)

Transmission
Gearbox: 4-speed selective sliding gear (sliding mesh)
Clutch: Single dry plate with pedal adjustment to compensate for wear; self-aligning, compressed graphite clutch-release bearing
Ratios
    1st: 7.22:1
    2nd: 3.5:1
    3rd:1.7:1
    4th:1:1
Final drive: WHB: single fully enclosed propeller shaft
WLB: twin propeller with intermediate universal joint
Rear axle: Spiral-bevel, ratios: 5.83:1 (WHB), 6.2:1 (WLB)

Suspension and Steering
Suspension: Semi-elliptic leaf spring, front and rear
Steering: Semi-irreversible worm and wheel, with adjustable ball joints on the track rods and drag link
Front axle: Forged I-beam with inclined swivel pins; hubs carried on taper-roller bearings
Wheels: Pierced steel disc wheels with integral rim, singles at the front and twin at the rear
Rim width: 5 × 32in
Tyres: 6 × 32in

Brakes
Type: Drums with self-servo action shoes, mechanically operated by rods and cables
Size: 11.5 × 1.75in (front); 16 × 2.5in (rear)

Dimensions
Track
    Front: 61.5in (1,562mm)
    Rear: 61in (1,549mm)
Frame: WHB: 6.375 × 2.25 × 0.22in (155mm × 57.14mm × 5.55mm)
WLB: 7 × 2.25 × 0.22in (178mm × 57.14mm × 5.55mm)
Wheelbase: WHB 10ft 9in (3,327mm); WLB 13ft 1in (3,987mm)
Overall length: (over bumpers) WHB 18ft 3in (5,607mm); WLB 21ft 3in (6,502mm)
Width: up to 7ft 6in (2,286mm) overall

Electrical System
12v with Lucas starter and CAV dynamo with constant voltage charging

Another operator to favour local bodywork was A. Livermore of Barley, Herefordshire. The twenty-seat bus body on Livermore's 1934 WLB was built by Thurgood of Ware. It is pictured in Baldock Street, Royston, which has changed little over the years, though the post office, like so many others, is now gone though the building remains in use as the Jolly Postie pub.

Bodies

Duple was by a good margin the most popular choice for bodies on the WHB chassis, but other coachbuilders who built bodies for the WHB included Grose, Heaver, Mumford, Rees & Griffiths, Robson, Thurgood, Waveney and Willowbrook.

A WLB body typically had twenty seats, to either bus or coach standard, though there were examples with fourteen seats and others with a range of seating capacity between twenty-one and twenty-five. One example is claimed to have seated thirty-eight in a front-entrance body by Duple but this may be an error in the data, or the chassis may have been modified. The vast majority seem to have been front entrance, though for over 300 bodies the door position is not recorded – this from around 1,281 chassis for which data are available.

For the WLB chassis, once again the largest proportion of bodies were built by Duple, at over 400, though other coachbuilders who built significant numbers (sixteen or more) of bodies on the WLB included Robson, Waveney, Thurgood, Willmott, Burlingham, Economy, Willowbrook and Mumford, in approximate order of quantity. Plaxton of Scarborough displayed a twenty-seat bus body on a WLB chassis at the 1933 Commercial Motor Show and possibly the first body that this soon-to-be-famous concern had built on a Bedford chassis. It is not recorded if Plaxton built further bodies on the WLB, but the published data suggest that over 400 bodies were built whose builders were not recorded – a significant number when considering the proportions of bodies built by individual manufacturers – so it is not beyond the bounds of possibility that they did so.

Sales and Production

The very first purpose-built Bedford PSV was a WHB, finished as a fourteen-seat bus by Waveney. It was completed in August 1931 and sold to local operator J. E. Woodham of Melchbourne, Bedfordshire. Registered TM 9347, it gave good service until 1956, when it was withdrawn. Remarkably, it has survived and is now part of the Vauxhall Heritage Collection and is kept at Luton. Export orders did not materialize in any quantity for the WHB, only eight being sold abroad, and total production appears to have been only 102. The WLB, on the other hand, was somewhat more successful and 464 were exported out of over 2,000 recorded built.

The increasing demand for luxury coach tours during the 1920s and 1930s ensured a steady increase in sales for Bedford passenger chassis; however, at the same time demand for smaller-capacity vehicles was falling off, so no WHBs were built after June 1933, with a production total of just over 100 recorded. The 2-ton (2,032kg) range remained in production until 1935, when the WT 3-ton (3,050kg) range was introduced. Radiator surrounds were chromed, unlike their goods counterparts, which were enamelled black. When production of the WHB ended, Bedford was able to reduce the price of the WLB chassis such that a complete Duple-bodied twenty-seat bus dropped in price from £550 to £510 and the sun saloon coach was reduced from £590 to £555, making a Bedford PSV an even more attractive proposition for the smaller operator.

Available figures suggest just over 2,050 WLBs were sold between 1931 and 1938, with the largest number being built in 1932, though almost as many were built in both 1933 and 1934. The WLB sold new mainly to independent operators, who in many cases bought just one or two examples – this being more a reflection on the size of the operator rather than their satisfaction with the model. While the records are incomplete, some interesting figures emerged from analysing the available sales data; for example, F. O'Boyle of Dublin bought four in 1933 and another one in 1934; King of Long Clawson, Leicestershire bought four, as did Moore's of Kelvedon, Essex in the period 1932–5. R. Johnson & Sons of Southsea, Hampshire bought five, starting with two in 1931 and buying the last one in 1934.

Cumberland Motor Services Ltd, a large territorial operator half-owned by the British Automobile Traction group and generally a Leyland customer (and to a lesser extent AEC), bought around five WLBs from 1932 and acquired others from absorbed operators – most of these were used by Cumberland, some passing to the War Department during the Second World War for further use elsewhere in a variety of roles. Cumberland had also bought Chevrolets at the end of the 1920s. Businesses took to the WLB for staff transport: the Anglo-Iranian Oil Co. of Persia (now Iran) took half a dozen and the Trossachs Hotel Co. Ltd, Callander bought four. Exports included thirty for the Chekiang Highway Bureau, China, though very little information is recorded about these. Another operator to take more than the usual ones and twos was D. Hardwick of Snainton, North Yorkshire. Famous operator names to adorn Bedford WLBs included MacBrayne's Ltd of Glasgow, Davies Bros of Pencader, southwest Wales, Greenslades Tours Ltd of Exeter – a WLB was its first Bedford, in May 1935 – and Walter Alexander of Falkirk.

The largest home market sales, however, seem to have been to Scottish Motor Traction Co. Ltd (SMT), who bought twenty-six in 1934, mostly with twenty-seat bodies by Burlingham but some with its own SMT-built twelve-seat bodies.

On the Road

To start the engine, the driver needed to retard the ignition slightly, using the 'Spark' knob on the instrument panel, then depress the starter switch with his foot, the switch being mounted in the centre of the pedal board on the floor. Gear changes were apparently quite easy to accomplish, despite the design of the gearbox and the absence of synchromesh. The method of meshing the gears and the way they were cut gave rise to a melodic howl in the intermediate gears, characteristics shared with many 1930s (and even later) gearboxes of similar design. To an engineer it is not an unpleasant sound but perhaps less appealing to the average passenger. In fourth gear the gearbox was commendably quiet. For the size of vehicle, the brakes generally were considered to be good, though the steering was less highly regarded.

WTL AND WTB

The need for more seating capacity resulted in some three-ton Bedford WTL lorry chassis being modified to enable bus bodies of twenty-six seats to be fitted. The WTL was a larger version of the WLG goods models and was introduced in 1934. Bedford, preferring to supply a properly designed PSV chassis for this purpose, rapidly introduced the WTB bus chassis, which appeared in 1935. This was a derivative of the WTL and WLB with a wheelbase of 13ft 11in (4.2m). The WTL and WTB were of semi-forward control design, where the driving position was moved forward to be partially alongside the engine. In practice this was accomplished by also moving the engine forward in the chassis so that its centreline was located over the front axle. This resulted in a shorter bonnet and a generally more compact look about the front.

The fuel tank was located half-way down the chassis on the right-hand side, hung from chassis outriggers and parallel with the chassis frame. The fully floating rear axle and differential casing were mounted at an angle of 45 degrees to provide more ground clearance under the banjo-shaped axle casing and to enable larger (and hence stronger) spiral-bevel gears to be fitted.

Revisions

A facelift for both the WTB and the WTL arrived in the summer of 1938; changes included an all-metal cab and

Front end of the WTB chassis showing how the engine cowl and dash were integrated into the front end of the chassis. GM

View of the rear axle of the WTB showing how the nose of the differential was angled down at 45 degrees to provide a lower floor line. GM

redesigned front wings. The radiator grille and bonnet assembly became much more rounded and more modern-looking, pointing the way for the OB chassis that would appear in 1939. Mechanical changes included an uprating of the engine from 64bhp to 72bhp (RAC rating 28hp), following the work done by Alex Taub on the Stovebolt

BEDFORD WTL AND WTB

Layout and Chassis: Single-deck bus or coach with 20–26 seats. Frame: pressed-steel channel section

Engine
Type: 6-cylinder petrol
Capacity: 194cu in (3.2 litres)
Max. power (DIN): 64bhp at 2,700rpm; from 1938 onwards 72bhp at 2,700rpm
Fuel capacity: 20gal (91ltr)

Transmission
Gearbox: 4-speed selective sliding gear (sliding mesh)
Clutch: Single 10in dry plate with pedal adjustment to compensate for wear; self-aligning, compressed graphite clutch-release bearing
Ratios
   1st: 7.2:1
   2nd: 3.5:1
   3rd: 1.7:1
   4th: 1:1
   Reverse: 7.1:1
Propeller shaft: Twin Hotchkiss open tubular propeller shaft with Hardy Spicer needle-roller universal joints
Rear axle: Spiral-bevel, ratio: 6.71:1
Front axle: Forged I-beam with inclined swivel pins; hubs carried on taper-roller bearings

Suspension and Steering
Front: Semi-elliptic leaf spring, 38 × 2.25in, nine leaves
Rear: Semi-elliptic leaf spring, 60 × 2.5in, progressive type with seven primary and three secondary leaves
Steering: Worm and wheel, ratio 15:1
Wheels: Pierced steel disc wheels with integral rim, singles at the front and twin at the rear
Rim width: 4.33 × 20in
Tyres: 7.50 × 20in

Brakes
Type: Drums with self-servo action shoes, vacuum-servo-assisted mechanical
Size: 14 × 1.75in (front); 16 × 2.5in (rear)

Dimensions
Track
   Front: 64.5in (1,638mm)
   Rear: 64in (1,626mm)
Wheelbase: WTL 13ft 1in (3,987mm); WTB 13ft 9in (4,242mm)
Overall length: (over bumpers) WTL: 18ft 4in (5.607mm); WTB: 21ft 3in (6,502mm)
Width: 7ft 6in (2,286mm)

Electrical system: 12v 85Ah battery with Lucas starter and CAV dynamo

MacBrayne's fleet no. 70 was a WTL with Duple twenty-seat bus bodywork with a rear mail compartment, delivered new in June 1935. It subsequently passed to Lowland Motorways as fleet no. 11 in 1942.
A. CROSS

Six. The new front end was devised in conjunction with Duple, which gave the WTB/Duple Vista coach a modern, coherent look. The design was carried on to the OB that followed, and to the untrained eye the last WTBs and the first OBs were hard to distinguish, the most noticeable difference being that the OB had a visible radiator cap atop the grille where the WTB's was concealed under the bonnet.

Bodies

The WTL was, in the event, something of a stop-gap chassis and the WTB soon became the commonest form of the WT range to be bodied as a PSV. Duple and the usual range of coachbuilders built both bus and coach bodies on the WTL chassis, but when the WTB was introduced Duple reinforced its strong commitment to the Bedford make by offering nine different variants of its body. There were four service buses, a dual-purpose 'bus-cum-coach' – Vauxhall's

The WTB chassis. GM

Livermore's obviously liked its first Bedfords as the firm later purchased this 1937 WTB with a twenty-six-seat coach body by Thurgood of Ware. Here it is at the Fox and Hounds in Barley, which is still there, as is the magnificent overhead sign, though the current structure is not the one seen here.

own description, the bus industry having yet to embrace fully the term dual-purpose – two 'De Luxe' coaches and two 'Super De Luxe Coaches'. Not surprisingly the cheapest was a twenty-seat bus and the dearest the 'KD Super Deluxe Coach' at £785. The chassis on its own could be purchased for £290.

Duple built its first body with the name 'Vista' on the WTB in 1937. This was a luxurious twenty-five-seat coach, successor to the 'KD'. Once again Duple was by far the most common supplier of bodies on the WTB chassis, though the Dutch coachbuilder Den Oudsten en Domburg built fifty bodies on chassis exported to the Netherlands for GVU Utrecht (Utrecht Municipal Transport). The name Plaxton appears for the first time as a quantity producer of bodies for Bedford chassis, a single twenty-five-seat coach appearing in 1936, but by 1939 over sixty had been built on the early WTB chassis, a further forty-seven appearing on the facelift chassis in 1938 and 1939. Notable amongst these were a number of full-fronted bodies featuring a forward-control conversion of the chassis. Several different styles of body were fitted to the forward control conversion and Duple also built a number of similar bodies.

Most of Plaxton's bodies seated twenty-five or twenty-six, though some were more spacious, with only twenty seats. The full-fronted conversion does not seem to have amounted to more than four or so on the early chassis and perhaps twenty on the later chassis. Some of these were able to seat thirty passengers. The vast majority of bodies on the early WTB were twenty-five-seat coaches, the facelift models increasing this to twenty-six seats. Of the bus bodies, the most common were twenty-six seats with a front entrance, though for both coaches and buses the seating capacity could be anywhere between twenty and twenty-six depending on the operator's needs; one or two even managed to squeeze in as many as thirty-three, if the data are to be believed!

Plaxton was emerging as the number two body builder for Bedford on the WTB chassis. While the total was small compared with the number built by Duple, it was significantly larger than most of the others – though Thurgood of Ware came a close third. Apart from those already mentioned, coachbuilders who built twenty or more bodies on the WTB included: Grose; Robson of Consett, Co. Durham; Willmott of Shepherds Bush, London; and Willowbrook of Loughborough. Robson and Willmott had both built bodies on Chevrolet chassis at the end of the 1920s.

Sales and Production

The WTL was not bodied as a passenger vehicle in any great numbers, just over 200 being built as such in 1935 and 1936, but the WTL chassis continued to receive passenger bodies in ones and twos until 1939. Ones and twos also describes the numbers bought by most operators, though Walter Alexander of Falkirk bought at least five and at least eight were exported to the Netherlands, both in 1935. Vauxhall had at least four for staff transport, also in 1935. The vast majority of passenger bodies on WTL chassis were built by Duple, but Plaxton built several in 1939. Robson, Thurgood, Willmott and Willowbrook also built a few and those exported to the Netherlands were bodied by Werkspoor of Amsterdam and Jurgens.

The WTB became very popular and before long accounted for 55 per cent of the bus and coach market in Great Britain; the usefulness of the Bedford as a rural bus is demonstrated by the fact that by 1936, Bedfords accounted for 80 per cent of privately owned buses in Scotland.

Once again the WTB tended to be bought by independent operators, who would take one or maybe two examples new. Of those that took more, notable quantities went to the Anglo-Iranian Oil Co. Ltd, who seems to have been the largest customer with approximately fifty-two purchased between 1936 and 1939, the majority being the facelifted models with Duple bodies. Keith & Boyle, trading as the famous Orange Luxury Coaches of London, had six facelifted models in 1939 and gave them names – Cecilia, Eugenia, Fidelia, Sophronia, Sophia and Zenobia, generally names that would instil confidence in travellers (perhaps with the exceptions of Cecilia, which means 'blind' or 'not seeing', and Zenobia which means 'worn by an ancient queen').

Keith & Boyle had taken up a Bedford dealership from

Devon General Omnibus & Touring Co. Ltd bought this WTB in June 1937 and had it fitted with a body by Birch Bros of Cathcart St, Kentish Town, London NW5. CTT 660 displays the long tradition of painting buses in cream or white when intended for use at seaside locations.

In September 1936 G. Jorden of Peterstow, Herefordshire, bought this WTB with a Duple twenty-seat coach body and roof luggage carrier, seen here on the A49 near Craven Arms en route for Shrewsbury. The slush on the road and the snow on the hills add a chill to this winter scene. VH

around 1935 and also held a controlling interest in Shamrock and Rambler Motor Coaches Ltd of Bournemouth. Thus Shamrock and Rambler became another Bedford customer, taking twenty WTBs in the years 1936–8. Essex County Coaches had five, Greenslades Tours had eight, including two facelifted models. Others with fleets of six or more WTBs included Lansdowne Motors Ltd of Fleetwood; Rippondon & District Motors in the West Riding of

Yorkshire; Lamboll & Ingham Ltd, trading as Ruby Cars of Paignton; and the well-known and much-missed Yelloway Motor Services Ltd of Rochdale, Lancashire.

The WTB was an extremely successful product for Bedford and by the end of 1936 Bedford was claiming that they were responsible for 50 per cent of the new buses and coaches licensed in Great Britain in the preceding year. While the majority of sales were to the independent operators, some of the larger bus groups and municipal operators also found the Bedford WTB useful. The Till-

ing-controlled Western and Southern National Omnibus Companies, based in Exeter, bought a significant quantity – around sixty examples – of WTB chassis with Duple bodies in the period 1937–9, of both the original series and the facelifted models. It was unusual at that time for the Tilling Group to purchase anything other than Bristol chassis, but the 'Nationals' were operating in the narrow country lanes of Devon, which were more suited to smaller vehicles than those available from Bristol, so the Bedford proved ideal – Dennis Ace and Mace chassis were also bought for

J. C. 'Johnny' Arnold started his coach business initially as a taxi firm in Dosthill, Tamworth, Staffordshire in 1920. He bought his first coach, an REO, in 1926. By 1937 the business was sufficiently well established that he could afford to buy this late Series I WTB with standard Duple twenty-six-seat body. Johnny Arnold died at the early age of 58 in 1960 and the business was acquired by the L. F. Bowen Group in 1961. VH

This semi-forward-control conversion of the WTB was built by Plaxton. It was new to Arthur Heeley, of New Tupton, Derbyshire in May 1938 and is seen on a day trip to London around 1955. VH

ARV 920. An interesting rear view of Liss & District Omnibus Co. Ltd's 1938 Series I WTB with a quite sleek-looking twenty-five-seat coach body by Arthur Mulliner and Co. of Northampton. Liss & District was the operating name of C. E. Cartwright of Liss Forest, Hampshire. VH/A. MULLINER & CO. LTD

Thurgood of Ware built the twenty-six-seat coach body on this Series 2 WTB in July 1938 for W. H. Vaughn of Chippenham, Wiltshire. VH/THURGOOD

the same reason. Bristol Tramways, another Tilling company and closely associated with the 'Nationals', took nine WTB/Duple twenty-seat buses in 1939 and Southern Vectis on the Isle of Wight took three. Scottish Motor Traction (SMT) of Edinburgh also bought a quantity, as did its Kilmarnock counterpart, Western SMT. At the opposite end of the UK, Bournemouth Corporation Transport was another customer who took both the first version and facelifted WTBs, building a fleet of twenty-five Bedfords. Luton Corporation bought one and in New Zealand, Wellington Corporation bought ten.

Export destinations included China, Malta, the Netherlands and New Zealand, in addition to those that went to the Anglo-Iranian Oil Company in Iran.

Perhaps the most unusual version of the WTB was built from two chassis joined back to back to form a railcar for the Kowloon-Canton Railway. Another unusual version had an additional rear axle and extended rear body for operation by the Danish State Railways.

By the time the WTB was produced, the idea of luxury coach travel had taken hold in the country. As a result, the tendency was now for bodies with more luxurious seating to be fitted to the WTB compared with those fitted to earlier chassis. In many cases operators used their vehicles in a dual-purpose role according to their needs and the traffic available, a pure bus-bodied vehicle being less appealing to passengers for long-distance travel. As a result, there were fewer WTBs bodied as plain buses. Despite this, Duple did produce a standard bus body for the chassis, based on the 'Hendonian' coach.

Many WTBs lasted well into the 1950s, some being converted to diesel engines – the Dorman 4DS being found to be suitable.

Rear views are fairly uncommon so we are lucky to have this one of Bournemouth Corporation's 1939 WTB with Burlingham twenty-five-seat dual-purpose body, one of four similar vehicles purchased that year. The front end is standard Series 2 WTB as seen on AJT 176, the style being continued with the OB introduced in 1939.

Young's Bus Service of Paisley, Scotland was the first owner of this 1939 Series 2 WTB with Duple twenty-six-seat coach body, seen heading north through Ardlui on the A82 in the direction of Crianlarich. In the background is a rare WHG with passenger bodywork. VH

IN PRESERVATION

1938 Bedford WTB/Willmott AJT 176

Year new: 1938
Engine: 194cu in (3.2-litre) petrol (late 28hp version)
Gearbox: Bedford four-speed
Body: Willmott, twenty-seat 'Lincoln' bus, 7ft 6in (2.29m) wide
Current owner: Dave Prosser

History

This bus was purchased new by Herb Vincent of Thornecombe, Devon in 1939, where it remained in service until 1963. It was then taken out of service and laid up in Vincent's yard until bought by the late Colin Shears in 1972 for the West of England Transport Collection at Winkleigh. Shortly after this, AJT 176 passed to Doug Allen of Ross-on-Wye, who did some work on the bus for a few years until it was purchased for use as scout transport. By this time, however, the bus was in need of restoration so it was passed on to the Cheltenham Bus Preservation Group, who performed some serious restoration before selling it on in 1983 to Derek Barwell of Droitwich. Derek kept the bus at the Birmingham and Midland Omnibus Trust (BaMMOT) museum at Wythall, where further restoration work was carried out, including repairs to the wooden frame and the roof.

By now in quite a reasonable state, the bus quickly passed through two owners in Essex before passing to the Watts family until around 2005, when it once more changed hands and the current owner bought it from Tim Wotton, the well-known owner and restorer of Bedford OBs.

Dave Prosser's superb Series 2 Bedford WTB is the only surviving example with a Willmott body. It was new to H. A. Vincent of Thorncombe, Devon, in May 1939.

Owner's Experience

One is immediately struck by Dave Prosser's infectious enthusiasm for vintage vehicles and it is clear that the unique Bedford bus that is AJT 176 is in good hands. A short ride in the beautiful Worcestershire countryside reveals that this little bus is currently mechanically very healthy as well as being in first-class condition bodily. The ride is harsh, as one expects from fairly short leaf springs, but not uncomfortable; the engine is noisy by modern standards but this is not surprising as the rear end of it intrudes into the body of the coach and is protected only by an uninsulated metal cowl. The bus rides well, bumps are felt but absorbed reasonably well by the suspension and, given that the bus is sixty-eight years old, the performance feels very lively. Dave's expert driving allows the gearbox to sing its familiar song with only the occasional slight crunch during the first few changes from a cold start to indicate any stubbornness from its primitive sliding selector mechanism. This tends to be a feature of the 28hp box until the oil warms up a little.

The Willmott body, believed to be the only survivor, is virtually rattle-free and the interior has a welcoming look to it. The seats, albeit recently retrimmed, are as comfortable as any modern service bus and not far from luxury coach standards, so the bus would have been equally at home on local stage services and excursions and tours. Having only twenty seats, there is plenty of legroom and the interior is quite spacious – Dave recalls that Herb Vincent always referred to it as 'the twenty' and it was used for everything from school runs and excursions to local services around Chard, Axminster and Crewkerne. Vincent's deliberately timetabled its stage services not to start before 10.30 to allow for the bus to come back from the school run in good time.

Dave Prosser's own interest in Bedfords – he currently owns seven, including a Martin Walter CA Workobus – has matured over forty years. Initially his interest was drawn to military vehicles because, he says, 'you get a lot of metal for your money!' His motivation has always been about saving vehicles for posterity that would otherwise be lost – in short, true preservation.

On the road, Dave says the bus will cruise all day at 45mph (72km/h) and return about 16mpg (17.7ltr/100km) on a run. It will do around 55mph (89km/h) flat out, but the noise and vibration becomes uncomfortable, especially for the driver. Long distances, he says, are best accomplished at night, when there is little traffic around and you can average 35mph (56km/h) on longish runs. Moving off is best undertaken in second gear on the flat, as otherwise at road junctions you have barely pulled out before you have to change up. Dave mentions that drivers of more modern vehicles often underestimate the ability of the bus to slow down with its rod-and-cable brakes (although they are servo-assisted) and this can cause problems when they overtake and cut in front approaching road junctions and roundabouts. However, Dave takes all this in his stride, and says that as long as one employs good driving techniques and plans ahead, the bus is straightforward to drive. The chassis and track is quite narrow, so the cab itself is slightly narrower than the body and this can catch you out if you aren't paying attention!

Dave uses the bus for his own and his family's enjoyment and for film work and rallying and says he is always looking for an excuse to take it out for a run. It attracts a lot of attention, as the author discovered while setting up for the photo shoot for this piece. Dave recalls that when he brought the bus home to Worcestershire, his neighbour saw it and asked 'is that from Thorncombe? My mother used ride to school on it!'

The neat and welcoming interior of Dave Prosser's Willmott-bodied WTB.

CHAPTER THREE

THE OB AND OWB

The Bedford OB was introduced as a replacement for the Bedford WTB in August 1939. An increased wheelbase of 14ft 6in (4.4m) meant that bodywork accommodating twenty-six to thirty-one or thirty-two passengers could be fitted. New developments included a drive-line offset to the left to allow a lower centre gangway, the chassis cross-members being mounted lower to achieve this, requiring the rear cross-member in front of the rear axle to be cranked upwards over the propeller shaft. The differential was offset 11in (28cm) from the chassis centreline towards the left-hand side. Two open tubular propeller shafts were employed, the rear end of the front propeller shaft being supported in a double-row ball-bearing mounted on top of the intermediate chassis cross-member. Three Hardy-Spicer needle-roller bearing universal joints allowed the freedom of movement necessary for the two propeller shafts. The fuel tank was mounted in front of the rear axle, parallel with and outside of the chassis frame on the right-hand side. The pressed channel-section frames were cranked upwards in a smooth curve over the rear axle.

The rear axle was fully floating, with a cast steel differential housing. Steel tubes through which the axle half-shafts ran were pressed into the differential housing. Spring saddles were welded to these at the outer ends inboard of the wheel hubs and brake drums. The rear hubs were supported on two taper roller bearings, the half-shaft flanges being secured to these by studs in the hubs and nuts.

The engine capacity was increased to 214cu in (3.5 litres) and now produced a useful 72bhp at 3,000rpm. The electrical system included a new distributor with combined vacuum and centrifugal automatic ignition advance and retard.

The OB's brakes were hydraulically operated drum brakes based around Lockheed components. Front and rear brakes had two shoes per wheel, those at the front being arranged as a two-leading-shoe brake to provide a self-servo action when the brakes were applied with the vehicle travelling forward. Those at the rear also provided the handbrake – the only permissible adjustment of the handbrake was via the adjustment of the shoe to drum clearance, set by means of notched wheels positioned under the hydraulic cylinders for that wheel and accessible through rubber flaps in the brake back plate.

The hydraulic system employed a tandem master cylinder with two bores, one for the front and one for the rear brakes. The master cylinder was bolted to the top of a brake servo, which provided power assistance for the driver's foot. The servo was powered by engine inlet manifold-derived vacuum. In the event of failure of the vacuum system, this system still allowed for the brakes to be operated via the hydraulic system but without power assistance. The dual-circuit arrangement of the brakes added a further safety factor and had been only recently introduced by Lockheed in 1937. Even after the war it was still quite an advanced concept as only a few car makers, notably Saab and Jaguar, were employing dual hydraulic circuits in their brakes at the time, though these were of the diametrically opposed form – one front and the opposite rear brake per circuit.

While mechanically very similar to the five-ton goods models, the OB suspension had semi-elliptic leaf springs designed specifically for passenger work, the front having nine leaves while those at the rear were of the progressive type with seven primary and three secondary leaves.

The OB chassis, showing the offset differential and split propeller shaft. The apparent curve in the rear half of the prop shaft is an optical illusion.

BEDFORD OB AND OWB

Layout and Chassis: Coach or bus, 26–29 seats (OB) or 32-seat utility specification bus (OWB). Frame: reinforced pressed-steel channel section, 6 cross-members

Engine

Type: Bedford 214cu in (3.5-litre) 6-cylinder ohv petrol

Fuel capacity: 20gal (91ltr)

Transmission

Clutch: Single dry plate friction type with ball-race thrust bearing, 10in diameter

Ratios

    1st: 7.22:1

    2nd: 3.47:1

    3rd: 1.71:1

    Top: 1:1

Transmission: Two propeller shafts with three needle-roller universal joints

Rear axle: Spiral-bevel differential ratio: 6.17:1

Suspension and Steering

Suspension: Semi-elliptic leaf springs; front 38 × 2.25in, 9 leaves; rear progressive with 7 primary leaves and 3 secondary leaves

Steering: Worm and full wheel

Front axle: I-beam section, reverse Elliott type with inclined swivel pins and taper-roller front hub bearings

Tyres: 1939 OB: 7.50-20 front and twin rear; 1942 OWB and OB from 1946: 7.50-20 front, 8.25-20 twin rear

Brakes

Type: Lockheed dual-circuit hydraulic, separate front and rear circuits; handbrake operates on rear wheels via bisecting expanders; cast iron brake drums

Size: Total lining area 373sq in (2,406.5sq cm)

Dimensions

Track

    Front: 64.0625in (1,627mm)

    Rear: 70in (1,778mm)

Wheelbase: 14ft 5in in (4,420mm)

Overall length: typically 24ft 3in (7,417mm)

Width: 7ft 6in (2,286mm)

Electrical system

12v positive earth dynamo, CAV type D5 LFA-10 with compensated voltage control

The 12v electrical system incorporated a CAV dynamo with compensated voltage output that used a separate control box to regulate the field winding current of the dynamo. The regulator ensured that as the battery became fully charged, the output from the dynamo was reduced to avoid overheating the battery and damaging the electrical system. This was achieved by magnetic cut-outs in the associated control box that caused the dynamo field current to be interrupted as the difference between the dynamo output voltage and the battery voltage was reduced. Four 25-amp fuses protected the electric system, with an additional wire link fuse in the control box to protect the field windings of the dynamo.

Visually, the OB had a slightly narrower windscreen than the WTB, which produced a more angular front end.

OB SALES AND PRODUCTION – 1939

Production of the OB started in August 1939 but was halted almost immediately by the outbreak of the Second World War. Quoted figures for production vary, but the maximum seems to be seventy-five, so not many were made before production stopped. Of these, not all are accounted

A genuine OWB, albeit with Roe thirty-two-seat body, was new in January 1943 to Worthen & District Motor Services of Worthen, Shropshire. R. H. G. SIMPSON

for in the published data but it is recorded that almost a third went to the Tilling Group, Western National taking eight and Southern National taking eleven. Both companies had previously operated the Bedford WTB. Orange Luxury Coaches, London SE11 continued its interest in Bedford by taking four; once again these received classical-sounding names – Astoria, Athenia, Claudia II and Thalia – the names being painted on the driver's side front mudguard. In terms of bodies, the largest recorded supplier was Duple, almost all being twenty-six-seat coaches, though several twenty-nine-seat coach bodies were also built.

OWB

The OWB came about as a result of the Ministry of War Transport (MoWT) recognizing the importance of new buses in meeting the needs of civilian transportation in con-tributing to the war effort. Bedford's Luton factory was already under the control of the Ministry of Supply (MoS), set up at the start of the Second World War to ensure the supply of resources to the armed forces. The MoWT had already designed a 'utility' specification double-deck body that could be fitted to suitable chassis from Bristol, Guy, Daimler and the other heavy bus chassis manufacturers, so early in 1942 they set about commissioning a corre-sponding utility single-deck bus. Bedford and Duple were by far the most prolific of the pre-war manufacturers of lightweight buses of this type so it is not surprising that the ministry turned to Bedford and Duple for a prototype.

Built on the OB chassis, the Duple body seated thirty-one with a five-person seat across the rear and had upholstered seats throughout. The emergency door was on the right-hand side and located just behind the driver.

The MoWT accepted the prototype design with a few amendments. The most significant was the relocation of the emergency door to the rear, aligned with the central gangway and resulting in a three-section rear window. The loss of a single seat at the rear was compensated for by adding an extra pair of seats behind the entrance door on the left-hand side. This necessitated squeezing up the gaps between the seats with resultant loss of leg room. This was in contravention of the Construction and Use regulations so a dispensation had to be applied for and granted – a not uncommon event in wartime.

The production version of the wartime chassis was named the OWB, although the differences from the OB were minimal – no chrome trim was allowed, the cover over the starting handle opening was omitted from the radiator grille, smaller headlights more suited to the blackout (but less suited to road safety) were fitted and the carburettor was changed from the Zenith downdraught to the Solex type. OWB buses carried Ministry of Supply identification numbers on the chassis, prefixed with a B for Bedford.

Bodies

The Duple-designed thirty-two-seat bodies fitted to the OWB were very austere, with as few as possible curved panels and economy seating – wooden slats in many cases instead of the pre-war Vista's sumptuous upholstery – and leg room was tight. At £810 complete, what Bedford described as an 'Economy Type Bus' or 'War Time Bus' did not seem to offer as good value as the pre-war Vista-bodied

This very early post-war OB has a Thurgood body to Duple's thirty-seat Ministry of War Transport design. It was delivered to Theobald's of Long Melford, Suffolk, in December 1946.

OB at roughly the same price, but the wartime economy suffered from inflation and in comparison with 1939 prices for similar seating-capacity buses from Leyland, AEC and Bristol, the OWB represented reasonable value for money.

Bodies were built to the Duple design under MoWT contracts by Charles H. Roe Ltd of Leeds, Mulliner Ltd of Birmingham and Scottish Motor Traction Ltd (SMT) in Edinburgh, thus providing good geographical coverage of the country for the regional supply of wartime bus bodies. The few that were exported in 1945 were generally bodied locally and with different seating from the home models; New Zealand Motor Bodies was one such builder. All those for the home market were supplied painted in a semi-matt bauxite brown colour, though individual operators often repainted them into their own livery. Some operators also replaced the economy seating with more comfortable items from life-expired pre-war buses, in some cases reducing the seating capacity slightly, though in doing so the operator risked incurring the wrath of the Traffic Commissioners – 'Don't you know there's a war on?' was a phrase commonly heard between 1939 and 1945, oft repeated both by the author's late maternal grandmother and the immortal Hodges of *Dad's Army*.

Not an OWB, having been built in 1950, but this **OB** has a **Whitson** twenty-eight-seat body to MoS specifications. Looking rather battered in June 1973, its first owner was actually the Ministry of Supply. It was later owned by the 1st Bromsgrove Scout Group in the 1970s, in whose livery it is seen here. It later moved south to St Michael's Church in Woburn Sands. It was restored in the mid-1990s but has apparently since fallen on hard times.

Sales and Production

The Ministry of War Transport had decreed that the Bedford OWB would be the only single-deck bus available to operators during the war, so many operators who had previously not been Bedford customers found themselves with Hobson's choice for new single-deck buses. By far the largest recorded customers for the OWB were the Northern Ireland Road Transport Board (NIRTB), with over 170, and Walter Alexander of Falkirk, with 100. Of the major bus groups, there were a number of companies who had taken Bedfords in the 1930s – Lincolnshire Road Car, Western National and Southern National – and who all took quite large quantities of the OWB. Lincolnshire Road Car in particular had been a customer of GM since the days of Chevrolet for its light buses and bought over fifty OWBs. Western and Southern National had bought both the WTB and the pre-war OB in quantity and between them bought thirty OWBs. Similarly SMT in Edinburgh took sixty and Western SMT at Kilmarnock took over twenty. Bristol Tramways took fifty and Red & White Services in Chepstow took thirty. Neither had been Bedford customers previously. Other large territorial operators to buy the OWB included the Caledonian Omnibus Co. Ltd, Dumfries and Cumberland Motor Services of Whitehaven. Cumberland had been a Bedford customer pre-war.

Many independent operators found themselves with a great increase in work during the Second World War as a result of industry and agriculture being largely turned over to the war effort. Civilians needed to be transported to their places of work and most private cars were taken off the road during the war years as a result of the non-availability of petrol for private use. Such operators used the OWB to build up their fleets during the war years – for example, Worthington Motor Tours Ltd, based at the Station Garage, Stafford, were amongst the top ten customers, with thirty-eight. Enterprise and Silver Dawn, of Scunthorpe, increased the total in use in Lincolnshire by

IN PRESERVATION

1949 Bedford OB/Duple MHU 49

by Mike Walker

Year new: 1949
Engine: 214cu in (3.5-litre) petrol
Gearbox: Bedford four-speed
Body: Duple thirty-seat bus
Current owner: Mike Walker

History

The Bristol Tramways & Carriage Company received thirteen Bedford OB buses in 1949 and 1950, all but one with Duple thirty-seat bus bodies, having received a large number of the OWB Utility buses during the war. As the Tramways' own chassis building plant resumed bus production (from war work) just after the war, one would have thought that their current single-deck chassis, the Bristol L, would have fulfilled the company's needs. There are two possible explanations for receiving the Bedfords: first, the bus factory had also to supply other Tilling Group companies with the L chassis, meaning that demand outstripped supply; or second, it is quite possible that there was a requirement within the company for a smaller bus than the thirty-five-seat L, especially as the post-war period saw an upsurge in passenger demand and the consequent increase in the operation of services, including in deep rural areas. Interestingly, however, the company also received a further eight OBs, but this time with Duple's Vista coach body.

Most of the Bedford OB buses lasted seven or eight years in Tramways' service before being sold on, although a small number lasted until the early 1960s, serving the very narrow roads around Stroud in Gloucestershire.

MHU 49, fleet number 207, was the first of these buses to enter service, and operated initially at Weston-super-Mare (hardly on rural narrow roads!), linking the railway station with the seafront and Kewstoke Woods, and it is almost certain that she was worked with a conductor. She was withdrawn in 1958 and then worked for over twenty years with Mid Wales Motorways, where she was fitted with a driver-operated door control. After passing into preservation, she was acquired by the well-known preservationist William Staniforth in 1988, who kept her under cover until I acquired her in 2009.

Owner's Experience

MHU 49 was recovered from storage on a low loader and sent to TDC bodyshop at Lydney, in Gloucestershire, where she was completely restored. Much of the wooden framework was replaced and, along with all the exterior panelwork, a new floor was fitted and the seats were retrimmed (by a retired Longwell Green Coachbuilders trimmer!) and refitted, while her mechanical units were refurbished where necessary and she was fitted with the more powerful 32hp (RAC rating) engine taken from a Bedford TK lorry. After receiving several coats of Tilling green and cream paint, she passed the MOT test in 2012 (her first for thirty-five years!) and was unveiled at the Bristol Vintage Bus group/Avon Valley Railway at Brislington, Bristol in that August, carrying passengers on several trips between the Brislington Park and Ride site and the Bristol Vintage Bus Group premises at Flowers Hill.

Later that month she was entered in the Wedmore (Somerset) Harvest Home Vehicle Festival, winning best in class, and then taken to nearby Cheddar, where she almost certainly at one time operated, and was photographed there with a suitable destination display.

When driven she exhibits the characteristic Bedford petrol engine whine, and shows an easy acceleration, reaching a top speed of around 50mph (80km/h), although her brakes were never too good compared with other OBs.

She was used at the Crosville Motor Services open day in July 2014, when she operated around her old haunts of Weston-super-Mare, operating many trips to and from the town centre, but it became clear that her brakes were definitely not effective, and on examination she was found to need work on the brake servo and wheel cylinders. Consequently she was taken off the road and a thorough brake overhaul undertaken at a professional PSV repairer in Bristol. When she was

Bought by the Bristol Tramways & Carriage Co. Ltd in 1949, this OB/Duple bus spent some time with Mid-Wales Motorways, based in Newtown, Powys, before passing into preservation in 1971. It has recently undergone a full restoration by current owner Mike Walker and looks absolutely splendid in its original livery of Tilling green and cream. M. WALKER

collected it became clear that, although the Bedford OB was a very simple design, modern vehicle technicians find it difficult to come to terms with 'old' technology and although all of her working brake parts had been replaced, the brakes were not balanced and still not effective. In addition, although she ran perfectly well when being delivered to the workshop (she just wouldn't stop!), on collection the engine was now no longer giving adequate performance and just would not pull. So unfortunately I was forced to take her off the road until I could get someone with the appropriate knowledge to look again at the brakes and, now, the performance of the engine.

She was laid up while a number of people tried to cure her problems, including by the replacement of all of her electrics (points, plugs, condenser, leads, distributor and so on), but to no avail, and her engine and braking systems are now being stripped down again with the hope that her problems can be identified and she can be returned to the road.

When in use the bus attracts a great deal of attention and is great fun to drive, as well as being small and manoeuvrable enough to take almost anywhere: in addition, as a Bedford OB service bus, she is quite rare on the rally circuit as most people associate the OB with the twenty-nine-seat coach that Bedford enthusiasts have grown to love. I am hoping that MHU 49 will now be in good health to attend many local and national events in 2016, to reinforce the slogan that 'You see them everywhere'!

twenty-five. In Staffordshire, Brown's Motor Company of Tunstall had eighteen. Greenslades, Highland Transport Ltd of Inverness, Morlais Services Ltd, Merthyr Tydfil and Hereford Motor Co. Ltd had ten or more.

Municipal operators who ran OWBs included the corporations of Belfast, Bournemouth, Cardiff, Coventry, Douglas, Edinburgh, Exeter, Merthyr Tydfil, Portsmouth, South Shields and West Hartlepool. Of these, the biggest fleets were Belfast (thirty), Edinburgh (twenty) and Portsmouth (ten).

Many OWBs were put to use in the service of the government. The Admiralty and other government departments accounted for at least 160, while the Navy, Army and Air Force Institutes (NAAFI) had thirty-four. That most secret and important of places, GCHQ at Bletchley Park, had twenty-four for its own use, each given an alphabetic identification code, presumably to encourage the residents in their endeavours, and even the BBC had four. The British Overseas Airways Corporation, better known by its initials as BOAC, had been relocated from London to Bristol at the start of the war and was allocated nine OWBs during 1945 to help them maintain Britain's air connections with the colonies and the free world.

As conditions eased, many OWBs found their way back to the government. By the spring of 1945 the situation had improved enough that the MoWT was able to allow some OWBs to be exported, the majority to New Zealand although a good quantity also went to Ceylon.

Many that stayed in private hands received new or rebuilt bodies in the 1950s. Often these resembled the post-war OB, but some received very modern bodies (for the time) built by coachbuilders such as Burlingham, Willenhall Coachcraft of Willenhall, Staffordshire, Lee Motors of Bournemouth and others. There were also a number of forward-control conversions of OWB chassis, probably in the hope of convincing the travelling public that they were riding on the most up-to-date of vehicles!

Of those that were rebuilt to look like OBs, there was very little to distinguish them externally. The most obvious difference was in the radiator grilles, the missing cover over the starting handle aperture being a give-away. However, the OB also had a removable cover over this aperture that could disappear over time, so it wasn't a guaranteed method!

Some OWBs were dismantled in 1947 to provide running units and engines for use in new lightweight aluminium integral buses built by J. C. beadle and Co. of Spital St, Dartford. At the time these were referred to as 'chassisless' buses and were part of a project instigated by Tilling in search of economy of running costs per vehicle, the project culminating in the group building its own integral bus, the Bristol LS.

On the Road

Despite the wartime seating, the OWB was not particularly uncomfortable. The petrol engine was smooth-running compared with the diesels that were common in the buses of the late 1930s and the gearbox, while making itself heard, was no louder than those of the pre-war Leyland and Bristol products, for example. The ride was good due to the OB having been intended as predominantly a coach chassis, and passengers in territories where the Tilling Group were the major operators would probably have found the OWB a more comfortable and quiet experience overall than riding in a Bristol JO5G or L5G bus.

THE OB POST-WAR

Bodies

The post-war OB body production generally continued where it had left off in 1940. The Duple Vista twenty-nine-seat front-entrance coach body was to all intents and purposes identical in appearance to that of the 1939 version. Of the post-war production, Duple built by far the largest number of bodies, at just over 4,800 recorded. Of these, the majority were coaches of around twenty-nine seats, though versions were produced with seating capacities ranging from fourteen to twenty-eight, twenty-seven seats being the next most popular after the usual twenty-nine seats. Duple also built over 600 bus bodies, with seating ranging from sixteen to thirty-six, the lower capacities often including space for carrying parcels and, in a few cases, the Royal Mail. Production of normal Vista bodies was interrupted in late 1948 due to a shortage of some materials; an alternative was offered by Duple in the form of the Mark V Service Coach, which was somewhat less well appointed and without the sliding sunshine roof and some of the external decoration of the Vista.

In 1947 Duple built fifteen special luxury bodies for the Overseas Touring Co., Nairobi, to be operated by the UK subsidiary Overseas Motor Transport Co. Ltd, Pall Mall, London, SW1. Eleven had fourteen seats, the remainder sixteen. These required some chassis modifications, including twin 20gal (90ltr) petrol tanks and shock absorbers both front and rear, several years in advance of Bedford's adoption of this arrangement. Two spare wheels were carried in a fabric container mounted to the right of the driver's cab. The bodies were specially designed to give improved ground clearance, while better ventilation was provided

A 1945 Duple publicity shot of an export OWB bus for Sri Lanka (then known as Ceylon). VH/DUPLE

JXX 487. A 1950 OB with thirty-seat Duple body, new to the Ministry of Supply. Despite the 'Wendover' destination this image was most likely taken during its sojourn in Pembrokeshire. The Duple Almet body was very similar to this design. This bus survives in preservation and is under restoration at the time of writing.

Duple brochure for Bedford OB/Almet kit-form bus.

by wind-down windows, six roof ventilators and Rawlings 'Vortex' extractors. A waterproof and dust-proof rear luggage boot was provided, with additional baggage space in containers mounted over the rear wheelarches. A partition with a sliding door separated the cab from the passenger compartment.

The body frame was of African timbers and, except for the steel scuttle and rear corner panels, panelled in aluminium. The roof and side panels had Isoflex insulation between the double skins to provide some protection from the relentless heat of the Nyriri desert.

Duple also built an all-metal kit-form body called the Almet. Intended for home or export sales and based on Duple's wartime experience with manufacturing major assemblies for heavy bombers and bodies for the OWB, the Almet was built in six major assemblies with no timber used anywhere in the body. Special paint was employed to protect against corrosion, making the body suitable for use in tropical and humid conditions. The kit was designed to be assembled with the minimum of tools – no welding or specialist metal processes were required; not quite just an allen key, but not far off! The frame structures were manufactured in steel, with aluminium outer panels locked to the frame by ingeniously designed beading strips that allowed damaged panels to be removed and replaced easily. Quarter panels were in mild steel for additional impact resistance; in the same vein, floor-height triangulated steel mouldings were fitted around the periphery of the floor to transmit side-impact forces into the floor.

The next most prolific builder was Mulliner, with over 1,200 bodies, mostly buses with seating capacities in the range sixteen to thirty-three, though there were around seventy bodies with coach or dual-purpose seating. The basic design of the Mulliner bus body was produced by Duple, and some buses were built under a subcontract arrangement with Duple; it has been suggested that two bodies were sent to Mulliner to assist in producing jigs. Following the subcontracted batch, further orders were passed by the Vauxhall dealers directly to Mulliner, many of which were exported, often purchased by oil companies in the Middle East or South America. Many other Mulliner-bodied OBs were built for British military or welfare use, signs of a burgeoning relationship between Bedford and such users.

SMT – the operator, who became separate from SMT the dealer when the Scottish bus companies were taken into

MHU 193 and LHW 139. Mulliner of Birmingham built bus bodies to a Duple design on the OB. Clifton College in Bristol used these two OB/Mulliner thirty-one-seat buses to transport boys from Clifton to the school's sports ground at Abbots Leigh, where the two buses are pictured on 2 December 1978. Farthest from the camera is MHU 193, now preserved in the livery of Bristol Tramways. Nearest is LHW 139, which dates from October 1948, while MHU 193 dates from September 1949. MHU 193 was quite spartan inside, with wooden slatted seats reminiscent of the wartime utility bodies. G. GOULD

seat bodies though there were around 100 with semi-forward-control full-front conversions with thirty seats.

Other coachbuilders to build in quantity on the OB included Thurgood of Ware (100), Pearson of Liverpool (ninety), Beadle (seventy-five) and New Zealand Motor Bodies, Auckland (NZMB; sixty).

In 1953 Scottish Omnibuses (operating as SMT) substantially rebuilt twenty OB chassis to a forward-control layout with the driver beside the engine. They were then fitted with twenty-four-seat Burlingham Seagull bodies and used for extended tours around the highlands and islands of Scotland until 1961–2. At least one of these survives in preservation.

In the late 1950s, Lincolnshire Road Car purchased four Duple-bodied OBs from Western National

government ownership in 1949 – built over 300 bodies for its own use, mostly coaches but between seventy and eighty buses. SMT also built a mobile bank, shop, livestock carrier and a number of vans on the OB – standardization being the name of the game.

Plaxton had emerged as a coachbuilder on Bedford chassis towards the end of the 1930s. However, there was still some way to go before it would challenge Duple; just over 200 coaches were built on the OB, most with twenty-nine-

and converted them into replicas of the old 'toastrack' trams found in seaside locations of yore. Two were open on both sides, the other two being open on the nearside. These were used for seafront services at Skegness, the town made famous by the LNER for being 'so bracing' – a ride on one of those four OBs would leave you in no doubt of that, for sure.

Plaxton was not quite as prolific as Duple in building bodies for the OB. This example, photographed at Marine Parade, Hastings, in August 1966, belonged to Empress Coaches of Hastings.

Mrs A. Martlew operated this thirty-seat full-front semi-forward-control Plaxton conversion on the OB chassis. It was new in June 1947. Mrs Martlew was based in Donnington Wood, Shropshire and was a member of the Shropshire Omnibus Association, who pooled their services and operated them according to a rota. Around 200 of these Plaxton conversions were built on OB chassis. VH

Sales and Production

Production of the OB restarted in a small way in 1945 with forty-eight chassis, then from 1946 to 1950 averaged just over 1,400 per year according to some published records. These figures are at odds with Bedford's own claims for total production, which suggest that production should have averaged around 3,000 chassis per year with over 12,000 built in the period 1946–50. Production of the OB officially ended in 1950, though over 150 were registered in 1951 and three in 1952.

Some OBs were converted to diesel engines in the early 1950s. For example, in 1951 Perkins was offering its P6 74bhp at 2,400rpm diesel conversion, which included an exhauster for the brake vacuum system and a 300W dynamo for the electrics. Some impecunious operators contrived their own diesel conversions, often using the Perkins P6 or in some cases the Dorman 4DS or anything that could be shoehorned in.

Of the post-war production, the largest recorded fleet of OBs went to UK government agencies – over 100 to the Admiralty, just under 200 to the Air Ministry and over 100 to the MoS, mostly with Duple or Mulliner bodies. The Anglo-Iranian Oil Co. Ltd accounted for over 150, largely with Mulliner bodies, though some with Duple bodies. London County Council (LCC) built up a fleet of around sixty, mostly with Mulliner bodies. Crosville Motor Services Ltd of Chester had sixty-eight, around a third of which had Beadle bodies, the remainder having Duple bodies. The Southern and West-

This OB was delivered to the Eastern National Omnibus Co. Ltd with fleet no. 4067 in 1949. It was purchased by the Lincolnshire Road Car Co. Ltd in 1958 and its standard Duple Vista twenty-nine-seat body was converted to the form shown here for seafront services at Skegness.

ern National Omnibus companies had sixty-seven and sixty-three, respectively – Southern National taking fifteen with Beadle bodies, the remainder for both companies having Duple bodies.

An independent operator who bought an extensive fleet of OBs was Worthington Motor Tours Ltd, of Wolverhampton, around a third of its total having Mulliner bodies, the remainder Duple. Started by Jack Worthington, the fleet grew to considerable size during the war, providing transport for workers at ordinance factories in the West Midlands, with OWBs and later OBs. The business lasted into the 1970s, when it was taken over by NBC and absorbed into National Travel (Midlands).

Other large fleets included those of Keith & Boyle, Walter Alexander at Falkirk, and the Metropolitan Police, each with over forty. Fleets of between thirty and forty were built up by Fallowfield & Britten Ltd, London E8; Grey Green; Hanson's Buses Ltd of Huddersfield; Hants & Sussex Motor Services Ltd of Emsworth; Lincolnshire Road Car Co. Ltd of Bracebridge Heath; Northern Roadways Ltd of Glasgow; Scout Motor Service Ltd of Preston; and Shamrock & Rambler.

The OB went all over the world; estimated exports included over 150 to Greece via Alexandria, around 100 to Belgium and Malaya, just fewer than 100 to Finland and between 90 and 100 to Australia. Around seventy are thought to have been exported to Chile. Other export

Thurgood of Ware, Hertfordshire built many bodies on the OB. Here is an interior view of a Thurgood twenty-seat touring coach body, showing it to be quite spacious, light and airy. VH/THURGOOD

destinations included Paraguay, Pakistan, South Africa and New Zealand, all receiving fifty or more, and Sweden, Holland, Portugal, Mauritius and Ceylon. A large proportion of the New Zealand contingent went to New Zealand Railways Road Services with bodies by NZMB.

The OB was vastly popular with small independent coach companies and over 2,000 such operators bought just one or two, some perhaps as their very first purchases at the start of a new business. Such was the familiarity of the OB as a country bus that one was chosen to represent railway competition in the famous Ealing comedy *The Titfield Thunderbolt*; it was an OB with Duple Vista twenty-nine-seat body – GAM 338, starring in the blue and cream livery of the fictitious Pierce & Crump Bus Co. While the steam locomotives are undoubtedly the real stars of the film, for some enthusiasts it is a close-run thing!

Bedford OBs often led long and fruitful lives and as a result many survive in preservation, some still earning their keep with their current operators. It has been said that many OBs passed from service into preservation almost unnoticeably, their owner's attitudes to them changing from a workaday tool to a precious old friend as the years went by. Two notable examples were one owned by H & M Coaches of Chasetown, West Midlands, with the usual Duple Vista body, and another by Hulleys of Baslow, Derbyshire, with a rare Barnaby body (of which it is believed less than five were built on OB chassis), both of which were still in regular use at thirty-one years of age in 1979. Bedford claimed that when production ended, 16,164 OB chassis had been built, of which approximately 3,300 were wartime OWB versions. Of these, published records account for around

A standard OB/Duple Vista coach, new to J. Lamb of Upholland, Lancashire in August 1950, is seen here at Brassington, a village in the Derbyshire dales, on 19 December 1970, when owned by Webster's of Hognaston, Derbyshire. It serves to show how well the traditional OB/Duple coach blended into the rural environment.

8,500 OBs, including the few built in 1939. As this is being written in April 2015, there are at least eighty OBs still on the road in the UK.

ON THE ROAD

The narrow cab of the OB, derived as it was from the O-series trucks, could cause the novice driver some difficulty, as the bodywork behind the cab was generally quite a bit wider and constant use of the mirrors was necessary to ensure progress clear of verges and drain covers. For its time, the OB was nippy, easily reaching 40mph (64km/h), unlike many of its contemporaries, and even 60mph (97km/h) was rumoured to be possible (though inadvisable) on a down gradient. Brakes were efficient and sufficient for the weight of the vehicle, and the OB was said to be a joy to drive, especially in wet or icy conditions, compared with other vehicles. The gearbox, however, showed its prewar origins and double declutching was necessary, though it could be easily mastered with practice, after which clean and silent gear changes became a matter of pride. The characteristic gearbox whine was a familiar sound and instantly recognized all over the country. George Atkin says of the driving experience: 'The OB is a particularly nice vehicle to drive, almost car like, and has that wonderful iconic gearbox whine in third gear which says, come on! We're nearly ready to change up!'

This rather aggressive-looking body was built on an export OB chassis by Van Hool in 1949 and seen at the Brussels Motor Show. VH

IN PRESERVATION

OB/Duple Vista JDV 754

by Mark Withers

Year new: 1947
Engine: Bedford 214cu in (3.2-litre) petrol engine ('28hp')
Gearbox: four-speed synchromesh
Body: Duple Vista coach, twenty-nine seats
Current owner: Lewis Coaches Stalbridge Ltd

History

This 1947 Bedford OB coach was new to the Woolacombe & Mortehoe Motor Company in North Devon. In 1960 she moved to Barnstaple to work for Fred Guard, doing school contracts and private hire. When the Fred Guard business was sold to Streets Coachways of Barnstaple in 1966 JDV went too, but not for long.

By 1967 she had moved to Armstrong of Bletchley and was exhibited at the Brighton coach rally of that same year. Prior to the coach rally she had undergone extensive refurbishment, including removal of the sliding roof, which was replaced with Duple Super Vega-type opening skylights. A new headlining was fitted, along with twenty-three luxury seats plus a courier seat. In 1972 she was withdrawn from service and in 1978 she passed to coach dealers Erringtons of Leicester. By the mid-eighties she was owned by Douglas Butland from Towcester, and by the mid-nineties she was at Barry Biffin's garage in Melbourne near Derby.

Enter Mr Martyn Babb of Blue Motors, Minehead, who was working with one of his coaches in Derbyshire when it broke down. When his coach was towed back to the garage in Melbourne, Barry Biffin thought that Martyn might be interested to see the old coach. Martyn recognized this as a North Devon OB and thought that it would be a useful addition to his fleet. A deal was struck and JDV 754 was returned to Devon in 1997. After much restoration and renovation the coach was re-certified and started earning her keep in April 2000. Without doubt she was one of the hardest-working OBs during the first decade of the twenty-first century. As well as doing Exmoor tours and local excursions she visited places as far afield as Beachy Head and preserved railways in Wales. In 2011 Martyn decided to retire from coaching and sold JDV 754 to Lewis Coaches in Henstridge, Somerset. Some structural repair work to the bodywork and a repaint in Lewis Coaches colours has resulted in her looking somewhat different for her semi-retirement in Henstridge. Further restoration and renovation will follow as time permits.

Owner's Experience

For as long as I can remember I have been interested in Bedford coaches. My father and grandfather were coach operators in the 1950s. Most small family coach operators at that time used Bedford coaches. Their business was based at Chitterne on Salisbury Plain. The Bedford OB coach was a jack of all trades and would be used for forces weekend leave journeys as far away as Manchester, Liverpool and Leeds. During the week a bus service was operated through the Wylye valley to nearby Warminster and there was also private hire work for local clubs and schools. Summer excursions to the south coast were also popular. I well remember trips to the seaside being full to capacity and my mother having to sit on a stool in the gangway.

By 1960 a change of career for my father meant a move to the East Midlands, where he worked as a traffic examiner for the Ministry of Transport. During my school holidays we would visit operators in the local area and have a look at their coaches. By this time the OBs were disappearing and SB coaches were replacing them.

In 1968 I started work as an apprentice mechanic with Granville Tours of Grimsby. Their fleet of thirty or so coaches comprised mainly Bedfords. At that time, in addition to annual testing, coaches had to have a certificate of fitness. This was in effect a kind of super MOT. The coach in question would be given a thorough overhaul of brakes, steering and suspension.

Lewis Coaches (Stalbridge) Ltd of Henstridge, Somerset, maintains this superb OB/Duple Vista twenty-nine-seat coach and another in preservation. M. WITHERS

Steering arms had to be removed and polished until they shone – this was done to check for cracks. After all this work, if the coach was as good as new it would be given a certificate for a maximum of five years, though usually less.

After working as a mechanic for many years I decided it was time I had a PSV driving licence. By now I was married with two small children and living in Cornwall. With the help of friends at Roseland Motors, Veryan, a licence was obtained. Their fleet of coaches was of course all Bedfords.

In 1988 an advert in *Coach Mart* led to the purchase of Lewis Coaches, Henstridge, Somerset. Pat Lewis had decided to retire and sold the business as a going concern, together with vehicles and premises. The vehicles were fairly old and, with the exception of one Ford, were all Bedfords. The two older coaches had Duple Viceroy bodies, which tended to leak when it rained. Newer Bedfords soon replaced the older ones. About three-quarters of the work we did was schools related, the remainder private hire. My main job was to look after the coaches and keep the wheels turning. If you looked after your Bedford it would usually look after you. Spares were always readily available and not too difficult to fit. We worked long hours, very often seven days a week. Coaches were a way of life and not just a job. If you didn't like it you wouldn't do it!

Nostalgia isn't what it used to be, or so they say, but childhood memories of Bedford OBs stayed with me. Occasionally an OB would come on the market but, with little money and nowhere to keep one, it was a lost cause. Later in life that changed as we wound down our business and had a little more spare time.

Why an OB? Well for me it is probably early childhood memories as much as anything. The Duple Vista bodywork and the Bedford stubby nose look just right compared with today's straight edges and right angles. The bodywork was designed to look attractive as well as being functional. The whine made by an OB gearbox is also something you don't forget, particularly on a hilly route. The straight-cut gears become noisier the more you subject them to load. This is particularly noticeable if travelling in the front. Passengers further back can listen to the rear axle, as that also tends to whine!

Our first OB, KPW 986, was purchased in 2005 and is used mainly for weddings and special hires, though she sometimes goes to bus rallies and steam fairs.

In 2011 we were offered a second OB in the shape of JDV 754, which arrived from North Devon under her own steam. Although mechanically good, the bus's bodywork was starting to show signs of its age. A respray into fleet colours was quickly achieved with the help of my son. Soon afterwards she was used to carry entrants to the Cancer UK 'Race for Life' event at Sherborne castle. Pieces of pink feathers worn by the runners found their way into every nook and cranny. We are still finding bits of pink feather now!

The winter of 2013 saw the offside body panels removed and I replaced most of the timber framework. The window rubbers and channels were also replaced and my son fabricated a rear wheelarch.

The following summer it was decided to take the coach to Cornwall on holiday. Some of the seats were taken out and others turned around to face the rear, and a table was installed together with cooking equipment. Accompanied by my wife, daughter and two dogs a great time was had by all at the West of England Steam Engine Society at Stithians. JDV won a prize for best commercial vehicle.

Driving an OB in the twenty-first century can be a bit of a challenge. If the weather is too hot the fuel tends to vaporize and in cold weather the carburettor can ice up.

The suspension is firm with a vintage feel to it. On a good road a cruising speed of 40mph (64km/h) seems about right. The 6-cylinder petrol engine develops 72bhp, which is less than most small cars have these days. When climbing a hill, a change down through the gears will be required; third gear will be good for 25–28mph (40–45km/h). Hopefully second gear won't be needed, as this is a 15mph (24km/h) gear.

The steering won't win any prizes either – to keep the coach in a straight line requires constant attention. The steering is also heavy, particularly at low speeds; add a full load of passengers and things start to get quite physical.

Once you get used to the ways of the OB, though, it is actually a delight to drive, particularly when there is not too much other traffic about. Motorways are best avoided and other motorists don't understand your difficulties.

Sadly my wife passed away in 2015. Many happy memories of journeys taken together by OB will always stay with me. The idea of having two OBs was so that we could drive one each. This didn't really go according to plan but JDV will stay with the family for now at least. We are hoping to have many more OB adventures to make Bedford memories for the next generation. Besides, there is still more restoration and woodwork to be done!

CHAPTER FOUR

THE SB

The SB was introduced to the world at the Commercial Motor Show in September 1950. Over time it became something of a phenomenon for Bedford, remaining in production right until the end at Dunstable in 1986. The rugged simplicity of the chassis cannot be understated, and it is this no-frills, no-nonsense approach to engineering that was maintained, despite the chassis being revised and updated over the years, and was responsible for its continued popularity throughout the world.

The SB was the PSV version of the new Model S 7-ton (7,112kg) truck range, which was the heaviest range of Bedfords to date. The SB was Bedford's first normal control chassis; in its 1950 form it was powered by a new 300cu in (4.9-litre) petrol engine that gave 110bhp at 3,200rpm and was mounted vertically over the front axle. The chassis was fabricated from pressed-steel channel section. Two robust side members were cranked outwards just behind the gearbox and the frame was completed by five cross-members cold-riveted to the side members and positioned in the chassis to suit the mechanical units. The side mem-

bers were of constant depth from the centreline of the front axle to a point just in front of the forward rear spring mounting. From this point the side members were gradually reduced in depth, passing above the rear axle in a swan neck shape, curving down behind the axle until they were approximately level with the bottom of the differential casing. At this point they tapered rearwards to a very narrow section, allowing for the body to incorporate a low-loading boot floor with maximum clearance beneath it.

The gearbox and engine were unit-mounted and drive was transmitted by a three-piece propeller shaft supported in two places by resilient bearings in the chassis cross-members. The three sections of the propeller shaft were connected by Hardy Spicer mechanical universal joints.

Suspension consisted of long semi-elliptic springs front and rear, made of silicon manganese steel, shot-peened on the long side to increase fatigue resistance. The front spring dimensions were 50 × 2.25in (1,270mm × 57mm) with eleven leaves, the rears 60 × 2.5in (1,524mm × 63.5mm) with twelve leaves. The wheelbase was 206in (5,232mm), suitable for bus and coach bodies of the then maximum legal length, which was 27ft 6in (8.4m).

The gearbox was new, with synchromesh on second, third and top gears, second and third gears being of the single-helical type in constant mesh – the helical form being chosen for its general quietness in operation. Final drive was by hypoid differential with ratio options of either 5.833:1 or 6.8:1. The 26gal (118ltr) petrol tank was mounted on the right-hand side of the chassis in the centre of the wheelbase, two batteries for the 12v or 24v electrical system being mounted slightly forward of this position on the left-hand side.

Brakes were a combination of hydraulic and mechanical, a system that was finding some popularity at the time and which, in hindsight, was a backward step. The hydraulic system comprised a Lockheed master cylinder with two pistons in tandem and combined with a Clayton Dewandre vacuum servo. One piston operated the slave cylinders at the front wheels, while the other actuated the rear brakes through a system of rods and levers. The tandem master

The 1955 SB chassis, complete with dash and engine cover. GM

cylinder effectively provided a dual hydraulic circuit similar to that in the OB so that in the event of either front or
rear brakes failing in service, the other would continue to
provide some braking. The brake shoes were designed to
have a self-servo effect when travelling in both forward and
reverse directions.

Steering was by semi-irreversible worm-and-sector contained in a steering box bolted rigidly to the chassis frame,
the steering column being connected to the box through
a fabric universal joint. At the top the steering column
was supported in a rubber-bushed bracket attached to the
instrument panel. The cab itself formed part of a complete
unit that included the front wings, front cowl, radiator
grille and bumper. The front was Bedford's first effort at a
full-front design and was of bulbous though not unpleasing
appearance. In some parts of the world it was referred to as
the 'bull-nose' front, for fairly obvious reasons.

REVISIONS

As the years went by, opportunities were taken to update
the SB chassis in line with Bedford's other developments.
The first of these came in autumn 1953, when a diesel
engine option was introduced employing the Perkins R6.
This was almost certainly a direct result of the popularity

**Another of Moody's of Northfleet's fleet, this 1951
SB has a body by Thurgood of Ware. It is seen in
Portsmouth on 5 May 1974. It was later preserved
but is thought to have been exported to Holland in
the early 1980s.**

of a proprietary conversion introduced by Millburn Motors
Ltd, Millburn Street, Glasgow in 1952. This utilized the
Albion Chieftain E.N.286 diesel engine (known as an 'oil'
engine at the time), which was a 4-cylinder 4.9-litre engine
producing 75bhp. This particular engine had also been fitted successfully in Leyland and Thornycroft chassis by Millburn. Lowland Motorways Ltd of Glasgow was one of the
first operators to sample the conversion and found that both
performance and economy were very satisfactory, 20mpg
(14.2ltr/100km) being achievable. The only modifications
to the SB chassis were new front engine mountings and the
cost of the conversion was £675.

The Perkins R6 was generally available across the entire
S range and not confined solely to the PSV chassis, and this
would be the case with Bedford's own diesels in the future.
However, the Perkins engine suffered from some reliability problems, which may have put pressure on Bedford to
speed up development of its own diesel engine, though in
the event it was 1957 before the 300cu in (4.9-litre) diesel
became available. The Perkins R6 had meanwhile evolved
into a Mk2 version that addressed the reliability problems
of the earlier version and remained available as an option
on the SB. When the diesel option first became available, the two versions of the chassis were reclassified SBG
(gasoline) and SBO (oil) for the petrol and diesel versions,
respectively. The price for an SBG was £855 and for an
SBO £1,248, and this price differential remained fairly consistent throughout the period when both petrol and diesel
engines were options.

A major change took place in August 1955, when the
wheelbase was increased to 216in (5,486mm) to enable
bodies of the maximum legal dimensions of 30ft × 8ft
(9m × 2.44m) to be built on the SB. The increase of 10in
(254mm) on the wheelbase made it possible to increase the
overall length of the vehicle by 15in (381mm), allowing
the seating capacity of a typical coach body to be increased
from thirty-six to forty-one seats.

To maintain the turning circle of the new chassis a
greater lock angle was required, which necessitated an

BEDFORD SB

Layout and Chassis
Bus or coach body, typically 27ft 6in (8.4m) long × 7ft
6in (2.29m) wide, with 31–33 seats. Frame: pressed-
steel channel side members with five cold-riveted cross-
members

Engine
Type: Bedford 300cu in (4.9-litre) petrol
Later options:
Perkins R6 340cu in (5.8-litre) diesel (from 1953)
Leyland O.350 350cu in (5.7-litre) diesel
Bedford 300cu in (4.9-litre) diesel (from 1957)
Bedford 330cu in (5.4-litre) diesel (from 1962)
Bedford 330cu in (5.4-litre) normally aspirated (NA) or
turbo-diesel (from 1982)
Fuel capacity: 26gal (118ltr)

Gearbox
Bedford 4-speed, synchromesh on second, third and top
(1950)
Clutch: 12in diameter single dry plate when Bedford petrol
engine fitted, 13in diameter with Bedford diesels, 14in
with Leyland O.350 engine
Ratios for all engines except Leyland O.350:
   1st: 7.06:1
   2nd: 3.03:1
   3rd: 1.71:1
   Top: 1:1
   Reverse: 7.06:1
Standard when fitted with Leyland O.350 engine, optional
when fitted with late Bedford 330cu in (5.4-litre) normally
aspirated and turbo-diesel:
   1st: 6.5:1
   2nd: 2.86:1
   3rd: 1.58:1
   Top: 1:1
   Reverse: 6.5:1
Eaton five-speed direct top:
   1st: 6.92:1
   2nd: 3.98:1
   3rd: 2.37:1
   4th: 1.47:1
   Top : 1:1
   Reverse: 6.5:1
Eaton five-speed overdrive top:
   1st: 6.30:1
   2nd: 3.36:1
   3rd: 1.84:1
   4th: 1:1
   Top : 0.82:1
   Reverse: 6.5:1

Transmission
Three-piece Hardy Spicer propeller shaft
Rear axle: Fully floating rear axle with final drive by
hypoid differential, ratio 5.833:1; later options 5.286:1,
6.8:1; from 1957 the options included a 5.833:1 ratio and a
two-speed rear axle: high 4.89:1, low 6.8:1
Front axle: Drop-forged I-section beam with taper-roller
hub bearings

Suspension and Steering
Suspension: Semi-elliptic springs with double-acting
hydraulic shock absorbers
Steering: Semi-irreversible worm and sector
Tyres: 8.25 × 20in, 10- or 12-ply; later option 9.00 ×
20in, 10- or 12-ply

Brakes
Type: Lockheed hydraulic with Clayton Dewandre vacuum
servo assistance; later dual air over hydraulic with engine-
driven 9.5cu ft/min compressor
Size: 16 × 3.18in (front), 16 × 4.25in (rear)

Dimensions
Track
   Front: 74.5in (1,892mm); 76in (1,930mm) from 1955
   Rear: 69in (1,753mm)
Wheelbase: 17ft 2in (5,232mm); from 1955 on 18ft
(5,486mm)

Electrical system
12v, two 6v batteries in series, 500W compensated-voltage
dynamo (1950)

increase in the front track of 1.5in (38mm) and modifications to the steering comprising a new third-arm forging
and a new steering box with greater sector movement and
external adjustment.

The frame height was increased by 2.625in (66.7mm) to
answer complaints of insufficient clearance and the chassis side members lost their rearwards extensions and the
swan necks over the rear axle. The top of the frame was
now flat over the rear axle to the rearward mounting for
the rear spring. To provide clearance for the rear axle, the
side members were reduced in depth and tapered rearwards
along the bottom edge, starting at a point approximately
12in (305mm) in front of the rear spring forward mounting. The frame now ended immediately behind the rear

spring hangers, reducing the overhang behind the rear axle from 85.5in (2,172mm) to 49in (1,245mm) with a commensurate saving in weight. The net result of these changes for the coachbuilders was a higher floor level – coachbuilders apparently not having found the lower frame level of the original design of any practical advantage – a higher boot floor, giving more underside clearance at the rear, and a reduced overhang behind the rear axle.

From April 1957, the Leyland O.350 6-cylinder diesel engine was offered as a third option for the SB. This followed on from a proprietary conversion offered first in 1952 by the Arlington Motor Co. Ltd, Bedford dealers of Ponders End, Enfield, Middlesex, of the Bedford S-type goods range. The cost of conversion was expected to be recovered in 30,000–40,000 miles (48,000–64,000km), thereafter saving the operator 4.75d (2p) per mile. Some modifications to the chassis frame were required and an additional battery needed to power the 24v starter motor of the Leyland engine, as well as an exhauster pump and vacuum reservoir for the brakes.

The official adoption of the Leyland O.350 engine led to a revision of the classification system for the chassis. The 'O' changed to a zero so the original SBO chassis with Perkins R6 engine became the SB0, though in practice many still referred to it as the SBO. The SB with a Bedford diesel became the SB1, with the Bedford petrol engine it was the SB3 and, with the Leyland O.350, the SB8. A different set of gearbox ratios and larger 14in clutch were fitted to the SB8, while the other models also received a stronger 12in clutch. A 24v electrical system was fitted on those chassis with the Leyland and Bedford diesels, the Perkins diesel and Bedford petrol engines staying with the 12v system.

All models received thicker brake drums at this time to increase heat dispersion and discourage fade and warp when hot.

Also in 1957 a two-speed rear axle option was added to the specification, which provided 4.86:1 and 6.8:1 ratios and a further 5.833:1 single-speed axle ratio. Another new option was power steering. The Perkins R6 engine option was deleted late in 1957.

From late 1961, the more powerful Bedford 330cu in (5.4-litre) diesels became an option on the SB. In 1963 the more powerful Leyland O.370 engine became an option – chassis so fitted were then classified SB13. From this time the Leyland O.350 seems to have been dropped from the option list.

In 1968, the SB was given new identification codes in connection with computerization at Vauxhall, the diesel version becoming the NJM and the petrol the NFM. The

The final version of the SB chassis in the 1980s, which allowed the coachbuilder much more freedom around the front end. GM

brakes on the diesel chassis were air-assisted by this time, although the petrol chassis retained the engine-vacuum servo.

By 1982, the SB was available in three basic specifications, two diesel and one petrol. The two diesels were both classified NJM with additional suffices to identify the precise engine, and offered a choice of normally aspirated Bedford 330cu in (5.4-litre) diesel with 98bhp (73kW) or the Bedford 5.4-litre turbocharged Red series diesel with 107bhp (80kW). The petrol version was classified NFM and had a 300cu in (4.9-litre) 114bhp Bedford engine. The NFM version was not, however, available in EEC countries. The brakes were still hydraulic with a tandem master cylinder but assisted by air pressure provided by a single-cylinder compressor driven off the engine. Independent hydraulic circuits were provided for front and rear brakes, while the handbrake was now an air-operated spring parking brake. An Eaton five-speed gearbox was fitted to those chassis powered by the turbocharged diesel, but for the other options the gearbox remained the same wide-ratio box as the original 1950 chassis, although the close-ratio box as fitted to the VAS (see Chapter 6) was available on request.

For 1983, there was a stronger range of axles to match the higher power output for the more modern engines. Additional axle ratios were made available in the range 5.29:1 to 6.83:1, in order to eliminate the need for over-

A 1953 SB with the updated version of the thirty-three-seat Duple Vega body, identified by the deeper windscreen and rounded profile to its lower edge. Photographed in the service of Guscotts Coaches, Halwill, Devon while looking a little past its best in September 1975.

drive gearboxes in favour of the stronger, direct-top four- and five-speed gearboxes.

BODIES

When discussing bodies for the SB, it must be borne in mind that a huge number of chassis were exported during its production life. Many were bodied by local coachbuilders in the countries that received them – particularly in the Australasian countries – so to give a definitive account is not possible and may not ever be possible, though it would be a worthy piece of research if someone were to attempt it. This survey therefore primarily considers bodies built and sold in the UK, though often export orders were made up of complete buses and coaches.

Pictured in the garage at the premises of Norfolk's of Nayland, Suffolk, this SB was new to Orange Luxury Coaches, London N16 in 1954 and has coachwork by Harrington of Hove.

The SB shown at the 1950 Commercial Motor Show was fitted with a full-fronted, thirty-three-seat Duple body named the Vega. This was an entirely new body and Duple had clearly worked closely with Bedford to integrate the bulbous front cowl into the body to give a coherent and tidy appearance to the whole coach, which for its time looked sleek and modern. The change in the regulations limiting the maximum dimensions of bodies meant that coachbuilders were able to build slightly longer bodies on the SB than had originally been envisaged, so for the 1952 Commercial Motor Show, the Duple Vega and new 'Super' Vega (with a higher standard of interior trim) were offered with an overall length of 28ft 11.75in (8.8m), allowing the seating capacity to be increased to thirty-five or thirty-seven. The restriction on maximum overhang initially prevented bodies of the then legal 30ft (9m) length being built on the SB, leading to the longer wheelbase version of the chassis introduced in 1955. The new Duple Vega body seated thirty-three passengers and curves abounded, including curved glazed panels in the front corners. The body was constructed with a good deal of steel – the upright pillars, truss panels to add stiffness to the frame, interior stress panels and bearers all being made from this material, though a fair bit of wood was still in evidence in the body's construction. The intermediate pillars were trimmed with stainless steel for appearance. The shape of the SB chassis frame at the rear meant that the Vega was able to incorporate a 66cu ft (1,870ltr) luggage locker, with two smaller cupboards in the sides of the body providing further luggage accommodation. Additional refinements included toughened-glass roof quarters, an optional sliding roof, special tubular luggage racks with interior lighting, heater unit and radio.

A 1953 SB owned by Blue Coaches of Ilfracombe and used on its bus service from Woolacombe to Ilfracombe via Mortehoe. Pictured at the seafront stance, Woolacombe in 1969, this was the bus that sparked the author's interest in Bedford.

A 1954 SB with Duple Vega thirty-eight-seat coach body, new to Fountain Coaches of Twickenham but seen here in the smart livery of Moody's Coaches, Northfleet, Kent while on hire to Maidstone and District Motor Services. It later passed to Williams of Burgess Hill, West Sussex.

The SB was soon finding favour as the basis for a medium-sized bus, Mulliner introducing a lightweight, minimum-cost bus body in 1951. The body was capable of carrying forty-eight passengers in certain configurations although the usual specification was for seating for between thirty-four and thirty-six passengers. The all-metal bus body was available in widths of both 7ft 6in (2.29m) and 8ft (2.44m) and weighed around 4 tons (4,000kg), with an overall length of 28ft 9in (8.76m). The body was constructed in welded and bolted steel, framed with rolled-steel sections although the upper exterior panels were in aluminium. It is likely that Mulliner intended to incorporate more aluminium to keep the weight down, but the material was expensive and in short supply at the time. The floor was made from tongue-and-grooved softwood and the seats were tubular-steeled frames with Vynide leathercloth covers to the cushions and squabs, the overall package being somewhat utilitarian.

The whole recipe does not sound like a vehicle intended for a particularly long life yet the author clearly remembers seeing one of these vehicles in the back yard of Morris dealers TT Motors in Chipping Sodbury in the early 1970s, still apparently in good original condition, though what it was doing there remains a mystery.

From April 1952 a new series of Duple bus and coach bodies was introduced for the SB, the revised regulations for maximum dimensions allowing the new bodies to be extended from the original 27ft 6in (8.4m) to 28ft 11.75in (8.8m) with maximum allowable overhang. Seating capacity could now be thirty-seven in the bus, which was known as the Duple Mark VI, although the thirty-three-seat shorter version was still available. The longer coach was able to seat thirty-five. Both bodies could be built to either 7ft 6in (2.29m) or 8ft (2.44m) width. The new range included the more luxurious Super Vega, which was introduced later in the year. Prices stayed the same, however – £2,530 complete for a 7ft 6in (2.29m) body and £2,565 for the 8ft (2.44m) body. Prices in the two widths for the other bodies were as follows: Mark VI bus, £2,345 and £2,380; Super Vega coach, £2,690 and £2,725. The framing for the new bodies consisted of steel pillars and bearers with timber

Rare Gurney-Nutting 7ft 10in (2.4m)-wide coachwork is fitted to this 1953 SB of Bicknell's of Guildford, Surrey. The coach was new to Essex County Council. R. H. G. SIMPSON

Vaggs of Knockin Heath, Shropshire, was known for its eclectic collection of vehicles. This 1956 SBG/Duple Vega coach was purchased by Vaggs from A. T. Brown of nearby Trench in 1964. Brown was another member of the Shropshire Omnibus Association and operated on the Wellington–Trench–Donnington route. Alongside the coach is a vehicle closely related to the SB mechanically, if not in appearance or comfort – former Eastern National Bristol SC 603 JPU.

Seagull and Corgi pose for the camera. ODV 122 was a 1953 SB with a Burlingham Seagull luxury coach body. The Seagull body was introduced in 1950, the same year as the SB chassis, so this combination would at the time have been a very modern coach. Hookways was an Exeter-based company who survived until August 2011, when the firm collapsed, apparently with debts of £3.5m. The directors blamed increases in fuel costs and the bout of severe weather that had afflicted the southwest of the UK earlier that year.

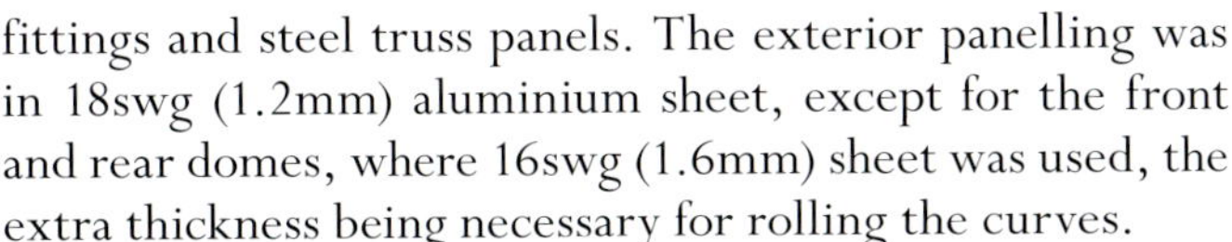

This superb vehicle, typical both of Barton's predilection for the unusual and its attention to presentation, is a 1961 SB1 with Burlingham forty-one-seat coach body.
P. BATESON

Another version of the Plaxton Venturer body is seen on this 1955 SBG belonging to J. Davis of Hawkhurst, Kent. It seems to have suffered the ravages of the weather somewhat.

fittings and steel truss panels. The exterior panelling was in 18swg (1.2mm) aluminium sheet, except for the front and rear domes, where 16swg (1.6mm) sheet was used, the extra thickness being necessary for rolling the curves.

The 'super luxury' to be found in the Super Vega comprised polished timber interior mouldings, veneered roof panels and matching decorative motifs in moquette under the parcel racks. The interior panels were also trimmed in moquette to match the upholstery and the seats were of an improved type with individual head rolls.

A half-height bulkhead separated the saloon from driver's cab, which incorporated a new dash panel of improved layout. Plastic floor mats and a padded leathercloth engine cover were included as standard. Surprisingly for a super luxury coach, heating was an extra, as was a radio and curved-glass quarter panels in the roof. If the latter were specified then tubular luggage racks instead of the cantilever solid type were fitted.

Other coachbuilders were soon taking advantage of the new chassis, a thirty-five-seat version of the famous Burlingham Seagull being produced for the SB in 1952, with an additional super luxury version with armchairs seating only thirty-one; the Plaxton Venturer was also introduced in 1952 and was somewhat similar in appearance to the Burlingham body. The Plaxton body had seating for thirty-five to thirty-seven passengers and had a rear luggage compartment of 90cu ft (2,549ltr) capacity. The body was of composite construction with the sides panelled in aluminium. A sliding entrance door was fitted immediately behind the front axle, as with almost all the other contemporary bodies on the SB. The interior trimming was described as

'luxurious, with waist-high lining panels covered in Plaxide' – Plaxide apparently being Plaxton's in-house brand of plastic leather cloth. The seats were trimmed in moquette and the coach weighed a little under 5 tons (5,000kg). A Plaxton Venturer/SB coach won the Prix d'Honneur for long-distance coaches with thirty seats or more at the International Coach Rally and Concours at Nice in 1954. In 1956, Plaxton introduced the Consort body, which was advertised as being available for the SB. The Consort would evolve into the Embassy body in 1961.

Another coachbuilder to see the potential of the SB was Gurney Nutting Ltd, of Lombard Road, London SW19, a company more famous perhaps for its bespoke bodies on Bentley and Daimler motor car chassis. Shown at the Commercial Motor Show in September 1952, Gurney Nutting's thirty-six- to thirty-eight-seat body was developed in conjunction with dealers and operators Keith & Boyle. Marketed by Keith & Boyle under the name Skyview, it had several novel features, including fixed windows that allowed the interior side panels to be recessed to provide more room for passengers. Ventilation was provided by swivelling panels above the main windows that were mounted on offset hinges so that they could either direct air into the saloon or extract air from it. The Skyview name came from the glass panels with retractable sun-blinds fitted in the roof; the front dome was glazed in Perspex. Maximum use of the rear overhang was made by incorporating a 75cu ft (2,124ltr) luggage locker. Overall length was 29ft 4in (8.9m) and the width an unusual 7ft 10in (2.38m).

For the 1953 season Duple had improved the thirty-five-seat Super Vega, which now had a ramped floor, revised front end and rear-wheel covers, the latter not always being popular with fitters and mechanics, and the luggage locker space was increased to 80cu ft (2,265ltr). A sliding sun roof was now available as an option, perhaps prompted by the appearance of the Gurney Nutting Skyview of the previous year, and on the standard body larger glazed roof panels were included to let more light in.

These often quite small changes were typical of the way coachbuilders competed with each other; updating their bodies in minor ways on an annual basis to try to gain an advantage. Thus for 1954 a restyled version of the Duple Super Vega appeared that did away with the Bedford cowl,

New in 1958 to Halley of Sauchie, Clackmannanshire, this SB3 with forty-one-seat Plaxton Venturer Mark III coachwork served with its first owners for over twenty-five years. It survives in preservation and is currently undergoing restoration. Despite being a Mark III Venturer, it retains the windscreen style of the earlier Venturer bodies.

HMS 227. This 1956 SBG with thirty-five-seat Burlingham Seagull body was new to Alexander (Midland) as fleet no. MW260. In 1968 it passed to Leasks of Shetland then subsequently to Johnson Brothers (fish farmers) of Shetland, where it was photographed on 31 May 1976.

producing a much smoother outline to the front profile with an understated oval radiator grille. Late in 1954 Duple made further revisions to the Vega and Super Vega. A new chromium-plated front grille in the now-familiar butterfly shape appeared, while new front and rear bumpers, bolder exterior mouldings and heavier-gauge exterior panels completed the cosmetic changes, and for the first time the driver had the luxury of flashing traffic indicators with a self-cancelling switch. At the rear the lighting was revised to give a combined stop, indicator, reflector and tail light unit. The double-hinged Perspex ventilator panels in the roof remained as before.

A forty-two-seat version of the familiar Duple bus body was shown at the 1956 Commercial Motor Show; built at the Duple (Midland) factory, it was specifically designed for overseas use with ten side window pans (a form of construction where the window frame and glazing is attached to the body frame separately as a single unit) with full-depth sliding glasses. The windscreens could be fixed or opening, with the open position being lockable by side quadrants. A two-panel folding entrance door was provided, while the emergency door was located alongside the driver's seat. The passengers sat on the usual tubular-steel framed seats with foam-filled cushions and rubberized horse-hair squabs covered with plastic-based leathercloth. Alternative seating arrangements and trimming were available as an option.

The latest version of the Duple Super Vega was unveiled at the 1958 Commercial Motor Show. This showed several major changes of appearance; gone was the attractive butterfly front grille, to be replaced with what can only be described as a large grin. The grille was a bold statement and clearly took its cues from the 1957 Vauxhall Cresta PA – the familial appearance is unlikely to have been coincidental. At the rear the two wrap-around, glazed corner panels were replaced by a three-piece slightly curved screen, the centre panel of which formed the emergency exit. The front windscreen was now a wraparound two piece item mounted in rubber, the regulation requiring coaches to have an opening windscreen having recently changed. Seats were mounted on slides, the exposed parts being in-filled with rubber strips so the seating pitch could be easily adjusted; the version of the Super Vega/SB on show had five single seats across the rear of the coach and two pairs of seats facing rearwards immediately opposite with a pair of tables in between them. Interior panels were trimmed with a plastic ersatz wood finish, as were the tables.

Duple's biggest facelift on the SB body theme to date came in 1962, with the introduction of the Bella Vega forty-one-seat coach as the successor to the Super Vega. The Bella Vega replicated the distinctive styling introduced the previous year with the Bella Vista body for the Bedford VAS chassis. Overall dimensions of the new body were 30ft 4in (9.2m) long by the now-allowable maximum 8ft 2.5in (2.5m) wide. Composite construction was employed, with emphasis on ventilation and heating arrangements. The rear portion of each version of the new bodywork incorporated fixed windows with forced-air ventilation. On the example of the Bella Vega exhibited at the Commercial Motor Show for 1962, the Smith's refrigerated ventilation (air-conditioning) system was incorporated as an indication of possible future options.

Yeates

Yeates produced a striking-looking body in 1953, notable for its large amounts of polished aluminium mouldings. Seating thirty-five to thirty-eight passengers and named the Riviera Super Luxury, it made its first appearance at the 1953 Commercial Motor Show. Extras included a public address system and a Radiomobile radio. The body was updated in 1954 and the emergency exit repositioned at the rear on the off side, in anticipation of a change in the construction and use regulation governing the distance between the emergency and entrance doors.

On the Yeates stand at the Commercial Motor Show of 1956 was its new Europa coach body, with forty-one seats. The Yeates Europa was innovative in appearance, eschewing the curvaceous nature of the Duple Vega, Plaxton Venturer/Consort and Burlingham Seagull bodies in favour of a more businesslike outline. The front end was dominated by a bold, fibreglass moulded 'cheese-cutter' grille that included the headlamps and fog and spot lamps. Coloured Perspex panelling was let into the roof. While opinions on its attractiveness are subjective, it was certainly different from its contemporaries. Yeates utilized composite construction in its bodies, with light alloy and timber framing, aluminium external panels and glass-fibre mouldings for the front and rear ends.

Seeing a gap in the market created by the growing popularity of coach and single-deck bus chassis with under-floor engines, from 1960 Yeates offered a conversion of the SB chassis that placed the driver and the passenger entrance door ahead of the front axle. Known as the FE44 Continental, the end result was a well-balanced product, modern in appearance and in line with current thinking regarding the arrangement of the entrance on single-deck buses and coaches. Front-entrance coaches were available from the heavyweight competition and clearly of interest to operators for bus work, where the possibility of driver-only operation was of economic appeal. The conversion was achieved by moving the front axle rearwards, thereby making space for a front entrance and set of steps forward of the front axle. This was not approved by Vauxhall, and Bedford itself did not offer a vehicle in this configuration until the introduction of the VAM in 1965. Problems arose with some of the Yeates conversions, as the SB chassis was not designed to support the engine without the axle underneath it, though warranty claims on Vauxhall were not accepted as the modification was not officially approved. The Yeates bodies were also offered under the Fiesta, Europa and Pegasus names, all of which were of similar distinctive appearance.

The ubiquitous forty-one-seat Duple, Plaxton, Burlingham, Harrington and Yeates bodies on the SB became a common sight on the roads of Britain and by 1962, the range of bodies available for the SB included the Duple Bella

This is an example of the Yeates FE44 forty-four-seat front-entrance conversion on a 1960 SB1 chassis; later models of this body had a more restrained frontal appearance. P. BATESON

Vega, the Duple (Northern) Firefly, the Plaxton Embassy II, the Harrington Crusader Mk III with either thirty-seven or forty-one seats and the striking MCW Amethyst. These typically cost around £3,000, though for some reason those intended for the SB5 diesel-powered chassis were slightly more expensive than those for the SB3 with the petrol engine.

MCW

MCW was more associated with double-deck bodies, popular with municipal and BET group operators. The Amethyst was, therefore, something of a departure for MCW and unconventional. It employed MCW's lightweight metal construction pioneered on its Orion double-deck bodies and at only 4 tons 9cwt (4,521kg) unladen, it weighed typically 10cwt (508kg) less than most other bodies for the SB. An example was displayed on an SB3 chassis at the Commercial Motor Show for 1962. Despite its lightweight construction, the body displayed no apparent flimsiness, with comfortable seats and a fairly striking appearance. In many ways it was reminiscent of contemporary single-deck bus practice and perhaps a little out of date; ventilation was by top-sliding windows and the interior finish was plain. Maybe because of this, or perhaps because it just appeared a half-hearted effort, the Amethyst did not sell well and few were built.

Plaxton, Duple and Harrington Through the Years

The range of bodies for the SB continued to be developed by their manufacturers throughout the 1950s and early 1960s, with various improvements, typically in seating, heating and ventilation, with some bodies incorporating fixed windows and forced-air ventilation that was not universally popular with passengers. Air conditioning was becoming more popular in motor vehicles and early examples applied to coach bodies on the SB chassis included Smith's refrigerated air ventilation system. Some changes in overall dimensions occurred, though bodies continued to be available in 7ft 6in (2.3m) width form for those operators whose journeys took them down narrow rural lanes, while the general trend was to utilize the full legal width of 8ft 2.5in (2.5m); for 1962, Plaxton's Embassy II body was offered with 8ft 2.5in overall width and a slight increase in length to 30ft 2.5in (9.2m), while the Yeates Fiesta Continental forty-four-seat body was available with overall length of 31ft 2in (9.5m) on the SB5 chassis.

The Plaxton Consort had appeared in 1956. Several evo-

Plaxtons brochure cover for the Bedford SB-based Consort. The registration number of the coach in the picture is shown as FWP 57, the initials of Plaxton's founder, Frederick William Plaxton, and the digits represent the year of introduction – 1957. PLAXTON

lutions turned it into the Consort IV, which then formed the basis for the new Embassy body in 1961. The Embassy also evolved and Embassy III appeared in 1963, along with a competitor in the shape of the Harrington Crusader Mark IV, the latter having dimensions of 30ft 5in (9.3m) long by 8ft 2.5in (2.5m) wide. A 100cu ft (2,832ltr) rear luggage locker was provided. In line with contemporary trends, ventilation was forced air using the Smiths Jet-Vent system, although double top-sliding opening windows were provided. The body was built using the traditional composite framing.

Duple (Northern) introduced the Firefly forty-one-seat coach body in 1963, a design that was quite different in styling from the Bella Vega produced at Hendon. Fluorescent lights made their appearance on the Duple Bella Vega body in 1964, as did larger panoramic windows on the Plaxton Embassy IV introduced the same year. Plaxton had engaged the services of Ogle Design, probably most famous for its work on the Reliant Scimitar GTE sporty shooting brake, to update the Plaxton Panorama, and these styling changes brought the Embassy body into line with the new Panorama. Plaxton would at that time incorporate combinations of features, particularly front grilles from either body on request or for necessity, so to the uneducated eye the only identifying feature was often the badge.

The Embassy IV body was replaced in 1965 with a version of the Panorama for the SB. Visually very similar to the Embassy IV, the Panorama body on the SB had fixed

There continued to be low-volume alternatives to products from the larger coachbuilders throughout the 1950s and 1960s. This 1958 SB1 had a thirty-nine-seat Thurgood Forerunner body. New to Knight of Hemel Hempstead, Hertfordshire, it was owned by Norfolk's of Nayland when seen at Colchester bus station on 29 June 1974. T. WALKER

windows with no sliders and forced-air ventilation. The other visually distinguishing feature was a larger polished moulding below the driver's window. The Panorama was available in several alternative forms for the SB, all basically similar in appearance, known as the Panorama and the Panorama I, II, III and IV. The Panorama II could be identified by the absence of the polished moulding below the driver's window, while the Panorama III introduced a new-look front end, much more upright with a peaked dome, leaving behind the echoes of the Embassy body possessed by the other Panoramas. The last base model Panoramas were built on SB chassis in 1971. The Panorama I and II were built on SB chassis for 1968–9; the III and IV were built on SB chassis in 1972–3. The Panorama range for the SB was discontinued in 1974 in favour of the Supreme. The last Plaxton bodies on the SB chassis were supplied to Tatlock's Coaches, Radcliffe, Lancashire in the summer of 1979. They had Supreme forty-one-seat bodies and carried registrations WBN 7T and WBN 8T.

Duple continued to produce the Bella Vega body until 1970, by which time the design was looking dated. Continuing demand for the SB/Duple combination prompted a new body based on the Viceroy design for the VAM and VAL. This was introduced for 1970 and known as the Vega 31. Overall length of the Vega 31 was 31ft 4in (9.6m) and the body was available in either 7ft 6in (2.29m) or 8ft 2.5in (2.5m) widths. Evidence that demand remained for the narrower bodies lay in Duple's order books for 1970, which included around thirty 7ft 6in (2.29m) bodies on the SB chassis. In addition to the external restyling, other improvements over the Bella Vega included an increase in

Rover Bus Services (J. R. G. Dell) of Hemel Hempstead, Hertfordshire operated this 1955 SB with Duple MkV service bus body on service 316 jointly with London Transport Country Services from Hemel to Amersham. It was photographed in Chesham in October 1972. Bodies to the exact same design were also built by Mulliner on behalf of Duple when the latter was too busy to fulfil all its orders.

seat pitch, resulting in a spacing of 29in (737mm), providing additional legroom for passengers. The Vega 31 was not destined to have a long production life, however; Duple's products were beginning to look a little outdated when compared with those from Plaxton, so in 1972 the Dominant range was launched. The Dominant clearly took its cues from the Plaxton Panorama while being an all-new and very attractive design. Designed from the outset to be easily adapted to fit a wide range of chassis, forty-one-seat examples soon began to appear on the SB chassis.

Welfare Bodies

Welfare and utility type bus bodies were common on the SB chassis right from the early days. Having been somewhat less active in the PSV field in recent years, Strachans re-entered the market in 1964 with its Pacesaver body. Aimed at welfare users, it was available with seating capacities of generally thirty-five to forty-one seats, though more could be accommodated with a little ingenuity. Eleven were sold to West Suffolk County Council in 1972 for use as school buses. The buses seated fifty-one by utilizing seats in a compact three-and-two arrangement with a narrow gangway. Three were fitted with luggage compartments to make them suitable for school days out and field trips. The buses were painted in a tangerine high-visibility livery, undoubtedly inspired by CIE's Bedford school bus fleet, and were supplied by O. G. Barnard & Son, Stowmarket.

A growing awareness of the needs of people with disabilities led the proprietor of Mascot Coaches, Norwich, a Mr L. Votier, to design a coach purpose-built to carry such passengers in the same sort of comfort their more able-bodied compatriots had enjoyed in the past. The coach was built in 1966 by Bonallack Refrigerated Vehicles Ltd of Norwich on a SB3 chassis; known as the 'St. Christopher Coach', it was the first such vehicle of its kind built by Bonallack. Of particular note were the double doors at the rear of the vehicle, where was fitted a full-width US Industries battery/hydraulic tail-lift. Seating could be altered to suit requirements but the usual pattern provided room for

Tudor Williams, who traded as Pioneer Coaches of Laugharne, Carmarthenshire, acquired this 1958 SB1 with Duple (Midland) bus body in 1961 from Thomas of Llangadog.

twelve wheelchairs and twelve seated passengers. Bars were provided at the rear of the vehicle so that wheelchairs could be secured and the forward entrance was provided with five shallow steps 39in (1m) wide with sufficient grab rails for passengers and helpers to make their way into the coach. Fixed seats were supplied free of charge by the Eastern Counties Omnibus Co. Ltd of Norwich. Overall dimensions were 27ft 6in (8.4m) long by 7ft 6in (2.29m) wide. The coach cost £3,500, financed by donations, of which £2,000 came from Norwich City Football Club supporters.

A Bedford from the Western Isles. This SB with forty-two-seat Duple (Midland) bus body dates from June 1961. It was new to Mitchell's of Stornoway but by the time this photograph was taken in June 1974 it was working for Lochs Motor Transport of Cameron Terrace, Leurbost, in whose livery it is seen at Leurbost waiting to depart for Callanish in the Isle of Lewis.

Such was the usefulness and popularity of the coach that it was in demand seven days a week.

The SB also played its part in the foundation in 1967 of CIE's huge school bus fleet, with high-capacity bodies designed and built by CIE itself and mounted on SB5 chassis. Of 31ft 6in (9.6m) overall length and 8ft 2.5in (2.5m) wide, the bodies could squeeze in a remarkable sixty-seven children – sixty-seven remarkably small children, given the space each would have to occupy – or forty-five adults. The skeleton framing for the bodies was supplied by Metal Sections Ltd of Birmingham (METSEC) and finished at CIE's Inchincore works.

Marshall showed a metal-framed body for schools transport and similar at the Commercial Motor Show in 1976. This body featured twin-panel glider doors, unstressed panels in fibreglass, Stelvetite PVC-coated steel ceiling panels, melamine sidewall panels, 3kW Smiths saloon heaters and forced-air ventilation. The metal framing was phosphate-dipped for full corrosion protection.

At the same show and in similar vein, Van Hool McArdle Ltd of Spa Road, Dublin (formed in 1972 to construct buses for CIE) had a new 'multi-purpose' forty-three-seat single-deck body for the SB with an overall length of 31ft 2in (9.5m). Interesting features included a stepped-down windscreen on the passenger side for improved kerb-side visibility and a larger than usual area of glass. A two-panel folding entrance door was fitted. Two Clayton QH17 saloon heaters were fitted inside and the seats were of the same pattern as those fitted to contemporary double-deck bodies from Van Hool McArdle. Twin headlamps and fog and spot lamps completed the specification.

In 1980, Wadham Stringer Coachbuilders of Waterlooville in Hampshire announced a new range of bodies for city and inter-urban buses. Known as the Vanguard, the prototypes were built on a Ford T152 (a shortened Ford R1014), Leyland Cub and Volvo B58 chassis, but the first production models were built on the ubiquitous SB.

SALES AND PRODUCTION

The 17ft 2in (5m) wheelbase SB initially sold for £690 as a bare chassis or around £2,000 with a Duple Vega body fitted and was popular right from the start. In the first year of production over 2,000 were built. By 1952, a complete Duple Vega/SB thirty-seven-seat bus cost £2,380; in comparison, a used 1950 OB/Duple Vista could be purchased for £1,485 and a 1939 OB/Duple Vista was a mere £175. This was at the time when the average price of a house in the UK was about £1,800.

In 1957 a Bedford SB fitted with forty-one-seat Duple Vega coachwork and powered by the Perkins R6 Mk2 diesel engine cost a total of £3,620, with power steering available for an extra £60; the two-speed axle option cost £185.

By August 1960 the cost of a Duple Vega coach on a diesel SB chassis had risen from £3,620 to £3,953; in 1961 the same coach cost £4,100, and in 1963 it cost £4,275, while the price of a complete forty-one-seat coach with Plaxton Embassy body and SB3 chassis was £4,571. Chassis price in 1963 was £1,200; by 1980 this had risen to £8,353.

The Suez crisis was at its height in 1957, yet despite the threat of petrol rationing in 1958 71 per cent of UK market SBs still had petrol engines; conversely, or perhaps perversely, 53 per cent of export SBs were diesel powered. This was despite the clear advantage of fuel economy displayed by the diesel-powered SB, suggesting that operators were loath to forgo the acceleration and smooth running available from the petrol engine. In time, of course, operators would be forced by harsh economics to favour diesel over petrol.

For the chassis alone in 1962, the operator would have paid £1,025 for an SB with a petrol engine; the version with the 330cu in (5.4-litre) Bedford diesel was £1,155 and if you wanted a Leyland O.350 diesel engine in your SB then you needed to pay almost £300 more, at £1,450. By this time, the diesel-versus-petrol paradigm was looking more sensible; only 35 per cent of UK sales were petrol, compared with 43 per cent of those exported. There is some logic to the export figures as petrol in overseas territories was generally cheaper than in the UK.

In the 1950s, a major customer for Mulliner-bodied SB buses was the Admiralty; similar buses were exported to Trinidad for use in the oil and petrochemical industry. By the end of the 1950s the SB had established itself as a firm favourite with operators, with its choice of petrol or diesel engine and 8ft (2.44m) or 7ft 6in (2.29m)-wide coach bodies. The George Ewer group, having in recent times favoured heavier chassis from Leyland and AEC, was by 1960 purchasing quantities of SB8, which they found suited their needs better, despite the potentially shorter life of the Bedfords.

Notable sales in the first half of the 1960s included 200 SB5 chassis for the Inland Transport Authority, Egypt, in 1964. These had Egyptian-built bus bodies. Orders continued unabated at home, too. The forty-one-seat SB/Duple Bella Vega combination was very popular – Progressive Motor Coaches (A. E. Harris), of Cambridge, ordered nine; United Service Transport Co. Ltd, of London SW17, six; and five each went to Stanley Spencer and Happiways Tours, both Manchester companies, later to be merged and eventually to become part of the Shearings empire. Ten more on SB13 chassis went to the George Ewer group and five on SB5 chassis were ordered by Wilts & Dorset Motor Services, one of the few Tilling Group orders for Bedfords. Wessex of Bristol preferred the look of the Duple Firefly body and had five mounted on SB5 chassis.

In 1965, orders for export included ten SBs with Marshall forty-two-seat bus bodies for Barbados Transport, then in 1966 an order was received from Afghanistan, a country much less in the public eye in those days. This was for five SB5 chassis with fifty-one-seat Duple bus bodies of particularly utilitarian finish, though exceptionally robustly built to cope with the local road conditions.

The SB remained as popular at home as ever through the second half of the 1960s; in 1968, Duple produced around fifty Bella Vega bodies on SB chassis and still demand outstripped supply; by the autumn of 1969 a further 100 bodies on SB chassis were already sold to operators or dealers in the UK for 1970 production.

During the 1960s, sales of the SB5 with its diesel engine eventually overtook the SB3 petrol-powered chassis. Despite this, in the early 1970s, operators were still buying good quantities of SBs with petrol engines. Operators in the Channel Islands seemed to prefer them, and Salopia Saloon Coaches Ltd, Whitchurch, Salop, also bought

Murphy's Coaches of Bray, Co. Wicklow, Ireland was the first owner of this 1962 SB with Duple Super Vega coachwork.

New to International Progressive Coaches of Cambridge, this 1965 SB5 carries the Duple Bella Vega body, which was introduced in 1961 with the similarly styled Bella Vista body for the VAS. It is shown here at Sudbury, Suffolk, in the livery of Chambers of Bures.

Harrington's 1960s product on the SB is illustrated by another of Vaggs' fleet. This 1965 SB8 has a Harrington Crusader MkIII body to the specification of its former owner, Barton Transport. It was photographed on 26 May 1974.

Vega 31-bodied examples with petrol engines. However, by 1978 the party was over for petrol and the economics of the diesel ruled supreme; from that time onwards, very few SB3s were sold annually, though even as late as 1984 there was still a small demand.

The Australasian countries formed a large export market for the SB – the New Zealand Railways Department bought over 1,200 SBs, making them owners of the probably the largest SB fleet in the world.

Generally speaking, the range of engines and gearboxes offered by Bedford satisfied its customer's needs, but the final batch of SBs purchased by the New Zealand Railways were to special order and had 210bhp Caterpillar C7 441cu in (7.2-litre) engines and Allison transmissions.

In the UK, the Ministry of Defence bought a large fleet of SB3s and SB5s and deployed them with all three services, though on the available figures the Army seems to have had the largest number. Other examples of operators who bought sizeable fleets of SBs new included Blue Coach, Jersey; the Inner London Education Authority; Salopia, Whitchurch; Shaw, Maxey; Tantivy, St Helier; and West Suffolk Education Authority. The Isle of Wight and the Channel Islands were both Bedford strongholds, with around 80 per cent of the Guernseybus fleet in 1984 consisting of SBs with bodies by Reading of Portsmouth or Wadham Stringer, all of a utilitarian appearance and dating from the 1970s.

The last Plaxton body built on an SB coach was supplied to Tatlocks Coaches of Manchester in 1980. Thereafter Plaxton concentrated on its updated Supreme range on other chassis. Duple was still building the Dominant, and at £27,000 for a forty-one-seat coach it was the cheapest luxury coach available in Britain at the time. The SB remained Bedford's primary export passenger chassis and by May 1980 over 54,000 had been produced, according to Bedford. Of these, only 17,482 were bought to operate in the UK; 37,368 were sold abroad, the chassis being a top

RCT 2. This SB3 with Yeates Europa forty-one-seat body was new to The Delaine of Bourne, Lincolnshire; however, it only spent a short while there before joining the fleet of Mid Wales Motorways of Newtown, Powys, with whom it remained for many years.

This SB5 with Plaxton Embassy III forty-one-seat body was new to Cooke's of Guildford, Surrey (based in Stoughton). It was one of five identical coaches Cooke's purchased in October 1963, registered 471 JHO–475 JHO.

This 1967 SB5 with a Plaxton Embassy IV body was new to MacBrayne but is seen here in the livery of Highland Omnibuses as its fleet no. CD82. The Embassy IV body was introduced in 1965 and shared some features with the new Plaxton Panorama body, in particular the long side windows and the front grille and headlight arrangement, as styled by Ogle Design.

seller in most British Commonwealth countries. In the UK, the SB continued to be popular in the school, welfare, military and staff transport markets, its simplicity combined with adequate performance being cited as the reasons for its continued popularity.

Examples of countries where the SB continued to sell well included Malaysia, Pakistan, and Bangladesh – fixed-fare operating stringencies imposed by the government in Malaysia in particular made the SB highly attractive for

The Strachans Pacesaver bus body was popular in the utility and welfare field, but this thirty-nine-seat example on a SB5 chassis was new to Bebbs of Llantwit Fadre. It is shown here in service with Ashley's of Telford, Shropshire. Ashley operated a number of bus services in the Telford, Dawley and Wellington areas of Shropshire.

operators. The SB could be found providing bus services in such diverse locations as India, Jersey, Malta and Nigeria. In the UK, the SB's popularity had waned in the luxury coach market largely due to the fact that larger coaches provided more passenger comfort, were more economical as a whole to run and easier to drive. However, after thirty years in production no one could argue that Bedford had not had its money's worth out of the SB and it was still selling well – indeed, the SB outsold all other Bedford passenger chassis by a significant margin in 1983, though largely as a result of export orders.

Published Bedford production figures for the SB suggest that by June 1965 over 28,000 SBs had been built. Post-1965, available records account for only 2,418 chassis, which is probably a meaningless figure. By 1985, the SB had been in continuous production for thirty-five years, a record probably never surpassed for a PSV chassis. Even with the storm clouds gathering at Bedford, there was still optimism in the UK industry for the old SB; with government deregulation of bus services in sight, there were those who thought the model might still have a future with operators of rural bus services, and there was even an SB on show at the 1985 Commercial Vehicle Show. Appropriately, perhaps, the body fitted was an all-aluminium school bus body by Robert Wright of Ballymena. Described as a 'high-capacity bus', it had been built for the London Borough of Havering; a fitting reminder of a role that the Bedford SB had played for so many years.

Dodd's of Troon, South Ayrshire, bought this SB5 with forty-one-seat Duple Viceroy body in May 1971. Dodds were involved in a service-sharing arrangement with other operators on the Ayr–Ardrossan route (known as the AA Service), similar to that of the Shropshire Omnibus Association.

ON THE ROAD

The new SB in its original form with Duple Vega luxury coach body was road tested by L. J. Cotton MIRTE for *Commercial Motor* in June 1951. Cotton enjoyed his time with the coach, both as a passenger and an observer, in the former role finding it very comfortable to travel in. The conditions on the day were ideal for testing, it being a moderately warm, calm and dry day and the test was conducted in the company of a Vauxhall works demonstration driver. The vehicle had done just about 3,000 miles (5,000km) from new so could be considered to be 'run in'. The suspension was praised, little roll being evident, and the long semi-elliptic springs provided a good ride with the frame being well-insulated from wheel movements and vibration. What with a radio, and a head roll to the seat, Cotton felt this was 'vehicle testing deluxe'!

New to Hornsby of Ashby, South Humberside, this June 1971 SB5 with Duple Viceroy forty-one-seat body passed to Longstaffs of Mirfield, West Yorkshire. The bus is seen here when owned by G. D. Byrne of Bradford, in September 1977.

Images of in-service military buses are quite rare. This SB5 was allocated to the army and is seen here conveying former British soldiers (Old Comrades) on an outing. It has a thirty-seven-seat body built by Marshall of Cambridge.

When it came to his turn to drive, Cotton found the performance in respect of acceleration and speed to be of a very high standard – 'almost of saloon car standard' – with 30mph (48km/h) coming up in 21.2 seconds and 40mph (64km/h) being achieved from rest in 38 seconds. For comparison, similar measurements for a state-of-the-art 1952 Austin A30 small family saloon were 11.1 seconds and 19 seconds. Fuel economy was good, whether performing as a touring coach or service bus with regular stops every mile or so, with touring consumption of 10.85mpg (26.08ltr/100km) at an average speed of 33.5mph (54km/h) and bus-duty consumption of 9.33mpg (30.33ltr/100km) at an average speed of 28mph (45km/h). Not bad for a petrol-engine coach of this period – by comparison, contemporary diesel-powered single-decks could manage 15–18mpg (16–19ltr/100km). The 33.5mph (54km/h) touring average suggests that coach had little trouble reaching, maintaining and exceeding the legal limit of 40mph (64 km/h) then in force for vehicles of this class. A maximum speed of 55mph (89km/h) was achieved on the test and under favourable conditions it appeared that 60mph (97km/h) would have been attainable. For bus duties requiring frequent stops, such as an urban service, a test of stopping and restarting every 400yd (366m) was undertaken, which increased the consumption to 6mpg (47ltr/100km) – quite creditable where a heavy diesel single-deck bus would have achieved around 8mpg (35ltr/100km) for the same duty. Taking into account the full purchase price of £2,145 for the Bedford Duple thirty-three-seat bus, this would have been an attractive proposition to an independent operator of provincial and town services who might have otherwise turned to an older, second-hand heavyweight diesel bus near the end of its life.

Cotton found his SB/Vega easy to drive, the gearchange being enhanced by the synchromesh fitted to the upper three ratios of the gearbox. The helical-cut constant-mesh intermediate gears were quiet in operation and in top gear the gearbox was effectively silent. The gearbox enabled swift

Coachbuilder Wadham Stringer was the successor to the business of Reading of Portsmouth via its acquisition of Sparshatts. Guernsey Bus (formerly Guernsey Motors/Guernsey Railways) had a tradition of purchasing bodies built by Reading, so it is not surprising to find this striking-looking thirty-nine-seat Wadham Stringer body on a 1978 SB5 chassis, one of the very last Bedfords bought by Guernsey Bus. Fleet no. 125 had more luxurious seating than its outward appearance might suggest.

Here is the Willowbrook version of the Duple bus body seen previously on **UAX 639**, this time mounted on the 1976 **SB5** chassis belonging to Chaloner's of Wrexham. This design of body had been in continuous production for over twenty years by the time **PCA 331P** was built.

changes to be made between gears, and top gear could be engaged at 28mph (45km/h), a factor in the coach's overall economy. Conversely, a speed in excess of 30mph (48km/h) was obtained in third gear at maximum engine revolutions.

Such was the torque available from the engine that top gear could be engaged at 10mph (16km/h) and the coach was still able to accelerate smoothly to reach 30mph (48km/h) in 23.9 seconds from the rolling start. The petrol engine showed no signs of pinking (pre-ignition knock) or hesitation at low rpm, nor any protests from the transmission, the

SB taking it all in its stride and going on to reach 40mph (64km/h, the legal limit) in 41.3 seconds. The acceleration achieved was felt to be well up with the best of the competition, the 21 seconds to 30mph (48km/h) figure being considered very good for a coach with a full load. Cotton's opinion was that by greater use of the indirect gears a further second might have been shaved off the 0–30mph time.

Hills were negotiated without drama, a half-mile climb at 1-in-10 with a section at 1-in-6 providing little challenge, and second-gear was only required on the steepest

A December 1971 **SB5** with austere-looking Strachans forty-five-seat body in service with the Isle of Wight Education Department on 18 March 1976. The radiator grille reveals evidence of a problem with over-cooling of the 330cu in (5.4-litre) diesel engine.

section. Even while hill climbing, there was no tendency for the engine to overheat, the peak water temperature never exceeding 163°F (72°C), showing that the SB was well cooled. A hill start on the 1-in-6 section was easily achieved.

The brakes were described as 'adequate', which is perhaps not quite the impression the tester sought to convey, judging by the test results; the SB had a brake lining area of 70sq in per ton of laden weight, which was significantly better than that of the equivalent S-type goods chassis. Using the brakes to control the descent of the coach on a hill revealed no noticeable loss of efficiency when the bottom was reached. A brake test on a level, dry surface showed the coach was able to stop in 22ft (6.7m) from 20mph (32km/h) and in 45ft (13.7m) from 30mph (48km/h), evidence of a sharp response to movement of the driver's pedal. A Tapley meter was able to record readings of 66–68 per cent, proving there was little or no wind-up of the springs or other unpleasant behaviour likely to compromise safety or impair passenger comfort. The handbrake was able to lock the rear wheels when applied from 20mph (32km/h) with sufficient power to stop the coach in 38ft (11.6m). The Tapley meter readings for the handbrake tests averaged 38 per cent.

Brake fade was tested by continuously accelerating to 30mph (48km/h) and braking hard to a stop, taking note of the maximum Tapley readings each time. The cycle of accelerating from rest, braking, noting readings and starting off again took about 40 seconds in more than five stops per mile for 7 miles (11km). Initial Tapley readings showing 63–65 per cent efficiency after the first twenty stops in a period of 13 minutes showed no increase of pedal travel or reduction in efficiency. After twenty-seven emergency applications, the efficiency dropped by 5 per cent on the meter, unnoticeable by the driver. Soon afterwards the pedal travel had increased slightly, but after thirty-six stops in only 35 minutes, the efficiency reading had fallen to only 50 per cent. The handbrake was still effective when tested with hot drums at the end of the trials. For a vehicle of this class in 1951, this was an impressive set of results.

The position of the handbrake and the low ground clearance were the only points that came in for criticism, the latter being considered inadequate for private hire situations, where the coach was likely to be driven off road.

A further extended road test took place in March 1959. This time the subject was the longer 18ft (5.5m) wheelbase, level frame SB as introduced in 1957 and fitted with the Bedford 300cu in (4.9-litre) diesel – even at this late date still referred to by Bedford as an 'oil' engine – and a 30ft (9m) long by 8ft (2.44m) wide, forty-one-seat body. The chassis of this particular coach was also fitted with the two-

IN PRESERVATION

Bedford SB3/Duple Super Vega 107 GYC

Year new: 1960
Engine: 300cu in (4.9-litre) petrol
Gearbox: Bedford four-speed
Body: Duple Super Vega with thirty-three seats, 7ft 6in (2.29m) wide
Current owner: Roger Chambers, Bristol

History

107 GYC was new in 1960 to Bowerman's Tours of Taunton, at that time a subsidiary of Greenslades Tours of Exeter, Bowerman's having been acquired by Greenslades in 1958. The bus was operated under the Bowerman's name and was one of a batch of three (107–109 GYC) of 7ft 6in (2.29m) width, bought for travelling along narrow West Country roads. It passed to Berry's of Taunton in 1964 and then to Martin Perry of Bromyard. It was subsequently acquired by an operator in Ashbourne, Derbyshire who intended to operate 'classic' coach tours in the Dales. Roger Chambers bought it from them in 2005.

Owner's Experience

Roger Chambers' connection with Bedford, like so many enthusiasts of his generation, goes back to his earliest days. Growing up in Devon until 1954 brought him into contact with the coaches of Greenslades Tours of Exeter. The family did not own a car and holidays were day tours by Greenslades coach, often on Bedford OBs. Having moved to Bristol, schooldays meant regular trips on the Bedford SBs of Wessex coaches, as his school's playing fields were situated a short distance from the city of Bristol at Failand in Somerset, and further trips as a member of the school's hockey team. Attending University College Hospital in London after school usually meant return trips home on a Bristol Greyhound RELH, which provided an interesting contrast and served to widen his interest in coaches. The things that give us pleasure as children remain firmly embedded in the psyche, and in time thoughts turned to perhaps owning a former Greenslades coach. As is the way of these things, finding one of the right generation proved difficult; Roger had joined the West of England Historic Omnibus and Transport Trust (WHOTT)

Roger Chambers' 1961 SB3/Duple Super Vega coach in November 2015. It is currently nearing the end of a thorough restoration.

in 2000, and subsequently met the redoubtable William Staniforth, possibly the greatest facilitator and friend of bus and coach preservation since Prince Marshall invented the concept. Being aware of Roger's interest and knowing of Bowerman's connection with Greenslades, William thought that 107 GYC would be of interest. The coach was bought and transported down from Ashbourne by Simon Munden, son of the famous one-armed Len Munden, the well-known Bristol coach operator and driver.

Having no personal workshop facilities, Roger was forced to store the coach away from home, initially at Wick St Lawrence near Weston-super-Mare, then later in Devon at WHOTT's facility, so working on the coach was a challenge of logistics. In order to attempt to hasten restoration progress, the coach was moved to premises just outside Bristol. Restoration is nearly complete and has been lengthy, as is often the case, with Roger doing what he could himself and calling in professional help when required. For example, the wind-down windows needed special complex steel sections to be made to frame the glass, the originals having rusted away. Upholstery was refurbished by South West Upholsterers in Bristol, using moquette that was fairly close to the original pattern. Surprisingly, very few areas of rotten woodwork were encountered.

Some mechanical work has been done: the gearbox and brake cylinders have been overhauled and the clutch renewed, also the fuel pump, carburettor and fuel tank. Parts from Bygone Bedford Bits have been crucial in completing these jobs.

So what is the coach like to drive? Roger comments, 'It is relatively light to drive without a load and so there is no need for power steering. The petrol engine is responsive and as she was only really used for local trips, a petrol engine was much quieter.'

Roger says the biggest challenge was having to store the vehicle away from home. 'Ideally you want to be no more than ten or fifteen minutes away, and you need somewhere with good lighting conditions and obviously a power supply.'

To conclude our survey of the SB, here are three views of export models, starting with Nelson Suburban Bus Lines fleet no. 28, which is a 1967 SB3 with NZMB thirty-seven-seat dual-entrance body. Note the row of hooks under the windscreen. New Zealand buses traditionally had these for hanging bicycles, pushchairs, shopping baskets and other impedimenta on the front of the bus. Doubtless the practice was killed off by modern health and safety legislation.

speed rear axle. The results make for an interesting comparison with those from the test of the 1951 petrol-powered coach; maximum speed had risen to in excess of 65mph (105km/h), no doubt as a result of the high ratio of the rear axle, but the real news was the fuel consumption. Where the petrol engine had given economy just slightly worse than a contemporary heavy diesel bus, the new diesel Bedford was returning 17.8mpg (15.9ltr/100km) over touring duty, with an average speed of 31.8mph (51.2km/h), compared to 10.3mpg (27.5ltr/100km) at 33.5mph (54km/h) in 1951. Bus duty cycle was not recorded, but the acceleration figures had suffered in the name of economy; with the rear axle low-ratio engaged, 0–30mph was achieved in 26.3 seconds (compared to 21.2 seconds in 1951), 0–40mph in 45 seconds (compared to 38 seconds) and 10–30mph in 26.6 seconds (23.9 seconds). Summing up the latest test, the coach was considered to be 'a good speculation' for operators, combining reasonable performance with good fuel economy.

From the passenger's point of view, the rear suspension was criticized for being harsh and inducing travel sickness in those prone to that malady and gearbox noise was intrusive in the intermediate ratios. In contrast, the engine was commendably quiet. Braking figures revealed slightly poorer performance under some conditions compared with the 1951 test, probably due to the slight increase in weight of the later coach compared with the earlier.

A common complaint from drivers regarded the set-back gear lever position on the early chassis, causing some coach drivers to suffer from what became known as 'SB driver's elbow', but over time this was modified to provide easier operation. The unsophisticated remote control linkage, however, remained until the end.

George Atkin describes the SBG/SB3 as 'an unpretentious workhorse', pleasant enough to drive but somewhat wearing for the driver, with that 330cu in (4.9-litre) 'lump' throbbing away noisily just behind one's left ear — a useful summing up of the Bedford SB.

This **SB5** is operating for **TCM** on the shuttle service between **Macau City** and **Taipa** across the bridge that links the two islands. It was one of a large number of Bedford 'high capacity' buses purchased between 1974 and 1980, which also included some **VAS** chassis with similar bodies.

One of a large quantity of SBs with New Zealand Motor Bodies coachwork, this 1978 SB3 (NFM) of New Zealand Railways Road Services with thirty-eight-seat dual-entrance body is pictured in November 1978 shortly after delivery. An older SB can be seeen behind.

CHAPTER FIVE

THE ENGINES

The range of engines fitted into Bedford bus and coach chassis divides into three categories: the Bedford petrol engines, other manufacturer's diesel engines and Bedford's own diesel engines. All the engines fitted to Bedford chassis from new were in-line 6-cylinder engines, from the start of production in 1931 to the end in 1986, though enterprising individuals have succeeded in fitting a variety of other engines, including Cummins V8s, into Bedford buses and coaches after the fact. Prior to the Second World War, all PSV chassis left Dunstable with a 6-cylinder petrol engine and the same applied in the years immediately after the war and for the first few years of the 1950s.

All Bedford petrol and diesel engines, and those of proprietary manufacture used in Bedford chassis, had cast-iron cylinder heads and blocks, and were of overhead-valve layout. All were water-cooled, using a belt-driven vane-type water pump and conventional front-mounted radiator.

Diesel (or 'oil') engines were developed by the automotive industry during the 1930s, the leaders in the field in the UK being L. Gardner and Sons Ltd of Patricroft, Manchester, Leyland Motors Ltd and AEC Ltd of Southall, all of whom had successfully introduced production diesel engines by the end of the 1930s. The slowness of response to technological change that dogged Bedford throughout its life, coupled with the war, prevented Bedford from engaging with the development of diesel engines and it was some time before Bedford got around to building its own. Thus it first turned to outside suppliers, notably Perkins and Leyland, in the early 1950s for compact diesel engines that were suitable for powering a range of Bedford chassis. This move was stimulated to some extent by the activities of after-market dealers and traders, who developed a number of successful conversions in the early 1950s as described elsewhere in this book. Bedford finally produced its own diesel engine in 1957. This chapter attempts to describe those engines most commonly fitted to Bedford chassis from 1931 to 1986.

Figures for power and torque quoted in this chapter are gross, unless otherwise stated.

THE BEDFORD PETROL ENGINES

The Chevrolet Stovebolt Six – the prototype for all Bedford petrol engines – seen here in a 1932 Chevrolet pick-up.

Bedford 194cu in

Applications	Bedford WHB, WLB, WTL, WTB
Cylinders	6 in-line
Bore and stroke	3.3in × 3.8in (84.1mm × 95.3mm)
Capacity	194cu in (3.2 litres)
Firing order	1, 5, 3, 6, 2, 4
Compression ratio	5.6:1
Carburettor	Zenith U-type
Max. power	57bhp at 2,700rpm
	From 1934: 63–64bhp at 2,800rpm
	From 1938: 72bhp

The 194cu in 6-cylinder engine was based on the Chevrolet ohv, four-stroke Stovebolt Six used in many General Motors goods and passenger vehicles. The design was modified at Vauxhall by Harold Drew under chief engineer C. E. King to incorporate pressure lubrication, a four-main bearing crankshaft (compared with the original Stovebolt Six's three-bearing crankshaft) and to use locally sourced components, such as Lucas starters and CAV dynamos. This engine had also appeared in the 1929 Chevrolet LQ in this modified form. The crankcase and cylinder block were cast as a single integral unit and the cylinder head was cast separately. The original Stovebolt Six design was later updated again by Alex Taub, an Englishman who had gone to work for Chevrolet in the USA and had been involved in the design work for the early versions of the engine. Taub worked on the design further during the early 1930s, which led to the introduction of a four main-bearing version of the engine – presumably either identical or very similar to the Bedford version. Taub was an expert in the combustion properties of engines and as a result the later Bedford engines were capable of very good fuel consumption compared with those from their rivals.

Cylinders were six in-line with cast-iron solid-skirt pistons fitted to the connecting rods with bronze-bushed gudgeon pins. Four main bearings of babbit-lined gunmetal bearing shells supported the crankshaft. Big-end bearings were also of babbit, in this case bonded directly to the rod and cap, which therefore needed to be machined together when the bearing needed replacement. The engine had a belt-driven water pump and cooling fan. Ignition was by Lucas 12v coil and conventional distributor. Fuel was delivered by an AC pump to a Zenith U-type carburettor. Lubrication was by pressure from a sump-mounted oil pump to the bearings, timing chain, pistons and valve gear, the pump being driven by the distributor shaft, which itself was driven by a helical gear from the camshaft mounted half-way up the cylinder block.

Further improvement saw the 1934 version adopt a down-draught Zenith carburettor mounted above the manifold to replace the original up-draught type fitted below the manifold. This contributed to an increase in power output to 64bhp at 2,800rpm; further improvement took place in 1938, when the bore and stroke were increased to give a capacity of 214cu in (3.5 litres), which enabled the power output to be increased to 72bhp.

The Stovebolt Six had a long life, being manufactured from 1929 until 1962 in various forms and was used to power many thousands of GM small trucks and buses throughout the world.

Bedford 214cu in

Applications	Bedford OB, OWB, VAS (and MS/ML)
Cylinders	6
Bore and stroke	3.4in × 4in (85.72mm × 102mm)
Capacity	214cu in (3.5 litres)
Firing order	1, 5, 3, 6, 2, 4
Compression ratio	6.22:1
Carburettor	Zenith downdraught; Solex (OWB)
Max. power	OB, OWB: 72bhp at 3,000rpm VAS: 100bhp at 3,600rpm
Max. torque	OB, OWB: 161lb ft at 1,200rpm VAS: 184lb ft at 1,200rpm

This enlarged version of the 6-cylinder petrol engine was developed for the OB and OWB, then further up-rated for the 1961 VAS. It is sometimes referred to by its RAC rating of 28hp, which is also used to describe the late 194cu in engine, so confusion can occur. The 214cu in engine had three-point rubber mounts and a fully balanced four-bearing crankshaft with steel-backed white-metal shell bearings. The pistons remained in cast iron with cast piston rings, as in previous versions of the engine. Lubrication was a pressurized force-feed system and the connecting rods were drilled to enable lubricating oil to be sprayed into the bores. Three holes at an angle from the vertical centreline of the connecting rods were drilled in the top of the big-end bearings to ensure that the cylinder bores and pistons were lubricated immediately on start-up from cold, thus ensuring the longevity of the engine.

The 214cu in engine installed in a Bedford ML.
V. NYYSSONSEN

An oil filter was fitted with a replaceable cartridge-type AC filter. As before, the oil pump was a simple twin-gear type driven by an inclined shaft engaged with the distributor centre shaft. Oil was drawn into the pump via a tube submerged in the sump, the end of which had a cylindrical wire gauze strainer fitted to filter the oil. A twin-gear oil pump works by creating vacuum at the inlet port as the gears come out of mesh. Oil is drawn into this space and then trapped by the gear teeth as they rotate and forced around the inside surface of the pump casing surrounding the gears. Oil is carried to the outlet port by the gear teeth, where it is forced out under pressure. The principle is still in common use in engine oil pumps today. The body of the oil pump also incorporated a spring-loaded oil-pressure relief valve, and a pressure switch operated a warning light in the cab if the oil pressure fell below a safe level.

The four main bearings were fed with oil directly from the pump, oil then passed to the connecting-rod big-end bearings through drillings in the crankshaft.

The camshaft was supported in four white-metal bearings, supplied with pressurized oil from the crankshaft bearings though drillings in the crankcase and cylinder block.

A Zenith down-draught carburettor with accelerator pump for instant mixture enrichment was fitted, though versions of this engine fitted in the OWB had a Solex carburettor. Fuel delivery to the carburettor was by an AC mechanical pump of the lever-operated, positive displacement diaphragm type so familiar to owners of British cars until the widespread adoption of electric and electronic fuel pumps.

Bedford 300cu in

Applications	SB, SBG, SB1, VAM5
Bore and stroke	3.9in × 4.3in (98mm × 108mm)
Capacity	300cu in (4.9 litres)
Firing order	1, 5, 3, 6, 2, 4
Compression ratio	7.0:1
Carburettor	Zenith 481R downdraught
Max. power	SB: 110bhp at 3,200rpm
	VAM5: 133bhp at 3,400rpm
Max. torque	SB: 234lb ft at 1,200rpm
	VAM5: 267lb ft at 1,200rpm

Introduced in 1950 for the S-range of truck and bus chassis, this vertical in-line ohv cast-iron engine had removable dry cylinder liners for easy replacement and a seven main-bearing crankshaft with induction-hardened bearing journals. Main and big-end bearings were fitted with

The 300cu in petrol engine installed in the **WHOTT WTB/Heaver EFJ 382**. This engine was fitted many years ago to replace the original 194cu in engine when it was no longer serviceable, and no doubt provided a noticeable improvement in power-to-weight ratio.

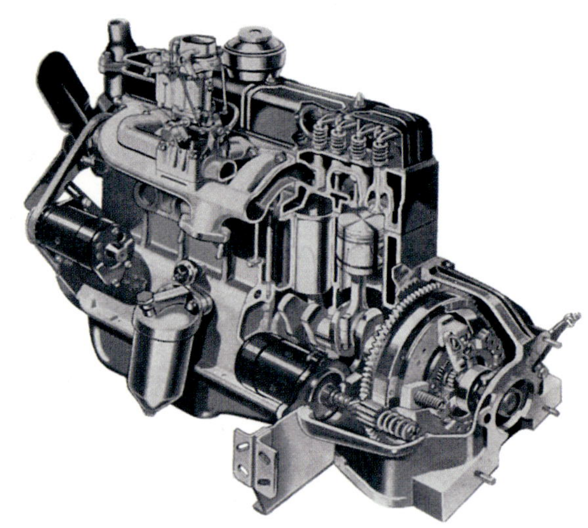

Cutaway drawing of the 300cu in petrol engine. GM

replaceable copper-lead bearing shells. The pistons were flat topped and made of aluminium alloy. Fuel was supplied by a camshaft-driven AC pump to a Zenith type 48IR carburettor with oil bath air filter. Ignition was by an AC Delco oil-filled ignition coil and distributor driven from the camshaft by a helical gear.

When the 300cu in diesel was introduced in 1957, many of the up-rated components from that engine were incorporated in the petrol engine, improving its strength and durability.

The 300cu in engine was capable of long service with careful attention to oil and filter changes and general servicing; operators reported that 150,000 miles (240,000km) was possible between overhauls and only minimal crankshaft wear was detectable at that mileage.

OTHER MANUFACTURERS' DIESEL ENGINES

Perkins R6 and R6 Mk2

Applications	SBO, some OB conversions
Cylinders	6
Bore and stroke	4in × 4.5in (102mm × 114mm)
Capacity	340cu in (5.6 litres)
Max. power	104bhp at 2,500rpm
Max. torque	240lb ft at 1,500rpm

The Perkins R6 was the first diesel to be offered by Bedford for the SB. It was a 6-cylinder, ohv engine with indirect injection. Early versions of this engine proved unreliable, though the faults were quickly rectified by Perkins and a slightly de-rated Mk2 version was soon introduced.

The Perkins P6 engine, though not installed by Bedford, was quite commonly found in proprietary conversions of OBs to diesel in the early 1950s. PERKINS

This partially sectioned example of the Perkins R6 can be seen at Dover Transport Museum.

Leyland O.350

Applications	SBO, SB8
Bore and stroke	3.9in × 4.8in (100mm × 121mm)
Capacity	350cu in (5.7 litres)
Max. power	SBO: 90bhp at 2,200rpm
	SB8: 105bhp at 2,400rpm
Max. torque	SBO: 240lb ft at 1,300rpm
	SB8: 255lb ft at 1,400rpm

The O.350 diesel had its origins in the original O.300 unit developed for the Leyland Comet. For the O.350, bore and stroke were increased from 96.5mm × 114.3mm to 100m × 121mm with a power increase of 15bhp. The O.350 was externally similar to the O.300 though slightly longer to accommodate the increased cubic capacity. The engine was a direct injection, ohv pushrod unit with a combined cylinder block and crankcase in a single monobloc iron casting. Pistons had toroidal crowns and were fitted in renewable liners that were a sliding fit in the cylinder block. The cylinder block and crankcase were flanged and ribbed to provide additional rigidity. A nitride-hardened crankshaft was carried in seven main bearings lined with thin-shell indium-coated copper-lead bearings. The centre bearing carried babbit metal-faced thrust washers, tongues being located in grooves in the bearing caps to prevent rotation of the washers. Centrifugal loading on the centre bearing was relieved by counterbalancing the crankshaft and equipping it with a rubber-bonded torsional vibration damper. Fuel delivery was by a CAV fuel-injection pump driven in tandem with a Clayton-Dewandre exhauster at half-engine speed and controlled by a vacuum governor.

For the O.350 version, the little-end gudgeon pin location was offset from the centreline of the piston by 1.5mm in an attempt to reduce mechanical noise. Cylinder head improvements included nitrided inlet and 'silichrome' exhaust valves, while the inlet valves seats were cut directly into the parent metal of the cylinder head, exhaust-valve seats being replaceable and made of 'Valmet'. Pistons were now Wellworthy low-expansion types.

The O.350 engine as used in the SB conversions and early SBO model was up-rated to 100bhp by increasing the size of the inlet ports and other minor cylinder head modifications in 1955.

The Leyland O.370 engine was used in the SB13 chassis from 1964. LEYLAND

The Leyland O.350 engine, designed for Leyland's own Comet range of goods and PSV chassis and used in the Bedford SBO and SB8 chassis. LEYLAND

Leyland O.370

Applications	SB13
Bore and stroke	4.1in × 4.8in (103mm × 121mm)
Capacity	370cu in (6 litres)
Max. power	106/110bhp at 2,200rpm
Max. torque	240lb ft at 1,200rpm

The Leyland O.370 engine was a development of the Leyland O.350 engine. Increase in cubic capacity was achieved by increasing the bore from 100mm to 103mm, although a still larger bore version – the O.375 – had appeared in the Leyland Super Comet truck in 1958. The O.370 first appeared in 1961, though was not sold in a new Bedford chassis until 1964.

Leyland O.400

Applications	VAL14, VAM14
Bore and stroke	4.3in × 4.8in (108mm × 121mm)
Capacity	400cu in (6.54 litres)
Max. power	125bhp at 2,400rpm
Max. torque	300lb ft at 1,600rpm

The O.400 engine was a further development of the O.350/O.370 6-cylinder direct-injection diesel, retaining the stroke of the O.350 at 121mm but with a new bore size of 108mm. The version used in the VAL was the 400/73 Mk2 with a governed speed of 2,600rpm. For use in the VAL the cylinder head was modified to allow the exhaust manifold to be mounted on the left-hand side of the head, the same side as the inlet manifold, which differed from the standard arrangement where the exhaust manifold was mounted opposite the inlet. When fitted in the VAM14, the standard Leyland cross-flow head was used.

BEDFORD DIESEL ENGINES

Bedford 300cu in

Applications	SB1
Bore and stroke	3.9 in × 4.3in (98.4mm × 108mm)
Capacity	300.7cu in (4.9 litres)
Max. power	97bhp at 2,800rpm
Max. torque	217lb ft at 1,400rpm

The 300cu in was Bedford's first diesel engine, introduced in 1957. GM

Bedford 330cu in

Applications	SB5, VAM5, VAS (PJK), SB (NJM)
Cylinders	6
Bore and stroke	4.1in × 4.3in (103mm × 108mm)
Capacity	330cu in (5.4 litres)
Max. power	99bhp at 2,600rpm
	Red series normally aspirated: 98bhp at 2,600rpm
	Red series turbocharged: 107bhp at 2,600rpm
	Red series Phase II turbocharged: 135bhp at 2,600rpm
Max. torque	234lb ft at 1,800rpm
	Red series normally aspirated: 227lb ft at 1,000rpm (net)
	Red series turbocharged: 253lb ft at 1,200rpm (net)
	Red series Phase II turbocharged: 299lb ft at 1,600rpm (net)

The 330cu in Red series turbodiesel. GM

The 300cu in diesel was Bedford's first venture in this field and was introduced in 1957. It was of 6-cylinder, direct-injection ohv design with pushrods and rockers, and featured toroidal bowl combustion chambers in the piston crowns, offset from the centreline of the gudgeon pin. Timing of valve events was by a gear-driven camshaft, which also drove the oil pump by skew gear. The CAV DPA distributor-type fuel injection pump was driven off the same gear train. End-to-end water flow through the cylinder head helped to maintain constant temperature at the gasket face, reducing the likelihood of head gasket failure, though stress and all coolant flow ports were outside the gasket compression joint area, thus eliminating any possibility of exhaust gas leakage into the cooling system. Water flow ports between the cylinder head and cylinder block were sealed with long-life synthetic rubber sealing rings.

The diesel engine was developed from the 300cu in petrol engine, with which it shared major dimensions, though most components were up-rated from the petrol design in order to meet the stresses of a high-compression diesel engine – this included new rocker gear, crankshaft, cylinder block and oil pump with a full-flow filter. By contemporary diesel standards, the engine was quite high-revving and tended to be rough-running and noisy, though long-lived and reliable.

The 330cu in engine appeared in November 1961 and was a basic enlargement of the 300cu in engine, which it replaced as the standard 6-cylinder diesel from Bedford. The 10 per cent increase in capacity within the basic form factor of the 300cu in engine was achieved by fitting Laystall Cromard thin-wall cylinder liners, which enabled the bore to be increased three-sixteenths of an inch (4.75mm) to 4.1in (103mm). The cylinder head to block joint was strengthened by using shorter and larger-diameter head studs.

The 330cu in engine continued in production right until the end of Bedford at Dunstable and grew up into the 'Red series' – so called because the units were painted red – in 1980, available in both turbocharged and normally aspirated forms. By this time Bedford was quoting power and torque as net – that is as installed with ancillaries, rather than gross figures as obtained on a dynamometer, so the increase in power for the turbocharged engines appears lower than one might expect. To allow for turbo-charging, the engine had stronger main-bearing caps, better cooling and a larger sump with an improved oil pump. All these improvements were also incorporated into the normally aspirated Red series engine, making that unit even stronger and more reliable. The turbocharger was a Holset 1B unit.

The normally aspirated option for the Red series was dropped from autumn 1982, with the introduction of the 'Phase II' Red series. A new 135bhp Red series engine was introduced but did not replace the 107bhp variant, which offered a lower-power option. The 135bhp engine featured increased turbo boost pressure, larger main-bearing cap bolts, new isoformic controlled-expansion pistons, a higher-flow oil pump and twin thermostats for improved cooling system efficiency.

The 70 Series

Applications	VAL70, VAM70, YRQ, YRT
Bore and stroke	4.6in × 4.8in (116mm × 121mm)
Capacity	466cu in (7.6 litres)
Max. power	VAL70: 143bhp at 2,800 rpm
	VAM70, YRQ, YRT: 150bhp at 2,800rpm
Max. torque	VAL70: 328lb ft at 1,600rpm (VAL70)
	VAM70, YRQ, YRT: 326lb ft at 1,000rpm

While retaining some design features of the 330cu in diesel that preceded it, the 466cu in diesel was a completely new engine. Labelled the '70 series' by Bedford, it was introduced in 1966 for the TK truck range and adopted for the VAL and VAM in 1967. Cylinders were now bored directly in the cylinder block, which was a new and stronger casting, dispensing with the liners used on the previous series of engines. The head and pistons were of similar design to its predecessors, with toroidal bowl combustion chambers in the pistons and a flat-faced cylinder head with overhead valves and pushrod-driven rocker gear. Also retained was the seven-bearing counterbalanced crankshaft and gear-driven camshaft. The 466cu in engine was the first of a new generation of Bedford diesels, which, with enlargement and other enhancements, would last until the end of production of Bedford vehicles.

The 466cu in 70 series diesel. GM

The 500 Series

Applications	YRQ2/3, YLQ, YRT2, YMT, YNT, VAM75 (non-EEC countries)
Bore and stroke	4.6in × 5.1in (116mm × 130mm)
Capacity	500cu in (8.2 litres)
Max. power	YRT, YRQ: 151bhp at 2,500rpm
	YLQ: 138bhp at 2,500rpm
	YMT: 157bhp at 2,800rpm
	Blue series, normally aspirated: 159bhp at 2,800rpm
	Blue series, turbocharged: 175/205bhp at 2,500rpm
Max. torque	YRT, YRQ: 377lb ft at 1,200rpm
	Blue series normally aspirated: 379lb ft at 1,200rpm (net)
	Blue series turbocharged: 410/504lb ft at 1,600rpm (net)

The 500 series was a logical development of the 70 series and was introduced in 1975. Bedford claimed in its literature that it was an entirely new engine, though many features of the 70 series were maintained. The increase in capacity was achieved by increasing the stroke of the engine from 4.75in (121mm) to 5.1in (130mm), requiring a new crankshaft amongst other minor changes to accommodate the new stroke dimension. Some attention to noise reduction had been paid in the new engine, with sound-deadening materials applied to the rocker cover, side panels and sump. The same type of pistons as used in the 466cu in engine were retained, with new piston rings, all chrome plated and a wedge-type top ring located in a cast-iron insert in the piston. With a view to meeting future smoke and emission standards, the newly introduced CAV DP15 fuel injection pump was fitted.

In its early form, the 500 series engine was available in a range of power outputs from 138bhp to 157bhp to suit different applications. This engine was ultimately developed into the 'Blue series' – so called because the engines were painted blue – which replaced the 500 series in February 1980. When fitted with a Holset H2B or Garrett TO/4B turbocharger and bigger valves, the Blue series 500cu in engine developed 206bhp, or 175bhp in de-rated form.

Bedford once again claimed this was an entirely new engine, though the ancestry was clear, but based the claim on the number of new and improved parts necessary to make the engine suitable for turbocharging. The Blue series was fitted with low-expansion alloy Mahle pistons but retained the same offset bowl-in-piston combustion chamber used in all the Bedford diesels. A return to cylinder liners was made, the Blue series items being centrifugally cast to achieve consistent bore hardness and hence slower wear. Two-stage honing improved running-in times for new engines, reduced wear and improved oil retention in the cylinders. Other improvements to enable the engine to withstand the power output achievable by turbocharging

The 500cu in Blue series 205bhp turbo was the final incarnation of the Bedford diesel engine. GM

included a stronger and stiffer induction-hardened crankshaft, reinforced crankcase, larger sump and oil cooler. Larger valves were fitted in the cylinder head to improve breathing; as with the Red series, many of these improvements were incorporated into the normally aspirated version. Minor differences in quoted net power outputs were the result of different ancillaries being fitted.

CHAPTER SIX

THE VAS, VAL AND VAM

THE VAS

The VAS was announced by Bedford on 18 August 1961. Designed for bodies of around twenty-nine to thirty-one seats, it was intended to replace the C4/C5 modified goods chassis that had been used in conversions since 1957 to provide a small coach in the twenty- to thirty-seat range. Two engine options were offered from the standard Bedford range – the 214cu in (3.5-litre) petrol engine and the 300cu in (4.9-litre) diesel as used in the SB. The wheelbase was 13ft 8in (4.2m), overall chassis length was 19ft 9.5in (6m), front track was 6ft 1.25in (1.9m) and rear track was 6ft 5.9in (1.98m).When bodied as a twenty-nine-seat coach, the gross vehicle weight rating was 6 tons 9cwt (6,210.3kg).

The chassis frame was flat-topped in the manner of the SB, with 9in (229mm) pressed-channel side members with top-hat section bracing and channel-section cross-members, the whole being of cold-squeeze riveted construction. The frame differed from the SB in the number and shape of the cross-members. On the SB these were depressed to allow a slightly lower gangway, but on the VAS they were flat and level with the top of the side frames. The clutch was a single dry plate item, 12in in diameter, though there was the option of a 13in clutch when the diesel engine was fitted. The gearbox was the same four-speed unit as fitted in the SB with a different set of ratios for chassis with petrol or diesel engines. A divided in-line propeller shaft took the drive to the rear axle, for which there were two standard final drive ratios, that for the petrol driven chassis being 5.43:1 and that for the diesel, 4.37:1. There was also the option of a 4.7:1 axle with both engines. The two sections of the propeller shaft were supported where they met by an under-slung mounting on the centre chassis cross-member. Rear hubs were mounted on taper-roller bearings. Suspension was by semi-elliptic leaf springs, those at the front being of eight leaves, 58in long by 2in wide (1,473mm by 51mm); at the rear, 60in by 2in (1,524mm by 51mm), with ten leaves. Telescopic shock absorbers were fitted at both the front and rear.

Steering was by Vauxhall semi-irreversible worm-and-sector with a ratio of 25.5:1, the front axle being of drop-forged I-section beam with steering knuckles fitted with lead-bronze bearing surfaces and steel-backed bushes. A fabric universal joint connected the steering column to the worm shaft in the steering gear case.

Hydraulic brakes were fitted, vacuum assisted on petrol models but air-pressure assisted on diesel versions. Foot-brake drums were 13in in diameter with 3.25in linings at the front and 4in linings at the rear. A drum transmission handbrake was mounted on the nose of the differential.

Road wheels were unusually small for a PSV, at only 16in in diameter compared with the 20in wheels fitted to the SB, but were in line with the lighter trucks in Bedford's contemporary goods range. The cost of a VAS chassis with a petrol engine was £850, and with a diesel engine fitted, £1,035.

Late-model VAS chassis with Red series diesel. GM

BEDFORD VAS

Layout and Chassis
Single-deck bus or coach with 29–31 seats, typically 23ft 5in–25ft long (7.14m–7.62m) and 7ft 6in, 8ft, or 8ft 2.5in (2.29m, 2.44m or 2.5m) wide. Frame: 9in (229mm) pressed-steel channel side members, top-hat section braces and five channel-section cross-members

Engine
Type: Bedford 214cu in (3.5 litre) petrol or Bedford 300cu in (4.9 litre) diesel
Fuel capacity: 26gal (118ltr)

Gearbox
Bedford 4-speed, synchromesh on second, third and top. Clutch: Single dry plate with spring-loaded centre, radial clutch release bearing; adjustable for wear clutch pedal
Ratios (4-speed)
Petrol engine
   1st: 7.06:1
   2nd: 3.33:1
   3rd: 1.7:1
   Top: 1:1
   Reverse: 7.06:1
Diesel engine
   1st: 6.50:1
   2nd: 2.86:1
   3rd: 1.58:1
   Top: 1:1
   Reverse: 6.50:1
5-speed (from 1962)
   1st: 6.30:1
   2nd: 3.36:1
   3rd: 1.83:1
   4th: 1:1
   5th: 0.82:1
   Reverse: 5.76:1.

Transmission
Two open propeller shafts in line with three Hardy Spicer needle roller bearing universal joints, 12in (petrol) or 13in (diesel) diameter
Rear axle: Fully floating rear axle with final drive by spiral bevel gear differential, ratio: 5.43:1 (petrol), 4.37:1 (diesel), 4.7:1 (diesel and petrol option)
Front axle: Drop-forged I-section beam, kingpins and swivels with taper roller hub bearings

Suspension and Steering
Suspension: Semi-elliptic leaf springs with hydraulic shock absorbers front and rear
Steering: Semi-irreversible worm-and-sector
Tyres: Radial-ply 7.50 × 16in; optionally 8.25 × 16in, 12-ply

Brakes
Type: Lockheed hydraulic with vacuum servo assistance (petrol); air-pressure concentric servo-assisted hydraulic with engine driven 9.5cu ft/min (269cu litre/min) compressor (diesel)
Size: 13 × 3.25in (front); 13 × 4in (rear)

Dimensions
Wheelbase: 13ft 7in (4,166mm)
Front track: 6ft 1.25in (1.86m)
Rear track: 6ft 5.9in (1.98m)

Electrical system
12v positive earth, two Exide 6v batteries in series; CAV 12v dynamo with current-voltage control

Probably the most familiar face of the VAS was that of the original 1961 Duple Bella Vista body. This example is in the livery of Island Coachways, Guernsey.

Revisions

Initially there were only two engine options, the 300cu in diesel, the chassis so fitted being classified VAS1, and the 214cu in petrol, fitted in the VAS2 chassis. From 1962, two further options were added, the VAS3 with the Bedford 300cu in petrol engine and the VAS5 with the 330cu in diesel. A five-speed overdrive gearbox became available as an option from March 1962, with ratios of first 6.30:1, second 3.36:1, third 1.83:1. Fourth was direct 1:1 as before, while fifth was an overdrive top at 0.82:1. Reverse was a fairly high ratio compared with the four-speed boxes at 5.76:1. The new gearbox was similar in design to Bedford's existing five-speed box as used in goods applications with a 1:1 fifth. First, second and reverse gears employed spur gears with sliding engagement, while third and fifth had helical gears engaged by a dog-clutch. By 1983, however, only the two four-speed gearbox options were listed.

A number of improvements to the VAS were announced by Bedford in 1974; these included floor-mounted pedals, new instrumentation, the gear lever repositioned and the rake of the steering column altered to bring the driver closer to the windscreen. At the same time, the VAS was incorporated into Bedford's computerized stores system, the diesel-powered chassis being allocated the letters PJK and the petrol engine chassis PFE. However, the chassis continued to be marketed as the VAS.

From 1983, the Bedford 3.6-litre and 5.4-litre Red series turbocharged diesels became available as options on the VAS (*see* Chapter 5). At the same time, the gearbox and rear axle options were updated to include the gearbox and rear axles used in the SB and TK and TL truck range.

Plaxton's first body style for the VAS was the Embassy, which in this form looks quite dated when compared with the contemporary Duple Bella Vista body. Twenty-nine seats was the usual quota. This example is currently preserved in the heritage fleet of Go Godwin Coaches of Manchester and is named Prince of Wales. M. RICHARDSON

Bodies

Both Duple and Plaxton introduced new bodies for the VAS chassis, seating a maximum of twenty-nine passengers. The Duple body was known as the Bella Vista and was essentially a smaller version of the Bella Vega for the SB. Similarly, Plaxton's initial offering on the VAS was based on its current body for the SB, in this case the Embassy II. The Embassy II was also available in a slightly longer,

TGE 202G. This VAS5 was new to MacBrayne in June 1969. It carries a twenty-nine-seat Duple Bella Vista body and is seen here in Midland Bluebird livery. The later Bella Vista body shared the same front panel and grille arrangement as the Venture body on the VAM, considered somewhat less attractive by some compared with the original Vista front end, though the twin headlamps were undoubtedly appreciated by drivers. Midland Bluebird was the 1991 incarnation of Midland Scottish Ltd, successors to Walter Alexander and Sons (Midland) Ltd.

This VAS had a twenty-nine-seat Thurgood Successor body, one of the last bodies to be built by the Ware coachbuilder. It is seen at the premises of Grey's Coaches of Ely, Cambridgeshire on 7 September 1974. Grey's bought the coach new in 1966. T. WALKER

thirty-three-seat form, which could be distinguished by an additional small side window towards the rear. The extra length necessitated the extension of the chassis frame side members rearwards, this operation being undertaken at Plaxton. The coachbuilder's records indicate, however, that few (maybe less than five) of these were built, perhaps due to warranty concerns, given Yeates' experience with modifying the SB chassis, or perhaps because there was no demand for a full-size coach option between the twenty-nine-seat VAS and the thirty-nine- or forty-one-seat SB.

An unusual coachbuilder for the VAS was Dennis Bros Ltd of Guildford, Surrey. Dennis was better known as a builder of chassis for goods vehicles and PSVs and the famous Bristol Lodekka clone, the Dennis Loline. Dennis produced a number of thirty-seat utility bodies on VAS chassis between 1959 and 1961 for London County Council, almost identical to those built on its own Dennis Pax chassis.

In 1962 Duple (Midland) produced a twenty-nine-seat metal-framed bus based on a VAS2 chassis intended for service with Texaco in Trinidad, notable for having an overall width of 8ft (2.44m) at a time when most Duple (Midland) products were of 7ft 6in (2.29m) width; at this time most Hendon bodies were 8ft 2.5in (2.5m) wide, the maximum allowable dimension. The standard Duple (Midland) bus body was built in quantity on the VAS and made a well-proportioned small bus.

Strachans produced a twenty-nine-seat bus body for operation in North Africa in early 1963, the body alone costing around £1,500, depending on exact specification. A coach version was also available costing around £2,000.

Low-volume coachbuilder W. L. Thurgood (Coachbuilders) of Ware Ltd had been producing a coach body design on modified Ford Thames goods chassis, which was found to be suitable for the VAS; known as the Forerunner, two twenty-nine-seat luxury coaches of the type were built in 1963 on VAS1 chassis. The Forerunners built on the VAS differed from previous bodies, with altered body lines and a raked-profile front with divided curved windscreen. Of very traditional composite construction, with steel-reinforced ash main pillars producing a fairly thin-wall body, the internal width of the body was 7ft 5in (2.26m) within an overall width of 7ft 10in (2.39m), producing a coach of internal dimensions more usual in an 8ft (2.44m)-wide coach but in a usefully narrower package. An interesting feature of the design was the rear chassis extensions added to enable a large luggage locker to be provided at the rear, reminiscent of the modifications made by Plaxton to accommodate a thirty-three-seat version of the Embassy body. Larger-profile Avon 8.25-16 two-ply tyres were another modification over the standard VAS specification. Total cost of a Thurgood Foreunner/VAS1 was £2,837 in the summer of 1963.

For 1964, the successor to the Forerunner, imaginatively named the Successor, was announced by Thurgood. Another twenty-nine-seat coach based on the VAS1 chassis, it was built in the same way as the Forerunner, with a composite ash and steel frame panelled in 18swg (1.2mm) aluminium. In appearance it was quite similar to the earlier Duple products and as such was therefore dated. The seats were of full luxury standard with double-density Dunlopillo cushions and rubberized hair squabs. Interior panels were trimmed with Formica plastics, with polished wood pillar and cant-rail trimmings. Solid full-length overhead parcels racks were fitted and ventilation was provided by four top double sliding windows, supplemented by roof-mounted vents. Interior lighting was by canoe-shaped light fittings in cod art-deco style, seven of which were distributed in the ceiling and luggage racks. A heater, demister and wheel discs rounded off the coachwork. Standard accessories provided with the coach included a clock, fire extinguisher, first-aid kit and tool kit. The successor to the Forerunner had overall dimensions of 23ft 6in (7.16m) length by 7ft 10in (2.39m) width, with an overall height of 9ft 9in (2.97m). The cost of the complete package in May 1964 was £3,250. The Successor continued to be available until Thurgood stopped building new bodies around 1966, though the company continued repairing and selling coaches until taken over by Plaxton in 1970.

Marshall designed and built a thirty-seat bus body for the VAS, intended primarily as a school bus. Seven of these were purchased in 1965 by Coventry Corporation Transport (CCT), intended for operation by the Coventry Education Committee; it was stated that the buses would also be used on feeder routes and on normal services during off-peak times. They were given fleet numbers 502–508 (CRW 502C–CRW 508C) in the general CCT bus fleet.

The prototype for an interesting twenty-eight-seat bus on the VAS chassis appeared in 1965. This was made by Cravens Homalloy Ltd of Sheffield, producers of ambulances, vans, trailers and other similar products of all-metal construction. As an extension of a range of what were described as 'large-capacity personnel carriers', basically small buses of fifteen to twenty-seven seats for a variety of chassis including the Bedford VAS, the new bus had an overall length of 22ft 11in (6.98m) and was 7ft 6in (2.29m) wide. It was fitted with an air-operated folding entrance door in the usual position for a VAS. The one known example was finished with twenty-two seats and was acquired by Sheffield Corporation Transport Department for use as a committee coach.

In the mid-1960s, Seddon Motors of Oldham, Lancashire built some boxy bus bodies on the VAS for Jersey Motor Transport. Seddon was a small producer of goods vehicles but had a limited flirtation with PSVs from the late 1940s until the early 1980s. Its bodies were usually

J 34653. Jersey Motor Transport operated this 1966 VAS with unusual Seddon Pennine 4 thirty-seat bodywork.

sold under the Pennine Coachcraft label; the body on the Jersey Bedfords, however, bore little resemblance to any other product bearing the Pennine name. Later Seddon bus bodies on the VAS were not dissimilar in appearance to Reebur bodies on the same chassis.

Duple continued to supply its thirty-seat bus body virtually unchanged for 1966, but the Bella Vista twenty-nine-seat coach received some revisions for the 1966 season. The side profile remained the same but the side mouldings were simplified with a flash outlined in stainless steel. The front grille was also modified with a new anodized mesh grill in a stainless steel surround of the same style as that fitted to the Bella Venture body for the VAM. The body was increased in overall length by 15in (38cm) in the autumn of 1966, with a corresponding increase in window size, which emphasized the 24ft 9in (7.54m) length of the body. At the same time, the interior decor was revised. Bella Vista bodies continued to be available in 7ft 6in (2.29m) and 8ft (2.44m) wide forms. For 1967, the body length was increased to 25ft (7.6m) and renamed the Vista 25, though still with twenty-nine seats. A major restyle of the Vista 25 occurred in 1969, a general facelift adding features to bring it into line with the Viceroy body on the VAM. These included the Viceroy grille, all mouldings in stainless steel and new bumpers incorporating rubber corner sections for increased safety for pedestrians in the event of a collision.

In November 1969 a radically new, spacious and attractive body appeared for the VAS; named the Sintra, it had the usual twenty-nine seats, but was built by the Portuguese coachbuilder Salvador Caetano. The sole concessionaire in Great Britain and Eire was dealer Alf Moseley. The

KWA 811D. This is the Cravens-Homalloy all-metal bus produced on the VAS as a speculative venture by Cravens of Sheffield. It is seen here in service with Sheffield Corporation Transport. T. WALKER

Sintra featured all-metal construction with arc-welded, jig-assembled, box-section frames. Outer panels were made from heavy-gauge aluminium. Three-section front and rear bumpers were made of stainless steel and other brightwork was of anodized aluminium; other interior and exterior metal parts were chromed brass. Panoramic toughened-glass side windows were also fitted and interior fittings included full-length parcel racks housing forced-air ventilation outlets. Even the side windows had individual demister

This 1970 VAS5 with a Plaxton Embassy IV body was new to Scott's Greys of Darlington, whose coaches carried the message 'Glorious Runs and Safe Returns' emblazoned on their rear panels. When this photograph was taken on 30 January 1978, it was looking a little tired in the yard of its owners, Eynon's of Trimsaran in Carmarthenshire.

The Vista 25 was the successor to the Bella Vista body from Duple and shared its front-end arrangement with the larger Viceroy bodies for the SB, VAL and VAM. This VAS5 was new in February 1973 to H. Atkinson of Northallerton, Yorkshire. It was in service with Battersby's of Morecambe, Lancashire.

vents. Individual reading lights were provided, along with diffused night lights and overhead fluorescent main lights. Curtains at the windows, a radio and public address system were all standard features.

For 1970 Strachans introduced a new version of its Pacerider all-metal body on the VAS. Intended for welfare use, the new body had side loading for wheelchairs, considered to be safer than the usual rear-loading arrangement. The manually operated, double-folding, fully glazed side door was situated between the axles, approximately 8ft (2.44m) from the front of the bus. The door aperture was 5ft (1.52m) wide. A Ratcliffe electro-hydraulic lift platform could take one wheelchair at a time along with an attendant, power for the lift being provided by the vehicle batteries so the bus passengers could embark without the engine running. Three inward-facing wheelchairs and one forward-facing chair could be accommodated along the offside of the bus. For securing the wheelchairs, lashing rails and flush brass drop rings were provided. There was also provision for a rear luggage locker of 80cu ft (2,265ltr) to be fitted. Overall length was 25ft (7.6m), width 7ft 8in (2.34m), with twenty-one forward-facing seats and space to accommodate four wheelchairs. An alternative version of the body was available without wheelchair accommodation and with the usual twenty-nine seats.

Another development of the Strachans welfare/school bus body was known as the SC, which first appeared in 1970. Options included an additional folding door on the offside for speedy loading and unloading in one-way streets, though at a cost of four seats. Length was a little short of the Pacerider at 24ft 1in (7.34m), although the body could still be fitted with a tail-lift and other equipment for loading and carrying wheelchairs. Seating capacity was typically between thirty and thirty-four, depending on requirements.

Dormobile Ltd of Folkestone, best known for its mobile home and camper conversions of light vans, produced a school bus body for the VAS. This was of all-steel construction with the exception of the corner mouldings, which were in fibreglass. Safety features included driver visibility aids with a nearside kerb-view window and jack-knife door that was remotely locked and unlocked by the driver. Seating capacity was thirty-one.

Wadham Stringer also built bus bodies for welfare and school use, optionally fitted with its own tail-lift at the rear. A typical body on a VAS was able to provide transport for twenty-six passengers or fourteen wheelchairs plus a driver and attendant.

Reeve Burgess offered an attractive and contemporary-looking 7m service bus body on the VAS in the early 1980s, typically with thirty or thirty-one seats and available in a number of configurations for use as a coach, service bus or welfare bus with wheelchair accommodation and side- or tail-lifts.

By 1974, the Duple and Plaxton bodies on the VAS were becoming outdated in aspects of their design and construction, so both companies introduced all-metal bodies suitable for the VAS in that year. Retaining the twenty-nine-seat format as the maximum acceptable in a luxury coach of the size suitable for mounting on a VAS, Duple's offering was a smaller version of the Dominant body introduced in 1972. Built in what was referred to as Duple's 'phase 2' construction method, the new body had a jig-built, all-steel tubular frame with no wood.

The Dominant body for the VAS received a facelift in 1975; now known as the Dominant I to distinguish it from the updated and larger Dominant II model, changes included a new front grille, wraparound front and rear bumpers, gas struts for the servicing access panels, larger exterior mirrors, pantograph-type windscreen wipers and repositioned direction indicator lights.

Plaxton's new body for the VAS also bore similarities to its existing range, as might be expected; christened the Panorama Supreme, it employed a modified form of Plaxton's traditional construction, which formed an intermediate stage in the progression to all-metal construction for the entire range. The Supreme utilized all-steel body bearers, roof sticks and cant and waist rails. U-section steel pillars formed the uprights, with wood inserts for mounting the external panels; those below the waist were aluminium while the front and rear panels were in fibreglass. The side and roof skins were insulated to provide some control over the internal temperature and minimize noise. A new kind of swivelling entrance door was fitted, with power opera-

tion offered as an option. The emergency door was at the offside rear and featured a double-claw lock with an easily operated handle, the unit having been specially developed by Plaxton. The intention was to replace the uprights with box-section pillars in due course when the Supreme range was extended to replace the existing Elite design. Front and rear screens were in double-curvature laminated glass and interchangeable, thus reducing the need for large stocks of spare glass. The main difference in appearance from the Elite was in the side profile, with taller windows and a restyled front end.

The next major update for the Plaxton Supreme body for the VAS came in 1980, when the body was restyled to bring it into line with the larger bodies in the Plaxton range. During Bedford's last days as an active PSV manufacturer, Plaxton built a special compact version of its stylish Paramount II body on a 1986 VAS for Stewarts of Dalavich, which remained unique.

Based on the available figures from all its factories, Duple built bodies on at least 808 VAS chassis in the period between 1964 and 1985. Prior to 1964, the figures suggest production was running at an average of five or six VAS bodies per year, so an approximation for the total number of bodies built on the VAS chassis would be around 832.

Plaxton's figures for 1960 to 1987 indicate that around 896 bodies were built by that concern on VAS chassis, remarkably close to the estimated figures for Duple.

Sales and Production

The VAS proved very popular and second-hand examples were sought after and held their price well, some operators apparently paying more for a four-year-old example than the first owner paid when it was new – a quite notable feat even taking into account a rate of inflation that varied between 3 and 5 per cent from 1962 to 1970. Available data show that the residual value of a coach tended to remain quite high throughout the first five years of its life.

Purchasers of significant quantities of VASs from new tended to be in the welfare field and included the London Borough of Croydon (thirty-one, 1967–87); the Greater London Council (GLC) and its successors on behalf of the

This 1977 VAS5 with Duple Dominant twenty-nine-seat coach body was new to Northern Motor Rentals of Sunderland, Tyne and Wear, in October 1977. It later passed to Alexandra Coaches, in whose livery it is seen here, and then to McColl's Coaches of Dalmuir, Clydebank, Scotland.

Inner London Education Authority (ILEA), who bought over 300 between 1966 and 1978; the Metropolitan Police; the MoD; Lincolnshire County Council (sixty-eight, 1974–85); and Strathclyde Regional Council (eighty-four, 1975–87). Other London boroughs to buy fleets of VASs included those of Greenwich, Croydon and Haringey. Bermuda Aviation Services bought at least twenty between 1970 and 1986.

Coach and bus operators tended to buy in lesser quantities; repeat customers for the VAS included Abbeyways of Halifax (at least eleven in the period 1966 to 1979); Alpha of Brighton (twelve, 1968–82); David MacBrayne of Glasgow, who favoured Duple thirty-seat bus bodies (twenty, 1966–9); East Kent Motor Services (ten in 1967); Hodson of Penkridge (thirteen, 1966–82, though the records suggest they simply replaced their existing VASs with a new one every year); Marton of Harmondsworth (fourteen, 1970–80); Rendell of Parkstone (fourteen, 1967–78); Richmond of Epsom (eleven, 1966–72); Tindall of Low Fell (nineteen, 1971–80); and Wallace Arnold of Leeds (ten, 1972–80).

From 1967 the Commonwealth Expedition (Comex) bought repeated quantities of VAS-based coaches for its Asian Highway expeditions, over sixty being purchased from the late 1960s to 1980.

By a good lead, the VAS5 was the most popular variant, followed by the VAS3; the VAS1 and VAS2 sold less than the others but in about equal quantities of each.

A VAS with a luxuriously appointed Plaxton body spent over four months touring the USA in 1962, during which it covered over 9,000 miles (14,000km). The coach, which had been supplied by Arlington Motors Ltd, was fitted with reclining seats, each individually lit under the control of the passenger and air-conditioning with aircraft-style outlets. A cocktail bar was built into the rear of the saloon and a tape recorder – a fairly bulky and inconvenient item in the days before the onslaught of the compact cassette – provided music and perhaps other entertainment. The tour was sponsored jointly by World Wide Coaches Ltd of London SE5 and I. T. Coach Operators Ltd. The coach returned to the UK via Southampton aboard the SS *American Forester*. It was said that all the Americans who inspected the coach and its interior were 'surprised at the standard', which probably says more about the general perception of the UK in the USA at the time than about the joint efforts of Bedford and Plaxton.

The VAS soon found a place in the world market. Twenty chassis were exported to Sudan for use in Khartoum in 1964; traditionally, public transport in the Sudan had been based on converted lorry chassis with locally built bodies with more emphasis on function than form. The twenty

Not all VAS PSVs found themselves with coach operators; this Plaxton Supreme twenty-nine-seat body on a VAS5 chassis was new to Durham Police in June 1976. It was serving with Durham Ambulance Service when photographed in December 1992. It clearly has the blues, but does it have the twos, too, we wonder?

VAS provided the chassis component of complete bus kits for local assembly in the Sudan, with bodies supplied by Metal Sections Ltd (METSEC), of Oldbury, Birmingham, with thirty more to follow. The kits were ordered by Mitchell, Cotts & Co. (Middle East) Ltd, who specified kit form as the cost of importing complete buses was considered prohibitive, and so made a saving of around 15 per cent on the total price.

By October 1965, the petrol-powered VAS chassis cost £890 and the diesel version £1085, approximately £175 less than the SB.

Available records covering the period 1965 to 1987 account for sales of 3,012 VAS chassis. Prior to June 1965, sales figures indicate that around 1,152 had been sold. The post-1965 figures are considerably less than would be the case if the figure of 750 units per year production claimed by Bedford in 1974 was accurate, with 80 per cent of these chassis being sold in the UK. Even assuming that production started modestly and increased year on year, the figure is likely in reality to be much higher.

Continental Touring Economics Favouring the VAS

The VAS was a good economic choice for continental touring, particularly for those whose tour destinations were Austria, Greece or Yugoslavia, as the routes inevitably took them through West Germany, where a circulation tax (replaced by a Heavy Vehicle Tax in December 1968) was in force. Three tax rate bands covered vehicles with a gross weight of 7,500kg–15,000kg (16,500–33,000lb), 15,000kg–20,000kg (33,000–44,000lb) and vehicles over 20,000kg (44,000lb). The VAS fell into the first band, which was the cheapest by two-thirds over the next tax band, which would apply to the majority of larger coaches. Belgium, France and Italy also levied various taxes for visiting coaches.

The VAS for School and Welfare and in the Community

The VAS soon found favour as the basis for utility buses for school and welfare duties. Manchester Corporation Welfare Services Committee purchased two VASs in 1963, with bodies by Able Bodywork Co. Ltd of Bolton. The bodies were mounted on diesel-powered chassis with larger than usual tyres of 8.25 × 16in. There was space for twelve seated passengers, four wheelchairs and two stretchers. The wheelchair positions were fitted with safety locking devices. An EdBro-Pilot electro-hydraulic lift was fitted at the rear and each coach was intended to be operated with a driver/attendant, and an attendant/relief driver. A supply of drinking water, first-aid equipment and blankets was also carried. The buses were intended for taking disabled passengers on holidays in May and September of each year.

Wheelchair accommodation was also provided in the first ten school buses for the London Borough of Haringey. Strachans thirty-two-seat Pacerider bodies were fitted to the chassis, which were supplied by Capitol Motor Co. Ltd of Tottenham, London.

The VAS also formed part of the huge CIE school bus fleet, being used to build a medium-size bus with dimensions 25ft (7.6m) long by 7ft 6in (2.29m) wide. These could carry forty-nine children or thirty-three adults. The bodies for these were built on frames supplied by Metal Sections Ltd and completed by a consortium of three bodybuilders, McArdle, Duffy and Murphy, all of which were based in Dundalk. The livery was the standard CIE school bus colours of golden brown with a white band.

The VAS found uses other than as a pure people carrier; Wiltshire County Council purchased a VAS with a body built by Longwell Green Coachworks Ltd, Bristol, for use as a mobile library. Longwell Green was a well-established low-volume coachbuilder who employed traditional methods of construction. Wiltshire's mobile library had composite framing with external panels in aluminium, except for the front dome, which was in glass-fibre and shaped to give a coach-like appearance. Reading capacity was 2,500 books; the number of borrowers that could be accommodated simultaneously is not recorded, but is unlikely to have led to a shortage of reading matter.

The Metropolitan Police found the VAS a useful tool for rapid force deployment and bought forty with Willowbrook bus bodies in 1970. Also in London, the ILEA, working with the GLC, bought seventy-seven VASs with petrol engines and Dormobile bodies for school bus use in 1972. A further five VAS were bought by the ILEA in the same year; these had Strachans SC bodies with both nearside and offside entrance doors.

OVB 188F. An irresistible picture that suggests the photographer's main interest was not the small Bedford. Fortuitously creeping past Routemaster RM656 is this Strachans-bodied thirty-two-seat VAS5 belonging to the London Borough of Haringey.

A. STRONG

The Duple (Midland) bus body sat well on the VAS chassis and is worth comparing with the Strachans body seen in the previous image. This 1965 VAS1 was fleet no. 51 in MacBrayne's fleet and has thirty dual-purpose seats. It later became fleet no. CD60 with Highland Omnibuses.

The VAS in Scotland

The VAS proved to be just as popular with Scottish operators as its larger, and indeed, smaller, Bedford brethren. David MacBrayne and Highland Scottish Omnibuses Ltd (formerly Highland Omnibuses Ltd) both found a use for the VAS, and some of these found their way to East Kilbride in 1974, where they were operated by the Scottish Bus Group on behalf of Greater Glasgow PTE on feeder bus services to a direct rail link to Glasgow city centre. Five twenty-seven-seat VASs were used on the service. That the VAS could have just as long a useful life as the products of heavier chassis manufacturers was demonstrated by Western SMT in 1979, when three VAS midi buses, with ages ranging from thirteen to fifteen years, were introduced on off-peak shopping services at Bargarran. The VAS was chosen specifically because of the narrow streets in the town's shopping area.

Scotland also proved to be one of the last destinations for brand new VAS chassis in 1987; these were four VAS coaches with Reeve Burgess bodies for Lowland Scottish Omnibuses Ltd (formerly Eastern Scottish Omnibuses Ltd) and were built after Bedford had ceased production. Reeve Burgess, a subsidiary of Plaxton since 1980, probably built the very last VAS-based buses and coaches during this time, with over £800,000-worth of vehicles based on the chassis being in production at Chesterfield. These included twenty-two coaches for the MoD and a twelve-seat, wheelchair-equipped body with a side lift for Doncaster social services department. The chassis for the Doncaster bus was supplied by Kirkby Bus & Coach Ltd.

THE BEDFORD VAL

The VAL was launched at the Commercial Motor Show at Earls Court in September 1962. Two examples were shown, bodied by Plaxton and Duple, respectively. What captured the imagination of the industry and the public, though, was the three-axle layout of the VAL. With its smaller than usual 16in-diameter wheels, shared with the VAS, and twin-steering front axles, it seemed to represent the future and was very typical of the forward-looking attitudes prevalent in the early 1960s. Three-axle PSV chassis were not new, but were fairly rare – the most common variants being double-deck trolleybuses, though there were a few pre-Second World War high-capacity double-deckers, and Leyland made a three-axle variant of its Tiger single-deck chassis. All of these had twin axles at the rear. The adoption of the three-axle layout was generally to allow the completed vehicle to be built to the maximum permitted dimensions allowed by the UK Construction and Use regulations.

This 1987 VAS5 with Reebur dual-purpose seventeen-seat body was amongst the last Bedfords built. Lowland Scottish fleet no. 714 demonstrates the final stage of evolution of the bus body on the VAS chassis and was photographed at Galashiels in June 1993.

More significant in the Bedford story was the Leyland TEC2 Gnu, of which only a few were made. The Gnu had a front-mounted vertical engine and differed from the other three-axle chassis by having twin front-steering axles, so in mechanical layout, the Gnu was the closest the VAL had to a progenitor. Walter Alexander and Sons Ltd had two with their entrances ahead of the front axles, so these were also similar to the VAL in that respect. The Gnu too had been designed as a high-capacity coach, but it is said that operators disliked the twin front-wheel steering. It is notable that the Gnu had standard-sized front wheels, which would undoubtedly have made for heavy steering. The VAL addressed this by having smaller than usual wheels and power-assisted steering.

The use of existing Bedford axles with 16in wheels was almost certainly a major factor in the decision to build the chassis with three axles; the demand for a maximum-dimension coach was clear, yet a two-axle design with the same components in such a large vehicle would have been under-braked and the axles and tyres subjected to greater loads than those for which they were designed. A further consideration was safety in the event of a front tyre bursting, the driver being able to maintain control of the steering much more easily with the twin steering axles. A further advantage was the low frame height that resulted from smaller diameter wheels, with less intrusion into the body space. At 29in (737mm) the VAL frame height, measured from the ground to the highest part of the level frame, was approximately the same as the VAS and 7in (179mm) lower than the SB. On paper, at least, then, the VAL looked set to be a world-beater.

TRAVELLING THE ASIAN HIGHWAY BY BEDFORD – THE COMEX EXPEDITIONS

Possibly the most exacting road tests ever performed on a Bedford VAS were the Commonwealth Expeditions of the late 1960s and early 1970s. The Commonwealth Expeditions grew out of an initiative first proposed by the Indian government in April 1964, as a part of the Indian Universities' Youth Festival. Students from all the commonwealth countries were invited to join in the festival; initial response was poor, though, and, with political problems in India, the festival did not take place in 1964. It did come to fruition in 1965, however, and a party of 210 young men and women from the UK, under the patronage of the Duke of Edinburgh and sponsored by Massey Ferguson (UK) Ltd, travelled nearly 6,500 miles (10,500km) in six Ford coaches. The expedition was repeated in 1967 and from then on took the appellation Comex.

Drawing on experience from the first event, the organizers decided to buy eleven brand-new Bedford VAS fitted with Duple Vista bodies modified to include cooking facilities and luggage space. The members of each contingent were allocated specific roles, navigators, drivers, mechanics, cooks, diarists, and so on. Those selected as mechanics underwent special training provided by Bedford at Luton. Those chosen to drive were trained to PSV standards and had to pass a PSV driving test – undoubtedly a useful asset for their CVs. PSV training was undertaken locally, for example the Durham contingent was trained by United Automobile Services Ltd, the local Tilling Group bus company. The decision to buy brand-new coaches was largely based on the principle that they would be less likely to need complex servicing and repairs during the journey. The VAS was chosen because it was more compact than the Fords used previously, had simpler maintenance requirements and was considered easier to drive. The potential resale value of the coaches once the expedition was over was also taken into account, the Bedfords being considered more likely to appeal to new buyers than the Fords. The coaches were supplied by the Arlington Motor Co. Ltd of Potters Bar.

Comex 2 took 330 students of both genders on a trip that covered around 6,590 miles (10,600km). While most of the programme took place in India and Pakistan, the party visited more than fifty universities in fifteen countries, with the final destination being Delhi. Participants were drawn from all over the UK and included students from universities, colleges of further education and industry. Students from other commonwealth countries also took part. Sadly, the Comex 2 expedition was marred by a serious accident when a mobile crane in Yugoslavia crashed into the Durham coach. While the driver survived, a number of the passengers were killed. The driver was later exonerated of all blame by the Yugoslav government.

The Comex 3 expedition bought twenty VAS5s with Duple Vista bodies, which would originally have had twenty-nine seats but were modified for use on the expedition to provide space for cooking and storage. The twenty Comex 3 coaches had consecutive registrations KNK 341G to KNK 360G. Angela Velleman, who took this photograph of the London contingent somewhere in the former Yugoslavia, recalls watching the moon-landing in the TV studios in Kabul, Afghanistan – a more peaceful place then than today. A. VELLEMAN

Some of the places visited during Comex 2 included Amol, Tabriz, Tehran, Kabul and Kandahar; some of those names are now familiar for entirely different reasons in the turbulent second decade of the twenty-first century.

Despite the tragic accident, the programme was only briefly interrupted and Comex 3 in 1969 was an even more ambitious affair, with twenty coaches and 500 young people. The Bedford VAS with Duple coachwork supplied by Arlington was once again chosen as the vehicle for the expedition.

Some of the conditions the coaches and their drivers had to contend with along the expedition route included crossing the dried-up beds of rivers to avoid collapsed bridges, filling in holes in the road so the coaches could pass, driving along roads turned into rivers by rainstorms, dust clouds caused by travelling in close convoy and ascending and descending dangerous mountain passes. David Burn, of the Lancaster contingent, recalls that a heavy-duty twin horn was added to the specification in Pakistan and affixed to the flag-holder bracket. The horn proved very effective in scattering the cows, rickshaws and taxis that congested their route, though was clearly less effective at scattering hostile children in Turkey, where some of the coaches suffered broken windscreens and windows as a result of stones being thrown at the coaches.

Wear and tear suffered by the coaches included exhausts falling off, broken shock absorbers and binding brakes, among other difficulties.

The Comex 3 expedition covered a round trip of approximately 18,000 miles (30,000km); the only failures were six alternators, two starter motors, a leaking radiator, a broken transmission handbrake, a failed steering box and an airlock in the fuel system of one coach. Dust caused air filters to block easily and Bedford produced a modified air cleaner assembly as a result.

Some statistics for the trip included oil consumption of between 1.1 and 1.5 pints (0.63–0.85ltr) per 1,000 miles (1,600km) and an average fuel consumption of around 17mpg (16.6ltr/100km), which, considering the arduous and variable conditions, is impressive. Bedford's worldwide service network meant that at various points along the route major servicing facilities were available for the coaches, and items such as the steering box and transmission brake could be sourced and repaired at the roadside by the students.

The Comex 3 expedition arrived back at Dover on 8 October 1969. A short ceremony then took place, where a trophy donated by Duple was awarded by Mr A. Pant, the Indian High Commissioner, for the best-maintained coach. The winners for Comex 3 were the Liverpool contingent. Following this event, the coaches were then returned to Arlington for resale after having the missing seats replaced. Roger Phillips, a branch general manager for Arlington, commented at the time, 'If a coach driver returned his vehicle in the same condition after the summer season, coach proprietors would have nothing to complain about', which reflects well on both the way the coaches were looked after by the students and the quality of the Bedford/Duple product.

Experience gathered determined that while the Bedford VAS/Duple was once again the choice for Comex 4 in 1970, the coaches received some modifications before setting out. These included 45gal (205ltr) fuel tanks in place of the standard 26gal (118ltr) tank, raised silencers and body skirt panels to reduce grounding damage (holes of up to 3ft/1m deep having been encountered). Mechanical modifications included stronger tie-rod ends, reinforced shock-absorber brackets mounted higher in the frame, up-rated rear springs and three-piece wheels with 8.25 × 16in radial tyres, though the standard horn was retained. The chassis were fitted with the 330cu in Bedford diesel engine with the optional 13in clutch and five-speed gearbox. Seating capacity was reduced to twenty-five due to overloading problems experienced with the twenty-nine-seat coaches, and the space was used to accommodate stores for the journey. Spare parts carried included gasket sets and injectors for the engine and half-shafts for the rear axle, as well as brake linings, oil and other consumables, and each coach carried a Bedford workshop manual. A Pye Telecommunications Ltd two-way radio was fitted in each coach to allow the contingents to communicate with each other.

Comex 4 took place with twenty-five Bedford VAS/Duple coaches in 1970 and visited Pakistan, India, Ceylon, Malaysia and Singapore.

While essentially a private venture, the Foreign and Commonwealth Office maintained close contact with the organizers of the expeditions and for Comex 4 the MoD provided transport between Malaysia and India, while the government provided a grant of £1,000 towards the cost of the expedition. The programme continued throughout the 1970s, always using Bedford coaches – including some larger YRQs and YMTs – culminating in 1980 with Comex 13, which comprised two expeditions, one to Asia and the other to Africa.

The chassis frame was made in the usual Bedford way, with pressed-steel channel section 10in (254mm) deep with 3in (76mm) flanges and 0.22in (5.6mm) thick. The material used was EN2D steel and the chassis was braced with seven riveted cross-members and one removable bolted cross-member just behind the engine. The offside chassis member was completely straight from front to rear, but on the right-hand-drive chassis the first 35in (889mm) of the nearside member was joggled inwards by 3.5in (89mm) to provide clearance for an inward-opening door on a front-entrance body. Left-hand-drive chassis did not need this joggle in the corresponding right-hand member. Both side members were swept down by 5in (127mm) ahead of the leading axle, with the flanges reduced to just over 2in (508mm) along this length. At the rear, behind the rear axle the lower flanges were swept upwards to reduce the depth of the side member to 6in (152mm).

The first engine and gearbox combination chosen for the VAL was, perhaps, surprising, in that proprietary units were used; the engine was Leyland's O.400 diesel coupled to a five-speed overdrive synchromesh gearbox made by the Turner Manufacturing Co. Ltd of Wolverhampton, the gearbox being of an American design from the Clark Equipment Company. The models shown at Earls Court in 1962 had chassis in this form and were later classified VAL14. The engine and gearbox were mounted ahead of the leading axle in order to keep the engine and driving position well forward, thus leaving an unobstructed low-height frame of simple profile from the leading axle rearwards, with room for a front entrance ahead of the front axle. The engine and gearbox unit were supported by two rubber sandwich mountings at the front and two rubber-bushed links at the clutch housing suspended from the removable arched chassis cross-member immediately behind the engine. For right-hand-drive chassis the engine had a modified cylinder head with exhaust ports and inlet ports both on the left-hand side of the engine to provide more room for the driver and cab. The power penalty of a less efficient cylinder head design does not appear to have been great so the modifica-

tion was obviously considered acceptable, if not desirable. Left-hand-drive chassis were equipped with the standard head provided by Leyland with the exhaust manifold on the right opposite the inlet manifold. Engine cooling was by a front-mounted radiator pressurized to 7psi (0.48bar).

Drive was through a 14in-diameter Borg and Beck single dry plate clutch and four-piece propeller shaft connected to a Bedford hypoid spiral-bevel rear axle. The standard axle was a single-speed unit with a ratio of 5.3:1 with optional ratios of 4.6:1 and 5.8:1. The 5.3:1 ratio gave the VAL the theoretical ability to climb a 3.5:1 gradient. Alternatively, a Bedford two-speed axle with air-pressure shift mechanism and ratios of 4.86:1 and 6.63:1 could be specified. Sealed-for-life Hardy Spicer 1500-series needle-roller universal joints were used to join the four sections of the propeller shaft, the shaft being supported in three intermediate bearings on the chassis cross-members.

Braking was by a Lockheed air-assisted hydraulic system with 12 × 3in drums on both front axles and 13 × 4.18in drums on the rear axle. A tandem master cylinder providing a dual hydraulic circuit was employed, and power assistance was by a Clayton Dewandre 1/375 air servo. Because of the different loading on each of the front axles, different-sized hydraulic slave cylinders were employed on each of the axles, the leading one having 1.25in-diameter wheel cylinders, the second axle having 1.125in-diameter cylinders. The handbrake was an unusual arrangement consisting of a two-part parking brake system, with a 12 × 3in drum-type transmission brake mounted on the nose of the rear axle. This was operated by an umbrella-handle pull-up lever on the steering column. The other handbrake was operated by a lever mounted to the driver's left, which applied the brakes on both pairs of front wheels via cables. The lever incorporated a mechanical spring-servo made by Stopfix-Bremse GmBH. This provided some assistance for the driver's left arm with variable mechanical advantage from 4:1 to 16:1 at the end of the lever's pull. The combined handbrakes were capable of easily holding the coach on a 1:12 (8.3 per cent) gradient.

The front axles were the usual H-section beam type with stub axles from the Bedford TK truck range. Steering was by Burman recirculating ball steering box, and gave five-and-a-half turns of the steering wheel from lock to lock. Power assistance for the steering came from a Hydrosteer hydraulic ram servo, powered by an engine-driven pump. Despite the twin steering axles, the system was not overly complicated; two relay levers were mounted on the chassis the same distance ahead of each axle, these each being connected to the steering arm on their respective axle and together by a drag link to ensure the correct relative

The VAL chassis. GM

geometry was maintained as the steering turned. The forward steering arm was also connected by drag link to the steering box drop arm, the hydraulic servo ram acting directly on the steering box drop arm. All joints were made using Thompson sealed-for-life ball joints, so the only lubrication required for the steering was at the four kingpins for the steering swivels and stub axles.

Suspension consisted of semi-elliptic springs hung from brackets that were outrigged from the chassis so the springs did not sit immediately below the chassis frame, an unusual design for a PSV. Heavy-duty Metalastik bushes insulated the springs from their mountings at the front and shackles at the rear. The leading axle springs had seven leaves with an overall length of 4ft 2in (1,270mm) and width of 3in (76mm), while the second axle had only four leaves in a 4ft 4in × 3in (1,321mm × 76mm) spring, the chassis having been designed so that loading on the leading axle would be greater than on the trailing axle. Safety brackets were provided just behind the second axle to ensure that should a spring break, it would not foul the steering linkages.

The rear springs were 5ft 7in long by 3in wide (1,702mm by 76.2mm) with ten leaves. Six Girling telescopic hydraulic shock absorbers controlled the spring movement, those at the front having a 7.5in (191mm) stroke while the rears had a 9in (229mm) stroke. The front shock absorbers were outrigged from the side members to meet the axles at their extreme ends for additional roll stability, while the rears were located inside the frame.

Good ride quality was achieved, despite the simple leaf-sprung suspension and rigid axles, by careful choice of spring rates and shock-absorber settings, combined with the low unsprung weight of the relatively small wheels. The fact that the rearmost front axle was considerably more softly sprung than the leading axle was probably a significant factor in the overall ride quality. The small wheels gave the vehicle a lower centre of gravity, contributing to a more stable ride.

The fuel tank could hold 26gal (118ltr) and was mounted on the outside of the right-hand chassis member, immediately behind the rear wheels. The electrical system was 24v with four 6v batteries mounted centrally in the chassis frame; charging was by dynamo.

The chassis was designed from the outset for front-entrance coachwork, addressing a gap in the contemporary Bedford range, with the maximum allowable dimensions of 36ft (3cm short of 11m and generally referred to as 11m) long by 8ft 2.5in (2.5m) wide. The wheelbase dimension was 19ft 3in (5.87m), with a front overhang of around 6ft 4in (1.93m) and a rear overhang of 10ft 5in (3.2m).

The use of 16in wheels meant a relatively low floor height could be achieved with bodywork of up to fifty-six seats. While primarily intended for passenger use, the VAL was also supplied as a basis for goods bodywork such as furniture vans (pantechnicons). The Duple-bodied example at Earls Court weighed in at 6.5 tons (6,604kg) with a GVW of 10.25 tons (10,414kg), a substantial weight saving over other contemporary coaches of similar dimensions.

Top speeds with the various axle ratios were quoted as follows: 5.3:1 – 59mph (95km/h); 4.6:1 – 68mph (109.4km/h); and, with the two-speed rear axle, 47mph (75.6km/h) in low and 54mph (86.9km/h) in high ratio.

Maintenance was generally straightforward; the use of sealed-for-life ball-joints and universal joints meant that lubrication was kept to a minimum, only thirteen grease points, including kingpins, propeller shaft sliding splines and brake pivot points, requiring attention. Access to the engine air cleaner, dipstick and power-steering fluid reservoir was from inside the coach, by removing a cowl held in place by spring clips over the engine. The fuel lift-pump, injection pump and air compressor were somewhat less accessible, being below the line of the floor, and the dynamo was obscured by the two heater pipes passing directly above it, making fan belt adjustment somewhat awkward; but on the whole the VAL was not difficult to service and maintenance costs were relatively low.

The chassis was designed for radial-ply tyres, which meant that choice was initially limited to Michelin X 8.25-16in tyres; however, other manufacturers soon started to produce the new size in a radial ply. It was left to the body-builder to decide on the location and means of carrying of the spare wheel, though the recommended position was below the chassis frame, behind the left-hand rear wheels.

Throughout its ten years of production, from 1963 to 1973, the VAL was virtually unique; the only similar vehicle that appeared during that time was a twin-steer coach

Plaxton's prototype Embassy body on the VAL chassis appeared at the Commercial Motor Show at Earls Court in 1962, decorated for Worldwide Coaches of London.
PLAXTON

that was shown on the Padana stand at the Turin Motor Show in 1966. It is unclear, however, if this chassis went into production and it seems to have slipped into obscurity.

When introduced in 1962, the bare chassis cost a very competitive £1,775 and was available in both left-hand- and right-hand-drive form. At a price of around £1,000 less than any other British chassis suitable for 36ft (11m) coachwork, the VAL offered good value for money and brought a 36ft-long coach within the financial reach of a wide range of operators.

Revisions

Larger brake drums were introduced from autumn 1965 to address complaints from operators of poor brake performance and short lining life. An exhaust brake kit had been available from December 1964, which used air pressure from the braking system to operate a cylinder and piston assembly connected to the fuel injection pump stop-control lever, and also a cylinder and piston assembly mounted on

the exhaust front pipe to close off the exhaust system under braking. However, this was a costly extra so Bedford modified the standard brakes to give a claimed improvement of 100 per cent in lining life. This was achieved by increasing the diameter of the front drums from 12in to 12.5in and the width of the linings from 3in to 4in and the thickness from 0.25in to 0.312in. At the rear, the lining width was increased from 4.18in to 5.5in. These modifications in total increased the lining area from 499sq in to 646sq in. The lining material was changed for a heavier-duty compound to combat fading, and the brakes were now twin-leading shoe all round in place of the leading and trailing shoes employed previously. The rear drum material was also increased in thickness slightly from 0.47in (11.9mm) to 0.58in (14.7mm).

From 1967 the Bedford 466cu in (7.6-litre) diesel became an option for the VAL, chassis so fitted being classified VAL70. At the same time, the electrical system was updated and an alternator replaced the dynamo fitted to earlier models.

BEDFORD VAL (1963–73)

Layout and Chassis
Luxury coach or bus, 48–56 seats; typically 36ft (11m) long by 8ft 2.5in (2.5m) wide. Frame: pressed steel channel section with seven riveted cross-members and one bolted cross-member

Engine
Type: VAL14: Leyland O.400 6-cylinder diesel
VAL70 (from 1967): Bedford 466cu in diesel
Fuel capacity: 45gal (205ltr)

Gearbox
Turner 564-VO 5-speed synchromesh (overdrive fifth)
Clutch: Borg and Beck 14in (360mm) single dry plate
Ratios
   1st: 6.06:1
   2nd: 3.50:1
   3rd: 1.80:1
   4th: 1:1
   Top: 0.8:1
   Reverse: 6.0:1

Transmission
Four-piece propeller shaft with Hardy Spicer needle-roller universal joints
Rear axle: Bedford full-floating hypoid bevel-gear differential; ratios, single speed 5.3:1 (standard), 4.6;1,

5.8:1 (options); two-speed axle high ratio 4.86:1, low 6.63:1
Front axles: Twin I-beam with kingpins, axles connected by constant-geometry drag link

Suspension and Steering
Suspension: Rubber-bushed semi-elliptic leaf springs with Girling hydraulic shock absorbers on all axles
Steering: Burman recirculating ball with Hydrosteer ram-type power assistance
Tyres: 8.25 × 16in radial

Brakes
Type: Air-assisted Lockheed Hydraulic with twin leading shoes on front axle, leading and trailing shoes on rear axle. Two separate handbrake systems with 12 × 3in transmission drum brake and single-pull lever operated on steering axle brakes
Size: VAL14: 12 × 3in (front on both axles), 13 × 4.18in (rear)
VAL70: 12 × 4in (front), 13 × 5.5in (rear)

Dimensions
Track
   Front: 81.89in (2,080mm)
   Rear: 82.5in (2,096mm)
Wheelbase: 19ft 3in (5,867mm)

Electrical system
24v compensated-voltage control system, 4 × 6v 114Ah batteries

EXHAUST BRAKES – HOW THEY WORK

An exhaust brake utilizes the compression of the engine to act as a brake. There are several variations with additional controls, but the general method of operation is this: an electrical mechanism that closes off the exhaust system and shuts off fuel to the engine is controlled by microswitches operated by the footbrake pedal and the clutch pedal. Operating the brake pedal causes a microswitch (A on the diagram) to close, which allows current to pass to the exhaust brake solenoid. This solenoid operates a vacuum- or air-activated butterfly valve that closes off the exhaust outlet from the engine, preventing exhaust gases from being vented through the silencer. This has the effect of building up air pressure in the engine cylinders, causing the pressure to resist the vehicle's momentum as it attempts to drive the engine round and thereby acts to retard the vehicle's progress. The same solenoid and actuator also acts on the engine throttle control through a Bowden cable or series of levers to shut off the fuel supply to the injectors, thus no fuel is admitted to the engine while it is being used as a brake. Several other switches are included to ensure the safety of the system and to ensure the engine will restart when the brake pedal is released.

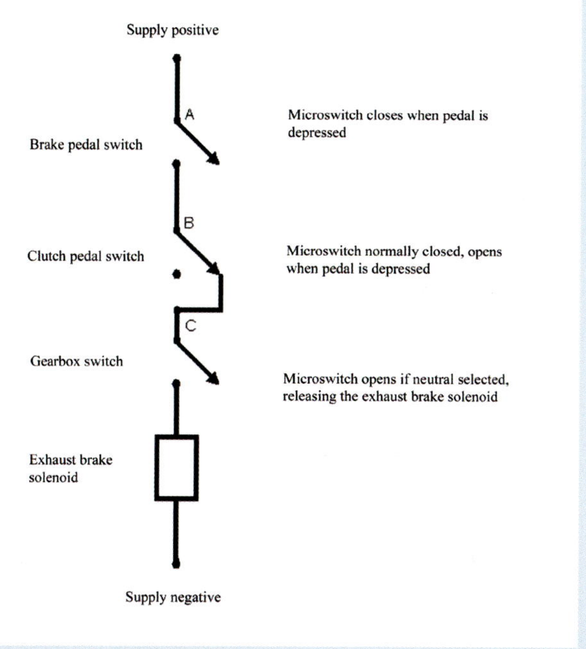

Generic circuit diagram for exhaust brake controls showing the various microswitches required for automatic operation.

Pressing the clutch pedal operates microswitch B, which opens and breaks the circuit to the solenoid. The solenoid is a spring-loaded device, which, when current is removed, moves back to its normal position, opening the butterfly valve and releasing the throttle so fuel is once again admitted to the engine. A further switch (C) on the gearbox ensures if neutral is selected, the exhaust brake is released. To engage the exhaust brake, the driver needs only to depress the brake pedal until the pedal switch operates, so the wheel brakes do not need to be fully applied.

Use of the exhaust brake has two major advantages. First, it reduces the need to use the normal wheel brakes, thus reducing wear on the brake drums and linings. Second, if the exhaust brake is used on, for example, a long downwards hill, the normal wheel brakes will not have suffered from 'brake fade' due to being heated over that distance, and so are still at maximum efficiency if required at some point during the descent.

Exhaust brakes tended to be very noisy in operation and of variable efficiency in some applications.

Bodies

The VAL was designed for coach bodies seating between forty-eight and fifty-three passengers, though higher capacities were achieved with bus bodies with more compact seats.

Although there was the option for goods use, in fact very few VAL chassis were used in this way. Approximately eight were built as pantechnicons and a further four as homing and racing pigeon transporters. The Road Transport Industry Training Board (RTITB) had one bodied by J. H. Sparshatt of Portsmouth as a van, and two were built as mobile TV units by L. V. Dove Ltd of Croydon for the National Coal Board. A further outside broadcast TV unit was built by Road Transport Services (Hackney) Ltd, in 1966. A flat-bed caravan transporter was built by Bedford dealer Chester Engineering Co. Ltd for Cheshire Caravan Transport Ltd of Winsford, Cheshire in 1965 – it was capable of carrying up to three 9ft–10ft (2.7m–3m) caravans, while the driver was accommodated in a comparatively luxurious cab.

Another interesting application was the 'Palletainer' delivery vehicle operated by Clarks Boxes Ltd of Mountsorrel, Loughborough, Leicestershire. It was specially designed for delivering 10,000 boxes in a single load, the boxes being on pallets with rapid loading and unloading.

CCU 277D. Barton's fleet no. 1124 is a 1966 VAL14 with the final version of the Duple Vega Major body, superseded by the Viceroy in 1967. P. BEST

The vehicle was a joint effort between the operator and local coachbuilders Crawford, Prince and Johnson Ltd of Syston, Leicestershire. The chassis was extended using folded channel-section steel members to give an overall length of 36ft (11m).

Duple and Plaxton

Returning to the VAL's primary role, the Duple body for the VAL14 was christened the Vega Major. The Plaxton body on show at Earls Court in 1962 was a version of its Embassy body that was also available on the SB and other manufacturers' lightweight coach chassis. This body featured Plaxton's recently patented variable seat anchorage, where the seat pedestals engaged with lipped rails to enable seat pitch to be altered quickly or seats to be removed easily.

Comparing the two initial bodies for the VAL, while opinion is subjective, the Duple Vega Major was to most eyes the more impressive and modern looking. Where the Plaxton body harked back to the 1950s, with its array of small side windows making it look somewhat cluttered, the Duple body looked forward to the new era of the 1960s, quite in keeping with the VAL's modernist pretensions. The Vega Major lasted until 1967–8 and the introduction of the VAL70 chassis; from then on the only Duple body available for the VAL was a specially designed version of the Viceroy body.

One common feature of the bodies on the VAL chassis that attracted favourable comment was the absence of intrusive wheel boxes over the front and rear wheels, another advantage of the smaller wheels used on this chassis.

At Duple's biennial Hendon showcase for 1963, the company presented a super-luxury version of the Vega Major with thirty-eight individual reclining seats. At the rear of the body were facing seats with tables set between them. There were no opening windows and ventilation was by a powered forced-air system.

A restyled service bus body was also on show. Features included overhead lighting by three 4ft (1.2m) fluorescent fittings with Formica interior trimmed side panels and pillars and stove-enamelled window frames. The bus body was offered at £2,920, making it possible to buy a fifty-four-seat service bus for less than £4,000.

A 36ft (11m) version of the new steel-framed Duple Viceroy body appeared at the 1966 Commercial Motor Show; this was Duple's intended replacement for the Vega Major, and the VAL body conformed to the standard for Viceroy, which included the Duple's latest type of seating and fluorescent lights. Seating capacity remained the same at fifty-two and the VAL body was later badged as the Viceroy 36. By the end of 1967, the total cost of a complete Viceroy 36/VAL coach was £6,369.

The Viceroy's update for 1968 was a new grille, previously seen on the Commander III body. The prominent sloping pillar of the Viceroy acquired a curve to it and was trimmed with a stainless steel capping. Solid-based parcel racks and the option of Jet-Vent ventilation in trunking or top-sliding ventilators, fluorescent lighting and opening roof lights were all included in the latest specification. Two luggage lockers were provided, a side locker of 35cu ft (991ltr) and a rear locker of 132cu ft (3,738ltr). The length of the Viceroy was increased slightly to 37ft 3.875in (11.38m) as a result of changes in the legislation limiting maximum vehicle dimensions; the new body was thus referred to as the Viceroy 37.

The 1965 Plaxton Panorama, announced at the 1964 Commercial Motor Show, was visually a great improvement over the Embassy, with only three long panoramic side windows and two smaller windows towards the rear. For the VAL, the Panorama retained the front grille from the Embassy body to accommodate the radiator necessary with the VAL's front-mounted engine. The Embassy body for the VAL remained available alongside the Panorama and was updated to become the Embassy IV. Both the Panorama and the Embassy IV were fitted with a new type of inward-opening entrance door.

For 1968, Plaxton's Panorama body for the VAL acquired the suffix 'Elite', and a forty-nine-seat version for Wallace-Arnold was displayed at the Commercial Motor Show. On the Panorama Elite the windows were deeper and curved in section. This, together with new side mouldings, gave the body a different and fresh look. The new body was 37ft 1.25in (11.31m), slightly shorter than the rival Duple Viceroy 37, the extra 70mm allowing slightly wider entrance and emergency doors to be fitted.

Harrington and MCW

By 1963 other coachbuilders were offering bodies for the VAL. A show staged by Arlington at London Transport's Potters Bar garage included the debut of the new Harrington Legionnaire fifty-two-seat coach and an example of a fifty-four-seat service bus from Willowbrook.

The Legionnaire was quite striking in appearance, built of light alloy and steel and with the usual fifty-two seats. Top-sliding windows and Smiths Jet-Vent forced-air ventilation and combined heating and demisting system were all part of the specification, which included two 40cu ft (1,133ltr) side lockers and a 72cu ft (2,039cu m) rear locker for £3,800, chassis extra.

MCW had developed a 36ft (11m) body for the VAL in 1962. Called the Topaz, a MkII version appeared for 1964 with seating for between forty-nine and fifty-two passengers. The body was steel framed with some light alloy sections, including side panels. Ventilation was by top-sliding windows and three two-way lift-up roof ventilators. An inward-opening entrance door was provided with optional manual control by the driver. The Topaz had a total luggage-locker capacity of 130cu ft (3,681ltr) in a coach of overall unladen weight 5 tons 15cwt (5,271kg). Intended to be built at Weymann's works in Addlestone, Surrey, a prolonged strike at MCW meant that the coach did not go into

The Duple group's bus body for the VAL is exemplified here by this fifty-four-seat Willowbrook body on a 1964 VAL14 chassis for Seaview Services Ltd of Ryde, Isle of Wight, seen here in 1968.

This VAL70 with fifty-three-seat Plaxton Panorama Elite II body was bought new by Naylor's Tours & Travel of Stockton Heath, Cheshire, in June 1972. Naylor's was run by husband-and-wife team Jack and Edna Naylor; their son George was a musician and appeared at The Cavern Club in Liverpool, where The Beatles also played in the early 1960s.

The Legionnaire body by Thomas Harrington of Hove was quite rare – only forty-three are recorded and all were built in 1964–5. This example on a VAL14 chassis was new to Yelloways Tours, Rochdale in May 1965 and was one of two purchased by the company. The Harrington Legionnaire/VAL combination is most famous for its appearance in the 1969 film _The Italian Job._

production for the 1964 season, which perhaps was something of an omen as very few were built. Two were ordered by Arlington for mounting on VAL chassis and these may in fact have been the only ones constructed. The Topaz was priced at £3,610 for the forty-nine-seat model and £3,650 for the fifty-two-seat model.

Strachans and Marshall

Ten Strachans fifty-two-seat bus bodies of a distinctive body style were purchased by North Western Road Car Co.

In 1964 Strachans built ten fifty-two-seat bodies for the North Western Road Car Co. Ltd with specially shaped roofs to allow them to pass under a canal aqueduct at Dunham Massey in Cheshire, on the route between Altrincham and Warrington. This example was somewhat off-route to the south when photographed at Lower Peover.

Ltd, in autumn 1964. The bodies had a special roof profile to enable the buses to pass under the Dunham Aqueduct on the Bridgwater Canal. Clearance under the bridge was only 10ft (3m), so the low build of the VAL chassis was advantageous. The roof of the Strachans body was designed in an unbroken arc from side to side and the overall maximum unladen height of the vehicles was 9ft 6in (2.9m). They replaced some elderly thirty-five-seat Bristol L-types that had themselves been modified to give a lower roof profile.

Strachans was also responsible for six fifty-three-seat buses for Curacao, South America, built on left-hand-drive VAL chassis in 1964. They were based on Strachans' 'Everest 63' Zintec-steel body frame designed for either buses or coaches. The buses were trimmed in a fairly utilitarian style with fibreglass seats in tubular steel frames, and wide gangways with a full-length handrail were provided to accommodate a large number of standing passengers. The exterior was slightly more luxuriously finished with chrome-plated bumpers, radiator grille and wheel embellishers. Side windows had top-sliding ventilators, and interior lighting was by recessed ceiling fittings.

During 1965, Marshall built ten airport buses on VAL chassis for BEA, one of the forerunners of British Airways (BA). These had forty inward-facing seats and room for a large number of standing passengers. Twin sliding entrance and exit doors were fitted both sides of the body in the centre of wheelbase to expedite rapid loading and unloading. A few more were built in 1966 and 1967 for other air-side operators and at least one is thought to survive in preservation.

Belgian Bodies for the VAL

International interest in the VAL was maintained by an example with a body built by Belgian coachbuilder Jonckheere, shown on the General Motors stand at the 44th Salon de l'Automobile, Brussels, in 1965. The body was quite distinctive to British eyes, with a flat roof line and deep side windows, though Jonckheere would not make significant inroads into the UK market until the 1980s and rarely on Bedford chassis.

Another Belgian coachbuilder with its eye on the UK market was Van Hool NV of Koningshooikt, near Lier. In cooperation with Alf Moseley, a prototype fifty-three-seat coach designed especially for the UK market was built on a VAL70 chassis in late 1968 and appeared early in 1969. The Van Hool body was of all-steel construction and followed the general outline of the coachbuilder's contemporary product line, though with an inward-opening entrance door and increased headroom as a result of the VAL's low chassis frame — the body was originally designed with a raised roof so a high floor could be fitted with luggage capacity beneath — and larger than usual side windows as a consequence of the lower floor line. One of the first production VAL/Van Hool coaches was a forty-nine-seat model, Van Hool's designation 3711, purchased by All Seasons Travel, London W2, which entered service on 23 August 1970.

Whether by accident or design, Duple and Plaxton built bodies for an almost equal number of chassis — approximately 825 each — and these were by far the majority. Small runs of bodies for the VAL were built by other coachbuilders. Harrington built forty-two coaches on VAL14 chassis in the period 1964–5, while Willowbrook built around thirty bodies, mostly buses with capacities ranging from fifty-three to fifty-six seats, though there was a run of thirteen dual-purpose fifty-four-seat bodies for the famous Blue Bus (Tailby & George) of Willington, Derbyshire.

The first Willowbrook bodies were built on the VAL in 1963 and the last in 1971. Salvador Caetano built twenty Estoril coach bodies over the period 1969–71, almost all with fifty-three seats. Marshall also built around twenty more bodies of the dual-entrance, forty-eight-seat bus type for BEA, who used them as airport buses, and one single-door, fifty-two-seat bus for Geddes of Brixham. Other notable coach-builders who built bodies on the VAL included Yeates in 1963–4, who built around eleven, including four dual-entrance fifty-seat coaches and three dual-entrance fifty-six-seat dual-purpose buses based on the Europa bodyshell for Barton Transport, of Chilwell, Notting-hamshire. The choice of Yeates for Barton is logical given the proximity of the two companies, the layout of the bodies less so!

Sales and Production

Production of the VAL spanned 1963 to 1973 and, from the published figures, appears to have reached approximately 2,000 chassis. Just over 1,200 VAL14 chassis were pro-duced by the time VAL70 was intro-duced to replace it in 1968. A fur-ther 700-plus VAL70s were built by the end of production in 1972. Pro-duction of the VAL14 ended in early 1968 with the final three chassis, but had averaged a healthy 225 annually over the period 1963–7. The VAL70 came on stream in early 1968 and averaged 150 per year until 1972, when production started to wind down in favour of the YRT, with only sixty-eight in 1972 and sixteen final chassis in 1973. A total of 1,945 are accounted for in the published records, so this can be assumed to be the minimum that Bedford pro-duced; based on the coachbuilders' records, somewhere between 110 and 150 were exported, many to

Australia and New Zealand.

The first eight chassis were bodied by Duple and based on the body numbers, the first completed was 592 PUR, for

This 1970 VAL70 has a forty-nine-seat Van Hool Vistadome body. It was new to All Seasons Travel of London W2. Very few VALs are recorded as having Van Hool bodies. H. ROSE

Another example of Barton's penchant for the unusual is demonstrated by its fleet no. 968, a 1963 VAL14 with Yeates dual-entrance body. Dual-purpose seating for fifty-six passengers was provided, despite the additional door. It was seen at Kidderminster in October 1990 after being restored to Barton livery. Before entering preservation it served with Mellor's Coaches of Goxhill, Lincolnshire, then later with H. A. Scutt & Son of Owston Ferry in the same county.

Premier of Watford; however, the first delivered was most likely to have been 7999 MD, chassis no. 1009 (numbers in this series started from 1001), delivered to World Wide Coaches Ltd of Coldharbour Lane, London SE5 in March 1963. Other operators who were quick to try the exciting new tri-axle chassis from Bedford included Creamline Motor Services Ltd of Bordon, Hampshire (three), Central Motors Ltd of Burnley, Lancashire (two), W. Robinson and Sons Ltd of Great Harwood, Lancashire (two) and Seamarks Bros Ltd of Westoning, Bedfordshire (one) – all ordered by December 1962.

Early purchasers of new VALs in quantity included Barton Transport (nineteen in 1963–4), BEA based at Northolt (thirty, 1963–7), Don Everall Travel Ltd of Wolverhampton (nineteen, 1963–5) and Wallace Arnold of Leeds (twenty-nine, 1963–5). Other operators who found the VAL to their liking and regularly bought new examples over a period of years included Bostock of Congleton, Edinburgh Corporation Transport, Jackson of Altrincham (seventeen owned in total, nine purchased in 1965–6),

Rendell of Parkstone (eighteen owned in total, ten purchased in 1969–70), Shearings of Altrincham (eighteen bought 1965–9) and Whittle of Highley (seventeen in total, nine in 1967–9). Other well-known operators who bought VALs new in more than penny numbers included Baddeley of Holmfirth, Banfields Luxury Coaches, London SE15, Bullock of Cheadle, Smith of Wigan, Manchester City Transport, Mann of Smethwick, Southern Vectis Omnibus Co. Ltd, Stockland of Brimingham, Tatlock of Whitefield, West Riding Automobile Co. Ltd, Wilts & Dorset Motor Services Ltd and Yelloways Tours of Rochdale; Yelloways replaced its VALs after around three years' service, so although they bought ten between 1963 and 1968 there were generally only around five in service together at any time, a situation probably typical of many larger operators.

The six bought by Manchester City Transport had Plaxton Panorama bodies, with a maximum seating capacity of fifty-two, though five seats could be removed to create additional luggage space. The coaches were used on the

A VAL70 with Caetano Estoril fifty-three-seat body, used as a demonstrator by the Alf Moseley Group. ALF MOSELEY GROUP

Duple's replacement for the Vega Major body on the VAL was the Viceroy, seen here on a VAL70 chassis. The fifty-three-seat coach was new to Edinburgh Corporation Transport in 1970 but is seen here in the livery of Aries Coaches.

thirty-minute journey linking Manchester Airport with the city centre. They were supplied by Shaw and Kilburn Ltd and cost in total £34,837. In 1965 a new VAL chassis had cost just £1,890.

Another Manchester-based venture for the VAL took place in 1970. City centre congestion was not a new phenomenon even forty-five years ago, but SELNEC PTE's effort to convert Manchester businessmen more used to chauffeur-driven limousines into coach-trip commuters seems hardly likely to have offered much of a respite for frustrated motorists. It was, however, an interesting use for a fifty-two-seat VAL with Plaxton Panorama Elite body. Operating on what was referred to as an 'Executive Express' commuter coach service along a route that lay between the millionaire stockbroker belt of Cheshire and Manchester city centre, the service ran Mondays to Fridays from Hale Barns to Deansgate, inward journeys starting at 8.05am and returning at 5.15pm with seven pick-up and set-down points along the way. In addition to the usual Panorama Elite refinements, a two-way radio enabled coach-riding executives to make phone calls to their offices en route, and there was piped radio to individual speakers to ensure that Jack DeManio on the Today programme could relay the business news in the morning and light music from Radio 2 in the evening for stress relief on the journey mansionwards. There are no records of the success, or otherwise, of the venture.

A Notable First for the VAL

A VAL was the first 36ft (11m) coach to operate on the Isle of Man, arriving on the island in the last week of May 1969. A fifty-two-seat Plaxton Panorama Elite body was fitted and the coach was refurbished and supplied by Kirkby and Sons (Sales) Ltd of South Anston, Sheffield. A special reception was given to mark the occasion and the coach was received by Mr M. Marshall, managing director of W. H. Shimmin (Tours) Ltd, who was to operate the coach on the island.

On the Road

When the VAL was introduced, the industry had very little experience of vehicles of the new maximum dimensions of 36ft (11m) long by 8ft 2.5in (2.5m) wide; however, drivers soon found that despite its size and layout, the VAL coach was no more difficult to drive than a typical 30ft by 8ft (9m by 2.44m) vehicle. Some drivers found the gear-ratio gap between third and fourth too large, to the detriment of acceleration. This gap tended also to be a disadvantage when negotiating fairly sharp bends on gradients. The direct-drive acceleration between 10 and 40mph (16 and 64km/h) was satisfactory, but some commentators found that between 9 and 14mph (14.5 and 23km/h) the coach tended to surge a little, indicating that the 5.3:1 axle ratio was a bit high for fourth gear below about 20mph (32km/h). Normal touring fuel consumption could be expected to be around 15mpg (18.9ltr/100km) with the standard 5.3:1 axle.

Vauxhall engineers had found the tyre pressures could be fairly critical in maintaining the correct loading on the twin-steering axles; 80psi (5.52bar) in the leading tyres and 50psi (3.45bar) in the tyres on the second axle were recommended, and some operators found directional stability was improved by exchanging the factory-fitted steel-belted radial tyres for textile radials. Surprisingly, some claimed that the textile radials wore better than the steel ones, too.

Alan Townsin rode in and drove the prototype VAL in 1962 and, while this was not a particularly exhaustive test, he noted that with around thirty passengers on board the coach was capable of cruising at 70mph (113km/h) on the M1 motorway, with occasional maximum bursts of around 75mph (121km/h) on downhill stretches. A favourite spot for Vauxhall and Bedford road tests was Bison Hill, 0.75 miles (1.2km) long with an average gradient of 1:10.5 (9.5 per cent) and a steepest gradient of 1 in 6.5 (15 per cent). Situated on the B4540 approaching Whipsnade Zoo in Bedfordshire, the hill was climbed confidently with a minimum speed of 11mph (18km/h).

Townsin felt that the ride quality at both the front and rear of the coach was good and closely approached what might be expected from more expensive coaches with more complex suspension, though his opinion regarding the ride at the rear was not universally endorsed by other passengers.

While driving, he found that the noise from the Leyland engine was intrusive though vibration-free when on the move, some vibration being evident while the engine was ticking over. The steering was light and responsive and the gearchange positive with good synchromesh. He noted that the brakes were progressive, though the pedal travel seemed excessive; a portent of trouble to come, perhaps.

A later production VAL14 with a few years' service and a reasonable mileage under its belt was thoroughly tested in March 1967 as part of a used coach survey Townsin conducted for *Bus & Coach* magazine. This particular coach was first registered in October 1963, and carried the Duple Vega Major body introduced at the Commercial Motor Show in September 1963 for the 1964 season. The coach tested, DME 976A, was provided by dealer Shaw & Kilburn and had had two owners from the new, last of these being Priory Coaches of Gosport, Hampshire. For the test the vehicle was in the condition in which it had arrived from the Gosport operator and had received no attention from the dealer. The recorded mileage was approximately 120,000 (190,000km), though some doubt was cast on the accuracy of this and it was suggested that the

mileage might have been nearer 80,000 (130,000km), without further explanation of how this discrepancy might have occurred. Apart from noting that the exterior paintwork could have done with a little polish, Townsin reported that the body was in good condition, though the seat moquette was slightly faded where heavily exposed to light through the roof quarter panels. The Formica that Duple used to trim the flat surfaces of the interior showed little sign of deterioration, as did the linoleum floor covering. The usual minor dings and dents were present that a three-year-old public service vehicle would have been expected to pick up.

On the road, interior noise from the Leyland O.400 engine was found to be less than expected, compared with most VAL coaches; noise meter readings taken at the centre of the coach indicated 77dB under acceleration with figures of 75–76dB when cruising at 45mph (72km/h) and 63dB at idle. Front-seat noise was appreciably higher, typically by 5db. Townsin commented that the actual mechanical sound quality of the O.400 engine made it seem noisier.

The engine itself seemed in fine fettle, with no difficulty in whipping the coach up to 60mph (97km/h) in a reasonable distance. The O.400 engine was noted for its tendency to consume oil, but this trait was not visually apparent during the test and an examination of the engine revealed little sign of oil leaks. The engine seemed to respond well to being revved, though there was sufficient torque available to accelerate away from 30mph (48km/h) in fifth gear.

Braking was described as 'fully adequate', despite predating the larger drums introduced in autumn 1965, and free from the vices of snatch and judder. The complex parking brake was found to be equally adequate and there were no problems in parking on a slope, though the tester commented on the difficulty of obtaining access to the driver's seat, which required negotiation of the various levers!

The power-assisted steering came in for praise, being described as precise, reasonably self-centring and with only a light touch needed making the VAL generally enjoyable to drive.

The Turner five-speed gearbox had developed a little slop in the gearchange though the gearbox seemed to work well, with effective synchromesh and smooth clutch action.

Townsin's strongest praise, however, was reserved for the ride quality, and he suggested that no contemporary vehicle could improve on it, repeating his views from the earlier test – this was all the more impressive given that the chassis used rigid axles and leaf springs. On offer at £4,250, the coach had much to commend it.

By the end of the 1960s, however, operators were beginning to find the VAL a little tired. There were reports in the industry press that operators were seeking for a replacement for the Bedford 466cu in engine as they were finding the VAL underpowered for its size compared with more modern designs.

Other road testers found various items to criticize, though often these could be laid at the feet of the coachbuilder rather than Bedford. For example, a common complaint was poor insulation of the engine compartment causing noise and fumes to find their way into the passenger space; screen washing and wiping equipment was found to be poor and the electrical switches poorly identified and located. On the other hand, those factors that were the responsibility of the chassis manufacturer were generally reported upon favourably. The VAL70, with the 466cu in Bedford diesel, was more lively than the Leyland-powered VAL14; less effort was needed to get the coach underway and top-gear performance was much improved. Maximum speed of the VAL70 with the standard axle ratio was 72mph (116km/h) compared with 58mph (93km/h), and its cruising ability at 60–65mph (96–105km/h), little affected by motorway gradients, made the VAL70 more suited for long-distance services. Some testers, however, found the transmission handbrake heavy to operate and the steering too light on the road, though perfect for manoeuvres in tight spaces, and the 466cu in engine a little thirstier, with an average fuel consumption of 15.9mpg (17.8ltr/100km). On the whole, though, the difference from the Leyland O.400 was really quite small.

Generally the VAL was considered very pleasant to handle, though some drivers found the steering a little vague until they got used to it, although the weak castor action sometimes proved troublesome in tight corners. Even so, the general consensus was that a VAL was at least as easy to handle as a vehicle half its size, though care needed to be taken in cross-winds, which could often make the coach yaw slightly without warning. The same tendency could be detected when overtaking large vehicles or emerging from the shelter of trees or embankments.

The reports of problems with brakes continued, despite Bedford increasing the size of the friction area of the brakes, and many VALs came to be fitted with Telma electro-magnetic retarders; indeed, some operators thought that a retarder was an essential fitment, though others found the cost prohibitive at typically £350 – and they were not approved by Vauxhall due to the additional load placed on the thrust bearings in the differential.

For the VAL14, Bedford offered an exhaust brake kit, though this device was only really effective when the engine was turning at quite high rpm and produced little or no braking assistance when travelling slowly in high gear. An alternative exhaust-brake kit was available from Smiths Industries, but no record of comparative performance has been found. Despite the adverse comments from operators, Vauxhall and Bedford service staff found that the most of the problems associated with VAL brakes were caused by poor maintenance and incorrect adjustment. In particular,

DV 1513. This VAL with MMB body was one of three new to Days Motors of Christchurch, New Zealand. Despite the size of the vehicle it seated only forty-three.
M. FOSTER

centralizing the brake linings was considered essential for long service between adjustments. Some operators found that textile radial tyres suited the VAL better than steel-braced radials, giving more even wear and greater directional stability.

There seem to have been few other recurrent issues with the VAL. Some operators found that kingpins wore more quickly than on other contemporary chassis, though generally they seem to have been very happy with their VAL-based coaches and buses. An operator could expect a VAL to return an average fuel consumption of around 16mpg (17.7ltr/100km) typically, which compared well with heavyweight rivals, such as the AEC Reliance at around 12.8mpg (22.1ltr/100km).

Afterlife and Fame

GM was proud of the innovative VAL, and rightly so; Vauxhall took a VAL/Duple Vega Major to New York to exhibit on the General Motors stand at the 1964–5 World Trade Fair. This particular coach, finished in a special two-tone gold/bronze livery, returned to be registered as EDL 783C with Moss Motor Tours, of Sandown, Isle of Wight, where it was named the 'New Yorker'.

The VAL was quite a popular vehicle for conversions, once its passenger-carrying service life was over. Apart from the usual crop of mobile homes, other second-use examples include racing car transporters and roadside rescue car-recovery trucks, the latter examples requiring significant and often quite ambitious re-engineering.

The VAL's first film appearance was in The Beatles' *Magical Mystery Tour* in 1966. The association with The Beatles' home city of Liverpool was maintained by tours operated by this VAL70/Plaxton Panorama fifty-two-seat coach decorated to look like the VAL used in the film. It was new to Gales Coaches of Haslemere, Surrey, in 1969, though it had migrated to Liverpool by the time this photograph was taken in July 1972.

RETARDERS – HOW THEY WORK

A retarder is an additional system for reducing the speed of the vehicle. It is a secondary system as it is powered solely by the electrical system of the vehicle to which it is fitted, and without electrical power it will have no effect. This is in contrast to the vehicle's primary braking system, which is mechanical, and while it may be assisted by additional force from air or vacuum actuators, the brake is always mechanically connected to the driver's foot brake pedal.

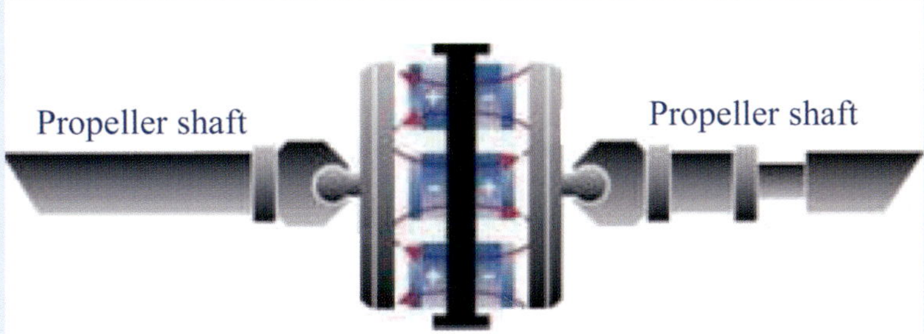

Simplified diagram showing the functional parts of an electric retarder. TELMA

A retarder consists of two parts – a stator and a rotor. The stator is fixed to the chassis and surrounds the propeller shaft. It carries a number of transformer-like coil windings of copper wire, rather like the field windings of a dynamo. The rotor shaft is supported in taper-roller bearings inside the stator and is fixed to the propeller shaft, which is mechanically fixed to the rotor, the rotor itself consisting of two electrically conductive discs either side of the stator. Eddy currents (also known as Foucault currents) are induced in the rotor discs when the stator coils are energized; by Lenz's law, eddy currents create a magnetic field that tends to oppose the magnetic field that is inducing the eddy current – that is, the magnetic field created by the stator coils. The net result is a magnetic force that opposes the direction of rotation of the rotor shaft (and hence vehicle propeller shaft) to provide retardation of the motion.

Control of the retarder is generally by a lever operated by the driver. This provides several positions, or 'notches', which energize different number of coils in the stator assembly, so the driver can control the amount of braking effort provided by the retarder. A typical retarder may have a three-position control that energizes eight, twelve or sixteen coils in the stator.

Some care in the use of the retarder by the driver was required due to the heavy current drain on the electrical system of coaches so fitted. Tests showed that descending steep hills in bad weather with lights, wipers and demisters all in action while the retarder was in constant use in the highest position (all coils energized) could drain the batteries sufficiently to prevent the vehicle from being restarted if stalled. Because of this, fitting a retarder to an older vehicle generally meant replacing the dynamo with an alternator (if the bus was not equipped with one already), the latter being capable of supplying almost full output at low engine revolutions and a typically higher current output than a similarly sized dynamo, thus eliminating the problem.

Retarders were an advance over exhaust brakes as their efficiency was independent of engine revolutions, the exhaust brake generally only being effective when the engine was turning over rapidly. A retarder not only increased the braking capacity of a vehicle but could, with careful use, considerably extend the life of the brake linings. The most common retarder in use with Bedford coaches was the Telma, but an alternative version from Klam was available from 1965, sold by Eesubrake Ltd, of Ashford, Middlesex. Available in several sizes to suit different GVW ratings, the Klam 3 and Klam 4 retarders were a popular fitment for the Bedford VAL14 and VAL70, respectively.

Telma retarder. TELMA

One 1964 VAL found further use in preservation as a mobile model railway exhibition, where the owner was able to combine his passion for vintage vehicles with another of his interests. The model railway layout had hundreds of feet of track, ran on two levels and was capable of running fifteen different trains simultaneously. The coach was a regular visitor at various rallies and events with the admission charge going to charity; it was also a big hit at Bedford's golden jubilee celebration at Luton in October 1981.

The VAL was truly a 1960s icon; it appeared in two major feature films: first in the 1966 film *Magical Mystery Tour*, which was directed by and starred The Beatles, and then in Peter Collinson's 1969 film *The Italian Job*, starring Michael Caine, Noel Coward and Benny Hill.

The vehicular star of *Magical Mystery Tour* was 1967 VAL/Plaxton Panorama URO 913E, hired from Fox Coaches Ltd of Hayes, Middlesex. The most memorable scene had The Beatles drummer Ringo Starr hurling the coach into a bend at high speed on a motor racing circuit while racing against an equally iconic collection of British sports cars – if Bedford had needed an advert for the road-holding of their legendary six-wheeler, they could have done no better. The coach featured throughout the film as The Beatles took a party of trippers on a mystery tour through the English countryside. While very much of its time, the quality of the film fell somewhat short of what the world had become used to in The Beatles' musical output. The coach was saved for preservation at The Beatles Exhibition Centre in Liverpool in 1984 and restored by Imperial Coachbuilders Ltd of Liverpool. It was subsequently used on tours of places in Liverpool associated with The Beatles. Its current location is believed to be the Hard Rock Cafe in Orlando, Florida, USA, though several replicas currently exist around the world.

The Italian Job was an altogether more creditable effort and featured a 1964 VAL14 with striking Harrington Legionnaire bodywork, ALR 453B. The story revolves around a criminal plot to steal a gold shipment in Turin by creating havoc by infiltrating the city's computerized traffic light control system. This enabled the perpetrators to escape in a fleet of Austin Mini Cooper cars, taking advantage of their small size to negotiate alleyways, sewers and other routes out of the city not blocked by the traffic jam. The film is notable for its very early depiction of criminal computer hacking and the high-speed car chase sequences, one of which included driving the Minis up a ramp into the rear of the VAL, a pair of rear doors having been fitted specially to facilitate this. Later in the film the Minis are unceremoniously dumped out of the rear of the coach over a cliff to dispose of them. After its brief career as a film star, ALR 453B returned to normal duties more befitting a luxury coach; in the 1970s it allegedly found use as a school bus with a coach company in Angus, Scotland and is believed to have been broken up for scrap in 1990.

Of those exported, many later underwent significant modifications to engines and transmissions to enable them to continue to work in local conditions; for example some could be found in Australia fitted with Japanese Hino engines.

The Beatles connection continued to keep the VAL in the public eye, in Liverpool at least; Liverpool's Cavern City Tours claimed it was carrying 50,000 passengers per year on its daily Magical Mystery Tours, which used a pair of VAL/Plaxton Panorama coaches. The coaches dated from 1965 and 1966 and were painted appropriately. The connection continues today in Germany; Simon Mitchell, who starred in the film as a child, has recently imported into Hannover a VAL70/Plaxton Panorama to add to a museum collection of Magical Mystery Tour artefacts and memorabilia in the town of Hameln. The coach was transported by ferry from Rosyth, Scotland to Zeebrugge in Belgium and then travelled under its own power to Hameln.

THE BEDFORD VAM

To some extent, Bedford, having the luxury of over 50 per cent of the lightweight bus and coach market, had been able to successfully plough their own furrow and create, rather than follow, trends in the industry. However, the Yeates front-entrance conversions on the SB chassis had awoken Vauxhall's engineers to the fact that there were alternative and better arrangements of wheel/entrance/engine that were more suited to some operators' needs than those provided by the SB and the VAS. The VAL was the first Bedford built for a front entrance ahead of the wheels, but this was really to address an opening in the market for a lightweight, 36ft (11m) coach rather than an indication of a general approach. The VAL therefore was an engineering solution that utilized mostly standard Bedford parts and construction methods to build a maximum-dimension vehicle. The industry in general had long since moved to under-floor, mid-mounted engines for heavyweight chassis and by the time the VAL appeared, chassis with the engines at the rear were starting to appear. Bedford had also been left behind in the forty- to forty-five-seat market and that gap needed to be filled; at the same time, Bedford needed to realign itself with current trends. Into this climate, the VAM was born.

Designed for bodies of around 32ft (9.75m) in length and 8ft 2.5in (2.5m) in width, the VAM provided a base for a coach or bus of around forty-five seats. The chassis frame was a typical Bedford ladder modified to provide for a low-step entrance ahead of the front wheels, as on the VAL and many other contemporary bus and coach chassis. The wheelbase was 16ft 1in (4.9m), with a front overhang of 6ft 8in (2.03m) to allow for a reasonably wide entrance door.

Pressed-steel channel frame side members were employed, the left-hand member being swept inwards and down at the front to allow for the entrance steps and the driving position. At the rear the bottom edge tapered upwards from the forward mounting of the rear springs to the rear end of the chassis, though the top surface was flat along its full length. The straight ladder frame had six cross-members and the top of the frame was level from the cross-member situated just aft of the engine to the rear of the chassis. The frames themselves were 10in (254mm) deep along the parallel length and the material was 0.22in (5.59mm) thick with 3in (76mm) flanges top and bottom. The engine was mounted vertically, forward of the front axle and low in the frame to provide a low entrance step. A removable front cross-member was provided to facilitate installation and removal of the engine when necessary.

It is curious that Bedford did not at this time take the opportunity to design the VAM with a mid-mounted horizontal engine as was common in the rest of the industry; perhaps, having redesigned the traditional Bedford chassis to accommodate a true front entrance, a new engine position was considered one step too far. The prototype VAM chassis had a kink in the frame so that the rear section was wider from just behind the front axle, so perhaps Bedford had been contemplating alternative engines and positions. The production VAM chassis frame was reasonably low even with a vertical engine, though still 3in (76mm) higher unladen than the SB at 39in (991mm), and 10in (254mm) higher than the VAL from the ground to the top of the frame at its highest.

Three engine options were initially offered, comprising the Bedford 300cu in 133bhp petrol engine, the 330cu in 107bhp diesel and the Leyland O.400 400cu in/131bhp diesel.

With the Bedford engines, the VAM was fitted with a four-speed wide-ratio gearbox with synchromesh on second, third and top gears. With the Leyland engine and later diesel options, a Turner five-speed, overdrive-top synchromesh gearbox was fitted with a larger 15in-diameter clutch. There was also a five-speed Bedford gearbox option only for the VAM3, which was described in some places as a direct-top synchromesh gearbox, although the quoted ratios in Bedford's literature suggested it was an overdrive-top gearbox. A single-speed rear axle was fitted with two ratio options of 5.83:1 or 6.83:1; a two-speed axle was offered as a further option with initially 5.3:1 and 5.8:1 ratios, later 4.86:1 and 6.83:1 ratios. Single dry-plate clutches with 12in, 13in and 15in diameters were fitted, the VAM3 having the smallest unit, the VAM5 and VAM14 the 13in unit and the VAM70 and 75 the largest.

The transmission consisted of a three-section propeller shaft, the rear ends of both the front and centre sections being carried in ball-bearing supports attached to the chassis cross-members. Universal joints were Hardy Spicer needle-roller universal joints.

The rear axle was fully floating with hypoid-bevel gear final drive in line with contemporary Bedford practice, and taper-roller rear hub bearings were fitted. Three axle ratios were offered, 5.3:1, 5.83:1 or 6.83:1; a two-speed rear axle was also offered, with high/low ratios of 4.86:1 and 6.63:1. An alternative two-speed axle was offered for the VAM3 chassis with high/low ratios of 5.83:1 and 7.95:1. With the 5.83:1 ratio, the claimed maximum gradient that could be climbed was 1 in 3.5.

Maintenance requirements were reduced by use of sealed-for-life steering joints and propeller shaft universal joints.

The front axle was of I-beam section, again similar to previous Bedford models. Steering swivels (knuckles in Bedford literature) were mounted on pivot pins secured in bosses in the axle beam by tapered cotter pins with a nut and lock washer, a thrust washer being interposed between each jaw of the steering swivel and the boss in the axle beam. The front hubs were mounted to the stub axles by two large adjustable taper roller bearings on each side. Steering was by Burman recirculating-ball steering box with pre-packed sealed-for-life steering joints.

Suspension was by semi-elliptic leaf springs all round, with telescopic, double-acting shock absorbers front and rear.

The brakes were power-assisted hydraulic, by vacuum servo on chassis with petrol engines and by an air-pressure servo on chassis with diesel engines. On the VAM75 they were a full air system. On the early chassis the brake servo was mounted just forward of the central point in the wheelbase and attached to the right-hand side member. The hydraulic system consisted of a tandem master cylinder with separate hydraulic circuits to the front and rear wheel cylinders. Front and rear brake drums were 15.25in in diameter with 4.25in front linings and 6in rear linings, giving a total brake-lining area of 600sq in, with 248sq in at the front and 352sq in at the rear. A conventional ratchet-lever handbrake

BEDFORD VAM

Layout and Chassis
Coach or service bus, 41–45 seats, with front entrance ahead of the front wheels; typically 32ft (10m) long by 8ft 2.5in (2.5m) wide. Frame: deep pressed-steel channel side members with six cross-members

Engine
Type: VAM3:Bedford 300cu in 6-cylinder petrol
VAM5: Bedford 330cu in 6-cylinder diesel
VAM14: Leyland O.400 6-cylinder diesel
VAM70 (from 1967): Bedford 466cu in diesel
VAM75 (from 1975, export only): Bedford 8.2/140D 500cu in diesel
Fuel capacity: 45gal (205ltr)

Gearbox and Transmission
Gearbox: Bedford 4-speed or 5-speed (petrol engines); Turner 5-speed synchromesh with overdrive fifth (diesel engines); Spicer 5-speed (VAM75)
Ratios
Bedford 4-speed
  1st: 7.059:1
  2nd: 3.332:1
  3rd: 1.711:1
  Top: 1.00:1
  Reverse: 7.059:1
Bedford 5-speed
  1st: 6.06:1
  2nd: 3.00:1
  3rd: 1.70:1
  4th: 1.00:1
  Top : 0.80:1
  Reverse: 6.00:1
Turner 5-speed overdrive
  1st: 6.06:1
  2nd: 3.50:1
  3rd: 1.80:1
  4th: 1.00:1
  Top: 0.80:1
  Reverse: 6.00:1
Spicer 5-speed (VAM75 only)
  1st: 6.06:1
  2nd: 3.00:1
  3rd: 1.70:1
  4th: 1.0:1
  Top: 0.80:1
  Reverse: 6.00:1
Clutch: single dry plate; diameter 12in (VAM3); 13in (VAM5, VAM14); or 15in (VAM70, VAM75)
Transmission: Three-piece propeller shaft with four sealed needle-roller bearing universal joints
Rear axle: Ratios, single speed: 5.3:1, 5.83:1 or 6.83:1; two-speed, early models: high ratio 4.86:1, low 6.63:1; VAM3 only 5.83:1 and 7.95:1
Front axle: Drop-forged I-beam section, taper-roller hub bearings

Suspension and Steering
Suspension: Semi-elliptic leaf springs front and rear with four double-acting telescopic shock absorbers
Steering: Recirculating ball
Tyres: 8.25 × 20in (early models); 9.00 × 20in (later standard and all export models)

Brakes
Type: Air-assisted hydraulic; VAM75 full air
Size: 15.25in diameter drums front and rear

Dimensions
Wheelbase: 16ft 1in (4,902mm)
Track
  Front: 78.5in (1,994mm)
  Rear: 72.62in (1,846mm)

Electrical system
12v negative earth, 2 × 129Ah 6v batteries connected in series (petrol engines); 24v negative earth, 4 × 129Ah 6v batteries connected in series (diesels)

---

was mounted on the driver's right and operated on the rear brake shoes.

The four 6v batteries were mounted in a tray between the chassis side members and just aft of the centreline of the wheelbase. A rectangular 45gal (205ltr) fuel tank was mounted roughly centrally between the front and rear axles and outrigged from the left-hand chassis side member.

With the VAM, Bedford returned to 20in wheels, which at that time were much more common in PSVs than the 16in wheels of the VAS and VAL.

Production began in August 1965, a prototype having been completed in June of that year, and finished in 1983, although from 1971 the VAM was available for export only. Available records account for 2,856 chassis but the records are very incomplete, so the final production figure is likely to have been much higher.

At the start of production the chassis cost £1,140 with the petrol engine option and £1,280 with a diesel engine fitted.

Caetano Cascais forty-five-seat coachwork is fitted to this VAM70, which was new to M. A. Hargreave of Morley, West Yorkshire in March 1969. Still with Hargreave, it is seen here at Hampton Court station. The London Transport RF in the background looks positively Orwellian in comparison to the crisp look of the Caetano body. Around twenty-seven Caetano bodies are known to have been built on the VAM chassis.

R. CRIPPS

Revisions

The first revision came with the Bedford 70-series 466cu in 143bhp 6-cylinder diesel engine, available for the VAM in 1967. The new engine increased the GVW of the VAM from 21,700lb (9,843kg) to 24,500lb (11,113kg). Chassis fitted with this engine were classified VAM70 and quoted GVW was actually 10 tons (10,160kg); the 300cu in petrol engine option remained available; when it was fitted, the GVW was quoted at 9.68 tons (9,835kg). A 15in heavy-duty clutch transmitted the power from the new engine through a Turner overdrive-top synchromesh gearbox, the four- or five-speed direct-top gearbox being fitted to chassis with petrol engines.

The final incarnation of the VAM was the VAM75, introduced in 1975 and available for export only. This variant featured a Spicer T5A-3255 five-speed gearbox as standard with synchromesh on all gears except first and reverse.

Bodies

The majority of contemporary coachbuilders built bodies on the VAM, the wheelbase and general dimensions being close to the heavyweight chassis from Leyland and AEC so current bodies available for these in the UK were relatively easy to adapt for the VAM. Those from the usual suppliers are considered below. Salvador Caetano produced its forty-five-seat Estoril body for the VAM from 1968. In Australia, indigenous bus builders Freighter, Ansair and Domino Hedges built some very attractive bodies on the VAM70 chassis, while in New Zealand the ubiquitous NZMB body could be found on the VAM, as could bodies built by Hess and Denning.

Plaxton

The prototype received a front-entrance Plaxton Panorama coach body, almost identical with those being fitted to the contemporary AEC Reliance mid-engine chassis and Ford R192, which was very similar in layout to the VAM, with a vertically mounted front engine. The VAM's design made it highly suitable as the basis for a lightweight service bus. Plaxton had introduced a facelifted version of its Derwent forty-five-seat bus body in 1966; in outline this owed a great deal to the standard design used by the BET companies and employed the same windscreen. An example of this body on a VAM70 chassis was on show at Alf Moseley's premises in October 1969.

Plaxton updated its Panorama to the Panorama Elite in 1967 and a version was produced for the VAM to the same length as the Duple Viceroy. Further updating took place in 1968 for the 1969 season and deeper windows, at 39in (991mm), were fitted to replace the 37.5in (953mm) windows carried through from the Panorama I (as the earlier body had become). The glass had a curve to it that gave the body a slightly barrel-sided appearance above the waist rail, and new side mouldings continued the freshening up of the appearance of the body. A wider, four-step entrance was fitted along with a two-piece curved windscreen, which that was shown on the Padana stand at the Turin Motor Show in 1966. It is unclear, however, if this chassis went into production and it seems to have slipped into obscurity.

When introduced in 1962, the bare chassis cost a very competitive £1,775 and was available in both left-hand- and right-hand-drive form. At a price of around £1,000 less than any other British chassis suitable for 36ft (11m) coachwork, the VAL offered good value for money and brought a 36ft-long coach within the financial reach of a wide range of operators.

Revisions

Larger brake drums were introduced from autumn 1965 to address complaints from operators of poor brake performance and short lining life. An exhaust brake kit had been available from December 1964, which used air pressure from the braking system to operate a cylinder and piston assembly connected to the fuel injection pump stop-control lever, and also a cylinder and piston assembly mounted on the exhaust front pipe to close off the exhaust system under braking. However, this was a costly extra so Bedford modified the standard brakes to give a claimed improvement of 100 per cent in lining life. This was achieved by increasing the diameter of the front drums from 12in to 12.5in and the width of the linings from 3in to 4in and the thickness from 0.25in to 0.312in. At the rear, the lining width was increased from 4.18in to 5.5in. These modifications in total increased the lining area from 499sq in to 646sq in. The lining material was changed for a heavier-duty compound to combat fading, and the brakes were now twin-leading shoe all round in place of the leading and trailing shoes employed previously. The rear drum material was also increased in thickness slightly from 0.47in (11.9mm) to 0.58in (14.7mm).

From 1967 the Bedford 466cu in (7.6-litre) diesel became an option for the VAL, chassis so fitted being classified VAL70. At the same time, the electrical system was updated and an alternator replaced the dynamo fitted to earlier models.

BEDFORD VAL (1963–73)

Layout and Chassis
Luxury coach or bus, 48–56 seats; typically 36ft (11m) long by 8ft 2.5in (2.5m) wide. Frame: pressed steel channel section with seven riveted cross-members and one bolted cross-member

Engine
Type: VAL14: Leyland O.400 6-cylinder diesel
VAL70 (from 1967): Bedford 466cu in diesel
Fuel capacity: 45gal (205ltr)

Gearbox
Turner 564-VO 5-speed synchromesh (overdrive fifth)
Clutch: Borg and Beck 14in (360mm) single dry plate
Ratios
    1st: 6.06:1
    2nd: 3.50:1
    3rd: 1.80:1
    4th: 1:1
    Top: 0.8:1
    Reverse: 6.0:1

Transmission
Four-piece propeller shaft with Hardy Spicer needle-roller universal joints
Rear axle: Bedford full-floating hypoid bevel-gear differential; ratios, single speed 5.3:1 (standard), 4.6;1, 5.8:1 (options); two-speed axle high ratio 4.86:1, low 6.63:1
Front axles: Twin I-beam with kingpins, axles connected by constant-geometry drag link

Suspension and Steering
Suspension: Rubber-bushed semi-elliptic leaf springs with Girling hydraulic shock absorbers on all axles
Steering: Burman recirculating ball with Hydrosteer ram-type power assistance
Tyres: 8.25 × 16in radial

Brakes
Type: Air-assisted Lockheed Hydraulic with twin leading shoes on front axle, leading and trailing shoes on rear axle. Two separate handbrake systems with 12 × 3in transmission drum brake and single-pull lever operated on steering axle brakes
Size: VAL14: 12 × 3in (front on both axles), 13 × 4.18in (rear)
VAL70: 12 × 4in (front), 13 × 5.5in (rear)

Dimensions
Track
    Front: 81.89in (2,080mm)
    Rear: 82.5in (2,096mm)
Wheelbase: 19ft 3in (5,867mm)

Electrical system
24v compensated-voltage control system, 4 × 6v 114Ah batteries

EXHAUST BRAKES – HOW THEY WORK

An exhaust brake utilizes the compression of the engine to act as a brake. There are several variations with additional controls, but the general method of operation is this: an electrical mechanism that closes off the exhaust system and shuts off fuel to the engine is controlled by microswitches operated by the footbrake pedal and the clutch pedal. Operating the brake pedal causes a microswitch (A on the diagram) to close, which allows current to pass to the exhaust brake solenoid. This solenoid operates a vacuum- or air-activated butterfly valve that closes off the exhaust outlet from the engine, preventing exhaust gases from being vented through the silencer. This has the effect of building up air pressure in the engine cylinders, causing the pressure to resist the vehicle's momentum as it attempts to drive the engine round and thereby acts to retard the vehicle's progress. The same solenoid and actuator also acts on the engine throttle control through a Bowden cable or series of levers to shut off the fuel supply to the injectors, thus no fuel is admitted to the engine while it is being used as a brake. Several other switches are included to ensure the safety of the system and to ensure the engine will restart when the brake pedal is released.

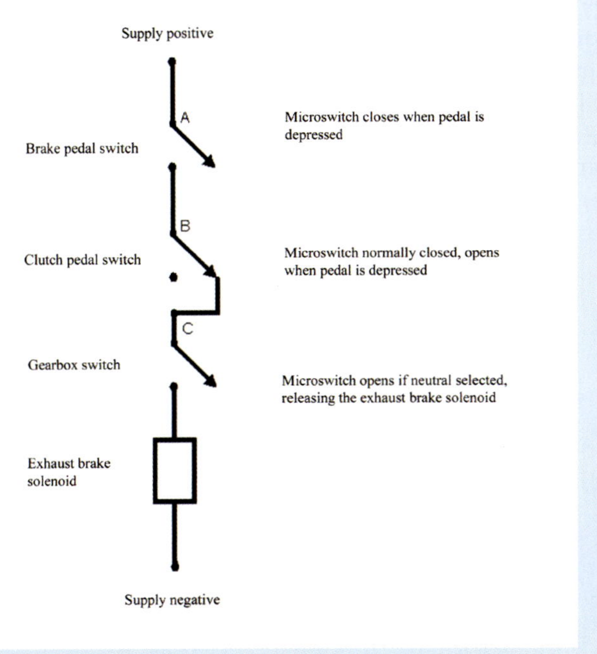

Generic circuit diagram for exhaust brake controls showing the various microswitches required for automatic operation.

Pressing the clutch pedal operates microswitch B, which opens and breaks the circuit to the solenoid. The solenoid is a spring-loaded device, which, when current is removed, moves back to its normal position, opening the butterfly valve and releasing the throttle so fuel is once again admitted to the engine. A further switch (C) on the gearbox ensures if neutral is selected, the exhaust brake is released. To engage the exhaust brake, the driver needs only to depress the brake pedal until the pedal switch operates, so the wheel brakes do not need to be fully applied.

Use of the exhaust brake has two major advantages. First, it reduces the need to use the normal wheel brakes, thus reducing wear on the brake drums and linings. Second, if the exhaust brake is used on, for example, a long downwards hill, the normal wheel brakes will not have suffered from 'brake fade' due to being heated over that distance, and so are still at maximum efficiency if required at some point during the descent.

Exhaust brakes tended to be very noisy in operation and of variable efficiency in some applications.

Bodies

The VAL was designed for coach bodies seating between forty-eight and fifty-three passengers, though higher capacities were achieved with bus bodies with more compact seats.

Although there was the option for goods use, in fact very few VAL chassis were used in this way. Approximately eight were built as pantechnicons and a further four as homing and racing pigeon transporters. The Road Transport Industry Training Board (RTITB) had one bodied by J. H. Sparshatt of Portsmouth as a van, and two were built as mobile TV units by L. V. Dove Ltd of Croydon for the National Coal Board. A further outside broadcast TV unit was built by Road Transport Services (Hackney) Ltd, in 1966. A flat-bed caravan transporter was built by Bedford dealer Chester Engineering Co. Ltd for Cheshire Caravan Transport Ltd of Winsford, Cheshire in 1965 – it was capable of carrying up to three 9ft–10ft (2.7m–3m) caravans, while the driver was accommodated in a comparatively luxurious cab.

Another interesting application was the 'Palletainer' delivery vehicle operated by Clarks Boxes Ltd of Mountsorrel, Loughborough, Leicestershire. It was specially designed for delivering 10,000 boxes in a single load, the boxes being on pallets with rapid loading and unloading.

Duple (Midland) built an attractive bus body for the VAM, which could be ordered in dual-purpose form with service coach seating and additional external brightwork. Optional extras for the bus body included solid-base luggage racks and a rear luggage locker. Willowbrook's contribution to the Duple group's range for the VAM was an express service coach body and a bus body from 1965. The service coach body had standard Duple group tubular-framed express coach seats and both bodies had the standard BET-style windscreen that was becoming common in the industry at the time. The outline of the bodies also owed something to the standard BET-federation single-deck body and was clearly targeted at the same market as the Plaxton Derwent.

The Duple Bella Venture was built at Hendon and was essentially a front-entrance version of the Bella Vega, with which it shared a similar side profile, particularly around the rearmost windows, and the same side mouldings as those fitted to the 1967 Bella Vega. A smaller and neater rectangular front grille with rounded ends was fitted, with the front lighting now incorporated in a horizontal moulding separate from the grille and situated just above the front bumper. The body was of composite construction – the front and rear panels, canopy and domes were in fibreglass. The entrance door opened inwards and there were two emergency doors – one full height at the front offside and a waist-depth emergency exit at the rear on the offside. A luggage compartment of 112cu ft (3,171ltr) capacity was provided behind the rear axle.

A version of the Bella Venture body was also built at Duple's Blackpool factory, where it was badged as the Viscount; it could be distinguished from the Bella Venture

Willowbrook built this stylish dual-purpose forty-five-seat body to the Duple group's standard bus design on a VAM14 chassis. It was new to Gibson Bros Buses of Barlestone, Hinckley, Leicestershire in February 1967 and was one of several similar buses in the fleet. It later passed to Monty Moreton of Attleborough in Leicestershire. It is seen here in Nuneaton in the early 1970s; the Fina garage and the Midland Red D9 double-decker in the background combine to make this a nostalgic West Midlands image.

by its vertical window pillars and larger panoramic side windows (similar to the Duple Commander body built on heavier chassis), though from the front the bodies appeared identical. Duple (Northern) continued to offer the Viscount for the VAM, though now updated to share the Viceroy's fluorescent lighting and new Duple standard seats. The interior of both bodies used decorative ersatz wood finish of Sapele and Walnut appearance, executed in Formica laminate on the waist and cantrail. The ceiling was trimmed Otaki Polar Green PVC-based leathercloth and the gangways were carpeted, while beneath the seats the floor covering was linoleum.

From 1967 the Viceroy replaced both the Bella Venture and the Viscount, with a completely restyled side profile featuring three large and one small side window at the front, the top edge of which was dropped to match the entrance door on the near side and the driver's side window on the offside, and to line up with the bottom edge of the top-sliding ventilators of the large windows. Gone was the backward-raked, sloping rear pillar of the Bellas' Vega and Venture, though the final grille style of the Venture was retained for the early Viceroy body.

The Viceroy for the VAM was updated in 1968 in line with the versions for other chassis. The modifications included a new, more rectangular stainless-steel front grille without a polished surround and with plain horizontal bars and new, deep polished mouldings that contained the front light clusters with twin headlamps and registration number plate. The moulding continued around the sides of the vehicle to the tail light cluster fairings at the rear.

Inside, the finish continued to be largely as on 1965 Duple group coaches, although the plastic trim panels around the windows and dash were now an imitation rosewood finish. Solid-based luggage racks replaced the open-mesh versions

of the earlier design and the new Viceroy was 32ft 6.375in (9.92m) long. The exterior styling was consistent with that of the Viceroy 37 body for the VAL and the Commander.

Also in 1968, Duple (Midland) produced a batch of all-metal bodies on left-hand-drive VAM3 chassis for the Iranian Oil Exploration and Producing Co. These were of similar specification to the MCW Superior body currently in production for the oil fields of Saudi Arabia, and seated forty-six passengers on slatted wooden seats.

The Viceroy body on the VAM continued pretty much unchanged through the last years of the 1960s until the end of production, though for the final year of VAM production the Viceroy received some improvements to the interior, which included new material for seating that provided better support and comfort for passengers while being more hard-wearing than earlier materials. A limited choice of interior colour scheme became available, these changes being introduced after Duple was taken over by Frank B. Ford & Co. Ltd.

Alexander

Walter Alexander of Falkirk was quick to see the potential of the VAM and built a service bus body on the VAM5 chassis that was exhibited at the 1965 Commercial Motor Show. Intended for use in the Scottish Highlands, the body had a larger than usual rear luggage compartment for carrying mail and parcels. The shell was based on the Alexander Y-type bus body that had been in production from 1962. The Y-type body was built on a wide variety of manufacturers' chassis as diverse as the Bristol RE, Albion Viking and Seddon Pennine 7. Around twenty-seven are thought to have been built on Bedford VAM5 chassis, including several with the coach version.

Seen in Thurso in the northern Highlands of Scotland in September 1972 is this 1966 VAM5 with twenty-four-seat Alexander Y-type bus body, adapted to enable mail to be carried in a compartment at the rear. Highland Omnibuses fleet no. CD13 was withdrawn from service in 1981.

In 1964 Strachans built ten fifty-two-seat bodies for the North Western Road Car Co. Ltd with specially shaped roofs to allow them to pass under a canal aqueduct at Dunham Massey in Cheshire, on the route between Altrincham and Warrington. This example was somewhat off-route to the south when photographed at Lower Peover.

Ltd, in autumn 1964. The bodies had a special roof profile to enable the buses to pass under the Dunham Aqueduct on the Bridgwater Canal. Clearance under the bridge was only 10ft (3m), so the low build of the VAL chassis was advantageous. The roof of the Strachans body was designed in an unbroken arc from side to side and the overall maximum unladen height of the vehicles was 9ft 6in (2.9m). They replaced some elderly thirty-five-seat Bristol L-types that had themselves been modified to give a lower roof profile.

Strachans was also responsible for six fifty-three-seat buses for Curacao, South America, built on left-hand-drive VAL chassis in 1964. They were based on Strachans' 'Everest 63' Zintec-steel body frame designed for either buses or coaches. The buses were trimmed in a fairly utilitarian style with fibreglass seats in tubular steel frames, and wide gangways with a full-length handrail were provided to accommodate a large number of standing passengers. The exterior was slightly more luxuriously finished with chrome-plated bumpers, radiator grille and wheel embellishers. Side windows had top-sliding ventilators, and interior lighting was by recessed ceiling fittings.

During 1965, Marshall built ten airport buses on VAL chassis for BEA, one of the forerunners of British Airways (BA). These had forty inward-facing seats and room for a large number of standing passengers. Twin sliding entrance and exit doors were fitted both sides of the body in the centre of wheelbase to expedite rapid loading and unloading. A few more were built in 1966 and 1967 for other air-side operators and at least one is thought to survive in preservation.

Belgian Bodies for the VAL

International interest in the VAL was maintained by an example with a body built by Belgian coachbuilder Jonckheere, shown on the General Motors stand at the 44th Salon de l'Automobile, Brussels, in 1965. The body was quite distinctive to British eyes, with a flat roof line and deep side windows, though Jonckheere would not make significant inroads into the UK market until the 1980s and rarely on Bedford chassis.

Another Belgian coachbuilder with its eye on the UK market was Van Hool NV of Koningshooikt, near Lier. In cooperation with Alf Moseley, a prototype fifty-three-seat coach designed especially for the UK market was built on a VAL70 chassis in late 1968 and appeared early in 1969. The Van Hool body was of all-steel construction and followed the general outline of the coachbuilder's contemporary product line, though with an inward-opening entrance door and increased headroom as a result of the VAL's low chassis frame – the body was originally designed with a raised roof so a high floor could be fitted with luggage capacity beneath – and larger than usual side windows as a consequence of the lower floor line. One of the first production VAL/Van Hool coaches was a forty-nine-seat model, Van Hool's designation 3711, purchased by All Seasons Travel, London W2, which entered service on 23 August 1970.

Whether by accident or design, Duple and Plaxton built bodies for an almost equal number of chassis – approximately 825 each – and these were by far the majority. Small runs of bodies for the VAL were built by other coachbuilders. Harrington built forty-two coaches on VAL14 chassis in the period 1964–5, while Willowbrook built around thirty bodies, mostly buses with capacities ranging from fifty-three to fifty-six seats, though there was a run of thirteen dual-purpose fifty-four-seat bodies for the famous Blue Bus (Tailby & George) of Willington, Derbyshire.

The first Willowbrook bodies were built on the VAL in 1963 and the last in 1971. Salvador Caetano built twenty Estoril coach bodies over the period 1969–71, almost all with fifty-three seats. Marshall also built around twenty more bodies of the dual-entrance, forty-eight-seat bus type for BEA, who used them as airport buses, and one single-door, fifty-two-seat bus for Geddes of Brixham. Other notable coach-builders who built bodies on the VAL included Yeates in 1963–4, who built around eleven, including four dual-entrance fifty-seat coaches and three dual-entrance fifty-six-seat dual-purpose buses based on the Europa bodyshell for Barton Transport, of Chilwell, Notting-hamshire. The choice of Yeates for Barton is logical given the proximity of the two companies, the layout of the bodies less so!

Sales and Production

Production of the VAL spanned 1963 to 1973 and, from the published figures, appears to have reached approximately 2,000 chassis. Just over 1,200 VAL14 chassis were pro-duced by the time VAL70 was intro-duced to replace it in 1968. A fur-ther 700-plus VAL70s were built by the end of production in 1972. Pro-duction of the VAL14 ended in early 1968 with the final three chassis, but had averaged a healthy 225 annually over the period 1963–7. The VAL70 came on stream in early 1968 and averaged 150 per year until 1972, when production started to wind down in favour of the YRT, with only sixty-eight in 1972 and sixteen final chassis in 1973. A total of 1,945 are accounted for in the published records, so this can be assumed to be the minimum that Bedford pro-duced; based on the coachbuilders' records, somewhere between 110 and 150 were exported, many to

Australia and New Zealand.

The first eight chassis were bodied by Duple and based on the body numbers, the first completed was 592 PUR, for

This 1970 VAL70 has a forty-nine-seat Van Hool Vistadome body. It was new to All Seasons Travel of London W2. Very few VALs are recorded as having Van Hool bodies. H. ROSE

Another example of Barton's penchant for the unusual is demonstrated by its fleet no. 968, a 1963 VAL14 with Yeates dual-entrance body. Dual-purpose seating for fifty-six passengers was provided, despite the additional door. It was seen at Kidderminster in October 1990 after being restored to Barton livery. Before entering preservation it served with Mellor's Coaches of Goxhill, Lincolnshire, then later with H. A. Scutt & Son of Owston Ferry in the same county.

skinned, with fibreglass insulation between the inner and outer roof panels. In standard form the seating capacity was forty-six, though a number of different versions were produced with seating capacities ranging from as few as thirty to forty-six. Three basic models were produced: a stage-carriage service bus (the Pacemax), an express service or dual-purpose bus (the Paceway Express) and a utility version for use as a personnel carrier. An interesting variation of the service bus body for city-centre and urban use had a front entrance and centre exit with seats for thirty passengers and standing room for up to thirty-four more where regulations and agreements allowed.

The Pacemax II body was mounted on a batch of four VAM14s for former Tilling Group operator Hants & Dorset Motor Services Ltd. These had thirty-three-seat dual-door bodies, something of a favourite style with this operator, who also had eleven VAM14s with very similar Willowbrook dual-door bodies. The Strachans bodies could accommodate twenty-five standing passengers, with the seats arranged such that the standing area was to the rear of the central exit. This was achieved by fitting eight single seats, four on each side of the bus immediately aft of the central exit door, giving an open area of 56in (1,422mm) between the seats. This put the majority of the standees in the rear half of the vehicle, reducing the load on the front axle and allowing for speedy loading and unloading with an unobstructed entrance door. At 3tons 9cwt (3,162kg), these buses weighed in at approximately half as much as similar-sized Tilling Group standard buses such as the Bristol MW and LS.

One of five VAM14s with Strachans Pacemax dual-door bodies supplied to Hants & Dorset Motor Services in 1967, fleet no. 825 (later 1502) was damaged by an engine fire in 1971 near Hurn Airport. It was photographed at Bournemouth bus station sometime in 1968.

NAH 661F. Eastern Coach Works (ECW) built a few bodies on both **VAM5** and **VAM14** chassis for the Transport Holding Company in 1967 to fulfil orders while the Bristol LH was coming into production. This example was new to the Eastern Counties Omnibus Co. Ltd. They seated forty-one passengers and apparently were capable of a good turn of speed though were very noisy compared with the under-floor-engine Bristols that were usually found in such fleets. It was seen here late in its life with Primrose Valley Garage & Coach Co. Ltd, based in the village of Primrose Valley in North Yorkshire.

ECW

Mention of the Tilling Group brings us to Eastern Coach Works (ECW), the favoured coachbuilder of that group. Twenty VAMs (six VAM14, fourteen VAM5) received ECW forty-one-seat bus bodies in 1967, of a style very typical of that coachbuilder. While the Strachans and Willowbrook bodies built for Hants & Dorset were based on the modern BET design, the two-piece flat windscreens and rounded rear dome of the ECW bodies harked back to a previous era. The VAMs with ECW bodies were distributed amongst Eastern Counties Omnibus Co. Ltd (two VAM5s, two VAM14s), West Yorkshire Road Car Co. Ltd (four VAM14s) and Western National Omnibus Co. Ltd (twelve VAM5s).

Sales

Significant early orders for the VAM included thirty-eight for J. T. Whittle and Son of Highley (delivered 1966–7), sixteen for the George Ewer Group and twelve for Salopia Saloon Coaches Ltd of Whitchurch, Shropshire, all with Duple Viceroy bodies. The Tilling Association Ltd, on behalf of the former Tilling Group companies, placed a relatively large order with Bedford for VAM chassis in late 1966 to be bodied by Duple, Plaxton, ECW, Strachans and Willowbrook. While those with Duple and Plaxton bodies were bought for use as touring coaches, the remainder were buses purchased as a stop-gap while the Bristol LH was being designed and put into production.

fuel consumption could be expected to be around 15mpg (18.9ltr/100km) with the standard 5.3:1 axle.

Vauxhall engineers had found the tyre pressures could be fairly critical in maintaining the correct loading on the twin-steering axles; 80psi (5.52bar) in the leading tyres and 50psi (3.45bar) in the tyres on the second axle were recommended, and some operators found directional stability was improved by exchanging the factory-fitted steel-belted radial tyres for textile radials. Surprisingly, some claimed that the textile radials wore better than the steel ones, too.

Alan Townsin rode in and drove the prototype VAL in 1962 and, while this was not a particularly exhaustive test, he noted that with around thirty passengers on board the coach was capable of cruising at 70mph (113km/h) on the M1 motorway, with occasional maximum bursts of around 75mph (121km/h) on downhill stretches. A favourite spot for Vauxhall and Bedford road tests was Bison Hill, 0.75 miles (1.2km) long with an average gradient of 1:10.5 (9.5 per cent) and a steepest gradient of 1 in 6.5 (15 per cent). Situated on the B4540 approaching Whipsnade Zoo in Bedfordshire, the hill was climbed confidently with a minimum speed of 11mph (18km/h).

Townsin felt that the ride quality at both the front and rear of the coach was good and closely approached what might be expected from more expensive coaches with more complex suspension, though his opinion regarding the ride at the rear was not universally endorsed by other passengers.

While driving, he found that the noise from the Leyland engine was intrusive though vibration-free when on the move, some vibration being evident while the engine was ticking over. The steering was light and responsive and the gearchange positive with good synchromesh. He noted that the brakes were progressive, though the pedal travel seemed excessive; a portent of trouble to come, perhaps.

A later production VAL14 with a few years' service and a reasonable mileage under its belt was thoroughly tested in March 1967 as part of a used coach survey Townsin conducted for *Bus & Coach* magazine. This particular coach was first registered in October 1963, and carried the Duple Vega Major body introduced at the Commercial Motor Show in September 1963 for the 1964 season. The coach tested, DME 976A, was provided by dealer Shaw & Kilburn and had had two owners from the new, last of these being Priory Coaches of Gosport, Hampshire. For the test the vehicle was in the condition in which it had arrived from the Gosport operator and had received no attention from the dealer. The recorded mileage was approximately 120,000 (190,000km), though some doubt was cast on the accuracy of this and it was suggested that the

mileage might have been nearer 80,000 (130,000km), without further explanation of how this discrepancy might have occurred. Apart from noting that the exterior paintwork could have done with a little polish, Townsin reported that the body was in good condition, though the seat moquette was slightly faded where heavily exposed to light through the roof quarter panels. The Formica that Duple used to trim the flat surfaces of the interior showed little sign of deterioration, as did the linoleum floor covering. The usual minor dings and dents were present that a three-year-old public service vehicle would have been expected to pick up.

On the road, interior noise from the Leyland O.400 engine was found to be less than expected, compared with most VAL coaches; noise meter readings taken at the centre of the coach indicated 77dB under acceleration with figures of 75–76dB when cruising at 45mph (72km/h) and 63dB at idle. Front-seat noise was appreciably higher, typically by 5db. Townsin commented that the actual mechanical sound quality of the O.400 engine made it seem noisier.

The engine itself seemed in fine fettle, with no difficulty in whipping the coach up to 60mph (97km/h) in a reasonable distance. The O.400 engine was noted for its tendency to consume oil, but this trait was not visually apparent during the test and an examination of the engine revealed little sign of oil leaks. The engine seemed to respond well to being revved, though there was sufficient torque available to accelerate away from 30mph (48km/h) in fifth gear.

Braking was described as 'fully adequate', despite pre-dating the larger drums introduced in autumn 1965, and free from the vices of snatch and judder. The complex parking brake was found to be equally adequate and there were no problems in parking on a slope, though the tester commented on the difficulty of obtaining access to the driver's seat, which required negotiation of the various levers!

The power-assisted steering came in for praise, being described as precise, reasonably self-centring and with only a light touch needed making the VAL generally enjoyable to drive.

The Turner five-speed gearbox had developed a little slop in the gearchange though the gearbox seemed to work well, with effective synchromesh and smooth clutch action.

Townsin's strongest praise, however, was reserved for the ride quality, and he suggested that no contemporary vehicle could improve on it, repeating his views from the earlier test – this was all the more impressive given that the chassis used rigid axles and leaf springs. On offer at £4,250, the coach had much to commend it.

By the end of the 1960s, however, operators were beginning to find the VAL a little tired. There were reports in the industry press that operators were seeking for a replacement for the Bedford 466cu in engine as they were finding the VAL underpowered for its size compared with more modern designs.

Other road testers found various items to criticize, though often these could be laid at the feet of the coachbuilder rather than Bedford. For example, a common complaint was poor insulation of the engine compartment causing noise and fumes to find their way into the passenger space; screen washing and wiping equipment was found to be poor and the electrical switches poorly identified and located. On the other hand, those factors that were the responsibility of the chassis manufacturer were generally reported upon favourably. The VAL70, with the 466cu in Bedford diesel, was more lively than the Leyland-powered VAL14; less effort was needed to get the coach underway and top-gear performance was much improved. Maximum speed of the VAL70 with the standard axle ratio was 72mph (116km/h) compared with 58mph (93km/h), and its cruising ability at 60–65mph (96–105km/h), little affected by motorway gradients, made the VAL70 more suited for long-distance services. Some testers, however, found the transmission handbrake heavy to operate and the steering too light on the road, though perfect for manoeuvres in tight spaces, and the 466cu in engine a little thirstier, with an average fuel consumption of 15.9mpg (17.8ltr/100km). On the whole, though, the difference from the Leyland O.400 was really quite small.

Generally the VAL was considered very pleasant to handle, though some drivers found the steering a little vague until they got used to it, although the weak castor action sometimes proved troublesome in tight corners. Even so, the general consensus was that a VAL was at least as easy to handle as a vehicle half its size, though care needed to be taken in cross-winds, which could often make the coach yaw slightly without warning. The same tendency could be detected when overtaking large vehicles or emerging from the shelter of trees or embankments.

The reports of problems with brakes continued, despite Bedford increasing the size of the friction area of the brakes, and many VALs came to be fitted with Telma electromagnetic retarders; indeed, some operators thought that a retarder was an essential fitment, though others found the cost prohibitive at typically £350 – and they were not approved by Vauxhall due to the additional load placed on the thrust bearings in the differential.

For the VAL14, Bedford offered an exhaust brake kit, though this device was only really effective when the engine was turning at quite high rpm and produced little or no braking assistance when travelling slowly in high gear. An alternative exhaust-brake kit was available from Smiths Industries, but no record of comparative performance has been found. Despite the adverse comments from operators, Vauxhall and Bedford service staff found that the most of the problems associated with VAL brakes were caused by poor maintenance and incorrect adjustment. In particular,

DV 1513. This VAL with MMB body was one of three new to Days Motors of Christchurch, New Zealand. Despite the size of the vehicle it seated only forty-three.

M. FOSTER

CHAPTER SEVEN

THE Y SERIES

The Y series was a range of mid-engine chassis introduced in 1970, the first version being the YRQ, and was Bedford's response to the industry's clear preference for a mid-mounted, under-floor engine for lightweight single-deck vehicles. The success of the Leyland Leopard and subsequently the Bristol LH (which was probably the closest to that which Bedford might have produced in the mid-1960s, with its Leyland O.400 engine and Turner Clark gearbox) had stolen a large proportion Bedford's market share. In choosing to install the amidships engine vertically in the Y series, Bedford's effort to take on the rival under-floor engine chassis might be considered somewhat half-hearted, as though it did not wish to depart too much from what had gone before. Perhaps it would have been too costly to modify the standard Bedford engines for horizontal mounting; a horizontal version of the Leyland engine was readily available but Vauxhall undoubtedly did not wish to be reliant totally on Leyland for its engines.

There would be a number of models bearing the 'Y' prefix intended for different classes of work but, apart from dimensions, they were all quite similar. The first model to appear was the YRQ, in September 1970. It was intended to replace the VAM in the Bedford product range and was suitable for 10m (32ft–33ft) coachwork.

THE YRQ

Described in Bedford's own literature as the 'mid-engined VAM', the Y-series chassis construction was very similar to that of the VAM and the current version of the VAS with the obvious difference being that the radiator, engine and gearbox moved from the front of the vehicle to within the wheelbase. The frame was slightly modified at the front but otherwise was the same as the VAM, as were the principal dimensions of wheelbase and front and rear overhang. Mechanically the YRQ was also very similar to the VAM, being powered by the Bedford 466cu in diesel mated to a Turner five-speed gearbox. Some modifications were necessary to the 466cu in engine in order to accommodate it

The forty-five-seat Duple Viceroy body, as shown here on this early 1972 YRQ, was externally unchanged from that on the VAM chassis. New to Owen's of Corwen, Denbighshire, it is seen here with Williams of Llangollen. Around 1983 it passed to Supertramp Trampolines Ltd of Uffculm, Devon for non-PSV use and later was used as a mobile home by a young travelling family. After such useful service it is sad to record it was broken up for scrap.

SPECIFICATIONS FOR BEDFORD YRQ/YLQ/YMQ/YMP

Layout and Chassis

Bus or coach, 41–47 seats, 33ft (10m) overall length. Frame: flat ladder with straight-through channel section 10 × 3in (254mm × 76mm) side members, six cross-members, cold riveted construction

Engine

Type: YRQ: 70-series 466cu in Bedford diesel
YRQ2/3, YLQ, YMQ: 500cu in Bedford diesel
YMP: 500cu in turbocharged Bedford diesel
Fuel capacity 45gal (205ltr)

Gearbox

YRQ: Turner 5-speed, overdrive top, synchromesh on second, third, fourth and top
Ratios
    1st: 6.06:1
    2nd: 3.00:1
    3rd: 1.70:1
    4th: 1:1
    5th: 0.799:1
    Reverse: 6.00:1
YRQ2 Eaton type 542 5-speed, overdrive top, synchromesh on second, third, fourth and top
Ratios
    1st: 6.40:1
    2nd: 3.05:1
    3rd: 1.75:1
    4th: 1:1
    5th: 0.78:1
    Reverse: 6.50:1
YMP: Spicer T5C 5-speed, overdrive top, synchromesh on second, third, fourth and top
Ratios
    1st: 5.29:1
    2nd: 2.72:1
    3rd: 1.49:1
    4th: 1:1
    5th: 0.74:1
    Reverse: 5.20:1
Clutch: Single dry plate 15in diameter, hydraulic operation

Transmission

Single propeller shaft with needle-roller universal joints
Rear axle: Bedford fully floating hypoid; ratio options 5.8:1, 5.43:1 or 5.28:1; optional Bedford two-speed axle, ratios 4.86:1 and 6.63:1
Front axle: I-beam section

Suspension and Steering

Suspension: Semi-elliptic leaf springs with rubber-bushed spring eyes; front: seven leaves 60 × 3in (1,524mm × 76mm); rear: nine leaves 67 × 3in (1,701mm × 76mm); double-acting telescopic shock absorbers (front and rear)
Steering: Recirculating ball, ram-type power assistance acting on relay lever, ratio 25:1 (optional on YRQ, standard on succeeding models)
Tyres: 9.00 × 20in, 12-ply

Brakes

Type: YRQ: dual-line air-assisted hydraulic
YRQ2 (from 1974, all models): full air, dual-line system, air-operated spring parking brake operating on rear wheels
Size: YRQ: 3.1875 × 13.6in (front), 6 × 13.6in (rear)
YRQ2, 1974–5: 6 × 15.5in (front and rear)
YMQ early: 6 × 14.2in (front and rear)
YLQ/YMQ, from 1976: 5 × 15.5in (front), 8 × 15.5in (rear)
YMP: 6 × 15in (front and rear)

Dimensions

Track
    Front: 78.35in (1,990mm)
    Rear: 83in (2,113mm)
Wheelbase: 16ft 1in (4,902mm)

Electrical System

24v, CAV AC5 alternator, four 6v ten-plate batteries, 137Ah rating

---

in its new position, principally to the shape of the sump to give more clearance under the engine, though this was still less than on other underfloor-engine models and the VAM. This was fine on the relatively smooth roads of Europe, but it is unlikely that it would have been sufficient in less well-developed territories where Bedford was a major supplier, and probably one of the reasons the VAM remained available for export.

Access to the engine was through a removable floor panel; removal required the engine to be lowered through the chassis with the vehicle raised on a lift.

A five-speed Turner gearbox was fitted as standard, the remote gearchange mechanism consisting of small-diameter steel bars articulated by several universal joints of the type common in car steering systems of the time, these being quite a bit smaller in size compared with those found on other mid-engine PSV chassis with manual gearboxes, and no doubt much cheaper.

One 1964 VAL found further use in preservation as a mobile model railway exhibition, where the owner was able to combine his passion for vintage vehicles with another of his interests. The model railway layout had hundreds of feet of track, ran on two levels and was capable of running fifteen different trains simultaneously. The coach was a regular visitor at various rallies and events with the admission charge going to charity; it was also a big hit at Bedford's golden jubilee celebration at Luton in October 1981.

The VAL was truly a 1960s icon; it appeared in two major feature films: first in the 1966 film *Magical Mystery Tour*, which was directed by and starred The Beatles, and then in Peter Collinson's 1969 film *The Italian Job*, starring Michael Caine, Noel Coward and Benny Hill.

The vehicular star of *Magical Mystery Tour* was 1967 VAL/Plaxton Panorama URO 913E, hired from Fox Coaches Ltd of Hayes, Middlesex. The most memorable scene had The Beatles drummer Ringo Starr hurling the coach into a bend at high speed on a motor racing circuit while racing against an equally iconic collection of British sports cars – if Bedford had needed an advert for the road-holding of their legendary six-wheeler, they could have done no better. The coach featured throughout the film as The Beatles took a party of trippers on a mystery tour through the English countryside. While very much of its time, the quality of the film fell somewhat short of what the world had become used to in The Beatles' musical output. The coach was saved for preservation at The Beatles Exhibition Centre in Liverpool in 1984 and restored by Imperial Coachbuilders Ltd of Liverpool. It was subsequently used on tours of places in Liverpool associated with The Beatles. Its current location is believed to be the Hard Rock Cafe in Orlando, Florida, USA, though several replicas currently exist around the world.

The Italian Job was an altogether more creditable effort and featured a 1964 VAL14 with striking Harrington Legionnaire bodywork, ALR 453B. The story revolves around a criminal plot to steal a gold shipment in Turin by creating havoc by infiltrating the city's computerized traffic light control system. This enabled the perpetrators to escape in a fleet of Austin Mini Cooper cars, taking advantage of their small size to negotiate alleyways, sewers and other routes out of the city not blocked by the traffic jam. The film is notable for its very early depiction of criminal computer hacking and the high-speed car chase sequences, one of which included driving the Minis up a ramp into the rear of the VAL, a pair of rear doors having been fitted specially to facilitate this. Later in the film the Minis are unceremoniously dumped out of the rear of the coach over a cliff to dispose of them. After its brief career as a film star, ALR 453B returned to normal duties more befitting a luxury coach; in the 1970s it allegedly found use as a school bus with a coach company in Angus, Scotland and is believed to have been broken up for scrap in 1990.

Of those exported, many later underwent significant modifications to engines and transmissions to enable them to continue to work in local conditions; for example some could be found in Australia fitted with Japanese Hino engines.

The Beatles connection continued to keep the VAL in the public eye, in Liverpool at least; Liverpool's Cavern City Tours claimed it was carrying 50,000 passengers per year on its daily Magical Mystery Tours, which used a pair of VAL/Plaxton Panorama coaches. The coaches dated from 1965 and 1966 and were painted appropriately. The connection continues today in Germany; Simon Mitchell, who starred in the film as a child, has recently imported into Hannover a VAL70/Plaxton Panorama to add to a museum collection of Magical Mystery Tour artefacts and memorabilia in the town of Hameln. The coach was transported by ferry from Rosyth, Scotland to Zeebrugge in Belgium and then travelled under its own power to Hameln.

THE BEDFORD VAM

To some extent, Bedford, having the luxury of over 50 per cent of the lightweight bus and coach market, had been able to successfully plough their own furrow and create, rather than follow, trends in the industry. However, the Yeates front-entrance conversions on the SB chassis had awoken Vauxhall's engineers to the fact that there were alternative and better arrangements of wheel/entrance/engine that were more suited to some operators' needs than those provided by the SB and the VAS. The VAL was the first Bedford built for a front entrance ahead of the wheels, but this was really to address an opening in the market for a lightweight, 36ft (11m) coach rather than an indication of a general approach. The VAL therefore was an engineering solution that utilized mostly standard Bedford parts and construction methods to build a maximum-dimension vehicle. The industry in general had long since moved to under-floor, mid-mounted engines for heavyweight chassis and by the time the VAL appeared, chassis with the engines at the rear were starting to appear. Bedford had also been left behind in the forty- to forty-five-seat market and that gap needed to be filled; at the same time, Bedford needed to realign itself with current trends. Into this climate, the VAM was born.

Designed for bodies of around 32ft (9.75m) in length and 8ft 2.5in (2.5m) in width, the VAM provided a base for a coach or bus of around forty-five seats. The chassis frame was a typical Bedford ladder modified to provide for a low-step entrance ahead of the front wheels, as on the VAL and many other contemporary bus and coach chassis. The wheelbase was 16ft 1in (4.9m), with a front overhang of 6ft 8in (2.03m) to allow for a reasonably wide entrance door.

Pressed-steel channel frame side members were employed, the left-hand member being swept inwards and down at the front to allow for the entrance steps and the driving position. At the rear the bottom edge tapered upwards from the forward mounting of the rear springs to the rear end of the chassis, though the top surface was flat along its full length. The straight ladder frame had six cross-members and the top of the frame was level from the cross-member situated just aft of the engine to the rear of the chassis. The frames themselves were 10in (254mm) deep along the parallel length and the material was 0.22in (5.59mm) thick with 3in (76mm) flanges top and bottom. The engine was mounted vertically, forward of the front axle and low in the frame to provide a low entrance step. A removable front cross-member was provided to facilitate installation and removal of the engine when necessary.

It is curious that Bedford did not at this time take the opportunity to design the VAM with a mid-mounted horizontal engine as was common in the rest of the industry; perhaps, having redesigned the traditional Bedford chassis to accommodate a true front entrance, a new engine position was considered one step too far. The prototype VAM chassis had a kink in the frame so that the rear section was wider from just behind the front axle, so perhaps Bedford had been contemplating alternative engines and positions. The production VAM chassis frame was reasonably low even with a vertical engine, though still 3in (76mm) higher unladen than the SB at 39in (991mm), and 10in (254mm) higher than the VAL from the ground to the top of the frame at its highest.

Three engine options were initially offered, comprising the Bedford 300cu in 133bhp petrol engine, the 330cu in 107bhp diesel and the Leyland O.400 400cu in/131bhp diesel.

With the Bedford engines, the VAM was fitted with a four-speed wide-ratio gearbox with synchromesh on second, third and top gears. With the Leyland engine and later diesel options, a Turner five-speed, overdrive-top synchromesh gearbox was fitted with a larger 15in-diameter clutch. There was also a five-speed Bedford gearbox option only for the VAM3, which was described in some places as a direct-top synchromesh gearbox, although the

quoted ratios in Bedford's literature suggested it was an overdrive-top gearbox. A single-speed rear axle was fitted with two ratio options of 5.83:1 or 6.83:1; a two-speed axle was offered as a further option with initially 5.3:1 and 5.8:1 ratios, later 4.86:1 and 6.83:1 ratios. Single dry-plate clutches with 12in, 13in and 15in diameters were fitted, the VAM3 having the smallest unit, the VAM5 and VAM14 the 13in unit and the VAM70 and 75 the largest.

The transmission consisted of a three-section propeller shaft, the rear ends of both the front and centre sections being carried in ball-bearing supports attached to the chassis cross-members. Universal joints were Hardy Spicer needle-roller universal joints.

The rear axle was fully floating with hypoid-bevel gear final drive in line with contemporary Bedford practice, and taper-roller rear hub bearings were fitted. Three axle ratios were offered, 5.3:1, 5.83:1 or 6.83:1; a two-speed rear axle was also offered, with high/low ratios of 4.86:1 and 6.63:1. An alternative two-speed axle was offered for the VAM3 chassis with high/low ratios of 5.83:1 and 7.95:1. With the 5.83:1 ratio, the claimed maximum gradient that could be climbed was 1 in 3.5.

Maintenance requirements were reduced by use of sealed-for-life steering joints and propeller shaft universal joints.

The front axle was of I-beam section, again similar to previous Bedford models. Steering swivels (knuckles in Bedford literature) were mounted on pivot pins secured in bosses in the axle beam by tapered cotter pins with a nut and lock washer, a thrust washer being interposed between each jaw of the steering swivel and the boss in the axle beam. The front hubs were mounted to the stub axles by two large adjustable taper roller bearings on each side. Steering was by Burman recirculating-ball steering box with pre-packed sealed-for-life steering joints.

Suspension was by semi-elliptic leaf springs all round, with telescopic, double-acting shock absorbers front and rear.

The brakes were power-assisted hydraulic, by vacuum servo on chassis with petrol engines and by an air-pressure servo on chassis with diesel engines. On the VAM75 they were a full air system. On the early chassis the brake servo was mounted just forward of the central point in the wheelbase and attached to the right-hand side member. The hydraulic system consisted of a tandem master cylinder with separate hydraulic circuits to the front and rear wheel cylinders. Front and rear brake drums were 15.25in in diameter with 4.25in front linings and 6in rear linings, giving a total brake-lining area of 600sq in, with 248sq in at the front and 352sq in at the rear. A conventional ratchet-lever handbrake

YMT from 1976: 7 × 15.5in (front), 8 × 15.5in (rear)
YMT (from 1982)/YNT: 7 × 15in (front), 8 × 15in (rear)
Dimensions
Track
   Front: 78.35in (1,990mm)

Rear: 84.25in (2,140mm)
Wheelbase:18ft 5in (5,639mm)
Electrical System
4v, CAV 60A alternator, four × 6v ten-plate batteries
137Ah rating

The **YNT** chassis with Blue series 500cu in (8.2-litre) turbocharged Bedford diesel engine. GM

Revisions

In order to signify general changes in engine options, the Y series underwent several recodes. In each case the final letter reflected the intended overall length – Q for 10m (33ft) chassis and T for 11m (36ft) chassis. In 1974, the troublesome Turner gearbox in the YRQ was replaced by a five-speed overdrive-top Eaton gearbox common to the YRT. In this form the chassis was classified as the YRQ2. Other modifications applied to bring the YRQ into line with the YRT included power steering fitted as standard, air assistance for the clutch and full air brakes. A two-speed rear axle with ratios either side of the standard single-speed axle was now an option on both chassis.

Both Y-series chassis received the new 500-series Bedford 500cu in (8.2-litre) diesels in autumn 1975, so the YRT became the YMT, answering the criticism from operators that the YRT was underpowered; to cope with the power, larger brakes were fitted. A de-rated 140bhp version of the 500cu in diesel was made available as an option on the YRQ2, which then became the YLQ. In 1980 the turbocharged Blue series of Bedford 500cu in diesels became available (*see* Chapter 5) and the YMT was produced with a 206bhp variant of this engine and sold as the YNT, a prototype of which was tested for twelve months by

This June 1978 YMT has an early Plaxton Supreme fifty-one-seat body. It seems to have lost its aluminium grille bars from the front panel at some point, though looks none the worse for it. Applebys Coaches of Conisholm, Lincolnshire bought it new and it still looked smart twelve years later when photographed in Broadgate, Lincoln in September 1990. The Broadgate Fish Restaurant in the background is now the Broadgate Dental Surgery, but the buildings are largely unchanged twenty-five years on.

This Duple Viceroy forty-five-seat coach on a June 1971 YRQ chassis was new to Edinburgh Corporation Transport. In 1975 Edinburgh Corporation Transport department passed to the Lothian Regional Council's Department of Public Transport and was renamed Lothian Regional Transport.

Tricentrol, the Dunstable operator and Bedford dealer, covering 50,000 miles (80,000km) prior to launch of the production chassis in October 1980. The prototype YNT was fitted with a Turner M6 six-speed gearbox, though production models were generally fitted with the Spicer T6 six-speed box. In 1982, the ZF S6-65 all-synchromesh gearbox, with slightly closer ratios than the Spicer, became an option on the YNT.

The YMT remained available with the less-powerful engine option of the normally aspirated 160bhp variant of the 500cu in diesel or a de-rated turbocharged version that developed 175bhp. One of the advantages of turbocharging is that it tends to make the exhaust quieter, a useful side-effect for a passenger vehicle application — it was now Bedford's intention that eventually all its engines should be turbocharged. However, it should be borne in mind that virtually all combinations of engine and gearbox could be had subject to special order — or, as Bedford called it 'non-RPO', non-regular production order. Thus specifications could vary quite widely from what might be considered 'standard'.

Bedford clearly suffered some difficulty in matching its engines with suitable gearboxes, as the variety of ratios and gearboxes that appeared through the life of the Y-series shows. This is reinforced by the comments of testers and operators, who complained of ill-matched ratios and difficult gear changes.

One of the minor revisions applied to the YMT was the replacement of the plastic locking collar on the spring parking brake lever with a metal item, the plastic version being prone to wear and breakage.

Demand for shorter (or 'midi') buses and coaches had become apparent with the success of the Bristol LHS and similar products, so in 1978 a short version of the YLQ was offered by Bedford, suitable for 8.2m (27ft) coachwork. This was not, however, a new chassis but a conversion carried out by Tricentrol Chassis Developments of Dunstable,

The shortened wheelbase of the YLQS is quite apparent in this photograph of Tricentrol of Dunstable's entry in the 1979 Blackpool Coach rally. CTM 85T was actually the prototype for the conversion, carried out by Tricentrol Engineering. The body is a thirty-five-seat Duple Dominant II. The coach later passed to Ambassador of Carsington, in the Peak District of Derbyshire, where it lost its original registration number and became KIW 7811.

in collaboration with Bedford engineers. The conversion involved reducing the wheelbase of the chassis by chopping a section out of the frame side members then welding the remaining sections together again. The joint was reinforced by additional plating Huck bolted and welded to the chassis side members. The result of this modification was that the engine was located 19.5in (495mm) further forward than previously. The propeller shaft was shortened then balanced and a smaller 36gal (164ltr) fuel tank fitted.

In this form the chassis was known as the YLQ/S; the prototype was registered CTM 75T and the conversion continued to be offered throughout the chassis' evolution as the YMQ/S and the YMP/S until 1987, the final twenty apparently being converted by Bedford at the Dunstable plant. At £11,714 in 1979, the YLQ/S was not cheap, but the resultant conversion provided a lively and versatile small coach that was an economic proposition.

Not content with creating shorter versions of the YLQ and its successors, Tricentrol also created a Vauxhall-approved 12m (39ft) maximum-dimension version of the YMT to meet a demand for larger touring and express coaches. Additional length was created within the wheelbase by inserting a new section 18in (457mm) long just behind the gearbox. The new section was reinforced well beyond its length by a flitch plate attached to the existing frame by Huck lock bolts. An extra cross-member was inserted into the chassis frame to carry a support bearing for an additional propeller shaft of the same length. The suspension was augmented front and rear using Aeon rub-

Marton's Coaches of West Drayton used this April 1985 YMP/S with Plaxton Paramount thirty-five-seat body on airport shuttles between Heathrow Airport and the Forum Hotel, Kensington.

ber springs, and larger tyres of 10.00 × 20in size were fitted. The chassis was then suitable for fitting with bodies of maximum legal length, though modifications were necessary to some 12m (39ft) bodies to enable the YMT to meet the requirements of the Ministry's tilt test and an extra 22in (559mm) had to be added in the rear overhang by the coachbuilder. The prototype, registered RGS 598R, was operated by Tricentrol for a number of years and is now preserved by the Eastern Transport Collection. The stretched YMT chassis is sometimes referred to as the YMT/L but this is not consistently applied. At under £35,000 bodied, the stretched YMT was the cheapest 12m (39ft) coach on the market by far.

Amongst many minor revisions, at some point in production there was a change in the rear hub oil seals from a Chicago rawhide type to a lip seal and O-ring to reduce the tendency for leakage.

The coding of the Y-series chassis warrants a brief explanation. Essentially, the second letter in the code represents the engine range employed, hence R for the 466cu in engine, L for the first series of 500cu in engine, M for the later 500cu in engine in 160bhp and 175bhp form and N for the 500cu in engine in 205bhp form. The third letter indicated the expected overall length, hence Q for 10m (33ft) length and T for 11m (36ft). An unexpected problem arose in 1981 when the National Highway Traffic Safety Administration in the USA introduced a standardized form of Vehicle Identity Number (VIN), which was required to be used by all vehicles sold in the USA and has since been

The 1982 10m (33ft) YMP chassis with centrally mounted Blue series engine.

adopted world-wide. General Motors, as an American-owned company, was naturally required to adopt this system immediately. The most noticeable effect was a further revision in chassis codes as the VIN number could no longer include the letter 'Q'; thus the YMQ became the YMP and the YMQ/S became the YMP/S.

After Bedford ceased manufacture of PSV chassis at the end of 1986, customers began to find support difficult. In particular, while the 500cu in engines could be successfully rebuilt by a competent engine remanufacturer, some parts were getting hard to find so other engine replacement options became viable. United Counties Engineering Ltd was a Cummins dealer established in 1986 and whose origins were the Central Repair Works for the former Tilling Group company United Counties Omnibus Co. Ltd. Trading as UCE, the company fitted a number of Y-series coaches with a specially adapted version of the Cummins 6BTA 360cu in (5.9-litre) turbocharged 180bhp diesel engine. The conversions included a Lipe ceramic clutch, a new power-steering pump and compressor. The cost was £5,900. A similar conversion of the Y-series using the Cummins 6BTA was also offered by Coombs Motors Ltd of Hastings, East Sussex. At least thirty chassis were modified in this way, the YMT being the most common.

BODIES

Despite the use of a vertical engine, the overall size of the Bedford diesel and the careful positioning of it in the frame meant that a level and reasonably low floor line could be achieved, though it would not have been possible for a bus-bodied Y-series to have met the accessibility regulations in force today. Coachbuilders were generally able to adapt their existing designs easily to fit the YRQ, having built bodies on chassis with mid-mounted engines from other manufacturers for many years; so for the first few years of Y-series production the casual observer would have been hard put to distinguish between an early YRQ and a late VAM without boarding the vehicle.

Duple, Plaxton and Willowbrook

Both Duple and Plaxton soon had bodies mounted on the YRQ and both were shown at the Commercial Motor Show in September 1970. Duple's body was naturally its current model, the Viceroy, though with an improved entrance with a power-operated door with safety sensing switches at the edge and an improved driver's cab. In common with current Viceroy specifications, as fitted to the VAM and other chassis, the lower corners were protected by rubber

XAW 509K. A later version of the Willowbrook bus body originally designed for the VAM, showing the restyled front panel and grille fitted to these bodies from 1971. Seen in May 1978, it is one of a number bought by Whittle of Highley on YRQ chassis in 1972. By the time this photograph was taken in May 1978, it was with Wiles of Port Seton, East Lothian, Scotland.

bumpers and the skirt panels were curved under at the bottom to minimize damage at kerb level. This latest version was known as the Viceroy 32 and seated forty-five in a body 32ft 6.375in (9.92m) long.

In 1972 the Viceroy gave way to the Dominant, available in both standard coach form and to New Bus Grant specification with power-operated glider doors under the control of the driver. In this form the body was known as the Dominant Express.

The Plaxton body for the Y series was a new version of the standard product, the Panorama Elite, now in its Elite II form and seating forty-five — and at 32ft 6in (9.91m) long, just 0.375in (9.5mm) shorter than the Viceroy 32! Changes from the Elite to the Elite II were fairly limited but included a refined front grille and pantograph windscreen wipers. The show model had two tables and peacock-blue curtains for Silverline Tours of Hounslow. The Elite II evolved into the Elite III and, as with earlier models of the Elite, it was available in New Bus Grant form as the Elite III Express. A number of Elite IIIs were built on late YRQ chassis.

Two new bodies appeared on the YRQ for 1971, both of the express or dual-purpose bus type, which was becoming quite popular with operators because they qualified for the government's New Bus Grant. Willowbrook brought out its unimaginatively named Express, an example of which formed the basis of a demonstrator. Registered EXE 276J, it provided useful service to Vauxhall, later being acquired by Blue Bus (Tailby & George) Ltd of Willington, who had a history of buying ex-demonstrators and clearly found them to be good value for money! A variant of the Express with a shallower roofline was also offered and known as the Expressway and fitted with full luxury coach seating. Both bodies were of all-metal construction and Willowbrook claimed that its product was the only all-metal body in volume production in the UK, a statement that could probably have been challenged by several coachbuilders had they felt

inclined. Vauxhall's other YRQ demonstrator SXE 663L was fitted with an Expressway body, with only thirty seats and a rear toilet compartment. The Willowbrook bus body as fitted to the VAM continued to be available with minor changes, including a slight increase in maximum seating capacity, for the YRQ.

The introduction in 1974 of a bus version of Duple's 1972 Dominant coach body was a significant event as many would be built on Bedford Y-series chassis. The Dominant bus body was built to Duple's Phase II standard of construction in all-steel with a tubular frame, with certain exterior panels in fibreglass. Unlike rival Plaxton's Derwent body, which had been based on a BET Federation design, the Dominant bus body looked to NBC's Leyland National for its influences, with its square cross-section and frontal aspect, while incorporating styling features such as the front grille and headlamps from the Dominant coach range to give a familial look to the product. With its large, flat, rubber-mounted side windows that gave passengers a good view of the countryside and a light, airy interior, it was an attractive package on the Bedford Y series and deservedly successful. Pillar spacing was identical with the Dominant coach and the wide-step entrance and air-operated door were to New Bus Grant specification, making the finances attractive to small operators. Mounted on the YRQ, the body seated forty-seven passengers and was 32ft 8in (9.9m) long and 8ft 2.5in (2.5m) wide, though a 7ft 6in (2.29m)-wide body was also available. The Dominant body proved adaptable: two YRQs were supplied to the social services department of the London Borough of Greenwich in 1976, the Duple bodies incorporating a Ratcliffe lift at the nearside to allow wheelchair passengers to board. The coaches had forty-three seats on rails, which allowed for easy removal to create more wheelchair space if necessary. The side-lifts were modified by Duple so the coaches could receive a full PSV Certificate of Fitness.

Cleveland Transit fleet no. 357 was a forty-seven-seat Duple Dominant/YRQ bus dating from December 1974 – at least it was, until Cleveland Transit performed major surgery on it to make it into a midi bus... A. STRONG

...and here is the result. Cleveland Transit fleet no. 357 after removal of the rear overhang and consequent reduction in seating capacity from forty-seven to thirty-six.

The **Willowbrook** bus bodies for the **YRQ** and **VAM** chassis were superficially very similar, but the extra length of the **YRQ** allowed an additional emergency exit to be fitted just behind the driver on the offside on some versions, as seen here on this 1973 example belonging to Chambers of Bures, Suffolk. The bus was in Sudbury when the photograph was taken.

Vauxhall had two **YRQ** demonstrators fitted with Willowbrook bodies. This one, shown here while operated by The Kings Ferry Bus & Coach Co. of Gillingham, Kent, had an Expressway body that originally seated only thirty passengers and had a toilet compartment in the rear. It is seen here on 14 May 1974 at Dover and was new in January 1973.

Willowbrook introduced a new range of coach bodies in 1972 for the 1973 season, all based on the earlier Expressway but more luxuriously appointed. All had the then fashionable square cross-sectional appearance and were of all-metal construction. The Expressway name was now dropped and the 10m (33ft) body for the YRT was now called the 002. The standard service bus body was revamped and now available for the YRT.

The YRT also formed the basis of a 12m (39ft) 002 executive coach from Willowbrook for Hutchison's of Overtown, Lanarkshire, the coach being intended for weekend charters from Glasgow to Paris. It seated thirty passengers, was fitted with a toilet, bar and television set and cost around £17,000 in December 1972. One of the advantages of the overall square cross-section aspect of the body was the excellent vision this allowed for both driver and passengers. Some of the extras available in the Executive version of the 002 included a stereo music system, Honda auxiliary generator, wash basin with hot and cold water, toilet and a Cona Coffee machine. When mounted on a YRT chassis, a fully specified 002 could cost in excess of £15,250. A peculiarity of the 002 was that even in Executive form it came with two-leaf power-operated folding doors ('bus grant' doors), which were reported to be a constant source of draughts and made it difficult to maintain an even temperature within the coach.

For the 1975 season Willowbrook showed its updated coach body in 11m (36ft) form on the YRT, now named the 008, at the Commercial Motor Show in September 1974.

YYB 967N. This September 1974 YRQ with forty-five-seat Plaxton Elite III Express coachwork was seen in Weston-super-Mare when new with Blagdon Lioness of Blagdon, Somerset. It was operating a contract bus service for Sainsbury's supermarkets at the time. It was later acquired by Phillips Coaches Holywell Ltd of Holywell, Flintshire. A. STRONG

The new model did not, however, continue the square look of the 002, reverting to barrelled sides and windows as employed in contemporary models from Plaxton. Allegedly styled by George Hughes, chairman of Willowbrook, the front end was particularly distinctive with a sharply raked (and non-industry standard) laminated windscreen swept up at each side to the level of the side waist rail.

Below the windscreen, the grille was finished in matt black with three headlamps on each side. A stainless steel bumper was fitted, mounted to the chassis, the bumper also holding the side, turn indicator and fog lights. The front registration plate opened to reveal the chassis-mounted towing eyes. At the rear, the single-piece window was set at an angle and the rear luggage locker arranged so that luggage could be loaded without having to be lifted over a sill. The 008 continued the all-metal construction of the 002, with solid-riveted steel frames and stress panels treated to resist corrosion. Exterior panels were in aluminium for the outer side panels and fibreglass for the quarter panels, front and rear panels, wheelarches and entrance step well. The floor was in fire-resistant plywood. From 1975 the 008 was renamed the Spacecar, the first batch all being built on YRT chassis. The Spacecar was replaced by the all-metal 003 body from 1980.

Plaxton's smaller Supreme body was updated and enlarged in 1975 to allow it to be fitted to the YRT in fifty-

Willowbrook's Spacecar body appeared in 1975 as the replacement for the firm's 008 body. The example shown here seated forty-nine passengers and was new to National Travel (South East) in April 1976. It was photographed on 16 July 1982, when owned by E. V. Wing of Sleaford, Lincolnshire. Wings was acquired by Sleafordian Coaches in 2005.

three-seat form. An example was on show at Plaxton's Scarborough and Ware sites in July of that year. An updated version, known as the Supreme Express, with a revised grille, entrance door, side mouldings, bumpers and external lighting, appeared in 1978 and in 10m (33ft) form was suitable for fitting on the YLQ chassis.

A new grille, side mouldings and entrance door were amongst other minor updates for the Plaxton Supreme range in 1978, and the company showed a 10m (33ft) Supreme Express body on a YLQ chassis at the Commercial Motor Show that year.

From April 1977 Duple's Dominant II body in both bus and coach form became available on the YMT.

Both versions of the Dominant coach were offered in express (New Bus Grant-compliant) form, had Ziebart anti-corrosion treatment to all steel work, adjustable tracks on the floor and body sides to enable the seats to be easily re-spaced and external access to electrical systems and fuses.

The Dominant continued to be available in service bus form for the YLQ and YMT. Basic specification of the single-deck bus body included power folding entrance doors, an illuminated 'Pay as you enter' sign for driver-only operation, interior parcel racks and multi-slat Treadmaster floor covering in the gangway. On all but the YLQ models the entrance door on the Dominant service bus was wider and Deans' two-leaf power-operated folding doors were fitted as standard.

Duple produced a special version of its Dominant coach body for 1978 and called it the Dominant Goldliner. The Goldliner was a joint exercise between Duple and National Travel Ltd and was built to meet some of the requirements of the GRSA (Group of Rapporteurs on Safety Provisions on Motor Coaches and Buses). Of all-steel Duple 'phase 2' electrically welded square-tube construction, the prototype had forty-nine seats and was built on a YMT chassis. It underwent trials in North Africa before entering service with National Travel (South East). A Goldliner body was also fitted to the YNT prototype tested by Tricentrol for Bedford in 1979.

Alf Moseley Group

Alf Moseley's body for the Y-series was the Portuguese Moseley Continental Porto, based on the standard Salvador Caetano coach shell but with a simpler finish. Sliding top ventilators were fitted to the 32in deep (813mm) side windows. The Porto body had four large ceiling-mounted fluorescent lights; the ceiling itself was trimmed in laminates and was fitted with five-way Weathershield lift-up roof

ventilators. The interior stress panels were also trimmed with laminates, styled in a grained wood finish, and the floor was covered with 0.125in (3.2mm) linoleum. A large luggage locker was fitted at the rear of the body. The driver was separated from the passengers by a full-height partition, and air-operated twin-leaf jack-knife entrance doors were fitted. Compared with the similarly priced Willow-

Wearing the striking livery of well-known coach firm Golden Miller, allegedly named after the race horse that won Grand National in 1934, this fifty-three-seat Plaxton Supreme IV body on a 1979 YMT chassis was delivered new to F. G. Wilder & Sons Limited of Feltham, Middlesex. Wilder acquired the Golden Miller business in 1955 and bought nine YMTs between 1977 and 1980.

'Bristol' dome and New Bus Grant doors are notable features of this fifty-three-seat Plaxton Supreme IV on Hedingham & District Omnibus Ltd's January 1981 YMT.

This 1980 YMT had a fifty-three-seat Salvador Caetano Alpha body. It was one of three identical coaches bought new by long-established operator Red Rover Omnibus Ltd of Aylesbury, Buckinghamshire, in May 1980. In addition to excursions and tours, Red Rover ran a number of local bus services in and around Aylesbury. The name is perpetuated by Arriva, currently the dominant operator in the area. FJO 144V later passed to Mil-Ken Travel Ltd of Cambridge. P. NICHOLAS

South Wales was notable for its multiplicity of small municipal bus fleets that existed until the early 1970s. Pictured on a wet day in Wales, this fifty-three-seat YRT was new to Gelligaer Urban District Council in December 1973. However, it did not remain with its first operator for long as the urban districts of Caerphilly, Bedwas & Machen and Gelligaer were merged in 1974 to form Rhymney Valley District Council, who became the primary operator in that area. RTG 221M has an early Duple Dominant Express body to New Bus Grant specification. Photographed in 1975, fourteen years later the coach was still in service with Brewers Motor Services Ltd of Caereu, Cardiff.

The Supreme body began to replace the Elite in Plaxton's range from 1975. This April 1977 YLQ with forty-five-seat Supreme body was still with its original owner, Yeomans Canyon Travel of Canon Pyon, Herefordshire when photographed in July 1988.

brook Express body, the Porto was well-specified though its gangway was 4in (102mm) narrower than Willowbrook's at seat cushion height; the seats, however, were slightly wider, at 18in (457mm) per passenger compared with the 17in (432mm) of the Express, and the luggage racks somewhat shallower. The unladen weight of the Porto on the YRQ was 17cwt (215.9kg) heavier than the Willowbrook Express, at 6 tons 19cwt (6,337kg). For the body only, the Porto cost £5,265.

Moseley showed an example of its 11m (36ft) Caetano Estoril II body on a YRT chassis at the 1972 Commercial Motor Show; this body was to Moseley's 'Continental Executive Pullman' specification with thirty-two reclining seats, side curtains, a lounge area with eight coach seats, hot and cold water systems, card tables, cocktail cabinet, television receiver and other luxury items befitting a coach of this class. Heating and ventilation were thermostatically controlled.

An interesting development in 1973 from the Moseley group was a forty-five-seat integral-construction coach based on a Caetano Cascais II body fitted with YRQ mechanical units. The engine was vertically mounted at the rear and drove through a standard Bedford axle. It did not find quite the popularity that perhaps it deserved and only around seven or eight were built, including one sumptuous example for the Texaco oil company. An extension of the executive theme, it had eight swivel chairs and a conference area at the rear, Sumak air-conditioning and a three-phase auxiliary diesel generator for kitchen and other electrical equipment.

Moseley was soon supplying fifty-three-seat 11m Caetano Estoril II bodies mounted on the YMT chassis, updated to include fully automatic thermostatically controlled heating and ventilation and a new layout of exterior colour schemes, Moseley now badging its bodies 'Moseley Continental'. The Moseley Caetano Continental Alpha was introduced in late 1978 on the YMT chassis and seated fifty-three. Of strikingly square cross-section, with very slim window pillars, deep windscreen and shallow roof line, the Alpha was clean and stylish in appearance and less fussy than earlier Caetano products.

The Y-Series Abroad

The YRT became the YMT in 1976, the YRQ becoming the YLQ in turn with the introduction of the new 500cu

169 YEV (formerly XPT 871R). Seen in Crawley on 20 April 1985 at the start of the Saturday Road Run for the 1985 British Coach Rally, is this Cedric's of Wivenhoe, Essex YMT with fifty-three-seat Jonckheere Bermuda body. New to Northern Motor Rentals of Sunderland, it is thought this was one of only two YMTs with this body. Dodds of Troon had the other. I. LAWSON

in engines from Bedford. With these new chassis came new body options, including the Belgian Jonckheere Bermuda for the YMT.

The Bermuda had a tubular steel frame and featured bonded, curved side windows, which formed part of the structure of the frame.

Bedfords had always sold well in Australia and a popular combination in the late 1970s was a special version of the Duple Dominant body on the YMT, the exporter being Arlington Motor Co. and the Australian importer being Smithfield Bus & Coach Pty Ltd of Sydney. The export Dominant was based on the Express version and was modified in a number of ways from its UK counterpart; a roof-mounted exhaust outlet required the exhaust plumbing to be routed up the rear of the vehicle, PVC seats were fitted to meet Australian fire regulations and front and rear lighting was also modified to meet the local regulations. A more obvious outward modification was a reduction in the length of the rear overhang causing a commensurate reduction in seating capacity to forty-nine.

New in 1978 and first seen at the British Coach Rally that year, was a Spanish-built Unicar body on the YMT chassis, distributed by the Alf Moseley group. Built by Union Carrocera, the steel-framed Unicar body featured full anti-corrosion protection, an entrance to New Bus Grant specification, large windows with drain slots for condensation to escape and an easy-clean flat floor. Gas struts were employed on all hinged opening panels. Electrical systems were fed from a dedicated illuminated and sealed cubicle located on UK vehicles at the front right-hand side of the body. Fuses were also located in the same cubicle, as was the screen-washer reservoir. Of the then-fashionable square-ish cross-section outline, a distinctive feature of the Unicar was a lowered roofline over the entrance and driving position. Although attractive and stylish (and described by Moseley as 'pleasingly competitive' in price), the Unicar

was somewhat more expensive than its UK counterparts. Nevertheless, a good number of Unicar bodies were sold in the UK.

Van Hool McArdle produced its 300-Line body for the YMT, with fifty-three moquette-trimmed seats. Based on a welded steel-tube frame, the body had external panelling in aluminium with fibreglass front and rear sections. The 300-Line was superseded in 1978 by the Aragon range, manufactured in Zaragoza, Spain.

Also from overseas, the Hungarian coachbuilder Ikarus,

Eighty-four Unicar bodies were recorded as built on Bedford chassis. The prototype was built on a VAS5, the remainder on YMT chassis. GAO 628V had body no. 17 in Unicar's Bedford series and was supplied new to Irvings Coach Hire Ltd of Carlisle, Cumbria, in January 1980. It was photographed at Newcastle on 25 March 1982.

Hungarian coachbuilder Ikarus offered its 238-series body on the YMT chassis from 1980 until 1986.
V. BELYAEVE

Golden Miller's first two YMTs were purchased in 1977. Registered PPE 661R and PPE 662R, they both had fifty-three-seat bodies built by Van Hool McArdle in Ireland and based on the 300-line range of bodies designed by Van Hool in Belgium.

SGS 509W. Looking very smart in the livery of E. J. Reid (Cedar Coaches) Ltd of, appropriately, Bedford, is this fifty-three-seat Duple Dominant II/YMT of March 1981. It was new to Armchair Travel of Brentford.

Enormous seating capacity could be achieved in an 11m (36ft) bus body on YMT chassis. This Wadham Stringer-bodied YMT seated sixty-one in a three-and-two arrangement. The bus was new to Maidstone Borough Council in March 1981. In December 1986 it came to Metrobus of Crawley, West Sussex (a company created from the assets of Tillingbourne in September 1983), then on to Caves of Solihull in September 1987, as pictured here on the 24 March 1988. Its final destination appears to have been Primrose Coaches of Leominster in May 1997.

based in Budapest, offered its Model-238 inter-urban bus on the YMT in left-hand-drive form from 1980 until 1986.

Van Hool's 1980 offering on the YMT chassis was the 11m (36ft) Alizee body, seating fifty-three. An interesting optional feature of this body was the full step-well for the offside emergency door that could be used as an entrance and exit on continental tours.

In 1982, the Spanish coachbuilder Ayats built an example of its D'Cotta Brisa lightweight fifty-three-seat body on the YNT, the complete coach costing £46,000.

Y-Series Buses

In addition to the current Plaxton Derwent, Duple Dominant and Willowbrook service buses, a number of other coachbuilders offered service bus bodies on the Y-series. Walter Alexander (Belfast) Ltd built a good quantity of forty-five-seat bus bodies on the YRQ chassis in a fairly plain version for Ulsterbus, and the parent company at Falkirk also built around ninety of the familiar and distinctive Alexander Y-type body, on YRQ and YRT chassis. These came in both bus and coach form with seating capacities ranging from thirty-eight to forty-five.

On the inter-urban bus theme, the 1980 Wadham Stringer Vanguard bus body was also available with fifty-three seats on the standard-wheelbase YMT, though this could be squeezed up to sixty-one seats by adopting two-and three-a-side seating, an arrangement that was not popular with passengers.

To challenge the Dominants of Duple, Plaxton introduced an all-new bus body with seating for between fifty and

The Alexander Y-type body was uniquely attractive and distinctive in its styling, reminding one instantly of Scotland. Perhaps one of the best bus and coach bodies of its era, certainly one of the most recognizable, this example had thirty-eight coach seats and was one of fifteen delivered in 1974. It was seen here in Eastern Scottish livery in August 1979.

The Duple Dominant styling worked well when applied to a bus body. This fifty-five-seat 1986 YMT was new to Arran Transport of Brodick, Isle of Arran in the Firth of Clyde. It was captured by the camera in June 1988.

fifty-five passengers for 1980 on the YMT chassis, named, somewhat more imaginatively than usual, 'the Bustler'.

The Bustler was based on the same framing that was used in the Supreme coach body but with a more obvious and not displeasing contemporary bus outline. Fifty-three standard Deans-type tubular-metal-framed bus seats were fitted along with a full-height driver's partition, a wide, air-operated four-leaf entrance door, fluorescent lighting and three saloon heaters. The high waistline betrayed the body's coach origins and made the side windows look rather smaller than they actually were; as usual with bus bodies on the Y series, the floor line was also high. The front end was best described as 'restrained' and lacked the style of the rival Duple Dominant.

A new Derwent body was also introduced in 1986, to replace the Bustler and derived from it. Distinguishing features of the second-generation Derwent body were deeper cove panels, square windows with very slim pillars as in the Paramount coach body and a redesigned front panel and radiator opening.

Robert Wright

Near the end of production of Bedford PSV chassis, the fifty-three-seat Wright TT all-aluminium bus body became available on the YMT. The TT body was of the by-then typical square cross-section, quite simply built with glazing set in rubber gaskets and with a somewhat odd-looking three-

Langley Park Motor Co. Of Durham traded as Gypsy Queen Coaches and bought this fifty-five-seat, first-generation Plaxton Derwent-bodied YRT bus in July 1976. The location of this photograph was Robert Miles County Junior School, Bingham, near Nottingham, and the date 12 May 1983. It was still in its original owner's colours despite being owned by Gilbert of Bingham.

piece front windscreen arrangement, with a large central, almost rectangular flat section and two vestigial polygonal windows set either side. Seats were generally trimmed in moquette but the covering could be specified by the operator and the interior was spacious, light and airy for passengers. The body was well finished and designed for a long life with quick and easy repair. With a potential capacity of sixty-one passengers, at £47,500 (1986) it represented good value for money. However, while the floor was completely flat, for a 1980s bus it was undeniably high to clear the vertical engine, necessitating four steps from the ground – quite a steep climb for the elderly or disabled. On the positive side, the entrance was wide with well-placed handrails, noise levels inside the body were low and the interior was attractively finished in light-coloured laminates. A single overhead parcel rack was provided down one side of the saloon and concealed lighting was fitted in the coving panels on the opposite side to the parcel rack. The whole gave a roomy and light appearance to the interior, clean and free from obstructions. It was certainly distinctive, but not unattractive to look at. At an on-the-road price of £47,500 it represented good value for money.

Wright also built its new luxury Contour body, developed jointly with Bedford stylists at Luton, on a Tricentrol-lengthened YNT chassis in 1982. Illustrated on page 165, the all-aluminium body was built on Alusuisse framing and was styled to give an aerodynamic, smooth look, helped by the carefully styled lift-up side locker doors, plug-type entrance door, spats over the rear wheel openings and flush-fitting, bonded windscreens and side glazing. Headlights were mounted behind a glass panel with wipers. Rubber flooring insulation and better engine encapsulation reduced interior noise levels and the seating was provided by fifty-three Chardon recliners. Capacity was generally fifty-one or fifty-three on a 12m (39ft) chassis, or forty-six with toilet facilities. Versions were also built on the 10m (33ft) YMP, some with thirty-four seats and toilet facilities, one of which was supplied to the Soviet Embassy in London. The Contour was undoubtedly in the vanguard of the new look for the 1980s.

The Last Words from Duple and Plaxton

Duple's answer to the Wright Contour for the 11m (36ft) YNT chassis was the conservatively styled fifty-three-seat Laser, built on steel frames with Ziebart anti-corrosion protection and aluminium external panels. The Laser featured bonded glazing, a body-coloured front grille and curved frontal aspect but, while of quite contemporary appearance, it was clear that Duple (by now part of the Hestair

This 1984 YNT carries a Duple Laser 320 body seating fifty-three passengers. It was new to S. Rae of Whitehaven in Cumbria but was owned by Rydal of Richmond, North Yorkshire when this photograph was taken in Darlington in July 1992.

RRT 110W. A YMQ/S with Duple Dominant thirty-five-seat body. This particular chassis is recorded as a YMQ in most lists, despite obviously being the short version. It was owned by JDW of Ipswich, Suffolk, when this photograph was taken at Cromer.

group) was struggling to compete. The general styling was fairly plain and understated, though driver vision was excellent through the large windscreen. Passenger vision was equally good, with slim side window pillars dividing the side windows that curved slightly inwards towards the roof. The Laser 2 replaced the original 1982 version in 1984. While the external changes were largely superficial, changes in construction meant that all external panels were now bonded together. A new thermostatically controlled heating system was now a standard feature. An Executive version of the Laser 2 was available, which featured a sunken toilet compartment at the rear of the body. Plaxton's mid-

1980s offerings, the Paramount (succeeding the Supreme in 1982), Paramount II and III were also built on Y-series chassis, including a special thirty-five seat Paramount III on a YMP/S for Gordon's of Rotherham.

SALES AND PRODUCTION

The Y-series was undoubtedly highly successful for Vauxhall and for the Bedford name. Ignoring the YNV Venturer, which is dealt with later, just a few hundred short of 10,000

A817 XCA (LIL 2104). This 1984 YMP with Plaxton Paramount forty-five-seat body was fleet no. 10 with Bostocks Coaches of Congleton, Cheshire. The Paramount replaced the Supreme in Plaxton's range from 1982. It later passed to Emma's Coaches, Dolgellau with a new registration number – LIL 2104.

Y-series chassis are recorded as being sold. Of these, the most popular chassis was the YMT, with over 3,200 recorded. The YRQ was almost equally successful, with over 2,400 recorded, and the YRT was just behind, with just over 2,000 recorded. Of the other Y-series chassis, a little over 800 were YNTs and over 700 were YLQs. Next were the YMP, with around 170, and the YMQ, with around 130. Of the Tricentrol-modified chassis, just three YLQ/Ss are accounted for and seventeen YMQ/Ss, ten of which went to Eastern National with Wadham Stringer thirty-three-seat bus bodies, and five to South Wales Transport with Lex Maxeta thirty-seven-seat bus bodies. Part of the problem of accounting for numbers is that the shortened chassis were not always recorded as such, so there are likely to be more of each type than accounted for. The longer Tricentrol chassis was perhaps not surprisingly more popular, given the price of the shortened chassis; twenty-one YMT/Ls and thirty-four YNT/Ls are recorded.

The Y-series was exported in small quantities. The available figures are probably wildly inaccurate, accounting for only just over 100 chassis. The most popular export destinations, roughly in order of quantity, were Cyprus, Denmark, New Zealand, Australia and Eire. Many more found their way overseas after service in the UK, often to Cyprus, Malta or Gozo.

Of the Y-series as a whole, the largest fleet in the UK was Barton Transport, with 208 recorded, followed by Whittle of Highley, Ulsterbus and Bexleyheath Transport (169, 169 and 110, respectively).

Alder Valley, successors to Aldershot & District Traction Co. and Thames Valley Traction Co., took two YMQ/S with Lex Maxeta thirty-seven-seat bodies in March 1985. This one carries fleet no. 303.

This YMQ/S was new to Eastern National Omnibus Co. Ltd of Chelmsford, Essex. It was one of ten with thirty-three-seat dual-purpose Wadham Stringer Vanguard bodies. Fleet no. 1054 was based at Enfield and was operating a service on behalf of London Transport when this photograph was taken.

YRQ

On release in September 1970, the standard YRQ without power steering cost £2,807 in the UK and was the lowest-priced mid-engine chassis available. With a forty-five-seat Duple Viceroy body, the total cost was £7,182. By comparison, in 1970 a loaf of bread cost 9p and a small terraced house averaged around £4,900. By 1974, the updated YRQ2 chassis price was £3,632; when fitted with a Plaxton Panorama Elite III body the total cost was £10,275.

Operators who favoured the YRQ included Whittle of Highley (who took seventy, mostly Duple but a couple of Willowbrook between 1971 and 1975, generally selling them on again after twelve months), Scottish Omnibuses (sixty-one, Alexander, 1971–5), United Counties Omnibus Co. Ltd, Northampton (thirty-five, Willowbrook, 1973–5), Hills of Tredegar (thirty-two, Duple and Plaxton, 1971–6), Barton Transport (twenty-one, Plaxton and Willowbrook, 1971), Ewer Group (Grey-Green; twenty, Plaxton, 1973–4), the Atomic Weapons Research Establishment (AWRE) at Aldermaston (eighteen, Marshall, Strachans and Willowbrook, 1972–7), Moor-Dale Group

Coaches Ltd (twenty, mostly Plaxton but a few Duple, 1971–3) and L. F. Bowen of Saltley, Birmingham (sixteen, Caetano and Duple, 1971–2). Operators who bought fifteen or more new included Jolly of South Hylton (Duple and Willowbrook), Park of South Hamilton (Duple, Plaxton and Caetano) and OK Motor Services, Bishop Auckland (Plaxton, Duple and Willowbrook).

Duple and Plaxton between them built the majority of bodies for YRQs, Duple being slightly ahead at around 1,100 with Plaxton responsible for just over 900. Willowbrook built over 200, while Caetano scored a respectable seventy-five and Alexander sixty-two. Van Hool and Wright managed twelve and seven, respectively.

Unusual purchasers were Nottingham Corporation Transport, who bought several YRQs with forty-nine-seat Willowbrook Expressway bodies to New Bus Grant specification in 1972. These were intended to assist in expanding the undertaking's private hire operations and were quite luxuriously finished. Interior panels were finished in ICI Vynair padded textured plastics.

The Scottish bus group ordered twenty YRQs in 1974 and tried a demonstrator fitted with GM-Allison four-

Rare Marshall Camair coachwork seating fifty-three passengers is fitted to this April 1973 YRT. Records suggest that it was possibly the only Camair body to be built on a Bedford chassis. It was bought new by Hedingham & District Omnibus Co. and was later acquired by Partridge Coaches of Hadleigh, Suffolk before being destroyed by fire in 1999.

speed fully automatic transmission with a CAV electronic controller.

A YRQ with an adapted Plaxton Panorama body was perhaps the most unusual Bedford sale for 1972; a London businessman, Mr T. Norman, had a luxurious mobile home created by Trevor Hazen Associates Ltd of Maldon, Essex with two bedrooms, a fully fitted kitchen and a spacious lounge. The vehicle came complete with a sophisticated electrical system and was probably the most expensive vehicle of its type to date. Also in 1972, the George Ewer Group ordered twenty YRQs with Plaxton Panorama Elite II bodies for its Grey-Green fleet, the largest order for Grey-Green since 1965.

Increase in tourism and the oil industry brought new interest in passenger transport in the north of Scotland; the largest bus operator on the island of Orkney at the time was James D. Peace and its very first brand-new coaches for its nineteen-vehicle fleet were two YRQs with Duple Dominant bodies. One of these made what was, for the region, a very unusual trip to the mainland via the ferry introduced in 1975 to take a local party to the south.

YRT

On introduction in 1972, the YRT chassis cost £3,250. Operators who bought substantial numbers of YRTs included Ulsterbus (118, with Alexander (Belfast) bodies, 1974–5) and Barton Transport as part of its major fleet renewal programme (117, Duple and Plaxton, 1973–5, many supplied through dealer Kirkby Bus & Coach Ltd). Others included National Travel (South East; twenty-six, Duple, Plaxton and Willowbrook, 1974–6), United Counties (twenty-five, Willowbrook, 1974–6), Fox of Hayes, Middlesex (twenty-two, Duple, 1974–5), Scottish Omnibuses (twenty in 1975), New Zealand Railways (eighteen, New Zealand Motor Bodies, 1974–6), Shaw of Coventry (seventeen, Duple and Plaxton, 1972–5) and Charles Rickards (Tours), Brentford, London (fifteen, Plaxton, 1973–5). The old-established firm of Timpson's of Catford bought ten in 1974, all with Duple bodies, for its London sightseeing tours.

Edinburgh Corporation Transport bought twenty-five, with Alexander and Duple bodies, in 1972–5. Ten were Duple Dominant-bodied Bedford YRTs to New Bus Grant specification in 1973 as part of an effort by the city planners to revitalize Edinburgh's bus services as part of a wider review of the city's transport needs.

Duple remained ahead with the YRT, producing bodies for around a hundred more than Plaxton, the latter's total being around 780. Willowbrook built ninety-three bodies for the YRT and Alexander (Belfast) 118, while Alexander (Falkirk) built around thirty Y-type bodies. In New Zealand, NZMB accounted for nineteen, Edgehill twelve and Hawke for a further four. Other coachbuilders contributing in ones and twos included Wright, Marshall and Van Hool.

Looking very well presented in August 1982 when in the fleet of Jones Motors (Login) Ltd of Whitland, Dyfed is this YRT with fifty-three-seat Plaxton Supreme body. The coach dates from January 1976 and was new to the Moor-Dale Group of Newcastle. The Supreme was the replacement for the Panorama Elite range and was introduced in 1975.

Another variation of Willowbrook's popular bus body is shown here on an April 1976 YRT chassis. This forty-five-seat bus was new to Squirrells Coaches of Hitcham, Suffolk and later passed to the Eastern Counties Omnibus Co. Ltd of Norwich with whom it carried fleet no. SB811. It was subsequently acquired by Dews Coaches of Somersham, Cambridgeshire at whose premises it was photographed on 6 May 2000.

YMT

A YMT with fifty-three-seat Plaxton Supreme body cost £18,311 in April 1976; the bare chassis cost £6,375 – almost £5,000 cheaper than an AEC Reliance. The first YMT chassis with a Plaxton Supreme luxury body was supplied to Harry Shaw Ltd of Coventry, one of eight YMTs and two YLQ chassis purchased by Shaw in 1976.

The largest purchaser of YMTs new was George Ewer for Grey-Green, clearly influenced by its earlier experience with the YRQ; sixty-six with Duple bodies were purchased between 1976 and 1979. Barton Transport was the next largest customer (sixty, Plaxton, 1976–80), followed by National Travel (East; forty-six, Duple, 1977–80), Shaw of Coventry (forty-one, mostly Plaxton but a couple Duple, 1976–80), Bexleyheath Transport Co. Ltd of Bexleyheath, Kent (forty, Duple and Plaxton, 1976–80), Bebb of Llantwit Fardre (thirty-nine, mix of Caetano, Duple, Plaxton, Unicar and Van Hool, 1976–80), Fox of Hayes (thirty-eight, Duple, 1976–9), Whittle of Highley (thirty-six, Duple, 1976–80), Smiths of Tysoe, Warwickshire (thirty-five, Plaxton, 1977–9), Armchair of Brentford (thirty-three, Duple, Plaxton and Van Hool, 1976–80), Maidstone Borough Council (thirty-three, Duple, Wadham-Stringer and Wright 1978–86). Other operators who bought more than twenty YMTs new included Cleverly of Pontypool, Doig of Glasgow, Jeffs of Helmdon, Moor-Dale of Newcastle, National Travel (South East) and Tappin of Wallingford.

In 1976, Nottingham City Transport replaced its last eight double-decks with Duple Dominant bus-bodied Bedford YMTs fitted with Allison fully automatic gearboxes. With two-and-three seating at the rear of the saloon and space for standees, they could accommodate sixty-nine passengers and were considered suitable for replacing seventy-seat double-decks.

Plaxton and Duple built the majority of bodies on the YMT, though Van Hool and Van Hool McArdle accounted for over 130 and Unicar for over eighty. Wright bodied seventeen and Willowbrook thirty-five. YMTs seemed to hold their prices well; a second-hand 1978 example with Duple body sold for £15,000 in 1980, showing barely £1,000 per year depreciation.

By 1972 Willowbrook was once again producing its own designs, having been separated from Duple though still sharing a common owner. A new range of coach bodies was introduced, the majority of which appeared on Bedford chassis at some point. This is an example of the fifty-three-seat 003 body, shown here on a 1980 YMT of Southern Vectis Omnibus Co. Ltd at Victoria coach station, London. Only four Willowbrook 003 bodies are thought to have been built on the YMT; three were bought new by Southern Vectis and the fourth by Excelsior Coaches (Yorkshire) Limited of Dinnington.

The YMT continued to be available until 1986, some of the last ones being bought by Metrobus of Orpington, Kent, who bought three with Wadham Stringer Vanguard bus bodies. The vehicles had fifty-three seats and space for fifteen standing passengers and all were fitted with GM-Allison automatic transmission. A number of YMTs with Unicar bodies found their way to Malta in the mid-1980s and gave good service on the island.

An unusual sale was to Saudi Arabia's Union Sporting Club football team, with a specially built luxury body by TDC of Rayleigh, Essex, and supplied by Len Street Ltd of Chelsea. The beautifully appointed coach cost around £50,000.

At the time of writing Jeffs Coaches are still a familiar sight on the roads of Northamptonshire and Oxfordshire. Very much a family business, Jeffs Travel was started by Jack Jeffs in 1958. This fifty-three-seat YMT with Duple Dominant II coachwork was new to Jeffs in March 1978 and was at Banbury on 13 July of that year.

IN PRESERVATION

Bedford YMT/Duple YMJ 555S

Year new: 1978
Engine: Bedford 6-cylinder 500cu in normally aspirated diesel
Gearbox: Turner Clarke five-speed gearbox
Body: Duple Dominant, fifty-three seats
Current owner: Andrew Lodge

History

YMJ 555S was new to Lodge's Coaches of High Easter, Essex, in 1978 and is currently part of the heritage collection owned by the same firm. The YMT was in regular service until 2003–4, having been cascaded down from front-line service over the years, latterly finding use on the school run.

Owner's Experience

Andrew Lodge started restoring coaches in 1989, with his first project being a Bedford SBG converted to diesel – so technically an SBO. He is currently responsible for maintaining the heritage fleet for Lodge's Coaches, which consists of two SBs, two OBs, one of which is the only surviving 'toastrack' body OB from the Lincolnshire Road Car fleet at Skegness, a pre-war WTL and a 1926 Chevrolet Q 1-ton charabanc, so the General Motors theme is strong. Andrew says that the heritage fleet contains a Bedford from every decade that Lodge's Coaches has been in operation and he has recently acquired a VAM, which is soon to be delivered.

Andrew's interest in coaches began when he joined the family firm, started in the 1920s by Andrew's grandfather. Andrew is the third generation of Lodges in the business, his father and his uncle – his father's twin brother – having carried on the business. His main skills are painting and body maintenance and repair, though he also drives in the summer and does a lot of private hire and film work with Lodge's heritage fleet.

Andrew says the coach still rides very well, with good steering and brakes with no need for a retarder or exhaust brake. It is quite well travelled, too, having been all over continental Europe – Germany, Holland and France, as well as Scotland and Ireland. These days it is kept in reserve for special occasions, but still appears on the odd school run now and then when the need arises.

While Lodge's have had several YMTs, another from only ten months old, YMJ 555S is special to Andrew because it has been in the family from new, and because of this he couldn't really let it go, parting reluctantly with the others instead. YMJ 555S has been very reliable since it entered preservation. It has not been modified from its original specification and there has been no major work done apart from the seats having been retrimmed with new covers and an external repaint. In fact Andrew can only recall one occasion in the coach's entire life when it had to be towed home, which speaks very well of both Lodge's maintenance and the general reliability of the Bedford Y-series. As the photo shows, it looks splendid and as good as the day it was delivered back in 1978.

Lodge's Coaches' YMT has been in the operational fleet from new. It looks absolutely splendid in this photograph taken at High Easter.
LODGE'S COACHES

The Duple Dominant II body was introduced in 1977. This example, on a YLQ chassis, was new to Silver Fox of Edinburgh. It is seen here during its time with Brownrigg's of Egremont, Cumbria, in company with another Bedford Y-series with Plaxton Supreme body.

YLQ

The YLQ did not attract quite the same loyalty as the YMT, though many operators with other Y-series coaches did take YLQs, including Bexleyheath Transport (fourteen, Duple and Plaxton, 1977–9), Armchair of Brentford (nine, Plaxton, 1979–81), Hills of Tredegar (nine, Duple and Plaxton, 1976–8) and Moor-Dale of Newcastle (ten, Plaxton, 1977–80).

Significant purchases were made by Ulsterbus (fifty-one, mostly Alexander (Belfast) but a few Duple, 1976–8) and Whittle of Highley (twenty-six, Duple, 1976–9). Other operators who found the YLQ a good buy included M&M Coaches Ltd of Kidderminster (thirteen, Duple, 1976–9), Corvedale of Ludlow (twelve, Duple, 1976–9), Alpha of Brighton and Bostock of Congleton, who had nine each with Duple and Plaxton bodies between 1976 and 1980.

Plaxton and Duple built around 300 bodies each on the YLQ, with Alexander (Belfast) coming in third with just under fifty; Caetano built fourteen and Willowbrook eight. Other coachbuilders contributed penny numbers on the YLQ, including Cypriot coachbuilders Askamax and Viamax.

This YLQ with Duple Dominant II forty-one-seat coachwork was bought new by Grey-Green in August 1979 and is pictured here a month later. Only six YLQs were recorded as having been bought new by Grey-Green, though the Duple Dominant body was popular with this operator.

YMQ

The YMQ sold mostly in twos and threes to existing Bedford customers, though the largest order came from South Wales Transport Ltd of Swansea, traditionally a user of more heavy chassis; eighteen with Duple bodies were purchased in 1980–1. By far the vast majority of YMQs had Duple or Plaxton bodies, in almost equal numbers at around fifty, though Wright built bodies for six and Lex built nine. Several went to Cyprus, receiving Askamax or Viamax bodies.

A new Derwent body was introduced in 1986 and is shown here with forty-seven seats on Hedingham and District Omnibus Ltd's 1986 YMQ, fleet no. L136, in September 1999. D136 XVW was bought new by Hedingham and District but later exported to Malta, where in substantially unaltered condition it became DBY 541.

One of eighteen similar buses delivered to South Wales Transport of Swansea in 1980, this YMQ had a Duple Dominant forty-five-seat bus body trimmed to dual-purpose standards. It was photographed at Swansea bus station in the early 1980s.

YNT

The YNT failed to attract such large orders as its predecessor, the YMT, and a good proportion of the top ten sales were made to operators who had previously purchased large fleets of earlier or concurrent Y-series chassis. Bebb of Llantwit Fardre returned to Bedford for twenty-one YNTs with Duple and Plaxton bodies between 1981 and 1986, as did Bexleyheath Transport (nineteen, Duple, 1982–6), Armchair of Brentford (eleven, Plaxton, 1983–4) and Barton Transport (ten, Plaxton, in 1981). Cleverly (Capitol Coaches) Ltd of Cwmbran bought ten YNTs with Duple and Plaxton bodies between 1981 and 1984 and a further twenty in 1985, Wainfleet of Nuneaton had seventeen Plaxton between 1982 and 1985, while Clarkes Coaches of London SE20 took eleven Plaxton between 1982 and 1983. Bedford regular Whittle of Highley took twenty-eight between 1981 and 1983, mostly Duple bodies but a small number of Plaxton and six with Wright bodies; other customers included Bostock of Congleton, who took just eight with Duple and Plaxton bodies, as did Claireaux of Hadleigh, Marchwood of Totton, Mayne of Buckie and Yeomans of Hereford.

Duple by this time was lagging well behind Plaxton, with only approximately 300 bodies built, compared with 500 by Plaxton on the YNT. Wright was the only other coachbuilder to make serious inroads on the YNT, with just twenty-two bodies. Caetano, Willowbrook and Van Hool all built very small numbers on the YNT, possibly only one or two each. As an example of prices, a 12m (39ft) YNT with Wright Contour body sold for £38,100 in standard trim and £42,350 for a luxury coach fully loaded with extras. By 1984, a Plaxton Paramount 3200-bodied 11m (36ft) YNT was listed at £57,000, but if one shopped around the dealers an example could be had for around £50,000 or even slightly less.

Built in the penultimate year of Bedford production and registered in January 1986, this YNT with fifty-seven-seat Plaxton Paramount 3200 body was new to Wreake Valley of Syston, Leicestershire.

The setting sun catches this April 1983 fifty-three seat Plaxton Derwent bus-bodied YNT, which was bought new by J. H. Hammel of Stanley, County Durham. Hammel traded as Diamond Bus Service. URG 318Y would have looked quite smart with a little attention from a hose and brush. Diamond was a fleet name used by a cooperative of several independent operators in County Durham. They gradually all faded away until only Hammel remained, later to be acquired by major operator Go North East.

YNT 141Y. Displaying an appropriate, though most likely fictitious registration number, is the prototype Wright Contour body mounted on a 1982 12m (39ft) YNT chassis. Those spats over the rear wheels must have been popular with fitters! GM

Duple built the bodies on all three of the 1979 YLQ/S chassis; two went to Grey-Green and the third, fitted with GM-Allison automatic transmission, went to Cleveland Transit.

Of the Tricentrol lengthened 12m (39ft) chassis, twenty-one were based on YMTs and all but one had fifty-seven-seat Duple bodies, the singleton having a Plaxton body. They sold mostly in ones or twos to regular Bedford customers, though one notable sale was to H. Svendsen of Akirkeby in Denmark. Regent of Redditch bought three in 1979 and Tricentrol kept two in its operating fleet. The remainder, thirty-four in total, were based on YNT chassis; eighteen had Plaxton bodies with either fifty-five or fifty-seven seats, fourteen had fifty-five- or fifty-seven-seat Duple bodies and two had fifty-seven-seat bodies by Wright.

The 11m (36ft) and 12m (39ft) YNTs did help to lift Bedford's fortunes and image in the early 1980s and the YRT/YMT/YNT range was very popular, outselling its closest rivals, the Ford R1014 and R1114 models by almost 100 per cent. While in many cases their service life with their first owners was quite short, resale prices remained high, indicating that operators considered that the vehicles were a desirable purchase. Maidstone Borough Council's YRQs and YRTs, for example, had a five- to six-year working life and were eagerly snapped up by operators looking for value-for-money when they came up for sale.

Some of the last Bedfords manufactured were the three YMP/S models, which were bought by Parks of Hamilton.

ON THE ROAD

YRQ

Road testers generally found little difference in the performance of the early YRQ compared with the VAM, though most commented on how much the interior noise was reduced.

In October 1970 Ron Cater tested what must have been a fairly early production YRQ, registered YXE 844H. The coach was fitted with a Duple Viceroy forty-five-seat body and he commented that it was amongst the quietest he had ever driven. The redistribution of weight resulting from the new engine position had eliminated the tendency of the VAM to pitch when fully laden and the ride was consistently good on the variety of road surfaces encountered on the test. Cater found the steering to be very sensitive and controllable, despite the lack of power assistance, even on uneven and rutted road surfaces. The gearchange was found to be somewhat less effective, with the linkage making the change feel 'uncertain'. Second gear in particular was dif-

ficult to engage, which caused the driver some problems in negotiating road junctions, the gearbox having been in neutral when the driver thought it was in gear. The other ratios generally engaged accurately, though there were occasions when these refused to drop in. This might have been excusable for a manufacturer's test hack, but for a demonstration vehicle upon which the industry press was let loose, it seems strange that Bedford was not on top of the problem.

The brakes were very sensitive, requiring some practice to achieve smooth stops, though no fade was evident even with harsh stops from 70mph (113km/h). Readings were, as usual, taken with a Tapley meter and produced the following results for stopping distance and efficiency: at 20mph (32km/h), 22.5ft (6.9m) and 81 per cent; 30mph (48km/h), 48ft (14.6m) and 82 per cent; handbrake from 20mph (32km/h) – 43 per cent, stopping distance not recorded. The handbrake held the coach easily on a 1:8 (12.5 per cent) gradient facing both up and down the hill.

Performance was very similar to the VAM, with the YRQ taking 0.3 seconds longer, at 8.6 seconds, than its predecessor to reach 20mph (32km/h) through the gears. In direct top, acceleration was 5 seconds quicker for all the times recorded. On the motorway, the YRQ's average speed was 10mph (16km/h) higher than the VAM while returning 3mpg (94ltr/100km) better fuel economy. These results were attributed to changes to the fuel injection system of the 466cu in engine. Commenting on these figures, Cater stated that the 'effortless progress', resulting mostly from the reduction in interior noise of the YRQ, misled one into thinking the vehicle was actually not quite as fast as the VAM, which was a significant comment on that which had gone before.

Hillclimbing was also a feature of the YRQ's effortless progress, a 1:13 (7.7 per cent) gradient being tackled easily in second and third gears, with the speed never dropping below 19mph (31km/h). A hill start was easily achieved at 1:8 (12.5 per cent) in both first and reverse. Adequate acceleration was present for overtaking in the traffic conditions of the day and this was considered by Cater to be an important asset of the vehicle. Maximum speeds in the gears were as follows: first – 9.8mph (15.8km/h), second – 19mph (31km/h), third – 33mph (53km/h), fourth – 55mph (88.5km/h) and fifth – 70mph (113km/h).

Fuel consumption was praised; on the M1 the vehicle achieved 12.975mpg (21.8ltr/100km) at an average speed of 64mph (103km/h); averaging 34mph (55km/h) on second-class A roads, 14.1mpg (20.1ltr/100km) was achieved, and crossing the Chiltern Hills on undulating roads 13.8mpg (20.5ltr/100km) was obtained. Overall consumption was calculated at 13.6mpg (20.8ltr/100km) for an average speed of 39.6mph (63.7km/h). Other testers reported similar or better figures, one test obtaining 16.7mpg (16.9ltr/100km) at a steady 40mph (64km/h). It would be difficult to achieve either of those figures with a modern coach of comparable size over the same roads today.

Other testers of the same coach repeated Cater's comments regarding the obstructive nature of the Turner gearbox, and it is worth noting that similar problems were reported with the Bristol LH, which used the same gearbox, so it is not surprising that Bedford looked to Eaton for a gearbox for the YRQ2 in 1974.

A further road test of a YRQ was conducted by Martin Hayes in June 1974, the subject this time being an updated YRQ2. In addition to the mechanical improvements brought in with the YRT, Hayes noted the introduction of new column-mounted controls for lights, wipers, washers and indicators. New instrumentation as per the YRT was fitted, which included air-pressure indicators for both brake reservoirs, a coolant temperature gauge, and warning lights for oil pressure, air pressure, temperature and fuel in addition to the usual turn indicators and high-beam light. A 'master electrics' dial included the alternator warning light and an indication of the state of the electrical system.

The test vehicle had the new, optional two-speed rear axle and a Plaxton Panorama Elite III body, and the test route was Vauxhall's usual tour through the Midlands, starting and finishing at Luton.

Hayes immediately noticed the easier gearchange; he noted that changes still had to be made quite slowly and deliberately, but incorrect selection of gears, a feature of the earlier test vehicle, was not an issue. On the M1 motorway, at that time encumbered by road works and heavy traffic, the coach was able to cruise at 70mph (113km/h) when conditions were favourable and averaged 61mph (98km/h) over the 16-mile (26km) section of the test route, though Hayes complained that there was some resistance from the throttle pedal at the fully open position. By changing down from fifth to fourth gear on motorway gradients, speed never dropped below 47mph (76km/h).

On normal A and B roads, Hayes found the fourth and fifth gear were poorly matched with the two-speed rear axle, because fifth gear in low ratio gave lower gearing than fourth with the axle in high ratio, so that when attempting to maintain speed up a gradient, fourth in high ratio had to be selected where fifth in low would have been a more suitable change. In high ratio, fifth gear was too high for road conditions where 30mph (48km/h) was likely to be the predominant speed. By contrast, in the lower ratios the two-speed axle proved very useful in filling the gaps between the gears, particularly in variable hilly conditions where the gap between third and fourth was noticeable, and third in high ratio was found to be a very useful combination for urban driving. Pulling away from a stand could be achieved in low second without drama though some careful

This forty-one-seat YRQ with the first version of Duple Dominant body was new in May 1974 to Shamrock & Rambler Motor Coaches Ltd of Bournemouth. It was tradition at Shamrock & Rambler to give coaches names, rather than fleet numbers, so ORU 290M was named 'Itchen' after the River Itchen in Hampshire. It is seen here on 2 February 1976 after passing to Eastern National, in use on the Stour Valley Post Bus service. The Stour Valley Post Bus was inaugurated in 1967 and proved very useful to the communities that it served in rural Essex. The service ceased in 1981.

clutch control was needed. A hill start on Bison Hill from about half-way up was easily achieved and an impressive 20mph (32km/h) speed at the summit was noted, in low third.

Brakes were not fully tested due to weather conditions, though Hayes found no tendency for the wheels to lock or the linings to fade and the parking brake held the coach without problem on Bison Hill. Hayes enjoyed the power steering, which gave good feedback from the wheels with precise control, while providing useful assistance for low-speed manoeuvring.

Fuel consumption overall was similar to that obtained with the larger YRT at 11.25mpg (25.2ltr/100km) and 2.35mpg (120.4ltr/100km) worse than the figure obtained when the first YRQ was tested in 1970.

The only significantly negative comment concerned the Plaxton-fitted air-operated pantograph wipers, for which the coachbuilder had bypassed the column-mounted switch and fitted a difficult-to-reach alternative on the instrument panel. The wiper installation leaked air continuously with an annoying hiss – though doubtless this could have been remedied by Plaxton, it proved a source of irritation for the driver on the test.

In comparisons with rivals, testers were generally of the opinion that while the early YRQ had some better features, overall it did not compare well with the Leyland Leopard, except on price, and was harder on the driver. Later versions of the Y-series certainly overcame some of the criticisms and put Bedford nearer to a level playing field for vehicles in the same class, particularly once a fully automatic gearbox became available.

YRT

A prototype YRT with 6.17:1 rear axle (production YRTs were fitted with either 5.83:1 or 5.29:1 axles) was tested by Trevor Longcroft for *Commercial Motor* in June 1974, again over the standard Vauxhall test route. The chassis was fitted with a fifty-three-seat Plaxton Panorama Elite II body, and, as with the YRQ tested two years earlier, the extremely low interior noise level was considered an outstanding feature of the coach and was attributed not only to the engine position but to the actual quiet running nature of the engine itself.

Longcroft found the driving controls without exception to be well placed, even for an unfamiliar driver. The driving experience, however, was more varied: the brakes, while demonstrating good results from high-pressure stops, seeming to require an inconsistent level of pedal pressure and travel in normal driving, pointing perhaps to

a fault with the air system. The tester was unable to lock the wheels during any of the tests, though stopping distances from 10mph (16km/h) and 20mph (32km/h) were significantly better than the VAL, a difference of 2.4ft (0.7m) and 17ft (5.2m) respectively being measured; the figures obtained compared well with those for the VAM and YRQ. At 30mph (48km/h), the stopping distance was 48.76ft (14.86m). Brake efficiency on the Tapley meter was consistently 77 per cent, with 20 per cent measured for the parking brake. The air-assisted clutch was, as might be expected, light in operation. The parking brake was able to hold the coach in both directions on a 1:4 (25 per cent) gradient at the Millbrook test circuit, and hill starts on the same gradient were accomplished without problem.

Surprisingly, in view of the criticism of the YRQ and the introduction of the Eaton gearbox, the gearchange on the YRT under test was troublesome and completely smooth changes proved impossible to achieve, despite several different techniques being employed. The ratios were not all to the tester's liking, either, there being a wide gap between third and fourth, which was exacerbated by a flat spot from the engine encountered when changing from third to fourth at maximum rpm, although the rest of the ratios were thought well spaced. Steering, despite the power assistance, was found to be heavy with much effort needed except at the extremities of the lock. The steering pulled to the left on the motorway part of the test, suggesting a problem with the ball joints, tyres or tyre pressures, which may also have affected the steering weight.

Overall performance was comparable with the YRQ, acceleration through the gears bringing 40mph (64km/h) up in 40.4 seconds and 50mph (81km/h) in 95.4 seconds. Average speed over the motorway section of the route was slightly lower at just below 60mph (97km/h). Top speeds in the gears were as follows: first – 6mph (9.7km/h), second – 16.5mph (26.5km/h), third – 30mph (48km/h), fourth – 51mph (82km/h) and fifth – 65mph (105km/h), though it should be remembered that these figures were obtained with 6.17:1 rear axle and would have been slightly higher with the standard ratios adopted in production.

Fuel consumption figures showed 10.6mpg (26.7ltr/100km) at motorway speeds, 12.6mpg (22.5ltr/100km) on mixed A roads in the Cotswolds and 12.8mpg (22.1ltr/100km) when prolonged cruising at 50mph (81km/h) was possible. An overall fuel consumption of 11.8mpg (24ltr/100km) was achieved. All figures are noticeably poorer than those obtained when testing the YRQ, though an example with a Willowbrook 002 body returned over 14mpg (20.2ltr/100km) unladen when tested by Martin Hayes in 1973.

Ride quality for passengers was good, with little pitch or roll at normal cornering speeds, though both could be induced by hooliganistic driving. The ride from a position seated over the rear axle was noted as 'a little hard'.

YMT

When the YMT appeared in 1976, a demonstrator with a Plaxton Supreme body was tested for *Commercial Motor* by Martin Watkins in April of that year. Although generally favourable, the ratios of the Eaton gearbox were still a source of criticism and comment. Watkins found the linkage stiff and had problems selecting second gear for moving off, though the common practice of lifting the clutch to spin the gearbox then attempting to reselect second was effective, suggesting the problem lay in the gearbox rather than in the Bedford linkage. Even so, the change was considered stiffer than that found on comparable chassis from other manufacturers. Selecting any gear while the gearbox was cold demanded patience and could not be rushed, and even with the torque available from the 500cu in (8.2-litre) engine, some clutch slip was necessary to get the coach underway in second when fully laden, although the coach could be held in second gear until the maximum speed of 20mph (32km/h) was reached.

This proved advantageous on hills where a change into third produced a noticeable drop in speed, as did the change from third to fourth; 34mph (55km/h) maximum could be reached in third but the coach would not pull up a hill in fourth at this speed. Hill starts were easily achieved on a gradient of 1:4 (25 per cent) but some odour of overheated clutch lining was apparent. Vauxhall engineers were aware of criticism of the gearbox ratios, but still maintained that the Eaton gearbox was the most suitable from the range of available proprietary gearboxes at the time. The problem would be addressed eventually by the use of a Spicer six-speed gearbox when the YMT was replaced by the YNT.

Improvements for the driver included the steering wheel from the KM truck range, considered a vast improvement on what had gone before, a key-operated start switch on the steering column, an audible repeater for the flashing direction indicators and a metal locking collar on the spring parking brake lever to replace the earlier plastic type, which was prone to wear and breakage. Brakes and clutch were light in operation; indeed the larger brakes (compared with the YRT) were very effective and pulled the coach up from 40mph (64km/h) in 20ft (6.1m) less than the rival Ford R1114. However, in other tests a slight side-to-side twitch was detected when braking from high speeds.

Noticeable performance improvements were gained from the 500cu in engine, acceleration from rest to 40mph (64km/h) taking approximately 38.5 seconds compared with the YRT's 40.4 seconds, and 50mph (81km/h) was reached in an impressive 60 seconds compared with 95 seconds for the YRT. However, in other road tests it was noted that performance was better at the extremities of the engine's speed range and lacking in the middle. Some smoke was noted when pulling away after idle, though there was none apparent when travelling at normal speeds. The tester noticed that the oil warning light came on under heavy braking, suggesting that there may have been a problem with oil circulation in the engine for this particular

Photographed in Guildford on 14 May 1994, this March 1987 YMT with fifty-three-seat Plaxton second-generation Derwent bus body was still in service with Tillingbourne Bus Company Ltd of Cranleigh, Surrey. Tillingbourne had been founded in 1924 under the name Tillingbourne Valley. The company established a network of routes around Cranleigh, Gomshall and Ewhurst in Surrey, extending into West Sussex and Hampshire. Tillingbourne ceased trading in April 2001.

coach. Faults were noted with the instrumentation, the speedometer, fuel gauge and temperature gauge all significantly under-reading, with the speedometer showing 60mph (97km/h) when the vehicle was actually travelling at 64mph (103km/h).

Fuel consumption, as might be expected, was poorer than the YRT, with an overall average of 10.74mpg (26.4ltr/100km) over the usual test route. Average speed over the motorway section of the test route was 62.5mph (100.6km/h), which was higher than the YRT, as was the overall average speed for the test circuit of 41.87mph (67.38km/h).

Almost at the very end of production, Noel Millier road tested a YMT with fully automatic GM-Allison MT543 gearbox and the de-rated 175bhp turbocharged 500cu in (8.2-litre) engine. The body was a Wright TT fifty-three-seat bus body, representing the new generation of aluminium bodies from this coachbuilder, and the bus was one of a fleet of Bedfords operated by Maidstone Borough Council. The test route on this occasion was around the north London suburbs, appropriate for a service bus. Fuel consumption overall average was 8.5mpg (33.3ltr/100km), though cruising at higher speeds produced better figures. The automatic transmission provided smooth gearchanges, though the change point for third to fourth was noted to be 30mph (48km/h); this meant that for most urban work the gearbox was always on the point of changing, with the result that the bus seemed most comfortable when travelling at just over the legal urban speed limit. The gearbox could be held in first, second or third gears, though it was only necessary to use this feature on the steepest hills, and for normal work the D position on the shifter was adequate. Gear selection was by a T-shaped shift lever that was illuminated when the sidelights were on. Performance for a service bus was good, with impressive acceleration from low speeds, which is important in a vehicle that is likely to spend much of its time travelling at around 30mph (48km/h) or less. Millier concluded that the combination of Wright TT body on a Bedford chassis offered an excellent package and one that would have sold very well in the UK post-deregulation environment had production not ceased in 1986.

YMT/L

The YMT in its Tricentrol-lengthened 12m (39ft) form was tested by Millier in February 1978. In many respects, he found the vehicle to be very similar to a standard YMT. The coach under test had a Duple Dominant II fifty-seven-seat body and had already seen two seasons' work with an operator. The chassis of the demonstrator was fitted with a two-speed rear axle, which in high ratio made 70mph (113km/h) cruising effortless. High ratio was found generally to be suitable for most road conditions apart from the severest of hills, but changing from high to low ratio required some skill and dexterity, as the engine revolutions needed to be maintained while the clutch was depressed and the control button operated. Changing from low to high was easier when the engine speed had dropped. The driver also needed to keep the clutch disengaged long enough for the axle to change ratio in order to avoid jerks and disconcerting noises.

Ride and handling were considered to be good, the larger tyres contributing to improved handling and reduction in road noise.

Steering was heavy, despite the power assistance, which was less effective at low engine speeds, though the superb lock made the coach very manoeuvrable considering its 12m (39ft) length.

Braking was perfectly adequate for a vehicle of its size and fully laden emergency stops were achieved in a straight line without drama.

Opinions varied as to whether the 12m YMT had sufficient power from its 500cu in (8.2-litre) engine, though most testers commented that hillclimbing was noticeably slower than contemporary mainstream 12m chassis. Despite this, overall average speeds over test circuits were around 42mph (68km/h), very similar to that obtained with the standard YMT. Fuel consumption figures varied a little across a number of tests but all reported overall figures of between 10.3mpg (27.5ltr/100km) and 11mpg (25.7ltr/100km), figures that were considered good for a fifty-seven-seat coach.

YLQ/S

Millier was in the driving seat again in September 1979, when he tested a YLQS with a Duple Dominant II thirty-five-seat body. The vehicle tested was the first YLQ to be modified by Tricentrol and the improved power-to-weight ratio offered by the reduction in size and the 500cu in (8.2-litre) engine was immediately apparent. The small coach was quite capable of ascending a 1:3 (33 per cent) gradient and restarted easily on a 1:4 (25 per cent) slope, something a similarly shortened Ford R1014 failed to do. The coach was fitted with an exhaust brake, though the tester found the brakes more than adequate and occasionally even violent, no doubt due to the reduced weight of the complete vehicle. The parking brake held the coach easily on the 1:3 hill.

Performance was lively, as already mentioned, cruising at 70mph (113km/h) on the motorway, and the climb to Shap summit on the M6 motorway was achieved without the speed dropping below 45mph (72km/h). On ordinary roads, 50mph (81km/h) was regularly achieved, courtesy of the improved acceleration. Overall fuel consumption was almost the same as for the standard YLQ at 12.1mpg (23.4ltr/100km), which is perhaps not surprising given the temptation for the driver to use all the available performance provided by the improved power-to-weight ratio. The test took place in windy conditions, which must be taken into consideration, and 12.5–13.5mpg (21–22.6ltr/100km) ought to have been achievable.

Ride quality was considered to be as good as or better than rivals with leaf-spring suspension. From the driver's point of view, the reduced wheelbase and overall length made for a pleasant and easy drive; of note was the combined exhaust brake and engine stop control, which was particularly well-positioned and easy to operate compared with previous Bedfords.

YNT

Millier was able to test a YNT with six-speed ZF gearbox and Plaxton Paramount 3200 body in 1984. He likened driving the turbocharged YNT to an old AEC Reliance, the new Bedford handling more like its heavyweight rivals than the previously tested YMTs and YRTs; the coach rode well, was responsive, 0–50mph (81km/h) taking 36 seconds, and the ZF gearbox gave predictable and positive gearchanges. Over the Scottish test route the YNT was no slower than any of its heavier rivals, while still showing the best fuel economy in its class, and it was capable of cruising easily at 70mph (113km/h) on the motorway with speed in hand. The best fuel consumption achieved was on fast A roads, where 14.3mpg (19.7ltr/100km) was achieved; the worst was 9.85mpg (28.7ltr/100km) on the M6 motorway climbing the long gradient over Shap between Kendal and Gretna Green. The test route was covered at an average speed of 52.7mph (84.8km/h), the fastest yet for a Bedford over this route, and the overall average fuel consumption was 12.07mpg (23.4ltr/100km), consistent with earlier Y-series chassis.

THE Y-SERIES IN RETROSPECT

The Y-series attempted to address two of the major criticisms that had been levelled at Bedford PSVs over the years – the high levels of internal noise and poor brakes. By placing the engine under the floor and improving silencing, interior noise was greatly reduced over the Y-series' predecessors and the later turbocharged engines were quieter still. Most road testers found the brakes to be more than adequate, though it could be argued that a one-day road test was not sufficient to combat the poor reviews of early chassis in that area. At least one road tester managed to sneak a Y-series demonstrator away from Vauxhall's watchful eyes and do a multiple-crash-stop brake fade test, during which it is alleged that the braking effort actually improved. However, the ghost never seemed quite to be laid.

From the final year of Plaxton Supreme production is York Pullman's fleet no. 175, a fifty-three-seat YNT dating from May 1982. Its first owner was N & R Coaches of Elsecar, South Yorkshire.

IN PRESERVATION

1969 Bedford YNT/Plaxton C307 UFP

by Andy McCarthy

Year new: 1986
Engine: 500cu in turbocharged 205bhp Bedford diesel
Gearbox: Six-speed ZF S6.65
Body: Plaxton Paramount built to 'one star' specification plus dress curtains, brown interior, fifty-three standard seats with footrests, ducted heating and single side locker
Current owner: Andy McCarthy

History

C307 UFP was bought new for my business, Roy McCarthy coaches. Various modifications have been applied over the years, in line with my experience of operating the YNT. The accelerator linkage was modified to part rod and part cable to overcome surge at constant speed on the motorway. The troublesome twin-plate 14in Borg and Beck clutch was modified to a single plate and diaphragm cover. To set this up involved changing the flywheel and adding a spacer collar for the release-bearing carrier.

The viscous cooling fan was modified to a Dynair system to overcome overheating problems when new. Bedford engineers discovered on Plaxton-bodied YNTs there was an air swirl created in front of the radiator at motorway speed. They discovered this by fitting a see-through hatch above the radiator. I can remember driving along the motorway and watching the temperature gauge slowly creep up above normal, at which point I would pull onto the hard shoulder (even if we were late – the Bedford was more important) and remove the front panel and put it in the boot, and this would cure the problem. The new Dynair cooling fan set-up solved the problem.

A stainless steel exhaust system has been fitted throughout for longevity.

The coach still works for its living; it is part of our fleet and regularly goes out, but only on selected jobs and with certain drivers! During the busy period it can be out every day, clocking up 3,000 miles in a busy month and this could be to Chester Zoo, to cover a swimming trip or on a school run. There are periods when it does very little, such as August. When it is out on the road, it does not matter that it is nearly thirty years old, it looks and is in better condition than some of the modern coaches you see in the area. Some of the school children we carry call UFP the 'retro coach', with its stylish seats and a handy doodling window, but more importantly they can see out through the windows, unlike some modern coaches where they are unable to.

Owner's Experience

My involvement in coaching started from an early age, accompanying my late father on many trips as he was a coach driver for local coach proprietor Fred Lomas of Macclesfield. Up until 1967 Fred ran an immaculate fleet of all black petrol-powered coaches. In 1967 he got his first diesel, a new Bedford VAL Duple Viceroy. I can still remember the old-fashioned hand-operated petrol pump they used – so many turns forward and then so many turns back to dispense each gallon!

Working for Fred Lomas was a good grounding for my father as he was obsessed with cleaning coaches! Fred retired in 1971 so father decided he would go it alone and looked for a coach of his own, a 1961 Bedford SB3 Duple Super Vega forty-one-seater – Roy McCarthy coaches was up and running. Consequently I became even more obsessed with coaches than I already was. I can remember helping to brush paint the blue panels on the bodywork at the side of the road where he parked on a local industrial estate lay-by. At the age of eleven I could not get enough of coaches and went with him whenever I could. Always ending up with brushing out at the end of the day (nothing changes!).

As time progressed my father swapped the SB3 for a Bedford VAM5 with Duple Viscount body of 1966 vintage and then progressed to a 1969 Bedford VAM 70 Plaxton; this was probably his favourite coach and really established the company's presence. As time went on he expanded and bought a Ford Transit minibus, then a twenty-seat Bedford J2 Plaxton Embassy. My brother-in-law then joined him and he bought a 1966 Bedford VAM 14 Plaxton for him to drive; not long after, another Ford Transit came along and my eldest sister came into the business to drive that on a regular contract.

I was always involved with maintenance and bodywork repairs and can remember weekends spent filling and touching up corrosion on one of the two Transits, as they were prone to rot.

By this time I knew the direction I wanted to go when I finished school. I wanted to work in our local commercial garage that was already looking after some of the maintenance and bigger jobs on our coaches. At the age of twenty-one I took my PSV driving test and worked with father with the aim of gradually taking over. Thirty-five years later the family business is still going strong with me at the helm and so is the Bedford YNT!

As for maintenance UFP has a safety inspection once a month and this includes greasing, oiling, adjusting and so on. My father was obsessive about cleaning where I am obsessive with maintenance. I have a saying '"that will do" won't do for me – it's got to be right!'

Mechanical work done on UFP has been the obvious: brake relines, new clutches, exhausts, fan belts, kingpins and bushes and so on. It has had one major engine change including a new turbo, reconditioned injector pump and injectors. The gearbox has had a new rear bearing and seals and was overhauled a few years ago. The prop shaft has been replaced. It has had new rear springs – the front nearside spring has never been off, but the offside had a new top leaf many years ago.

A major rebuild was completed two and a half years ago, with new stainless steel stretch panels, new lower aluminium panels and all new locker doors fitted. All lower steel work below the waist line, a section around the bootlid plus the boot inner panel work was replaced. The coach had a complete repaint and traditional sign writing was applied to the bootlid. The front sections of the stretch panels were also sign written with my father's initials, just as it had been when it left the factory on his birthday, 3 March 1986.

UFP is a dream to drive, although not all my drivers feel the same, as they have got used to automatic gearboxes, air suspension and air conditioning. It is always guaranteed to start, so if a modern coach fails due to an electrical or computer fault, the old faithful is brought out to rescue the day. It is a great drive around town and on motorways, it goes well up hills although you do need to be in the right gear and not miss one going down the box. The rule is twenty is plenty and come down the same speed as you have gone up.

We have taken UFP to a number of shows over the years; we attended the Plaxton centenary celebrations at Scarborough and the Bedford gathering in Ellesmere Port. Every year during the 1000 engine rally, it is used to transport visitors to the Anson Museum in Poynton – even lined up with two of our modern coaches, UFP is the first to fill up with enthusiasts.

Andrew McCarthy's YNT with Plaxton Paramount body.

A. McCARTHY

The Y-series was quite light compared with its rivals and the later engines produced a powerful coach or bus, suitable for the emerging traffic conditions of the 1970s and 1980s. As the private car got faster, so did the movement of traffic. The motorway network was well established and the volume of traffic not yet sufficient to choke it in the way we are used to in 2016, so long-distance driving at sustained high speeds was possible, and the Y-series, especially in its later turbocharged form, was a good performer. With the balanced weight distribution brought about by the amidships engine position, a more stable ride was obtained than with earlier Bedfords. The shortened YMP/S with 175bhp proved that power-to-weight ratio is the most important factor in outright performance by being exceptionally nippy; where the similar-sized Bristol LHS was considered to be over-powered for its chassis, the same criticism does not seem to have been levelled at Tricentrol's baby Bedford Y.

Operators found the early YRQ was capable of averaging 12.5mpg (22.6ltr/100km), the later YRQ2, YRT and YMT between 11.5mpg and 12.0mpg (24.6–23.6ltr/100km). Though these were the worst fuel consumption figures yet for a full-size Bedford PSV, these were also the most powerful chassis built by Bedford to date and the figures compared well with those for heavier chassis. In comparison with its main rival, the Ford R1114, the YRT/YMT was thirstier but both faster and quieter. Surprisingly, perhaps, the YMT was also thirstier than the Leyland National Suburban Express, which, though promoted as such, the latter never presented any real challenge in the Bedford market.

If the Y-series was not without its problems, these were often of a fairly minor though often irritating nature. For example, gearchange linkages soon wore and became sloppy, largely due to the small and insufficiently robust universal joints combined with unsympathetic drivers; this problem, compounded with the earlier gearbox in the YRQ, conspired to make gear selection very much a hit and miss affair. Some commentators noted that while the 500cu in (8.2-litre) engines gave sparkling performance at the top and bottom of the engine speed range, it was somewhat lacking in the middle. These engines suffered in time from failure of the bearings in the alternator/fan belt tensioner jockey wheel assembly, designed to automatically tension the alternator and fan drive belts. An improved bearing was made available but some operators replaced the whole assembly with a manually adjustable tensioner. It is fair to say that Bedford was not the only manufacturer whose engines were afflicted by this particular malady, brought about by an attempt to reduce maintenance costs. Failure to be aware of this potential fault could result in the cooling fan becoming detached from the water pump and damaging the radiator and coolant hoses, with inevitably terminal results, if not for the engine then for that particular journey.

Early YRQs could suffer a different problem with their Turner gearboxes, with a circlip on the mainshaft coming adrift and allowing the gear cluster to move backwards and forwards, the first symptom being a tendency for the vehicle to jump out of gear. While a cheap part to replace, it was a lengthy job to do, and if not caught early enough could mean a new gearbox had to be fitted, though this could be a blessing in disguise if the operator chose to fit the later Eaton gearbox as a replacement.

Bedford's reputation for poor brakes on its PSVs never seemed to go away and the Y series was not immune, despite the fact that the brakes grew in size over the years the series was in production. By 1981 Bedford was boasting that the YNT had 'the best brakes in the business', though some operators remained convinced this was a hollow claim. The spring parking brake actuators at the rear could seize if not properly and regularly maintained and some operators found this could happen after as little as a year's service – though a coach might cover as much as 20–25,000 miles (32,000–40,000km) in that time.

The fact that most road testers found the Y-series' brakes perfectly competent for their job suggests the real issue was not the design or principles of the braking systems employed, but the implementation. The size of the brake linings seemed to vary a lot during the production life of the Y series and this suggests that Bedford was trying to address this problem without much success.

It must be borne in mind also that road conditions worsened continuously from the early 1960s, when the private car became ubiquitous; the amount of traffic on the roads increased markedly every decade from then on, requiring adaptive styles of driving and attitudes from professional drivers. The Bedford PSV range was always a premium chassis, built in the way that gave best performance at a very good price. Perhaps too much emphasis on the latter resulted in the use of components in the braking systems that when in perfect (that is new) condition performed their jobs well, but wore quite quickly in such a way that reduced efficiency over time, while still appearing to be in reasonable working condition. It is known that some operators fitted softer linings, in the hope of gaining more 'bite' from the brakes, with the net result that linings wore out much faster, the harder linings originally specified being designed to work in conjunction with 100 per cent efficiency from the power-assistance actuators. If the overall efficiency of a number of brake components dropped even slightly over time, then the effect would be cumulative and result in generally below-par performance. The remedy was, as operators found but perhaps could not always afford, a much more intensive maintenance regime.

Retarders had been a popular fitment for the earlier VAL and VAM ranges and from 1977 a propeller shaft-mounted, Spanish-made electric retarder was available for the YRT from Jacobs Manufacturing and distributed by dealers the Kirkby Organisation Ltd. Operators continued to fit retarders to the Y-series, perhaps prompted by public opinion following a number of coach accidents in the 1970s. Crawthorne's Majestic Motors, Barnsley, South Yorkshire, ran four Bedford YRQs, all fitted with Telma retarders for just this reason.

There were grumbles from operators that fuel consumption of the YRQ and YLQ were poorer than the VAM, most seemingly obtaining consistently 12.5mpg (22.6ltr/100km) overall compared with 18.5mpg (15.3ltr/100km) for even quite elderly VAMs.

Despite the foregoing, the Y series was generally accepted as Bedford's best-ever product; it sold very well and was very highly thought of by operators and dealers. Newton's of Dingwall used a YRQ on its intensive oil-rig contract and found it to be the most trouble-free amongst a variety of vehicles of mostly Ford manufacture in use over a two-year period, which speaks well of the quality of construction. Back in 1980, K. E. Henderson, the chief engineer of Bebb's International Travel of Pontypridd, Mid-Glamorgan, was fulsome in his praise of the twenty-four YMTs that his company used on continental tours throughout the year, summer and winter alike, averaging 75,000 miles (120,000km) per annum and still giving excellent service. His view of Bedford's after-sales service was that it was 'second to none' and the company was happy to order fifteen YNTs for the 1981 season.

Other operators were not so fortunate and through 1981 there were reports of engine problems on brand-new YMTs; though these were not particularly common, they were often accompanied by reports of poor customer service from Bedford in resolving the problems. However, in general drivers liked them and operators found the Y series straightforward to service and repair and economical to run. Cyril Kenzie expressed the opinion to the author that of all Bedfords, the Y series was undoubtedly the best. Harry Hill of Hill's of Tredegar was quoted in a Bedford advert as saying of the Y series 'Operating costs are very good. On some runs we are getting up to 14 or 15 miles per gallon. With power-assisted steering they're excellent. There are no complaints at all from drivers. Excellent to manoeuvre in and out of tight situations. All round I think it is an excellent chassis'. Eighty per cent of Tricentrol's fleet were Bedford Y series in the late 1970s. Workshop manager Gordon Hoar said at the time: 'Bedford saves us money on our total operating costs particularly with the cost and availability of spares. They are one of the most straightforward vehicles to service and repair. We are able to do a full service on a Bedford Y in two hours in the morning before it starts work. Most other makes take much longer.'

The Whittle Coach and Travel Group had a fleet of over fifty and Ron Whittle said of them, 'The two areas where we think the Bedford "Y" is far superior to any of its competitors is in quality of ride and noise levels…substantially better. And this obviously makes for happy passengers.' The company found that even with intensive use, the Y series could go 30,000 miles (48,000km) or more without major attention.

Ken Barton, of Barton Transport, the largest independent bus and coach operator in the UK, echoed the comment from Ron Whittle. In conclusion, the passengers liked them; the drivers liked them; the operators liked them. What more is there to say?

This 1975 YRT with fifty-three-seat Duple Dominant bus body was new to Maidstone Borough Council and acquired from Maidstone by Richards Bros of Cardigan, Mid-Wales in 1981. Maidstone usually disposed of its Bedford rolling stock after five or six years' service. It is seen here in August 2002 somewhere along its usual route between St Davids and Haverfordwest. After twenty-seven years of use it still looks smart, which is a testament to the Y series and the traditional Bedford/Duple combination.

THE FINAL VENTURES – THE JJL AND YNV

JJL

The JJL urban midi bus had its origins in a project developed in the early 1970s by Marshall of Cambridge. Marshall had its fingers in a lot of automotive pies, being main dealers for Leyland as well as having its own coachbuilding division. The Marshall Midi was an integrally constructed 7.5m (24ft 7in) city bus, based largely around Leyland Terrier components, that had been in development since 1973. An example was demonstrated at the Yeates coach show in October 1975, the same month that Bedford announced it was considering taking over the project and re-engineering it to take the 330cu in (5.1-litre) Bedford diesel. The Marshall design already incorporated the GM-Allison AT540 automatic gearbox, which was retained, along with the Borg-Warner Morse Hy-Vo chain-drive components and spiral-bevel angle drive.

Bedford called the new bus the JJL, the chassis consisting of a low profile platform frame giving a low floor and low step entrance in an overall length of 7.5m. The 330cu in Bedford diesel drove through the AT540 gearbox unit-mounted with the engine and thence through a morse chain and spiral-bevel gear angle-drive transfer box to turn the drive through 90 degrees. A short prop-shaft then connected the angle-drive box to the conventional rear axle, mounted back to front so the drive entered the differential horizontally from the rear. Engine cooling was provided by a front-mounted radiator, and the fully enclosed engine

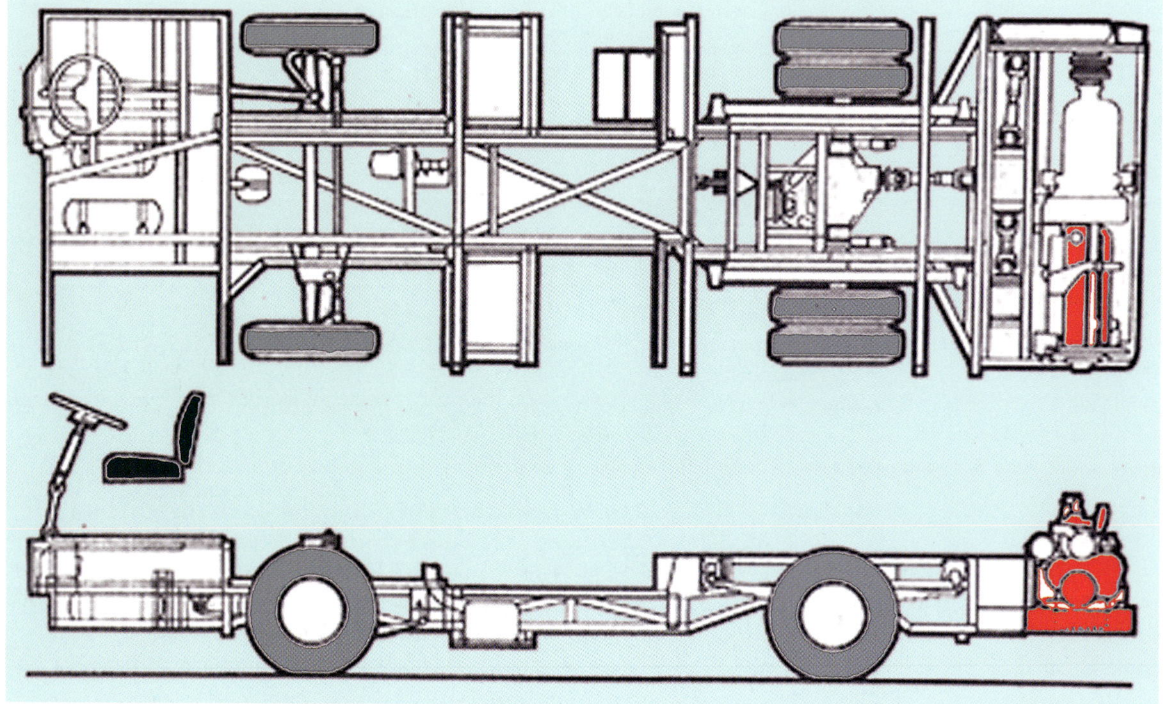

The JJL underframe in plan and side elevation showing the triangulated semi-space frame platform construction and position of the Red series Bedford diesel engine.

This was the first JJL produced after Bedford took control of the project from Marshall, seen here when new with Maidstone Borough Council Transport. Only the presence of the 1970s Ford Transit van lurking in the background gives any sense of period to this photograph – the JJL would not look out of place on the road today. L. SIMPSON

compartment was ventilated by an electric fan exhausting hot air to the atmosphere via grilles mounted high up the quarter panels.

Among the other unusual features of the design were 16in wheels, reminiscent of the smaller wheels fitted to the earlier VAS and VAL chassis.

Steering was by the usual recirculating ball steering box, surprisingly – given the small-diameter wheels, light weight and rear engine configuration – with power assistance. The JJL had a turning circle of 15m (49ft). Suspension was in Bedford's usual style with semi-elliptic leaf springs mounted with rubber bushes. Tubular hydraulic shock absorbers were fitted front and rear. Brakes were 12in drums front and rear, with dual-circuit air-assisted hydraulic actuation and spring parking brakes acting on the rear wheels.

Body

Marshall continued to work with Bedford on the project, developing designs for the body with a choice of interior layouts that catered for a mix of seated and standing passengers. Suggested options were twenty-seven seats or twenty-four with a luggage pen, with additional space for eleven standing passengers. It was intended that flexible seating arrangements would be offered – one suggested example had seats that would be mounted facing inwards in the front half of the body with seats facing forwards in the normal way in the raised rear half of the body and a full-width seat across the back over the engine. In practice, none were built with the seats arranged other than facing forwards and all had twenty-four seats.

Construction was described as integral, a method of construction where the underframe supporting the mechanical components is incorporated into and provides strength for the body structure. The JJL body was based on a square-section steel tube framework, including the underframe or floor platform. Rigidity was added using diagonal struts and steel web plates at frame joints. The body was panelled in aluminium at the sides, with high-quality fibreglass mouldings front and rear into which the lighting was recessed, so the general appearance was very smooth and there was little that protruded from the body. The roof was also moulded in fibreglass and the floor-to-roof clearance was greater than 1.8m (6ft) in consideration of the need for standing passengers.

A low step height for the entrance was another forward-looking feature, the first step being 13in (34cm) from the ground and the second 8.5in (21cm). An air-operated folding entrance door with two full-depth glass panels was provided. Large, flat windows contributed to the light and spacious appearance of the interior.

The body was styled by the Vauxhall studio and was pleasing to the eye. In many ways it was well ahead of its time – it certainly would not look out of place in the second decade of the twenty-first century and it is hard to believe that the JJL first saw the light of day forty years ago.

Production and Sales

The history of the JJL is one of fits, starts and ultimate disappointment; the first Marshall prototype, the involvement of Bedford, which came to nought, the abandonment of the project in 1978 then a brief re-emergence when Marshall took over some of Bedford's interests in 1986, only to fade once again into obscurity. Although there was interest from a number of operators, firm orders were not forthcoming and it seems the UK bus industry was not quite ready for the midi bus concept, at least in the form represented by the JJL. The relationship between Marshall and Vauxhall was clearly important in establishing production and there are stories of Vauxhall engineering executives being somewhat less than enamoured with Marshall's occasionally ad hoc assembly methods; they were used to the high precision required for the mass-production assembly line of the car industry while Marshall's craftsmen were perhaps more at home in the bespoke world of 'make it to suit' traditional coachbuilding. Given Marshall's aerospace connections, it does not seem as though this would have been an insurmountable problem, though economics may have played its part. Whatever the truth of the matter, the lack of will to work together

This was the last JJL built and one of the three that went from Maidstone to Brighton, seen during its time at the latter.

After its sojourn in Brighton, UKK 335X travelled north to Northern Bus of Anston, Sheffield, who had something of a reputation for having an eye for an interesting bargain. The photographer has thoughtfully provided us with a nearside view to complement the previous image.

combined with limited interest from industry meant that the project faltered.

In the event, four JJLs were produced over the period 1978–9 with consecutive Marshall body numbers, though the last was not registered until late 1980. Maidstone Borough Council were keen Bedford customers and was one of the operators who had shown interest in the project, so all four initially found a home there. After a short time with Maidstone, the JJLs were sold on, three to Brighton Buses and one, HKX 553V, to Bournemouth Transport Yellow Buses in 1983; the latter, after passing through several other owners, now survives in preservation.

On the Road

On test, it was found that the number of stops per mile that an urban service bus might make resulted in the brakes overheating leading to premature failure of the linings, due to the small drum diameter – a touch of déjà vu here perhaps – which slowed development down while different lining materials were found and tested.

YNV VENTURER

The YNV was added to the PSV chassis range in 1984 and announced on 26 September of that year. The final incarnation of the Y series, the YNV was powered by a mid-mounted vertical 204bhp version of the 500cu in (8.2-litre) turbocharged Bedford diesel. The YNV is significant principally because it was the first production Bedford PSV chassis to be fitted with air suspension. The failure of Bedford to include an air-suspended chassis in its range might have been

The YNV Venturer chassis was the pinnacle of **Bedford**'s technical achievement in the **PSV** field and a last-ditch attempt to recover the market it had once dominated. GM considered conservative back in the 1960s and expectations were much higher two decades on. Bedford had been lagging behind in current thinking for 11m (36ft) and 12m (39ft) coaches, and the YNV was intended to address the gap in its product range. The travelling public and operators were also expecting more in terms of performance and comfort from their vehicles; the latter in particular meant on-board services such as toilets and provision of hot drinks and food, all of which added to the weight of the vehicle, and doubt was expressed in some quarters as to whether 204bhp was enough for a modern, fully loaded 12m coach with a GVW of up to 16.25 tons (16,319kg).

Designed from the outset for 12m coachwork, it did not replace the YNT, which remained available for 11m bodies. By the 1980s, leaf-sprung coaches were well past their sell-by date; interestingly, a clue to Bedford's thinking had been seen in the shape of a YNT with rear air suspension conversion and Wright Contour 12m body shown at the Annual Bus and Coach Symposium in London in February 1984.

The YNV chassis was of Bedford's usual pressed-steel flat-topped ladder frame chassis, with seven cross-members, the two fore and aft of the engine being tubular in cross section. The frame was flared around the engine and gearbox to provide more space for access but was otherwise straight. The square-section fuel tank was mounted on the left-hand side of the chassis, approximately central within the wheelbase. Batteries were located between the frames and just forward of the rear axle. A spare-wheel carrier with access from the left-hand side was mounted below the batteries and offset to the left.

To reduce the cost of building the body and therefore make the YNV a more attractive proposition, all external cables were installed in such a way that no relocation should have been necessary during body construction, and all wiring harnesses were located in conduit and protected with heat-resistant insulating sheathing where they passed near the engine. For convenience and ease of servicing, all daily servicing points were grouped on the right-hand side of the chassis. The electrical system was 24v with the chassis connected to the negative side of the supply, the batteries being the usual four 6v 135Ah items. A key-operated master switch was mounted on the steering column, mimicking the ignition switch found in cars; this switch isolated the starter solenoid so the coach could not be started without the correct key. Similarly car-like were the windscreen wipers, indicators and lighting switches, which were mounted on stalks on the steering column. Ancillary switches were generally mounted on panels provided by the coachbuilder and installed on the driver's left side.

The gearbox was the same six-speed ZF S6-65, direct-

The YNV chassis was the first production Bedford to feature air suspension. The simplicity of the system can be seen in this view of the left-hand rear unit, showing the tubular rubber spring/air bag mounted between the suspension beam and the substantial bracket attached to the chassis. Front and rear double-acting tubular shock absorbers were mounted vertically on the YNV. GM

top synchromesh unit first seen on the YNT. Problems with the mechanical gearchange linkage on the YNT, which had plagued the entire Y series, led to the adoption of a cable-operated gearchange on the YNV. A hypoid rear axle was fitted with a standard final-drive ratio of 4.10:1, with an option of 4.38:1 for shorter distance work. Steering was by power-assisted recirculating ball, with a ratio of 20.4:1.

Air suspension was provided by six rolling-diaphragm spring units, two for the front axle and four at the rear. Two torque reaction rods were fitted in a V-shape from each chassis side member to a central mounting on the top of the differential casing. Tubular double-acting hydraulic shock absorbers were provided front and rear. A 'high rise' facility, operated by a switch on the dashboard, enabled the driver to raise the chassis by 75mm (3in) for traversing uneven ground, poor surfaces or for negotiating ferry ramps.

Braking was the usual drums-all-round system, in this case with Girling 'twin stop' self-adjusting shoes, fully air operated with two separate air-pressure circuits. An

SPECIFICATION FOR YNV VENTURER

Layout and Chassis
Bus or coach, 51–7 seats, overall length 12m (39ft). Frame: flat ladder with flat-top channel section with seven cross-members, two tubular, five of cold riveted construction

Engine
Type: 500cu in 204bhp turbocharged Bedford diesel
Fuel capacity: 59gal (268ltr)

Gearbox and Transmission
Gearbox: ZF S6.65 six-speed, direct top, synchromesh on all forward gears
Clutch: Twin plate 14in diameter, air-assisted hydraulic operation
Ratios
    1st: 8.88:1
    2nd: 5.11:1
    3rd: 3.08:1
    4th: 2.07:1
    5th: 1.42:1
    6th: 1:1
    Reverse: 8.34:1
Transmission: Single propeller shaft with needle-roller universal joints

Rear axle: Bedford fully floating hypoid, ratio 4.1:1 standard, optional 4.38:1
Front axle: I-beam section

Suspension and Steering
Suspension: Air suspension front and rear; two air springs at the front with twin-leaf axle location, four air springs at the rear; tubular double-acting hydraulic shock absorbers front and rear
Steering: Recirculating ball, power assisted, ratio 20.4:1
Tyres: 275/80R22.5 low-profile tubeless radials on 750 × 225 wheels; optional 295/80R 22.5 tubeless radials on 825 × 225 wheels

Brakes
Type: Full air, dual-line system; air-operated spring parking brake operating on rear wheels
Size: 8 × 15.5in

Dimensions
Track
    Front: 78.35in (1,990mm)
    Rear: 83in (2,108mm)
Wheelbase: 20ft (6,096mm)

Electrical System
24v, 100A alternator, negative earth; four 6v 135Ah batteries

Bedford had ceased production at Dunstable before this YNV first ventured onto the road with Classic Coaches (Lowestoft) Ltd of Lowestoft, Suffolk in August 1987. If it had entered service just a few days later it would have carried an F-suffix registration number. Fifty-seven seats were provided in the rather plain-looking Duple 320 body.

exhaust brake was a standard fitment, controlled by air-operated valves and operated by a floor-mounted foot switch, which doubled as the engine stop switch when the coach was stationary. Tyres were 275/80R tubeless radials, though lower-profile 295/80R tubeless radials were offered as an option. Other options included a choice of tachograph equipment (Veeder Root being standard, Lucas-Kienzle an option), tachograph recording instruments to monitor drivers' hours and speed having become a legal requirement in UK from 1979 (though they had been mandatory in some European countries for many years). Tachographs became mandatory by law throughout the EEC in September 1986.

Bodies

Bedford's own demonstrator received a Duple Laser 2 fifty-one seat body, as described in the previous chapter, though the chassis was designed to accept bodies of up to fifty-seven seats. Hestair Duple, as they were now known, produced the updated 320SL, which appeared in 1987, and a number were fitted to YNV chassis and sold through Yeates' dealership.

The Wright Contour body was also built on the YNV in limited numbers, an example being displayed on a proto-type chassis at the Commercial Motor Show at Earls Court in September 1985.

Plaxton announced its Paramount II 3200 body in 1985, available with fifty-three to fifty-seven seats and it was fitted to a good number of YNV chassis, as was the Paramount III, which appeared in 1986. The 3200 designation indicated the height of the body in millimetres, a 3500 high-floor version also being produced, though not fitted to Bedford chassis. Distinguishing features between the Paramount II and III bodies were a different window line – where the

It became fashionable in the 1980s for coaches to carry personalized or non-age-related registration numbers. This August 1985 Venturer carries a Duple Laser 2 body originally fitted with forty-nine seats and a toilet compartment, and was bought new by Whittle. The company was purchased from the Whittle family by East Yorkshire Motor Services in January 2004.

Plaxton's body for the YNV was the Paramount 3200, which went through several revisions during YNV production. The example shown here is a Paramount 3200 II. The Paramount II could be distinguished from the first Paramounts by the continuous moulding under the windows, which on the earlier version had been broken under the small side window near the front. C21 KBM was new to Yarranton Bros Ltd of Tenbury Wells, Worcestershire but was photographed here when serving with Midland Fox (successor to Midland Red) and carrying fleet no. 8050.

Paramount II had a sloping line along the bottom of the front window towards the driver's window, the Paramount III incorporated a stepped line with the first passenger window being almost the same depth as the driver's window, which in practice made the side view slightly more awkward-looking than the earlier model – and change in the front panel and grille arrangement. This latter was again not a positive change in some eyes and produced a more fussy-looking front end than the clean look of the Paramount II.

Caetano built the Algarve fifty-three- to fifty-seven-seat body, successor to the Alpha, on the YNV, which was very similar in appearance to the Plaxton Paramount II.

Willowbrook announced a new body in 1985 suitable for 12m (39ft) coaches and advertised as available on the YNV; in fact most were built on second-hand earlier Y-series chassis and one or two on other manufacturers' chassis. It appears that none was actually built on the YNV. Available records suggest that in practice the majority of bodies built on YNV chassis seated fifty-seven. A few seated fifty-five and at least one Plaxton body was built for dual-purpose use with sixty-nine seats, most likely with some seats arranged on a three-and-two plan.

Sales and Production

The YNV made its debut at the Birmingham International Motor Show in October 1984. Cost of the bare chassis in

1985 was £24,592, some £10,000 less than the nearest equivalent competitor. With a Duple Laser 2 body, a complete coach could be had for around £68,000. For comparison, the average price of a three-bedroom house in the UK was £31,000, showing that in real terms the final incarnation of the Bedford coach was around one-and-half times more expensive than the 1950 SB had been.

A YNV with Plaxton 3200 body formed an interesting acquisition for Sheffield Education Authority, when they were presented with the largest ever 'Sunshine' coach by the Variety Club of Great Britain in November 1986. The Variety Club was formed by actors and entertainers in the UK and provided many such coaches for the benefit of children with special needs, including wheelchair users. Usually these were twelve- to fourteen-seat minibuses, so a full-sized Sunshine coach was as rare in the UK as the phenomenon it was named after. The coach was supplied by dealer Kirkby Central of Sheffield.

As production spanned only two years and so few were produced, no one operator had the opportunity to build up a large fleet of YNVs. There were many examples of single purchases by operators and it was unusual to find fleets of more than three Venturers with one operator. Mayne's Coaches Ltd of Buckie, Scotland, obviously liked them as they had seven with Plaxton bodies in 1986–7, while Maybury and Sons Ltd of Cranborne, Dorset had six with Hestair Duple bodies, three in 1986 and three in 1987. Bexleyheath Transport had five, all with Hestair Duple bodies, three delivered in 1985 and two in 1986; Wainfleet's Coaches of Nuneaton, Warwickshire, had five with Plaxton bodies, the first in 1986 and the remainder in 1987. Arrowfleet of Bristol had three with fifty-five-seat Plaxton bodies, as did British Airways for use at Heathrow Airport, though fitted with fifty-seven seats.

The total number of YNV chassis for which data have been found is 152; remarkably, for such a recently built chassis, published data are scant and contradictory. Some sources suggest that over 200 were built, though others as few as 127. There are many missing chassis numbers so it is quite likely that the greater figure is more accurate. Of those recorded, sixty-three had Duple bodies, fifty-five had Plaxton bodies, thirty-four were by Caetano and just one by Wright. Searching down the list of operators who bought the YNV, it is apparent that they were almost exclusively already Bedford customers, which provides an insight into at least one aspect of Bedford's problems; the YNV brought in little or no new business and Bedford's existing market was dwindling as long-established customers retired, went out of business or changed their business tactics with the coming of deregulation. The result was that YNV became Bedford's last gasp in the PSV market.

On the Road

A YNV with Duple Laser 2 fifty-one-seat body was tested by Noel Millier for *Commercial Motor* in June 1985. The test started at the Motor Industry Research Association (MIRA) test track at Nuneaton, Warwickshire and included a thorough three-day road test over the Scottish circuit that had been in use since the early years of the Y series.

At the test track, which provided the full range of road conditions likely to be encountered in the UK, Millier found that the fully laden coach was stable and handled well, with good acceleration, hillclimbing abilities and braking. A restart on 1:4 (25 per cent) gradient was achieved relatively easily and the coach could be held safely by the spring parking brake on the same slope. Weather conditions meant that braking tests had to be carried out in the wet, but the coach behaved well in emergency stops from up to 50mph (81km/h), always pulling up in a straight line.

Acceleration through the gears showed the penalty incurred by building a larger coach based on the same mechanical units as the earlier YNT, the YNV taking a full 3 seconds longer to reach 50mph (81km/h) than the YNT with the same turbocharged 500cu in (8.2-litre) engine. Some smoke from the exhaust was noted, so perhaps the engine was not in a perfect state of tune. Good low-end torque from the engine made driving in traffic easy and pleasurable, no doubt helped by the air-assisted clutch, while the precise steering made it easy to negotiate the usual obstacles encountered in urban driving. Hilly conditions did not challenge the YNV over much and again the engine's torque proved its worth as speed could be easily maintained on switchback roads, though the YNV needed more gearchanges than some of its rivals to maintain progress. On the motorway, the legal maximum could be maintained with ease and 60mph (97km/h) could be maintained on dual carriageways without drama. Overall fuel consumption was 10.67mpg (26.4ltr/100km), which compared well with rivals the Hestair Duple 425 integral, at 9.67mpg (29.2ltr/100km) and the Bova Futura at 10.9mpg (25.9ltr/100km) when subjected to the same test regime.

Gear changes were accomplished with ease, and Millier's opinion was that the new cable linkage worked well, with no gear changes being missed throughout the whole three-day test. Steering and brakes overall were predictable and inspired confidence, though the exhaust brake was sufficiently noisy that Millier thought it would have been noticeable by passengers. Exhaust brakes on the whole tended to be noisy, so that fitted to the YNV must have been particularly so in order to elicit a specific comment.

One negative aspect of the YNV instrumentation was the lack of a tachometer – these were becoming more common in coaches and drivers found them a useful aid to extracting best economy and performance from the engine.

From a passenger's point of view, the ride provided by the air suspension was considered equal to the best of any rival manufacturer, though interior noise levels were described only as 'acceptable', suggesting there was room for improvement in this area. Apart from the minor niggles, such as the need to work on the engine from inside the coach, with the consequent danger of making a mess of the upholstery, and others previously mentioned, the YNV was in both performance and economic terms a good match for its rivals. Bedford had finally got around to building a chassis that, like the OB of 1939, could hold its own with allcomers while at the same time representing the economy and value for money expected from the Bedford name. It is to be regretted that production ceased after only two years.

Plaxton's third version of the Paramount 3200 is seen here on this March 1987 fifty-three-seat YNV for E. J. Reid's Cedar Coaches in May 1992. The Paramount III on the YNV typically had fifty-three to fifty-seven seats and featured bonded glazing, giving a clean look to the side of the coach. D102 SPP was with P. C. Coaches (Lincoln) Ltd by 1997.

CHAPTER NINE

GOODS CHASSIS CONVERTED FOR PSV USE

The modification of Bedford's goods chassis to create small PSVs was something of a tradition and goes right back to the start of the Bedford marque. An early example was the Rural Bus, a seven-seat model based on the 1932 Bedford VYC 12cwt (610kg) van modified with side windows and seats, the latter being removable so the vehicle could serve a dual-purpose role as a goods carrier as well as a passenger carrier. Similar conversions in the 1930s were carried out on the later WS van.

The tradition continued with the VXC and the WHG and WLG already described, through the K-, M- and O-series, the C4/C5 and J2 trucks, the CA van and later the CF van. Even examples of the QL military lorry chassis could be found under a bus body. Many small buses and coaches were turned out with these underpinnings, including the bizarrely named Spurling 'Spurmobus' on the K-series chassis. Described in Bedford and Spurling's literature as 'a vehicle of infinite uses', one can only assume its primary application was conveyance of naval personnel of low station.

Light van conversions were offered by coachbuilders such as Devon Conversions, Dormobile, Martin Walter, Kenex and Reeve Burgess (Reebur). These generally seated around ten to fifteen passengers. The mechanical components of the vans were in many cases drawn from Vauxhall's contemporary car range. For example, the VYC shared its 128cu in (2.1-litre) straight-six ohv engine with the Vauxhall Cadet of 1931. Pre-war, a common conversion was into a 'station bus' – typically of seven to ten seats and used by hotels for transporting guests to and from the local railway

AJB 635 is a 1937 WS with Churchill eleven-seat body. It was attending a rally and open day at Winkleigh Airfield, Devon, when photographed some years ago.

ABOVE: **The stark and forbidding entrance to Dartmoor Prison is the location for this photograph of a 1932 VYC of R. Finch & Sons of Princetown, Devon. It was in use as a school bus at the time, despite its location! The Finch business continues today as T. R. W. Finch Taxis of Princetown.** VH

A vehicle of infinite uses, though clearly not of infinite capacity. Spurling's diminutive Spurmobus was built on the early 1950s K-series and later T-series chassis. Spurling were almost next door to Duple and Vauxhall at the Hyde, Hendon. SPURLING

station in the era before private cars were commonplace. The advantage of such conversions was economy of operation where large numbers of passengers did not need to be carried, relatively easy maintenance and generally lively and car-like performance.

Chassis for bodying by other suppliers were usually suffixed with a C or a Z to indicate whether or not they were supplied with a cab (C) or just as a bare chassis (Z) and S or L to indicate short or long wheelbase where there were options. The earliest use of this nomenclature seems to have been applied to the pre-war K-, M- and O-series: thus the MLC was a long-wheelbase chassis and cab assembly, whereas the MLZ was the same chassis but minus the cab. Mechanically, goods chassis of a similar size generally shared the same engines, gearboxes and back axles with the contemporary PSV range, so pre-war and into the 1950s the 214cu in (3.5-litre) petrol engine predominated, with diesel becoming an option as time went on.

Builders of larger coaches, such as Plaxton and Duple, also offered miniature versions of their current ranges on suitable 1- to 4-ton (1,016–4,064kg) goods chassis such as the C4/5 and J2 derivatives, converting them where necessary to forward control. There was quite a wide range of chassis adapted in this way over the years, so this chapter is given over to a brief summary of the more common types. A fairly late venture was the BOV, based on the TM truck and introduced in 1983. A body for this chassis was designed by Robert Wright that incorporated the TM truck front-end panel work and was powered by the 500cu in Blue series diesel. It was intended for export, Nigeria being the most likely market; it has been suggested that around fifty were built, many of these receiving coachwork by Ikarus.

CONVERSIONS BASED ON LIGHT TRUCK CHASSIS

ML

The M series was introduced as a light, normal control goods chassis in 1939 to replace the WHG and WLG.

This 1947 MLC was new to Dorset County Council but has been in preservation for many years now. Photographed while surrounded by typical 1970s NBC buses of Bristol and Dennis manufacture, it has a rare Lee Motors body. Lee Motors was a small bespoke coachbuilder in Wimborne Road, Bournemouth.

There were two wheelbase variants, the MS, with a 10ft (3.05m) wheelbase, and the ML, with an 11ft 11in (3.63m) wheelbase. With the end of production of the WHB, there was no suitable chassis from Bedford to meet the demand for small buses in the twelve- to sixteen-seat range. The ML series was able to fulfil this role and did so until the introduction of the CA in 1952. The MLD was a dedicated drop-side lorry goods version, while the MLC and the MLZ were for general applications. The ML was rated at 2–3 tons (2,032–3,048kg) capacity and had a wheelbase of 11ft 11in (3.63m). Plaxton was thus able in the early 1950s to modify the MLZ to forward control and build a version of its Consort body, as used on small chassis from other manufacturers. Seating capacity of PSV bodies on the MLC/MLZ varied between fifteen and twenty-six.

OLAZ

The OLAZ was a long-wheelbase derivative of the O-series 3- to 4-ton (3,048–4,064kg) truck range introduced in 1950. The chassis was modified by Vauxhall for PSV use and had a 13ft 1in (3.99m) wheelbase. It shared the OB's 214cu in (3.5-litre) 6-cylinder petrol engine in 84bhp form, the gearbox being the standard OB item. Many had bus-style bodies built by Duple of around twenty coach seats and were generally similar in appearance to the OB, though shorter, at around 22ft (6.7m) long and 7ft 6in (2.29m) wide. Built between 1951 and 1953, the higher frame clearance of the goods chassis was particularly suited to narrow rural roads and ferry crossings. For this reason they were favoured by David MacBrayne Ltd, a loyal Bedford customer, who operated in the highlands and islands of Scotland, and adapted them to also carry mail. Duple also built a twenty-five-seat 'Woody' version of the body on the OLAZ, known as the 'Sportsman', with external wooden framing, as found on estate and shooting brake-type vehicles, and largely built of resin-bonded plywood. The model found few customers. British Railways also took OLAZ chassis with twenty-seat bodies from AllWeather Motor Bodies Ltd of Kilburn, London NW6 for staff transport.

Two OLAZ with Duple bodies from the MacBrayne's fleet are famously preserved by the MacBrayne Circle in Scotland, KGD 903 and KGD 904 (MacBrayne's 163 and 164).

In 1950, an OLAZ chassis cost £461, compared with an OB chassis at £533. The OLAZ was superseded by the C4/C5 model.

Duple's 'Woody'-style Sportsman body on the OLAZ did not sell in large numbers, despite its attractive appearance. VH

The **OLAZ** was introduced by Bedford in 1950 and could be considered as a slightly smaller and more rugged alternative to the **OB**. It was popular with operators who worked narrow and sometimes unmade rural roads. The extra ground clearance over the **OB** was no doubt quite appropriate for the use to which this example for British Railways was put. VH

Interior of the **OLAZ** shown in the previous image. The bus could seat twenty passengers and was built by **AllWeather Motor Bodies, Ltd, Canterbury Works, Canterbury Road, Kilburn, London, NW6.** VH

This 1955 (T)A2 with Spurling van conversion body played a small part in the 1960 film *A Look at Life: Girls Ahoy!*, about life as a Wren – the name given to members of the Women's Royal Naval Service – with the Royal Navy. It is seen here complete with a complement of cheerful Wrens.

TA Series

Often referred to as just the 'A-series', the TA2/3/4 chassis were a part of a range of small truck and van chassis introduced in 1953, notable for their normal-control Chevrolet-inspired cab and bonnet styling. The TA range could be had with either the usual 214cu in (3.5-litre) 6-cylinder petrol engine or a Perkins P6 diesel engine. With the petrol engine, fuel consumption of around 12–14mpg (20.2–23.6ltr/100km) was typical, the diesel giving 15–20mpg (14.2–18.9ltr/100km) if driven with care. An interesting feature of the A2 9ft 11in (3.02m) wheelbase 20–25cwt (1,020–1,270kg) chassis, among the otherwise typical amalgam of standard Bedford mechanical components, was the use of 16in-diameter wheels as used in the CA van, though of heavier construction in the TA.

From 1954, Spurling offered a thirteen-seat front-entrance bus based on the A2. A twenty-one-seat body was added to the range for mounting on the heavier-duty A3L chassis, which had a wheelbase of 11ft 11in (3.63m). These bodies were described as being of all-metal construction – in practice, this meant a steel frame with riveted aluminium outer panels. In the thirteen-seat model, seating was arranged with a full-width seat for four passengers at the rear, three double seats on the off side and three single seats on the near side. The seats were of the semi-coach type, with tubular steel frames. Squabs and cushions were padded with Dunlopillo and rubberized horsehair. Ventilation was provided by two top-sliding and two fixed windows in each side of the body. The Spurling conversions were popular export items, though a number were sold in the UK – Colwyn Bay Urban District Council took three A3Ls in 1954. Variations on the same theme were also built on the 13ft 11in (4.24m) 4-ton (4,064kg) A4S chassis.

TC Series

The TC range, as with the TA series, usually referred to as just the 'C-series' (not to be confused with the CA or CF vans), was introduced in 1957. For general use there were three models, the C4, C5 and C6. The C4 (4-ton/4,064kg) and C5 (5-ton/5,080kg) chassis were most commonly adapted for PSV use and shared a wheelbase of 11ft (3.35m). Engine options included the 214cu in (3.5-litre) petrol engine, the new 300cu in (4.9-litre) diesel engine and the 300cu in petrol engine. Additional numbers in the chassis code described the variant, the digits 1, 2 and 3 being used to indicate the engine option – 300cu in diesel, 214cu in petrol and 300cu in petrol, respectively. Thus a C4Z2 was a 4-ton chassis with 214cu in petrol engine supplied as a bare chassis suitable for PSV coachwork. Seating capacity of bodies on the C4/C5 was in the range twenty-eight to thirty.

Duple was offering a twenty-nine seat, 8ft (2.44m)-wide version of its Super Vista coach body on the C4Z2 petrol-engine chassis in the late 1950s and early 1960s, this being very similar in general appearance to the larger Super Vega body offered on the contemporary SB, though decorated with the butterfly grille of the 1956 Vega range.

Looking a little past its best is this 1958 C4Z1 with Duple (Midland) body in the fleet of Vaggs Coaches.

Norfolk's of Nayland's 1960 twenty-nine-seat Duple Vista-bodied C4, photographed in July 1974, was new to F. Yarranton of Tenbury Wells. It passed through several owners before arriving in Norfolk's fleet. It was later acquired by Fareline Bus and Coach Services Ltd of Wingfield, Norfolk and ended its days as transport for the 1st North Ormesby Scouts, Thornaby.

A similar twenty-nine-seat Duple body was also available on the C5Z1 chassis, and a number were operated by David MacBrayne in Scotland.

Between 1959 and 1961, Dennis built around twenty-seven thirty-seat utility bodies in the same style as those fitted to the Dennis Pax and Bedford VAS; these were on C4Z1 chassis supplied to London County Council.

The TJ Series

The TJ range, or J-series, was introduced in November 1958 with seven variants, numbered J1 to J6, based on the load-carrying capacity, which ranged from 1.5 tons (1,524kg; J1) to 7 tons (7,112kg; J6), although there were often several load ratings for each model. The 3 ton (3,048kg) J2 model was the most common variant, generally adapted to forward control by the coachbuilder for PSV use. The J2 continued the use of 16in (4.88m) diameter wheels as introduced with the A2. The engine options for the J2 were the usual 214cu in (3.5-litre) 85bhp petrol engine or a new 4-cylinder 200cu in (3.3-litre) 57bhp Bedford diesel engine. The diesel was enlarged to 220cu in (3.6 litres) and 70bhp from September 1961, and in time the 6-cylinder 300cu in (4.9-litre) petrol and 330cu in (5.1-litre) diesel engines became optional fitments. The gearbox for the J-series was a four-speed unit with synchromesh on all but first and reverse gears, with a choice of ratios to suit the intended application. The J2 was available with the same wheelbase options as the preceding A series, the J2S with 9ft 11in (3.02m) wheelbase and the J2L with 11ft 11in (3.63m) wheelbase. The J2L was very popular for small PSV use and production continued throughout the 1960s and 1970s, with a

LEFT: **This J2SZ10 with Duple (Midland) Compact nineteen-seat coach body was new to Noble Drilling Corporation's UK operation at Aberdeen in 1968.**

BELOW: **The J2 could make a luxurious coach, despite its relatively small size. Here is the interior of the Plaxton Embassy body on Cyril Kenzie's J2 KNK 373H.**

The island of Guernsey's two largest bus operators, Guernsey Motors and Guernsey Railways, were united in a single unit in 1974. In 1979 Guernsey's buses were taken over by Steiner Investments Ltd and a programme of fleet replacement was commenced; in 1980 a new company, Guernsey Bus, was formed to take over the island's buses. Both Guernsey Motors and Guernsey Railways had a preference for the J4 and this 1968 J4LZ5 was new to Guernsey Motors Ltd of St Peter Port. It has the distinctive thirty-five-seat body by Reading of Portsmouth that was commonly seen on the island's buses.

number of coachbuilders offering complete vehicles on the chassis. Production of the TJ series ended in 1975 for the UK market, though it continued for export only until the end of Bedford production at Dunstable in 1986. Almost all versions of the J, from the J1 through to the J5, chassis were bodied as PSVs, though the J2 and the J4 were by far the most popular choice for small PSVs in the thirty- to thirty-five-seat range. The J4, in particular, found a home on Guernsey in the Channel Islands, with bodies by Reading of Portsmouth and its successor, Sparshatt. There were also a number of bodies on Guernsey J4s built by Seddon Motors Ltd of Lancashire.

Duple (Midland) offered a forward-control fifteen- to nineteen-seat all-metal body called the Compact, which could be had in both service bus and more luxurious service coach form and from 1960 a twenty-three-seat kit form export version developed in conjunction with the United Africa Co. Examples of the nineteen-seat service coach were operated by British European Airways in Jersey. The Duple bodies were generally built to 7ft 6in (2.29m) widths. A twenty-seat version of this body was manufactured for the Southern Coach Centre in 1962 and sold as the JX20. With overall dimensions of 17ft 11in (5.4m) length and 7ft 6in (2.29m) width, the JX20 featured similar seats to those used in the contemporary Willowbrook Express service coach body and retailed for £2,019 for a petrol-powered version, a diesel engine costing approximately £50 more. With the petrol engine, an owner could expect fuel consumption in the region of 15–20mpg (14.2–18.9ltr/100km) and a top speed of 70mph (113km/h).

Plaxton built versions of its Embassy body for the J2, culminating with the Embassy IV body for eighteen to twenty-two passengers, available until 1971.

By 1974, the Alf Moseley group was offering what it claimed to be the only twenty-seat, purpose-built PSV body for the UK market. Named the Faro, it was a thoroughly modern-looking unit and built on a J2L chassis modified to forward control by Salvador Caetano in Portugal. Overall length was 19ft 1.5in (5.9m), width 7ft 4.5in (2.2m) and the body was all metal, based on a corrosion-proofed welded box-section frame. The stress panels that ran from window to floor level were in steel and all external lower panels were in aluminium. The front and rear panels were in fibreglass and the roof was a one-piece pressing.

CONVERSIONS BASED ON THE LIGHT VANS

CA

The CA was introduced in 1952 and remained in production until 1969. It was of semi-forward control configuration, with the driver located well forward but with the rear of the engine protruding slightly into the interior. Two length options were offered: the CAS, with 7ft 6in (2.29m) wheelbase and 12ft 10.1in (3.91m) overall length; and the CAL, with 8ft 6in (2.59m) wheelbase and 13ft 10in (4.22m) overall length. The CA was rated as a 10–15cwt (510–760kg) capacity van and formed the basis of a series of very popular minibus and minicoach conversions. The chassis was a simple pressed-steel A-frame with diagonal cross-bracing and two rear cross-members, fore and aft of the fuel tank,

The CA van formed the basis of the Martin Walter Utilabus and Workobus conversions in the 1950s and early 1960s. This is Dave Prosser's Workobus – these were generally somewhat more basic than the Utilabus conversions.

which was located behind the rear axle and below the floor. The engine was the 92cu in (1.5-litre) Vauxhall 4-cylinder ohv unit from the E-type Wyvern saloon, available in 6.8:1 and 7.4:1 compression ratios, giving 52bhp and 54.8bhp respectively. The engine was later enlarged to 97.4cu in (1.6-litre), as used in the Vauxhall Victor saloon, with 7.0:1 or 8:1 compression ratios, giving 58.5bhp or 62bhp. Initially only a three-speed gearbox was offered, a four-speed option arriving in the 1960s. Both gearboxes had synchro-mesh on all forward gears and the ratios were changed by a column-mounted lever, again as on the Wyvern and some models of the Victor. The rear axle was a hypoid unit with a final-drive ratio of 5.285:1, later models having additional options of 4.625:1 and 4.111:1 ratios.

The vast majority of conversions produced a vehicle of around twelve seats, and in the early years of production many were based on the short-wheelbase CAS variant. Probably the most prolific builder on the CA was Martin Walter Ltd of Folkestone, initially with a new version of its nine- or ten-seat body called the Utilecon, introduced in 1952 which had been built on the earlier Bedford PC 10–12cwt (510–610kg) van, which the CA replaced. The Utilecon, which was really a dual-purpose goods-and-passenger conversion as the seats could be folded up to provide goods space, was replaced for passenger-carrying use by the Utilabus in 1954. This seated twelve, including the driver. The twelve-seat model range was extended to include the Utilabrake conversion in 1956, which, like the Utilecon, was intended for use as a personnel carrier and generally not finished to meet PSV regulations. By 1958 Martin Walter was claiming 30,000 conversions had been manufactured on the CAS chassis; a new model, designated the Utilabus PSV and specifically aimed at the bus and coach operator, was introduced for the CAL chassis in that year. The chassis was fitted with the optional heavy-duty springs, rated up to 15cwt (760kg), and the high-compression version of the Wyvern engine. The seats were inward-facing benches, each seating five passengers, with one additional passenger and the driver seated in the front conventional car seats. The roof was single-piece translucent fibreglass moulding raised to give a 5ft (1.5m) interior clearance and fitted with two static air extractors. The interior and seats were trimmed in washable PVC and the Utilabus PSV cost £725 before purchase tax was added.

By 1962, the Utilabus PSV had risen in price to £783 for the 97cu in (1.6-litre) petrol version and £908 for the 4-cylinder diesel option.

Experience with moulded composites led to a radical introduction by Martin Walter in 1964. This was a one-piece moulded body in fibreglass, reinforced with timber

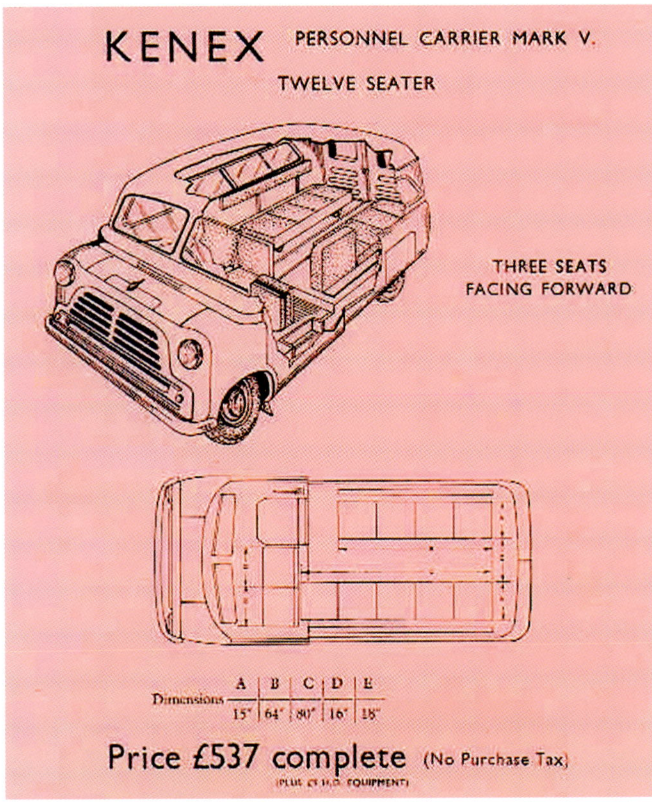

This advert shows the interior layout of the Kenex conversion of the CA van. KENEX

framing and steel inserts. The interior was fully trimmed, the side panels lined and the floor provided with a fitted carpet. A full-luxury version of the body is fitted to the CAL preserved by George Atkin and described below.

The Utilabus and the Utilabrake continued to be produced alongside the luxury body and were updated now and then throughout the 1960s. A twelve-seat Utilabrake Series II with the 97cu in (1.6-litre) engine road tested in 1967 showed that an operator could expect fuel consumption in the region of 22mpg (12.9ltr/100km) over varied driving conditions, including motorway usage. Although the example tested was not finished to PSV standards, the additional weight penalty incurred would probably not have much effect on the fuel consumption.

By 1966, Martin Walter had merged with Dormobile and was producing the eleven-seat Dormobile coach on the CAL, the same composite fibreglass body shell also being used for the caravanette (motor home) conversions to which the Dormobile name was more familiarly applied.

Marshall offered its twelve-seat 'Busette' conversion in 1958, with two bench seats upholstered in foam rubber and PVC, each seating three passengers, including the driver.

IN PRESERVATION

Bedford CAL/Martin Walter HCB 576F

Year new: 1967
Engine: Vauxhall 1.7-litre petrol
Gearbox: four-speed column-shift synchromesh
Current owner: George Atkin

History

HCB 576F was originally built by Martin Walter as an eleven-seat coach, plus the driver, in 1967. It was new to Aspden of Blackburn. It passed to a number of other operators then into private use, where it was converted into a caravanette. It passed to its current owner in this form in the spring of 2008.

Owner's Experience

George Atkin is one of those unassuming enthusiasts working quietly away in a draughty shed on cold nights to save historic buses and coaches for posterity. His fleet of superbly restored coaches would not disgrace the depot of a leading operator and the attention to detail paid in the presentation of his vehicles has to be seen to be believed. As well as completed projects, like the Duple Firefly/SB pictured on the front cover of this book (the restoration of this coach was substantially carried out for George by the Walsh and Kershaw brothers

of Manchester), there are a number of other Bedfords under restoration, including an OB with Duple Vista body and one of the rare forward-control conversion OBs with a Burlingham Seagull body. Following the mini-coach theme, there is a Plaxton Mini Supreme on a Bedford CF chassis well on the way to full restoration. How did he become interested in coaches? George says:

My father was a coach driver for most of his working life, so from being knee-high to a grasshopper I was perched in a coach… The owner of the business was Mr A. E. Brown, whose livery was pale blue and cream, hence the livery of my preserved coaches. Mr. Brown always bought an AEC coach for my father to drive, but it was in the days when you did not use your best coach on routine jobs! So there were OBs, early petrol-engined SBs and later 330 diesel-engined SBs with Plaxton, Duple and Yeates coachwork.

Mr Brown allowed me to go on many trips with my father and also to Yeates of Loughborough to pick up fresh coaches. On the trips to Yeates I was allowed in the factory to see the Europa and Fiesta bodies being built, all very interesting for a ten-year-old!

Upon Mr Brown's retirement he sold the business to R. W. Appleby of Conisholme and George's father transferred with the business. Appleby's had a mixed fleet, many of which were Bedfords of virtually every type – SBs, VALs, VAMs and VASs as well as the later Y-series range. George passed

George Atkin's superbly restored CAL/Martin Walter luxury coach conversion.

his PSV test with Appleby and went on to drive part-time for them and experienced all the different types of Bedford, the VAL being one of his favourite types to drive. Eventually George bought his own coach, a Bedford CAL with Martin Walter eleven-seat coachwork, similar to the one he owns now. He operated it for about five years, taking it as far north as Whitby and south to London's Victoria coach station, with a regular job being a Saturday night bingo run! Amongst George's fleet is a rare YMPS with thirty-five-seat Plaxton Paramount body and a restored thirty-seven seat NJM-spec SB/Plaxton Panorama.

When asked what was special about Bedfords, George says, 'I always considered Bedfords to be the workhorse of independent operators, which is where my interest lies. Not the fleetest of foot, but reliable, hard workers, which were economical to run and epitomized by the longevity of the SB, from the early fifties virtually to the cessation of Bedfords.'

When George acquired his current CA project, it had been in use as a caravanette (small motor-home conversion) so all the original internal fittings, lights, seats and luggage racks had been removed and replaced with both low-level and high-level cupboards in addition to seating and beds. During its working life it had various poor-quality repairs carried out to the fibreglass body using unsuitable materials, such as hardboard. The body is mounted on the CAL chassis cowl, which is made of steel. George found major corrosion

to most areas of the cowl but the chassis was sound, with the exception of the rear extension, which needed some attention. Major welding was carried out to the front cowl, including the reconstruction of both heater/demister ducts, the cab floor and the internal wheelarches. Other work included complete floor renewal, including the metal bearers and timber boarding, removal of the floor-change gearbox and replacement with a four-speed column-change gearbox to the original specification, which involved sourcing CA gearchange rods.

Some of the timber frame needed replacing and repairs were needed to the fibreglass body and bending new curved Perspex rear quarter-light windows. The interior had to be replicated in its entirety, luggage racks being cut down from standard Duple items, while seats were adapted from standard coach seats George had in stock, and these were retrimmed by Duoflex of Brackley.

Prior to its current restoration, George spent many hours driving the CA, saying, 'it is pleasant to drive with four-speed column change. It never ceased to amaze me how well it went for a 1700cc engine, cruising along at 50mph and pulling like a train – the gearing was just about perfect.'

Restoration took George about four years, interleaved with other work on coaches in his collection, and was largely all done on his own, though the coach was resprayed and the windows refitted professionally by CoBus Ltd of Bridlington.

The smart interior of George Atkin's CAL/Martin Walter coach. The level of trim and quality of seating would not disgrace a far larger luxury coach.

In the rear, two inward-facing triple seats made of wooden slats perhaps accounted for Marshall's description of the body as 'semi-utility'. Deep safety-glass side windows were mounted in polished alloy frames.

Another small coachbuilder who modified the CA was Walker and Son Ltd of Watford, Hertfordshire, whose Grosvenor twelve-seat personnel carrier was quite a luxurious vehicle, with pile carpeting, two-tone upholstery and oak-veneered cappings to the interior.

Kenex Coachworks Ltd of Dover was another volume builder on the CA, an early version being the 1956 twelve-seat Aristocrat, followed by the Kenebrake in 1958, though technically the Kenebrake was only an eleven-seat PSV, as, once again, the driver was included in the count! The seats were arranged with two three-person bench seats facing forward and two double seats facing inwards at the rear. Seat frames were of tubular steel with upholstery in Latex foam trimmed with Armoride PVC imitation leathercloth. The windows were mounted in weatherseal insert-strip rubber. The 1962 version of this body on the CAL chassis was known as the Kenebrake Super, though still only seating eleven passengers plus the driver.

CF

The CF was introduced in 1969 and was the successor to the CA in the 15cwt (760kg) Bedford range. Larger than the CA, the short 8ft 10in (2.69m) wheelbase version of the CF could accommodate up to 22cwt (1,120kg), the longer 10ft 6in (3.2m) wheelbase being rated at 25–35cwt (1,270–1,780kg), the 35cwt (1,780kg) version being fitted with twin rear wheels. The CF therefore neatly encompassed the CA market and overlapped with the J2. Clearly aimed at rival Ford's Transit model, the CF went on to form

CF production ended in 1987; having essentially been an entirely Vauxhall-based product, the CF no longer fitted into GM's plans to establish Vauxhall's range entirely on Opel platforms. This is Vauxhall's own publicity photograph from 1973 for the Dormobile Utilabus conversion on the CF. GM

Reeve Burgess was showing the compact Reebur 17 seventeen-seat body on the CF chassis at the Commercial Motor Show on 23 September 1976.

the basis of a very successful range of small buses and coaches and, in the words of one well-known coach company owner, 'became the saviour of many a rural independent operator'.

Mechanically, the CF was based largely on the Vauxhall Victor FD. The short-wheelbase CF was powered by the 98cu in (1.6-litre) 64bhp Victor FD engine, while the longer-wheelbase version had the 120cu in (2-litre) 85bhp Victor engine. Both these engines were relatively new designs, with a belt-driven overhead camshaft; they gave quite lively performance though some drivers missed the low-down torque of the CA's ohv engine. The two petrol engines were replaced by the 77bhp 107cu in (1.8-litre) and 88bhp 139cu in (2.3-litre) Vauxhall Magnum engines in 1972, which gave considerably enhanced performance to the CF. Two diesel

engine options were available, the 108cu in (1.8-litre) Perkins 4.108 4-cylinder providing an economical, if leisurely, drive from its 51bhp for the short-wheelbase model, while for the long wheelbase CF there was the 70bhp 154cu in (2.5-litre) Perkins 4.154 diesel. Opel diesel engines were fitted to the CF from the mid-1970s.

The Victor three- and four-speed gearboxes were both available with the smaller engines, though with the larger engines the four-speed was more commonly fitted. Around 1975 a superb ZF five-speed gearbox was fitted to some examples of the CF. Many of the five-speed CFs were later dismantled for their gearboxes, which were plundered by motorsport enthusiasts for use in competition cars. Independent coil-sprung front suspension and rack-and-pinion steering came again from the Vauxhall Victor, though the

IN PRESERVATION

Bedford CF/Plaxton Mini Supreme RNE 692W

by Terry Jones

Year new: 1981
Engine: 2-litre 4-cylinder GM diesel
Gearbox: ZF five-speed
Body: Plaxton Mini Supreme, seventeen seats
Current owner: Terry Jones

History

RNE 692W was new to Shearings Ribblesdale of Altrincham in April 1981, one of a batch of four used for tour feeder journeys and airport transfers. In April 1984 three of the four were sold to Coombe Hill Coaches, near Salisbury, and from there two went to L. F. Mayo Coaches of King's Stanley, near Stroud, Gloucestershire, in November 1988. RNE 692W was purchased by the current owner in 1993 from Mayo and believed to be one of only four Plaxton Mini Supremes on Bedford CF chassis still in existence.

Owner's Experience

Terry Jones became a preservationist in 1975, when he bought a 1950 OB with Duple Vista twenty-nine-seat coachwork, registered MFM 39. He subsequently turned his hobby into a business, Vista Coachways of Yatton, Somerset.

Terry writes: I owned that coach for over thirty years, using the OB as a PSV again from 1988 right through to 2014, for hire for special occasions.

As an enthusiast, I visited the 1979 British Coach Rally at Brighton. Two of the exhibits there were DJF 631T and BWB 61T, Plaxton Mini Supremes built onto Bedford CF chassis/cowls. I instantly fell in love with their design and 'bubble' characteristics. Thus when I needed a small coach for my business in 1992, I specifically set out to find one. Plaxton only built thirty-four of them, in their Special Services Division, about half being built at Scarborough and the others at Ware. With so few built it was not going to be easy to find one, but I was very lucky to be put onto two recently withdrawn examples, only about 40 miles (65km) from where I was based. I was able to persuade the owner to part with one of them, and so in September 1992 I became the proud owner of RNE 692W.

Over the following six years I acquired three more CF Mini Supremes, though none of them saw active PSV service with me. NPV 450W and EHE 526V were both acquired primarily for spares, but with a view to keeping one as a rally vehicle. In the event both were subsequently scrapped. The last one I acquired was HIL 7081 from Hilton's of Newton-le-Willows in 1998. I did put that coach on the road as a Class V for a time, before selling it on in 2006. The original identity of 'Hilton' was DJF 631T, one of those I first saw at Brighton in 1979. By the time I acquired it a Bedford 2.3-litre petrol engine had been fitted, in place of the original GM diesel. It made it quieter, but quite thirsty.

Back to RNE 692W (now christened 'Shearene'), she was an active member of my operational fleet from September 1992 to June 2010, and proved to be very robust and reliable, though quite slow on hills with passengers on board. She has a GM (Opel) 2-litre 4-cylinder diesel engine, with a five-speed gearbox, which has always been quite economical, consistently returning around 21mpg (13.5ltr/100km). It was, however, quite noisy, so I soon fitted carpet to the dashboard and footwells, to cut down the noise intrusion. When I first had her I found that she would break alternator brackets every fifteen to eighteen months, but after about the fifth new bracket I got somebody to look at the way it was set up and make a few adjustments. Since then, no more alternator brackets have been needed. Another thing I found was that unless she had been running within the previous hour she would crank for a good thirty seconds or more before firing, so a strong battery and good starter motor were essential. Over almost twenty-two years I asked various engineers to look at the starting system, but apart from fitting non-return valves into the fuel line, nobody ever got to the root of the problem, so I got used to the long cranking. That was until May of this year (2015), when I put her into a workshop on the Isle of Wight, for MOT preparation.

They sorted the starting out, and now she will fire into life almost instantly, even if she has been stood unused for a few weeks!

As I was regularly using Shearene on school journeys I had her fitted with seat belts in 1996. She has twelve retractor lap belts on the double seats, and five static lap belts across the back seat, so all seventeen passengers can be belted in. In 1997 I had her set of Plaxton seats retrimmed, as the original red moquette had faded to pink. The new grey moquette I chose for her was fitted by Duoflex at Brackley, and is still looking good almost twenty years on. When I first had her in 1992 I brush painted her into my Vista livery with Tekaloid coach enamel, and did my own sign writing by hand, and that paintwork still looks pretty good now, after twenty-two years of both active service and more recent storage.

Over the years Shearene has taken part in nineteen rallies or running days so far, but in the early years I noticed that most visitors walked straight past and ignored her. However, after a few years she started to attract much attention and interest, as she has become older and rarer. Between 1992 and 2000 she attended six of the annual rallies at the Dean Forest Railway, which included running free shuttle services between Lydney and the railway site at Norchard. She has also visited many events in the Bristol area. In 1997 she won the 'Best Bedford' trophy at Wroughton, near Swindon, and again in 1999 at Banwell, near Weston-super-Mare, beating my 1950 OB, which won the 'Runner-up in its class'. In August 2000 I took her to the Bedford Gathering at Somersham, near Cambridge, and more recently in 2007 and 2008 she visited Exeter twice for the annual WHOTT rallies at the Westpoint showground.

Shearene is now my only remaining coach. Today she is tested to Class 5, for 'social and domestic use' only, though she could easily be returned to Class 6 (PSV) if required. I hope I can keep her in preservation for many more years to come, as she has now been with me for twice as long as with her previous three owners put together.

Terry Jones' lovely CF/Plaxton Mini-Supreme in the livery of Vista Coaches, the business Terry established and ran for many years.

suspension was uprated to suit the weight of the larger vehicle. Rear suspension was by semi-elliptic leaf springs. A vacuum servo provided power assistance for the brakes.

By 1982, the short-wheelbase CF had become the CF250, with an option of the GM three-speed automatic gearbox and either 2.3-litre petrol or 2.3-litre GM diesel engines, while the long-wheelbase model was now the CF280, with the same engine options but with a ZF four- or five-speed gearbox. When twin rear wheels were fitted, the long-wheelbase CF was known as the CF350 and an even longer-wheelbase option, at 11ft 8in (3.55m), was now offered as the CF350L. All could be ordered from Bedford either as standard vans for conversion or as chassis-cab assemblies or chassis-cowl assemblies for custom coachwork to be fitted.

The CF became very popular for minibus conversions, with Deansgate, Reeves Burgess, Devon Conversions and Dormobile (formerly Martin Walter) all building on the CF. Seating capacity was typically between twelve and seventeen.

Examples of minibuses produced using the CF van included the twelve-seat (including driver) SL Utilabus on the CF and CF250, and B707 Long Utilacoach on the CF280, both from Dormobile, and the Walkerbus twelve-seat Personnel Carrier by B. Walker and Son. The Walkerbus featured full luxury seating, with all seats facing forward, and opening sliding rear side windows.

The Williams Motor Co. Ltd of Manchester's coachbuilding subsidiary, Deansgate, built a thirteen-seat (driver included) minibus on the CF, which it sold under the 'Mancunian' name. The Mancunian was a true twelve-seat PSV, with six tubular steel-framed bus double seats trimmed in vinyl, and fluorescent interior lighting. Deansgate also produced a seventeen-seat box-like conversion that retained the CF bonnet, grille and headlights. Four service bus-style passenger windows with top-sliding ventilators were provided in the workman-like body.

G. C. Smith Ltd of Loughborough, Leicestershire built a fourteen-seat version of its Whippet body on the CF350 and Dormobile built a fifteen-seat conversion on the same base; both had tail-lifts and were popular with the welfare fleets of local authorities.

Matt Ascough, the famous Dublin bus and coach dealer, built its neat Asco Clubman seventeen-seat coach body on the CF in the early 1970s, a design strongly reminiscent of Plaxton products. In a similar vein was Plaxton's own seventeen-seat Mini Supreme, built on the long-wheelbase CF and CF350 between 1979 and 1982; some of these were assembled at Plaxton's service depot at Ware in Hertfordshire, while others were assembled at Scarborough (in both cases by the Special Services department), but in all respects were true mini-coaches with a large windscreen, panoramic side windows and full luxury coach seats. The Mini Supreme retained the combined grille and headlight surround of the CF, revealing the coach's ancestry to the discerning eye. A design inherited by Plaxton was the Reeve Burgess Reebur 17 Minicoach, an angular design with a squared-off snout that owed everything to form but nothing to style – today's eyes would without difficulty place it as a product of the 1980s. The '17' in the name referred to the number of seats, which, despite the coach's external appearance, were quite luxurious.

Drivers found the light handling and precise steering made the CF a pleasure to drive, even fully loaded. Gear changing, as might be expected given the source of the components, was no more difficult than if one were driving a car. The CF was without doubt an attractive proposition for the operator with low volumes of traffic or regular small-party private hire work, just as its predecessor the CA had been.

CHAPTER TEN

PRESERVING A BEDFORD BUS OR COACH

The motor vehicle is so ingrained in the human consciousness that it is hardly surprising that there are those who consider it important to preserve examples for future generations to enjoy. Indeed, in talking to enthusiasts whose hobby is preserving old vehicles one is often struck by the passion and genuine affection they hold for what are, effectively, simple machines. Bedford played such a huge part in the development of mass transport and the building of an industry that many operators still retain one or perhaps two cherished examples, reluctant to part with old friends. That many preserved Bedfords are still working for their living, albeit in a slightly more relaxed way than when they were new, is testament both to the regard in which they are held and to their general ruggedness. Vintage coaches are also popular with the non-enthusiast public as any visitor to a bus and coach rally will testify. Those who worked or still work in the industry, like Andrew Lodge, Andy McCarthy and Cyril Kenzie, whose business was built upon Bedford foundations, demonstrate an unspoken regard for the workhorses that gave them a living for so many years by dedicating themselves to maintaining a collection of vintage Bedford coaches.

Love of old Bedfords is not the sole preserve of the industry, though; there is within the preservation movement a growing population drawn from those whose occupations were not directly connected with the transport industry. Our contributing preservationists, George Atkin, Roger Chambers and Dave Prosser, are outstanding examples of these. Others, like Terry Jones, became transport professionals as a direct result of their interest in preserving and restoring Bedford PSVs. The concept of preserving our heritage and the recognition of its importance in all walks of life is also growing; in any one weekend you will find people of diverse occupation and all genders digging out locks on derelict canals, cleaning steam locomotives at a heritage railway or taking their meticulously restored classic vehicles to rallies for the public and like-minded enthu-

siasts to enjoy. This chapter hopefully provides some insight and tips for the keen amateur who would join this thriving movement by preserving a Bedford bus or coach.

FIRST THINGS FIRST

Choosing a Vehicle

Having decided you want to enter the world of preservation, your choice of Bedford vehicle will be influenced by a number of factors – your favourite model, your budget, availability of vehicles, ease of maintenance and availability of spares and service items are just some of the things you might want to consider. One needs also to consider whether a restoration project or a going concern would be best for one's circumstances. If you fancy restoring a vehicle, you need to familiarize yourself with the skill set that is required and see how well it matches your own – are you a good mechanic, carpenter, panel beater and coach painter? These are just some of the skills you must have or will need to master if you are going to properly and safely restore an old Bedford bus or coach. Some work can of course be contracted out to specialists, though the budget will most likely determine just how much can be done professionally. There is a great deal of satisfaction to be gained from restoring a vehicle oneself, and the process can be therapeutic too. Skills can be acquired by experience, but time is often not on one's side, so searching out courses at your local further education institution can be profitable, and there will always be a health and safety awareness course available, which is something that should be a priority.

It would be fair to say that most competent mechanics will find little to challenge them in a Bedford chassis, but those whose first step in automotive problem solving is to plug a laptop into the OBD socket may need to adjust their expectations slightly. Repairing coachwork, on the other hand, requires a more diverse range of skills.

ABOVE: **Originally registered KLP 1D, this J2 has a Duple (Midland) Compact body built at the Willowbrook works at Loughborough. Bought for Royal Household duties it was kept at Buckingham Palace Mews and was used to transport the Queen Mother's staff between Clarence House and Sandringham. For those short of space, the J2/Duple Compact combination is a good choice of vehicle to preserve. It is also a relatively easy vehicle to drive and manoeuvre.**

LEFT: **Another compact prospect for the space-starved preservationist would be the MLC. Remarkably, this is another example with rare Lee Motors bodywork similar to FJT 96 shown previously. It too worked for Dorset County Council before being preserved.**

The intended use for the vehicle also needs consideration – is it just to be a show or rally entrant with occasional use for family outings and similar, or do you have in mind joining the growing ranks of Heritage and Vintage Tour operators? If the latter is your intention, then while a relatively modern Y-series coach requiring just a little tidying up might be easy to find and relatively cheap to buy, its attraction for your potential customers is likely to be less than, say, an OB or an early SB. Well restored examples of OBs are very popular with operators and as they represent a commercial investment prices are likely to by very high. The best examples typically start at around £40,000; a six-figure sum would not be a surprising amount to pay for the very best OB. A restoration project requiring a major rebuild might be yours for between £7,000 and £14,000, though at the cheaper end of this range onlookers are likely to question your sanity when the pile of sawdust, perished rubber, lichen and rusty metal you have purchased arrives on the back of a lorry!

Many SBs and VASs found a second use as mobile homes within the traveller community or were converted into luxury campers for occasional use for the less peripatetic. One such was offered for sale recently for £4,500, though this price took into account the special fittings that were included.

The C4Z/C5Z and the J2 models are not without their charm for the public and command somewhat lower prices, perhaps £10,000–£15,000 for a good example, less for restoration projects.

The VAL, being somewhat exotic and a favourite amongst enthusiasts, will be an expensive proposition, particularly as there are a limited number of survivors – an example in good condition though without a current test certificate changed hands in 2014 for £8,000. The size of the VAL may also make storage difficult, as you will need a space of at least 40ft (13m) in length in order to get round the vehicle safely when it is parked. Y-series coaches can still be found in service though value will depend on condition;

Restoration potential? This 1949 OB with twenty-eight-seat Mulliner body is worth saving, but projects like this need careful consideration of space, skills, finances and time. It last worked with Jessop's Coaches of Frinsted in Kent.

a YNV Venturer was advertised in autumn 2014 for as little as £800, though without a current MOT certificate. A 1970s Y series in roadworthy condition might also be found for less than £1,000 and a really nice example was for sale recently at £1,500.

Pre-war models such as the WLB and WTB are rarely advertised and tend to change hands by word of mouth; the participants in such transactions are understandably reluctant to discuss their financial business with outsiders, so to estimate the value of such a vehicle is a risky venture. It is a seller's market and the OB is beginning to move into this category.

Storage and maintenance facilities are very important; the latter were covered in some detail in the author's previous work on Bristol and Eastern Coach Works (*see* Bibliography). However, it cannot be over-emphasized that an understanding of both health and safety issues and proper storage should not be regarded as a luxury. If you want your pride and joy to last and you want to live long enough to enjoy it, then keeping it away from the ravages of sun, storm, variable temperatures and criminals in some form of secure covered accommodation with safe working conditions is necessary.

Where to Buy

To find a vehicle you will need to be fairly resourceful. Trawling the internet will often provide a number of adverts for Bedfords; Dick Gilbert's Classic Buses website has a healthy turnover of old buses and coaches for sale and there is a good advert section in *Bus and Coach Preservation* magazine. Getting to know Bedford owners by joining the online forums and going to rallies and the annual Bedford Gathering (*see* www.vauxhallclassics.co.uk) will acquaint you with people who will know when vehicles come up for sale. There are a number of collectors and dealers who save vehicles purely to prevent them from disappearing for good and are often willing to pass them on to those who are well-placed to restore them – the late Colin Shears, saviour of many west country buses and coaches, was a well-known example of this breed of collector. Treat such people with respect and do not expect them to part with a vehicle for a song simply because it looks down at heel. It has probably cost the current owner a small fortune in storage if they have owned it for a number of years and this will be accounted for in the selling price. It is quite likely you will be directed to one of these characters once whoever you are communicating with is convinced of your sincerity, though a secret handshake is unlikely to be necessary. Probably the best advice one can give is to buy with your

head as well as with your heart. Incomplete vehicles are best avoided, as there is a reason they are incomplete, and failing to source whatever is missing may be the undoing of the entire project.

Spares and Support

The general principles of preserving a Bedford bus or coach are no different from those of preserving any other make of bus and coach, though acquainting oneself with specialist Bedford suppliers, such as Norman Aish's Bygone Bedford Bits, should be a priority. Some patience may be needed because such specialist suppliers are few and the demands of their customers are many. A good range of new spares is still available for many models and for the Y series there are still some spares available off the shelf at commercial vehicle dealers and factors. Dave Prosser recalls that the vast usage of Bedfords by the military meant that up until 2004–5, there was still a good quantity of unused ex-military spares around, though he says this source is now drying up. Norman Aish has remanufactured many service parts for older Bedfords and continues to research suppliers and sources to meet the needs of Bedford owners. Currently he can supply parts for the WTB, WTL, WLB and WLG as well as OB, OWB and SB and also offers a parts tracing service. One of the most useful of Norman's products is the range of workshop manuals available to enable servicing and repairs to be carried out correctly. It cannot be over-emphasized that the safety of a large vehicle used on the road must be the owner's number one priority and having the correct servicing information is a vital part of this.

RESTORING A BEDFORD

Mechanics

Working on the majority of mechanical components of a Bedford is fairly straightforward and should be within the capabilities of a competent DIY mechanic, though some heavier-duty tools and a three-quarter-inch drive socket set will be very useful. The Bedford petrol engines and the normally aspirated diesels are easy to maintain and should hold no mysteries for anyone used to servicing and repairing their own cars and familiar with diesels. Engine parts availability is very good, especially for the later Blue and Red series diesels. Most local commercial-vehicle engine reconditioners will be able to carry out any machining necessary to rebuild one of these engines and probably supply or make any parts required. For the very early (pre-war) petrol engines, it is best to seek out an engine reconditioner

This preserved WLB with body built by Davies of Merthyr Tydfil, South Wales was seen at a Bedford Gathering at the Vauxhall Heritage Centre at Luton. VH

whose work is largely in the classic car field who will have the skills and know-how to rebuild a pre-war engine. Servicing the petrol engines is straightforward and no more difficult than servicing a 6-cylinder motorcar engine.

As many of the gearboxes used in the more recent Bedfords are proprietary, from manufacturers like Turner, Spicer and ZF, finding repairers and spares should not present too much difficulty. For Bedford's own gearboxes, especially the pre-war and 1950s production, these can often be stripped and rebuilt by the competent amateur mechanic. Finding parts may not be so easy, but one of the advantages of living in the twenty-first century is that facilities to manufacture parts from patterns using computer-controlled machinery are quite widely available, though it will undoubtedly be expensive.

A wide range of mechanical parts is available from Bygone Bedford Bits and a look at Norman's website is always worthwhile. Oil seals for engines and hubs are generally to standard sizes and can often be obtained direct from the manufacturers. Rubber seals and other parts for hydraulic braking systems are available from Norman and from other suppliers, though one should be wary of 'new, old stock' or 'NOS' items sold on eBay, as, while some parts are still in usable condition, others will have a shelf life that may have been long exceeded. With such items it is definitely a case of caveat emptor. Some pattern or reproduction rubber parts need to be chosen with care too, as many have a much shorter working life than those manufactured with the original materials and rubber compounds.

HOBBY TO BUSINESS

by Terry Jones

Most vintage vehicle owners consider, at some point, the possibility of turning their hobby into a business. Terry Jones, owner of the CF/Mini Supreme described in Chapter 9, did just that. In the following piece, he describes in his own words how this was achieved:

I have been a life-long bus and coach enthusiast, with fond childhood memories of my early years as a toddler, riding on the buses of Swindon Corporation, and then on Shotters Coaches on the Isle of Wight during our annual family holidays. As I grew older I became very interested in models of buses and coaches, but by the time I was eighteen I decided that I wanted my own coach for preservation. By then my main interest was in small independent coach companies. So it was that in 1975, at the age of just twenty, I purchased my Bedford OB coach MFM 39 for preservation. Many people thought I was too young at the time, and the novelty would wear off, but I think I have proved them all wrong, as I owned that coach for over thirty years and went on to form my business out of the hobby. Over the years since then I have also owned another twenty-three buses and coaches, mainly operated as part of the business.

The Bedford OB was originally new to Crosville Motor Services in 1950, where it operated tours and excursions from the North Wales coastal resorts for almost ten years. Although it was only twenty-five years old, it looked quite ancient when I

The former Crosville Motor Services OB/Duple Vista 'Bosworth' that inspired Terry Jones to take up running coaches professionally. Bosworth was seen at Shanklin Esplanade, Isle of Wight on 15 October 2012.

bought it because of the great step-change in coach design in the late 1960s. Today a twenty-five-year-old coach can still look quite modern, and still perform frontline work, if it is well cared for.

After three years of taking my OB to rallies around the country, I took her off the road at the end of the 1978 season for what I planned to be a 'major restoration' over eighteen months to two years. As this was mainly me, with help from friends mostly on Sunday afternoons, the project actually took eight years, with the coach returning to the road in August 1986. By that time I was working in the coach industry, as a driver and office manager for a small local company, and I was aware that around the country a number of operators were running Bedford OB coaches on wedding hires and other special occasions. So it was that I decided to get my own coach back to full PSV recertification standard, and run it commercially as an extension of my hobby. I contacted the local testing station, and had a visit from a senior vehicle examiner, who advised me on what I would need to do, beyond what I had already done for a Class 5 test. Work then started, as and when I could, and again with help from friends, together with professional help where necessary, and so in January 1988 I presented the coach for recertification and received a new COIF (Certificate of Initial Fitness). In the meantime, in late 1986 I purchased a home-study pack from Friendberry Ltd to study for the Operator CPC examination (Certificate of Professional Competence in Road Passenger Transport Management) and at the end of 1986 I visited their centre to sit the exam. By early 1987 I received notification that I had passed, and had my certificate.

In the early part of 1988, having my own CPC and the coach with a COIF, I obtained the forms to apply for a Standard National Operator Licence in my own name. Having satisfied the traffic commissioners that I was of good repute, sufficient financial standing, and had an offroad parking place that was suitable to be an 'Operating Centre', I received my licence and a blue disc, which took effect on 1 May 1988. Thus my business was born. I did not wish to trade under my own name, or with a name that was geographically specific, so that the business could develop in whatever way the future may lead. Thus, as the OB has a Duple Vista coach body, I came up with the trading name of 'Vista Coachways'.

For the first year I operated the OB part-time, while still working full-time elsewhere. However, in the summer of 1989 I was given the opportunity to tender for a home-to-school contract, which I won, enabling the business to add a more modern vehicle and become full-time from that September. From there the business grew steadily, and over the following years I increased my authorization from one vehicle, first to two, and then to four. The operation peaked in 1999, when I employed two full-time drivers and several part-time regular or casual drivers. However, I became so busy with admin that I found I was never out on the road any more myself, doing what I always enjoyed. At that point the business needed to either go up or down a notch, to maintain efficiency. Thus it was probably something of a relief when one of my schools contracts came to an end later that year, and the decision was made for me, to cut back the fleet and get back out on the road more myself. A steady period of quiet consolidation followed, until 2004, when I put in a successful tender to operate a council-supported local bus service. That meant buying buses, ticket machines, and a steep learning curve into the ways of local bus operation, rather than my more familiar world of private hire and tour work. However, it worked out well, and after a successful two years I re-tendered for a further two years. The service involved one bus, running around 135 miles (222km) per day, six days a week, but the great thing was that it was never more than 10 miles (16km) from the depot at the furthest point of the route. It also passed by the depot five times each day, so any problems with the vehicles could be quickly and efficiently dealt with.

From 1995 I took over the rental of a depot in my home village, which was very convenient. It had a pit and covered bays for five full-size coaches, so all light maintenance could be carried out on site. However, I knew that, while the landowner was initially in no hurry to sell, the site was in a residential area, and would eventually be sold for housing. Despite that, I had a good run, being there for around twelve years. By 2006 he was thinking of selling, so I reviewed my operations and decided that the time was right to cut back. Over the following year I sold the coaches, withdrew from private hire and just kept the bus service running. I also came to the conclusion that having owned my OB for over thirty years, it was realistically time to part with her, on a high. Through word-of-mouth she soon found a good home locally, and I was even able to keep her 'on fleet' and continue to use her through her new owner. Thus I had the best of both worlds! I eventually had to vacate the depot at the end of 2007, at which time the bus service contract had three months to run. My two Iveco buses were relocated to share space with a colleague 6 miles (10km) away, from where we saw the contract through. I was in the fortunate position of having enjoyed a good twenty years of operation, so I decided to take the opportunity then to finish daily operation. We went out 'on a high', running a number of privately owned local Class 6 tested 'heritage buses' (from 1950 to 1988) on the last two days of my tenure of the bus service.

Bodywork

It is surprising how many Bedfords from the 1950s and 1960s still survive in a basically unrestored condition, having been patched up over the years to keep them going as dictated by commercial need. In general, these are likely to be in better condition mechanically than bodily. Elderly coachwork can present a variety of problems, from corrosion in panelwork and steel-reinforced joints through wet rot in wooden framing to the need for new seat covers and retrimming the interior. Electrical systems became increasingly sophisticated through the years, though a competent auto-electrician should be able to fault-find on a Y series without too much trouble. Earlier models were much simpler and a basic understanding of Ohm's Law and the functioning of dynamos and alternators will stand you in good stead. Rubber- or fabric-covered wiring should be treated with suspicion and where possible replaced with modern material – one needs to be fearless in the face of sighs and moans from the rivet counters. An electrical fire in a wooden-bodied coach is likely to be terminal.

MHU 49 (2). This picture of Mike Walker's OB undergoing restoration illustrates clearly the probable lengths to which a restorer will need to go to return LKN 550 (see page 207) to pristine condition. M. WALKER

BXM 568. This 1935 WTB/Duple is being restored at Lodge's Coaches of High Easter, Essex.

Bodies from most coachbuilders from this period are largely wooden-framed, often built of ash or other relatively hard woods. Joints may be reinforced with steel flitch plates, which may have corroded. Having survived such a long time without full restoration, the body will almost certainly require stripping down to the frame for inspection and the replacement of considerable parts of the framework. To rebuild a wooden coach body frame is certainly not impossible for the amateur restorer, but at the same time it is not a job to be undertaken lightly. More modern coach bodies also contained a lot of wood, right up until the mid-1970s and will probably need similar levels of attention and repair.

The necessary skills can be learned and a course in joinery at your local college of further education will pay dividends, not least in familiarity with the tools required and methods to be employed. The alternative is to have the frame rebuilt by a skilled joiner or the whole or part of the job undertaken by professional restorers such as The Bus Works, at Brinwell Road, Blackpool, Lancashire or Cobus at Carnaby Industrial Estate, Bridlington, East Yorkshire. If you decide to have work done professionally, it is best to ensure – before you allow the work to proceed – that you know exactly how the work is to be done, what it is likely to cost, what materials are to be used and indeed, the standard of finish likely to be achievable. A Concours-ready, good-as-new rebuild will very expensive, but an acceptable result may be obtained in some cases at much less cost – it is a matter of balancing expectations against budget.

Panelwork is probably not as hard to repair as one might think; the complex front, corner and roof sections on post-war bodies are often fibreglass mouldings, which can either be repaired or replicated relatively easily. Working in aluminium is not too challenging if you have a good eye for measuring and cutting and much can be achieved with a jigsaw, electric pillar drill, a set of hole punches, a 4ft folder and a collection of hacksaws and files. Locating local small-volume forges and specialist welders is also useful. Their services will not be cheap, but if you do as much as possible yourself then it is worth spending a little money to get the remainder done properly.

During any strip-down process, it is vital to record the position of each and every component removed, making notes of how it is attached and taking many photographs to build up a good record. Any panels that can be reused should be removed and stored carefully to avoid damage, and marked on the underside in wax crayon to record their location. Curved metal panels are difficult to make without a wheeling machine, but there are specialist classic car repairers who can produce such panels, and perusal of enthusiast magazines will usually turn up one or two adverts; the internet is also a good hunting ground, as many such specialists now have an online presence and a Google search may throw up someone in your area with the necessary skills.

When considering replacement parts, it is important to realize that items such as external mouldings and polished castings were often unique to one model or year range of a particular model, so sourcing replacements for missing or damaged items is likely to be difficult. Some mouldings were made or adapted from standard sections, typically with Herzim infill strip, some types of which are still available, though this is largely a matter of luck. Some enterprising restorers have replaced pressed aluminium trim parts by taking moulds and having them cast in solid aluminium. There are a number of small forges who specialize in the classic car market, for example Whiteway Craft of Stroud (Unit F1c2/Bath Road Trading Estate, Stroud GL5 3QF, tel 01453 755344) can make high-quality small and medium-sized parts in aluminium and other metals. Cast and extruded aluminium parts were generally anodized when new, a finish that is hard to replicate, so will need to be repolished to a very good finish then protected with lacquer or regularly wax-polished to prevent corrosion.

Trim and Paint

Interior trim can be difficult to source, so some ingenuity in fabrication or trimming may be required. Upholstery can be restored professionally and the quality of work achieved often represents good value for money, though cost of the materials can be high. If you are handy at

The end product should be a superbly restored vehicle to be proud of. Kenzie's Bedford OB/Duple Vista, pictured as long ago as May 1969.

sewing, then purchasing an industrial sewing machine, which can then be sold on after the job is complete, will allow you to retrim seats yourself. Foam filling and materials are all readily available though some patterns of moquette are now extinct. They can be recreated from samples, but there will be a minimum order quantity so you may find that it is more economic to buy these materials in bulk in a combined order with several other people.

Painting the outside of the body offers a number of choices. Traditional white spirit-based coach paints are still available, and if used with care may be applied with a roller, brush or spray gun to obtain a very good standard of finish. The advent of cheap, high-speed (and relatively quiet) electric compressors brings spraying into the realms of the amateur restorer, though finding somewhere suitable to do the job might be more difficult. There is a wealth of information available from books and the internet on how to paint vehicles properly and it is worth spending some time researching methods and materials. In the author's experience, obtaining a good paint finish is generally a mix of basic knowledge and preparation, care, common sense and practice.

EFJ 382. When a vehicle has been in preservation for many years, however good the original restoration job was, the time will eventually come when it will need further attention. This picture shows the unique Heaver-bodied WTB formerly of Vic Tours, which spent its working life in the Scilly Isles before entering preservation. It is currently undergoing refurbishment by WHOTT.

If the idea of painting your coach or bus does not appeal, then there any number of professionals who will do the job for you, using modern materials and methods. Costs can be reduced by making sure you do all preparation yourself, though you will need to be able to visualize the end product while you are doing this in order to make sure the surfaces are prepared properly. Some paint shops will allow you to do the masking up yourself, which will save some labour costs, but you are still unlikely to come away with change from £4,000 or more for a good quality job. Carrying out a major restoration can be a time-consuming and at times, frustrating, job but there is no substitute for the feeling of satisfaction that will result when your pride and joy attends its first rally and attracts admiring attention from the crowds. Many amateur restorers have discovered they enjoy some of the tasks of restoration so much that they have given up their day jobs to focus on providing services to other restorers and enthusiasts, to the benefit of all concerned.

ON THE ROAD

If you choose to preserve a full-size Bedford PSV and intend to drive it yourself, it is well worth undertaking some commercial PCV training and perhaps even taking a PCV test; the latter will require you to achieve a Certificate of Professional Competence (CPC). Both this and your licence will currently need to be renewed every five years if you wish to remain qualified. However, if you do not license your preserved vehicle as a PSV then it is currently possible, providing you passed your practical car test prior to 1st January 1997, to drive it on a standard motorcar licence, providing you do not carry more than nine passengers including the driver. The Driver and Vehicle Standards Agency (DVSA) website should be consulted to find out the exact requirements for licensing and driving your vehicle.

If you are intending that your vehicle should only be for private use, then if it is eligible for the Department of Transport MOT test it needs only to be tested to Class 5 standards. For use as a PSV, then a special test certificate is required. For vehicles where a statutory MOT test is not required (licensed as a car and made before 1960), a voluntary roadworthiness test is available and is a highly worthwhile exercise.

Once you are on the road legally and safely, you will find there is a thriving rally scene for commercial vehicles, some dedicated to Bedford, such as the annual Bedford Gathering in July, which in 2015 was held at Ellesmere Port. There are other annual events and regular running days, one major example being the Showbus Rally, which is a very large event dedicated to buses and coaches, new and old, held

An enthusiast chats with the owner of this SB/Duple Vega at the annual Showbus rally, held in 2015 at Woburn House, Bedfordshire. Rallies provide an opportunity for like-minded people to meet to swap spares, share ideas, joys and woes and perhaps obtain leads on potential preservation projects.

generally at the end of September. Most localities will host at least one veteran and vintage rally at which your vehicle will be welcome, and in between events, what could be nicer than to take your friends and family on a leisurely drive into the countryside or to the sea to share an experience that their parents, grandparents and even great-grand-parents would have enjoyed in years gone by? A fully and properly restored Bedford will give years of reliable and trouble-free service for the kind of mileage that it is likely to experience in private hands, and will bring pleasure to all those whose eyes fall upon it. So, the only question that remains is, why haven't you bought one yet?

ABOVE: **A group of enthusiasts working together can provide opportunities for keen amateurs and beginners to become involved with preservation, learn skills and gain experience of working with larger vehicles. This VAL/Plaxton Panorama was restored and is operated by the Friends of King Alfred Buses, who prefer to be known as FoKAB.**

Lodge's Coaches' 1926 Chevrolet Q charabanc, predecessor of the LQ – the ancestor of all Bedford buses and coaches.

ENGINES FITTED TO BEDFORD BUSES AND COACHES

The post-war range of Bedford buses and coaches was characterized by the engine size and version employed. Each model variant was given a particular name and these are listed in the following tables.

Summary of SB Variants

Model	Engine	Size
SB	Bedford	300cu in (4.9-litre) petrol
SBG	Bedford	300cu in (4.9-litre) petrol
SB3	Bedford	300cu in (4.9-litre) petrol
SBO	Perkins R6	340cu in (5.6-litre) diesel
SB1	Bedford	300cu in (4.9-litre) diesel
SB5	Bedford	330cu in (5.4-litre) diesel
SB8	Leyland O.350	350cu in (5.7-litre) diesel
SB13	Leyland O.370	370cu in (6-litre) diesel
SBC	Caterpillar C7	441cu in (7-litre) diesel

Summary of VAS Variants

Type	Engine (all Bedford 6-cylinder in-line)
VAS1	300cu in (4.9-litre) diesel
VAS2	214cu in (3.5-litre) diesel
VAS3	300cu in (4.9-litre) petrol
VAS5	330cu in (5.4-litre) diesel

Summary of VAL Variants

Model	Engine (all 6-cylinder in-line)
VAL14	Leyland O.400 400cu in (6.5-litre) diesel
VAL70	Bedford 466cu in (7.6-litre) diesel

Summary of VAM Variants

Model	Engine (all 6-cylinder in-line)
VAM3	Bedford 300cu in (4.9-litre) petrol
VAM5	Bedford 330cu in (5.4-litre) diesel
VAM14	Leyland O.400 400cu in (6.5-litre) diesel
VAM70	Bedford 466cu in (7.6-litre) diesel
VAM75	Bedford 8.2/140D 500cu in (8.2-ltr) diesel

Summary of Y-Series Variants (not including YNV)

Model	Overall Length	Engine (Bedford 6-cylinder diesel)
YRQ	10m	466 cu in (7.6-litre)
YRQ2/3	10m	500cu in (8.2-litre)
YLQ	10m	500cu in (8.2-litre)
YLQ/S	8m	500cu in (8.2-litre)
YMQ	10m	500cu in (8.2-litre)
YMP	10m	500cu in (8.2-litre) turbocharged
YMP/S	8m or 8.5m	500cu in (8.2-litre) turbocharged
YRT	11m	466 cu in (7.6-litre)
YMT	11m or 12m	500cu in (8.2-litre) NA or de-rated 174bhp turbocharged
YNT	11m or 12m	500cu in (8.2-litre) turbocharged

BIBLIOGRAPHY

The following sources have been consulted in the preparation of this work:

Commercial Motor magazine, issues dating from 1929 to 1990
The *Commercial Motor* online archive
Motor Transport magazine
Old Motor magazine
Bus and Coach magazine
Buses Illustrated magazine and its successor, *Buses*, issues dating from 1959 to 2003
Classic Bus magazine
The Omnibus Society magazine

ABC British Bus Fleets series published by Ian Allan, 1959–67
www.buslistsontheweb.co.uk
Omnibus Society (New Zealand), Bedford SB buses website
Omnibus Society (New Zealand) – 'Bedford VAL Buses and Coaches'
The PSV Circle (2011), Bedford 1930s Production C1250 chassis list
The PSV Circle (2011), Bedford OWB Production C1251 chassis list
The PSV Circle (2011), Bedford OB Production C1250 chassis list
The PSV Circle (1989), Seddon Motors Ltd and Pennine Coachcraft BB133 body list
The PSV Circle (1991), Reeve Burgess Ltd BB134 body list
Broatch, S. F. & Townsin, A., *Bedford Volume 1 – Bedford and British Chevrolet 1923–1950* (Venture Publications, 1995)
Broatch, S. F. & Townsin A., *The Bedford Story Part Two – 1950–1986* (Venture Publications, 1996)
Brown, S. J., *Plaxton 100 Years: A Century of Innovation 1907–2007* (Ian Allan Ltd, 2007)
Furness, N. R. B., *The Buses and Coaches of Bristol and Eastern Coach Works* (Crowood, 2015).
Sims, C. G., *Duple Coachbuilders: from Domination to Demise* (Crecy Publishing Ltd, 2013)

Bedford OWB.

INDEX